Promising Faith for a Ruptured Age

Promising Faith
for a **Ruptured Age**

*An English-Speaking Appreciation
of Oswald Bayer*

EDITED BY
John T. Pless,
Roland Ziegler, AND
Joshua C. Miller

FOREWORD BY
Oliver K. Olson

☙PICKWICK *Publications* · Eugene, Oregon

PROMISING FAITH FOR A RUPTURED AGE
An English-Speaking Appreciation of Oswald Bayer

Copyright © 2019 Wipf and Stock Publishers. All rights reserved. Except for brief quotations in critical publications or reviews, no part of this book may be reproduced in any manner without prior written permission from the publisher. Write: Permissions, Wipf and Stock Publishers, 199 W. 8th Ave., Suite 3, Eugene, OR 97401.

Pickwick Publications
An Imprint of Wipf and Stock Publishers
199 W. 8th Ave., Suite 3
Eugene, OR 97401

www.wipfandstock.com

PAPERBACK ISBN: 978-1-5326-7492-1
HARDCOVER ISBN: 978-1-5326-7493-8
EBOOK ISBN: 978-1-5326-7494-5

Cataloguing-in-Publication data:

Names: Pless, John T., editor. | Ziegler, Roland, editor. | Miller, Joshua C., editor. | Olson, Oliver K., foreword.

Title: Promising faith for a ruptured age : an English-speaking appreciation of Oswald Bayer / edited by John T. Pless, Roland Ziegler, and Joshua C. Miller ; foreword by Oliver K. Olson.

Description: Eugene, OR: Pickwick Publications, 2019. | Includes bibliographical references and index.

Identifiers: ISBN 978-1-5326-7492-1 (paperback). | ISBN 978-1-5326-7493-8 (hardcover). | ISBN 978-1-5326-7494-5 (ebook).

Subjects: LCSH: Bayer, Oswald. | Theology.

Classification: BT30 P85 2019 (print). | BT30 (ebook).

Scripture quotations marked (NRSV) are taken from New Revised Standard Version Bible, copyright © 1989 National Council of the Churches of Christ in the United States of America. Used by permission. All rights reserved worldwide.

Scripture quotations marked (ESV) are taken from the ESV® Bible (The Holy Bible, English Standard Version®), copyright © 2001 by Crossway, a publishing ministry of Good News Publishers. Used by permission. All rights reserved.

Manufactured in the U.S.A.   11/14/19

Contents

Foreword by Oliver K. Olson / vii
Editors' Introduction / ix
Abbreviations / xiii
Contributors / xvii

1. The Bondage of the Will and Denials of the Existence of God / Jacob A. Corzine / 1

2. Johann Georg Hamann, *Biblische Betrachtungen* / Roy Harrisville / 17

3. Through the Cross Shattered Lens: A Cruciform Epistemology of Hope / John D. Koch Jr. / 37

4. Practicing the Promise: Confession and Absolution in the Wittenberg Circle, 1530–1590 / Robert Kolb / 49

5. Sanctification as Divine Order or Divine Gift? Simon Musaeus (1521–1576) and Simon Pauli (1531–1591) on New Obedience / Jason Lane / 66

6. The School from Which We Never Graduate: Luther's Exposition of Psalm 51 / Naomichi Masaki / 94

7. The Holy Spirit in Luther's Catechisms / Mark C. Mattes / 114

8. With Those who Weep: Towards a Theology of Solidarity in Lament / Joshua C. Miller / 136

9. The Eschatology of Forgiveness / James Arne Nestingen / 155

10. On Swearing and Certainty / Steven D. Paulson / 161

11. Sacraments in the Catechism: Promise, Gift, and Faith / John T. Pless / 181

12. Bayer's 21st Disputation Concerning Lament
    / GREGORY P. SCHULZ / 195

13. Hearing and Seeing [Eye & Ear], Word and Image in the Bible,
    Luther, and the Lutheran Tradition / JEFFREY SILCOCK / 209

14. Keep a Low Profile! Observations from a Translator
    of Oswald Bayer / THOMAS H. TRAPP / 227

15. Oswald Bayer on Postmodernism / GENE E. VEITH / 237

16. The Significance of *Oratio*, *Meditatio*, and *Tentatio* for Abraham
    Calov's Understanding of Theology / ROLAND ZIEGLER / 253

Oswald Bayer Bibliography / 269

Name Index / 277

Subject Index / 279

Scripture Index / 283

Foreword

Early during my second German stay I was invited by Oswald Bayer to the Ruhr University at Bochum to talk to his doctoral students about Matthias Flacius. In the discussion that followed I was extraordinarily taken with what Bayer had to say. I expressed my admiration by lending him my office. (In those enlightened days each Wolfenbuettel Stipendiat had one.) Later I had a better idea. I would spread his fame at home. It worked. This book, to my immense pleasure, is a validation of that judgment at Bochum. Meanwhile, age—nonage!—has done its thing. I can't remember what he said.

Nevermind. The word was already out. The hard part was to combine brashness with cash to revive *Lutheran Quarterly*. That done, everything worked. Though he speaks perfectly good English, a succession of translators went to work on his essays. Oswald Bayer became one of *Lutheran Quarterly's* most-published authors.

This book in praise of Bayer comes too late to connect it to the centennial. November 11, 1918, was the end of the war to make the world safe for democracy. And of the war to make it unsafe to speak German. In 1918 mobs killed at least 35 people for speaking the language of the Hun.

There is reason, however, for immediate praise, and it does relate to the language war. German was banned in libraries, public and private schools, newspapers, even telephone calls. In church, immigrant Catholics could listen legally to their mystical, non-German, words, but Lutherans were in danger. In the same year, 1918, Iowa Governor William Harding forbade German sermons. A similar ban was imposed in South Dakota by their Council of Defense. Absurd laws! Absurd war! What possible military advantage could be gained by calling a hamburger a liberty sandwich, by killing a dachshund or by silencing preachers?

Younger preachers have taken over. All of them have pledged allegiance to the flag. And to the republic for which it stands. But have they accepted the ideas for which the republic stands? Maybe in the future Christians will praise Bayer for his unhappiness with the half-pagan Enlightenment and the arrogant Enlightened. If enough people read his book about Johann Georg Hamann he might be the man who taught us to talk back to Jefferson.

At Armistice Day they used to say that the shooting war lasted four years, but that it would take a hundred years to wind up the barbed wire. Would it take a hundred years to undo the language war? It didn't help when the Governor of Montana posthumously pardoned the men who were hanged for speaking German. The change was permanent, irreversible. Those American places where once one had heard only German in the schools, stores, streets, churches no longer existed

How could they carry on church without *Lutherdeutsch?* How could the Lord's song be sung in a strange land? But it had to be done. Churches still raised money for missions and worried about passing the faith along to the young people. Theology students still read their books. Gradually, on the shelf next to tomes of the St. Louis *Werke*, appeared the red-cheerier!—volumes of translated Luther. For them we Scandinavians, too, are grateful.

But something had not been recouped—the connection that American Lutherans used to have with German theology. One thinks of Michael Reu in Dubuque. For complex reasons those ties are important. When would they finish winding up barbed wire? When would the theological break be healed? One well-meant attempt by a member of the Missouri Synod was to send free books to German pastors, exhausted and impoverished after yet another war. The initiative misfired, leaving behind bookstore bargains—unread copies of Pieper's *Dogmatics*.

But *Lutheran Quarterly* thinks that two events have been of help.

1. The unexpected decision by *Theologische Literaturzeitung* to review our articles.

2. The willingness of Oswald Bayer to write some of those articles. A Festschrift initiated in another country must be rare. This one, lieber Herr Kollege Bayer, is heartfelt, sent with thanks for what you have done for us.

Oliver K. Olson

Introduction

LUTHERANISM AROUND THE WORLD owes a debt of gratitude to Oswald Bayer. His work as both a Luther scholar and a Lutheran theologian have impacted the scholarly community as well as many pastors and teachers of the church. This collection of essays seeks to pay homage to Dr. Bayer and the insights his work has brought to Reformation studies and to the discipline of systematic theology. Moreover, in these pages, we seek to praise and thank God for Dr. Bayer's service to the preaching of God's creating and justifying word of promise in Jesus Christ.

Oswald Bayer was born in Nagold, Germany, on September 30th, 1939. Like many other German children of the era, Bayer lost his father during the Second World War, and he grew up under the care of his mother and grandfather.[1] In preparation for a life of study in service of theology, Bayer was educated in Bonn, Tübingen, and Rome. In 1970, Bayer defended his doctoral dissertation, written under the Luther scholar Ernst Bizer, and later published as his now famous work, *Promissio*.[2]

After his doctoral work, Bayer served as both a vicar and as a pastor in the parish of Tübingen, in the Evangelical Church of Württemberg. In 1974, Bayer began teaching systematic theology at Ruhr-University in Bochum. In 1979, he moved to teaching at the University of Tübingen, holding the position of full professor of systematic theology from then until his retirement in 2005.[3] Throughout this time, Bayer made exceptional contributions to the fields of Reformation studies, the study of Johann Georg Hamann, and Lutheran systematic theology.

---

1. Bayer, *Zeitgenossen im Widerspruch*, 2; "Selbstdarstellung," 305; Miller, *Hanging by a Promise*, 2–3.

2. Bayer, *Promissio*, 11; "Selbstdarstellung," 303; Miller, *Hanging by a Promise*, 2–3.

3. Bayer, *Was ist Das—Theologie?*, back cover; *Umstrittene Freiheit*, iii–v; "Selbstdarstellung," 301, 307; Miller, *Hanging by a Promise*, 2–3.

Since the publication of *Promissio*, Bayer has distinguished himself as one of the world's preeminent scholars of Martin Luther's theology. In this work, Bayer locates the particular reformational moment in Luther's life and theology as consisting of the Reformer's insight into the word of God in the gospel of Jesus Christ as a promise that does what it says, namely that it forgives, justifies, and reconciles the sinner to God by creating faith in Christ.[4] This evangelical breakthrough, says Bayer, took place amidst Luther's confutation with Cardinal Cajetan at Augsburg in 1518 and manifested itself fully in the *Babylonian Captivity of the Church*, wherein Luther argues that the words of institution in the sacraments constitute a performative promise that accomplish what they say.[5]

In his later work, *Martin Luther's Theology: A Contemporary Interpretation*, Bayer describes how this doctrine of performative justification by God's all-creating word of promise forms the center, basis, and boundary of Luther's entire theology.[6] In this work, he also explores Luther's experiential theological methodology of *oratio*, *meditatio*, and *tentatio*, demonstrating how the Reformer depicted the theologian as a passive character who is formed by God through the experiences of prayer, meditation on Scripture, and the spiritual attack of *Anfechtung*.[7] In his comprehensive study of Luther's theology, Bayer does not shy away from engaging with aspects of the Reformer's theology that are seen by some as controversial, such as Luther's teachings on the three estates and the hidden God.[8] Throughout all of his Luther scholarship, however, Bayer always relates the Reformer's thoughts to his central teaching of God's justification of sinners by his performative promise.

Bayer's original contributions to scholarship are not, however, relegated merely to the field of Luther studies, as he has also accomplished pioneering work in scholarship about the eighteenth-century philosopher and theologian, Johann Georg Hamann. In his works on Hamann, including *A Contemporary in Dissent*, Bayer identifies Hamann as a radical Enlightenment thinker, who is critical of the Kantian worldview, an outlook which still dominates intellectual life even today. According to Bayer,

---

4. Bayer, *Promissio*, 11–13, 225–29; Miller, *Hanging by a Promise*, 3–4.

5. Bayer, "Rückblick," 161; *Promissio*, 346; "Die reformatorische Wende," 107; *Martin Luther's Theology*, 50; *Martin Luthers Theologie*, 46; "What is Evangelical?" 5; *Zugesagte Gegenwart*, 26; Miller, *Hanging by a Promise*, 153; cf. *LW* 31:270–71; *WA* 2:13–14.

6. Bayer, *Martin Luther's Theology*, 44–67; Miller, *Hanging by a Promise*, 128–31.

7. Bayer, *Martin Luther's Theology*, 32–37, 42–43; Miller, *Hanging by a Promise*, 123–26.

8. Bayer, *Martin Luther's Theology*, 120–53, 196–213.

Hamann stands in stark contrast to others of his day, because he peers behind the rationalist façade and finds it wanting. Instead of reason as the basic category of life, Hamann posits that speech, particularly God's speech, is what constitutes reality.[9] This view of Hamann as a radical Enlightener has contributed in great part to a contemporary renaissance in the study of this enigmatic eighteenth-century Lutheran and has spurred others into exploring his thought.[10]

Perhaps Bayer's greatest contribution to the world, though, lies in his work in systematic theology. Here, one can find a confessionally-oriented Lutheran theology that utilizes a truly reformational approach to doing theology, preaches the gospel of Jesus Christ who comes in the fullness of his reality in the means of grace, recognizes both the goodness and brokenness of all creation, and gives real hope in the midst of evil and suffering. In all of this, Bayer undertakes theology the Lutheran way, using Luther's theology as a model for a contemporary Lutheran theology.

Bayer makes Luther's approach to theology his own, embodying the Reformer's assertion that God forms theologians through prayer, meditation on Scripture, and through the crucible of *Anfechtung*, the agonizing struggle and spiritual attack that drives the theology to trust in Christ alone for righteousness.[11] Bayer further demonstrates his allegiance to Luther by identifying the experience of being addressed by God through the law and the gospel as the divinely given data of doing theology.[12] Thus, for Bayer, theology is no neutral pursuit but entails a holistic formation in the faith through which God justifies.

For Bayer the heart, basis, and boundary of all theology is God's justification of sinners by his effectual word of promise in the gospel of Jesus Christ. This word, says Bayer, does not just describe but actually accomplishes what it says: forgiveness, faith, and salvation.[13] When God's promise comes to sinners in the present, in Scripture, preaching, and the sacraments, it actually renders Christ fully, bodily, creating faith in unbelieving hearts.[14]

---

9. Bayer, *Contemporary in Dissent*, 164–65, 197–200; Miller, *Hanging by a Promise*, 5–6, 137–41.

10. Betz, *After Enlightenment*, 2, 16.

11. Bayer, *Martin Luther's Theology*, 32–37, 42–43; *Theology the Lutheran Way*, 42–64.

12. Bayer, *Martin Luther's Theology*, 58–66; *Theology the Lutheran Way*, 17, 101–4; Miller, *Hanging by a Promise*, 136–44.

13. Bayer, *Martin Luther's Theology*, 53–54; "Justification as the Basis," 287; Miller, *Hanging by a Promise*, 127–30.

14. Bayer, *Martin Luther's Theology*, 116–18, 249–51; *Schöpfung als Anrede*, 18–19; Miller, *Hanging by a Promise*, 165–69.

One of the ingenious aspects of Bayer's theology is that he holds this teaching on justification together with the doctrine of creation. Justification and creation, says Bayer, belong together, because both are accomplished by God's gracious word of promise, which comes in, with, and under created means.[15] Furthermore, says Bayer, this word establishes the estates of created life: family, church, and state.[16] Bayer's work in this area stands as a helpful correction to those who have abused this teaching of Luther's by utilizing it as a justification for tyranny.

The most controversial of Luther's teachings embodied by Bayer, however, is that of the hidden God. While many modern theologians have shied away from this aspect of Luther's thought, Bayer adopts it and interprets it for contemporary believers by framing it as an alternative to theodicy. Rather than seeking to exonerate God for suffering and evil, Bayer employs the biblical exercise of lament in the face of this contradiction of God's love and mercy.[17] Here Bayer stands as one of the few theologians who hold in tension the paradox of the existence of evil and suffering with God's promise of love and new creation, proclaiming that believers must hold onto Christ in faith in the midst of contradiction, until God's final victory in the eschaton.

As we look forward to that day and continue our lives as pilgrims on the way, Oswald Bayer stands as a theological guide who helps us to do theology as Lutherans and to proclaim God's justifying and recreating promise in Jesus Christ. All of us who have contributed to this present work are indebted to Bayer's work in Luther studies, in Hamann studies, and in systematic Lutheran theology. At the same time, many of us have also been touched by the kindness of Dr. Bayer's friendship and the warmth of his Christian charity. This volume is intended both as a gift to Dr. Bayer, honoring him on his eightieth birthday, and as work of gratitude giving thanks both to Dr. Bayer personally and to our Lord, who has given to the church this servant of his creating and justifying word of promise.

The editors also wish to acknowledge the work of Vicar Berett Steffen of Our Savior Lutheran Church in Raleigh, North Carolina for his skillful assistance in preparing the manuscript for publication.

Joshua C. Miller
Advent, 2018

---

15. Bayer, *Martin Luther's Theology*, 95–97, 101–8; "Doctrine of Justification and Ontology," 45–47; Miller, *Hanging by a Promise*, 160–69.

16. Bayer, *Martin Luther's Theology*, 120–53; *Freedom in Response*, 90–118.

17. Bayer, *Martin Luther's Theology*, 20–21, 198–213; *Zugesagte Gegenwart*, 61–69, 111–24; *Schöpfung als Anrede*, 139; Miller, *Hanging by a Promise*, 218–22, 231–54.

Abbreviations

Ap	Philip Melanchthon, *Apology of the Augsburg Confession* (1531). Translated by Charles Arand. In *BC*.
BOC	*The Book of Concord: The Confessions of the Evangelical Lutheran Church*. Edited by Robert Kolb and Timothy J. Wengert. Translated by Charles Arand, Eric Gritsch, Robert Kolb, William Russell, James Schaaf, Jane Strohl, and Timothy J. Wengert.
BDAG	Walter Bauer, *A Greek-English Lexicon of the New Testament and Other Early Christian Literature*. 3rd ed. Edited by Frederick William Danker. Chicago: University of Chicago Press, 2000.
BoW	Martin Luther, *The Bondage of the Will* (1525). Translated by J. I. Packer and O. R. Johnston. Grand Rapids: Revell / Baker, 2000.
BSLK	*Die Bekenntnisschriften der evangelisch-lutherischen Kirche*. Vollständige Neuedition. Edited by Irene Dingel. Göttingen: Vandenhoeck & Ruprecht, 2014.
CA	*The Augsburg Confession* (1530). Translated by Eric Gritsch. In *BC*.
ELW	*Evangelical Lutheran Worship*. Minneapolis: Augsburg Fortress, 2006.
ESV	*Holy Bible: English Standard Version*. Grand Rapids, MI: Crossway, Good News, 2001.
ET	English translation

FC	*Formula of Concord*. Translated by Robert Kolb. In *BC*
FC Ep	*Epitome of the Formula of Concord*
FC SD	*Solid Declaration of the Formula of Concord*
FoC	Martin Luther, *The Freedom of a Christian*. Translated by Mark D. Tranvik. Minneapolis: Fortress, 2008
GD	Karl Barth, *The Göttingen Dogmatics: Instruction in the Christian Religion*. Vol. 1. Translated by Geoffrey W. Bromiley. Edited by Hannelotte Reiffen. Grand Rapids: Eerdmans, 1991
IJST	*International Journal of Systematic Theology*
JBT	*Jahrbuch für Biblische Theologie*
K&D	*Kirche und Dogma*
LBW	*Lutheran Book of Worship*. Minneapolis: Augsburg, 1978
LSB	*Lutheran Service Book*. St. Louis: Concordia Publishing House, 2006
LW	*Luther's Works*, American Edition. Edited by Jaroslav Pelikan and Helmut T. Lehmann. 56 vols. St. Louis: Concordia Publishing House and Philadelphia: Fortress, 1955–1986
LQ	*Lutheran Quarterly*
NJB	*The New Jerusalem Bible*. Standard Edition. London: Doubleday, 1998
NRSV	*New Revised Standard Version of the Bible*. Division of Christian Education of the National Council of the Churches of Christ in the United States of America, 1989
NZSTh	*Neue Zeitschrift für Systematische Theologie und Religionsphilosophie*
RGG[4]	Hans Dieter Betz et al., eds. *Religion in Geschichte und Gegenwart*. 4th ed. 8 vols. Berlin: de Gruyter, 1998–2007
SA	*Smalkald Articles*. Translated by William Russell. In *BC*
SC	*Small Catechism*. Translated by Timothy J. Wengert. In *BC*
SJT	*Scottish Journal of Theology*

TDNT	*Theological Dictionary of the New Testament.* Edited by Gerhard Kittel and Gerhard Friedrich. Translated by Geoffrey W. Bromiley. 10 vols. Grand Rapids: Eerdmans, 1964–1976
WA	*D. Martin Luthers Werke.* Kritische Gesamtausgabe (Weimarer Ausgabe). Weimar: Böhlaus, 1883–
WA TR	*D. Martin Luthers Werke, Tischreden.* Kritische Gesamtausgabe (Weimarer Ausgabe, Tischreden). Weimar: Böhlaus, 1883–
ZThK	*Zeitschrift für Theologie und Kirche*

Contributors

Jacob A. Corzine, MDiv, ThD, is Assistant Professor of Theology at Concordia University-Chicago, River Forest, Illinois, and author of *Erfahrung im Alten Testament: Untersuchung zur Exegese des Alten Testaments bei Franz Delitzch*.

Roy A. Harrisville, BD, ThD, is Emeritus Professor of New Testament, Luther Seminary, St. Paul, Minnesota. He is a translator and most recently author of *Pandora's Box Opened: An Examination of Historical-Critical Method and Its Master Practitioners*, and *Fracture: The Cross as Irreconcilable in the Language and Thought of the Biblical Writers*.

John D. Koch Jr., MDiv, ThD, is Associate Rector at Christ Church, Mt. Pleasant, South Carolina, where he is a pastor, speaker, and writer. He is the author of *The Distinction between Law and Gospel as the Basis and Boundary of Theological Reflection*.

Robert Kolb, PhD, is Professor Emeritus of Systematic Theology, Concordia Seminary, Saint Louis, Missouri, and author of several studies of Luther's and Late Reformation theology. Among his publications is the recent *Martin Luther as He Lived and Breathed*.

Jason D. Lane, MDiv, STM, ThD, is Assistant Professor of Theology at Concordia University Wisconsin, Mequon, Wisconsin, and author of *Luther's Epistle of Straw: The Voice of St. James in Reformation Preaching*.

Naomichi Masaki, PhD, is Associate Professor of Systematic Theology, Director of PhD in Theological Studies Program, and Director of STM Program at Concordia Theological Seminary in Fort Wayne, Indiana. He is author of *He Alone Is Worthy: The Vitality of the Lord's Supper in Theodor Kliefoth and in the Swedish Liturgy of the Nineteenth Century* and *Community: We Are not Alone*.

CONTRIBUTORS

Mark Mattes, MDiv, PhD, is Department Chair, Theology and Philosophy at Grand View University, Des Moines, Iowa, and the author of several books including *Martin Luther's Theology of Beauty: A Reappraisal*.

Joshua C. Miller, PhD, is Instructor in Religion at Augsburg University in Minneapolis, Minnesota, and author of *The Hidden God in the Theology of Oswald Bayer*.

James Arne Nestingen, MDiv, PhD, is Professor Emeritus of Church History, Luther Seminary, St. Paul, Minnesota, and Provost of St. Paul's Lutheran Seminary, online.

Oliver K. Olson, ThD, is Editor Emeritus of *Lutheran Quarterly* and author of *Matthias Flacius and the Survival of Lutheran Reform*.

Steven D. Paulson, MDiv, PhD, is Chair of Lutheran Theology at the Lutheran House of Studies at the Sioux Falls Seminary in South Dakota. He is the Author of numerous articles and books, including *Luther's Outlaw God*.

John T. Pless, MDiv, DLitt, is Assistant Professor of Pastoral Ministry and Missions at Concordia Theological Seminary, Fort Wayne, Indiana. He is the author of numerous articles and books including *Martin Luther: Preacher of the Cross* and *Praying Luther's Small Catechism*.

Gregory P. Schulz, DMin, PhD, is Professor of Philosophy at Concordia University-Wisconsin and author of *The Problem of Suffering: A Father's Hope*.

Jeffrey G. Silcock, BA, BTh, STM, ThD, is Emeritus Lecturer in Systematic Theology, Australian Lutheran College / University of Divinity, North Adelaide, South Australia, and author of numerous Luther articles, translator of Luther's *Antinomian Disputations* (LW 73) and Bayer's *Promissio* (forthcoming).

Thomas H. Trapp, MDiv, ThD, is Professor Emeritus at Concordia University in Saint Paul, Minnesota, and the translator of numerous works including those of Albrecht Peters and Oswald Bayer.

Gene Edward Veith, PhD, is Professor of Literature and Provost Emeritus at Patrick Henry College. He is the author of many books, including *Spirituality of the Cross* and *God at Work*. Most recently he co-authored *Authentic Christianity: How Lutheran Theology Speaks to a Postmodern World* with Trevor Sutton.

Roland Ziegler, ThD, is the Robert D. Preus Associate Professor of Systematic Theology and Confessional Lutheran Studies at Concordia Theological Seminary in Fort Wayne, Indiana.

1

✓ The Bondage of the Will and Denials of the Existence of God

Jacob A. Corzine

"Nur wenn man von der These ausgeht, daß die Gotteserkenntnis eben eine dem Menschen angeborene Möglichkeit sei, dann kann man den Zweifel am Dasein Gottes nicht verstehen und wird ihn als eine *Schuld* des Menschen ansehen. Aber wenn dies ist wie eine *Blindheit*, die dem Menschen 'angeboren' ist, dann wird man den Glauben als *Gnade* und *Wunder* ansehen, als Tat Gottes, und wird die Solidarität mit den Blinden nicht vergessen."[1]

*"Only if you presume the thesis that knowledge of God is an inborn potential of man can you fail to understand doubt in the existence of God and see it as a **fault** of man. But if this is like a **blindness** that is 'hereditary' to man, then you can regard faith as a **grace** and a **miracle**, as an act of God, and then you won't forget solidarity with the blind."*[2]

1.

It is not self-evident that Martin Luther's question about how to find a gracious God is still useful or relevant in Western society and those places where the influence of Western society is heavily felt. It is the question of certainty of salvation, of the insulation of divine promises of mercy and goodness from divine revocation resulting from an assessment of unwor-

---

1. Iwand, "Glauben und Wissen," 114.

2. It has not been possible to determine the exact year the lectures were given, but presumably the date was during his time in Göttingen or Bonn, therefore between 1945 and 1960. Iwand, "Glauben und Wissen," 7–8.

thiness. Put more simply, the question asks how I can be sure that God will treat me according to a judgment in my favor, when I can see clearly that the judgment should be made against me. This question has little meaning if there is no God.

Oswald Bayer, the *Jubilar* to whom these essays are dedicated, suggests in his book *Living by Faith* that there is a close relationship between Martin Luther's question and another, seemingly more foundational question: "How can I know that God exists?"[3] If these questions could be shown to be related, or even fundamentally the same when they are asked, it would seem to rescue the relevance of Martin Luther's question for today, or to confirm its legitimacy as a theological starting point.

This essay attempts to respond to a remark once made by Bayer and remembered by the author, that—I paraphrase, and out of my memory alone—Hans-Joachim Iwand's footnotes to the *Bondage of the Will* in the Munich edition of Luther's Works are among the best work on the subject. I say "respond," because I have not, in this article, directly followed the sign posted by Professor Bayer, pointing to those footnotes. Instead, I take up a series of lectures, published in the first volume of Iwand's *Nachgelassene Werke*, concerning *Glauben und Wissen—Believing and Knowing*. Therein, Iwand addresses differing grounds for the denying of God's existence and connects them to the fundamental problem of the bondage of the will, which for him expresses itself in an aggressive denial of God.

In the quote that opens this article, Iwand cautions against assuming that man is capable of acknowledging God at all. The consequence of this assumption is that the evidenced godlessness (using the word here not as a descriptor of great evil, but as a quality of a person who is literally "without God") is seen as a moral fault that must be corrected before one can proceed to Luther's search for a gracious God. Instead, Iwand speaks of blindness, an incapacity to recognize God at all. This could be perceived as absolving a person of guilt, but it's not intended that way. Rather, it changes the terms of the discussion by including in the things of the *Will* that is in *Bondage* not only the keeping of the law but also the acknowledgement of God's existence. The lectures on *Believing and Knowing* consider how this incapacity for acknowledging God has embedded itself in contemporary society.

---

3. Bayer, *Living by Faith*, xi–xii.

2.

In order to understand the *Believing and Knowing* lectures, it seems necessary to recognize a distinction between individual denial of the existence of God and the sort of denial foisted upon a person by subscription to particular schools of thought. Within the latter, collective sort of denial, three different forms of necessitated denial of God's existence are distinguished. These forms are closely related to one another and, in Iwand's depiction, are progressively more potent both in their forcefulness and in their potential for negative consequence. These three modes of thinking that press upon their adherents a denial of the existence of God, as named by Iwand, are:

1. Positivism (represented by August Comte, especially his *Positive Philosophy* (1830–1842)[4],
2. Sociology[5] as the culmination of Comte's hierarchy of the sciences, and
3. Ethics grounded in human freedom.

Each will be considered in the following paragraphs.

3.

Iwand traces the positivism to which he refers back to the work and thought of the French philosopher August Comte (1798–1857). Comte's positivism can be understood, on the one hand, in terms of its means of apprehending the world, and more broadly, of determining and then organizing that which

---

4. In this paper, I quote from Harriet Martineau's English translation of Comte's *Positive Philosophy* (1853), reprinted in the *Cambridge Library Collection* in 2009. See Comte, *Positive Philosophy*.

5. Iwand uses, apparently as synonyms, a variety of terms to refer to Comte's culminating science, including *social physics, socialism, scientific socialism, and sociology*. A certain difficulty is unavoidable when referring to concepts over three centuries and in three different languages, in particular when the concept is, in fact, quite young. In his 1967 article in the *Encyclopedia of Philosophy*, Bruce Mazlish credits Comte with coining the term "sociology," and probably with originating the discipline. Similar is Paul Weirich's assessment in the 1995 *Cambridge Dictionary of Philosophy*. With due deference to the complexities of the history of the present-day discipline of sociology, these articles demonstrate a standard English terminology when referring to Comte's work, which is accordingly mostly adopted in this article. Where more direct quotation of Comte occurs, it is occasionally nevertheless necessary to use the term "social physics," but the reader is entreated to regard the two as synonyms. See Edwards, *Encyclopedia of Philosophy*, 173–77; Audi, *Cambridge Dictionary of Philosophy*, 147.

can be intellectually apprehended.[6] The concept is embedded in a broader division of history in a manner similar to that presented in Herder's *Auch eine Philosophie der Geschichte zur Bildung der Menschheit* (1774) or Lessing's *Erziehung des Menschengeschlechts* (1780): phases of intellectual and conceptual development in human history are distinguished in a manner that parallels the intellectual and moral development of a human being.

This theory of history in Comte's *Positive Philosophy*, to which Iwand is chiefly referring, has come to be known as Comte's *Law of Three* Stages, and is referred to by Comte himself as the *Law of Human Progress*.[7]

> The law is this: that each of our leading conceptions, each branch of our knowledge, passes successively through three different theoretical conditions: the theological, or fictitious; the metaphysical, or abstract; and the scientific, or positive. . . . The first is the necessary point of departure of the human understanding; and the third is its fixed and definitive state. The second is merely a state of transition.[8]

Iwand gives particular attention to the *Law of Three Stages*, because it so explicitly motivates a denial of God's existence. The *Law* describes the development of each kind of knowledge as a movement from the *theological* through the *metaphysical* to the ultimate *positive*. The essence of the theological here is the supposition that "all phenomena [are] produced by the immediate action of supernatural beings."[9] Comte has something akin to superstition in mind here, rather than the modern-era discipline of theology. Nevertheless, the choice of words embodies a position on the value of the study of theology. The second stage, metaphysics, distills these supernatural beings into "abstract forces"[10] or moral principles inherent in the world. The final stage, positivism, frees itself of these inhibiting notions and focuses instead on the study of the laws which govern observable phenomena: "What is now understood when we speak of an explanation of facts is simply the establishment of a connection between single phenomena and some general facts, the number of which continually diminishes with the progress of science."[11]

Iwand describes it this way: "Here, only what is real counts, that which can be conceptually grasped and controlled for, which can be investigated

---

6. See *RGG4* 6:1509–512.
7. See Edwards, *Encyclopedia of Philosophy*, 173–77; Comte, *Positive Philosophy*, 1:1.
8. Comte, *Positive Philosophy*, 1:1–2.
9. Comte, *Positive Philosophy*, 1:2.
10. Comte, *Positive Philosophy*, 1:2.
11. Comte, *Positive Philosophy*, 1:2.

with the methods of natural science."[12] In this final stage, the laws that govern the phenomena of the world, either having been identified or being identified, progressively abrogate the motivation for belief in the existence of God. Iwand's description of Comte focuses on the human side. If the "scientification (Verwissenschaftlichung) of all processes" leads to the fall of God as "one of the great . . . fictions," Feuerbach's call for the exchange of theology for anthropology receives its affirmative response.[13] The result, if Comte's *Law of Three Stages* is an accurate model of the history of thought and belief, even if only with regard to the transition to the third stage, positivism, is a slow, practically unnoticed slipping away from faith in God. Scientists need launch no attack against the clergy, nor science against Christianity. The progression occurs with such subtlety that even the person in whose life it happens is hardly aware.

It is for this reason that Iwand cites not positivism alone as the motivation for denying the existence of God, but rather includes what comes into light when positivism is adopted: *God's invisibility*. This is the *[genommener] Anlaß der Leugnung*—the purported reason for denial.[14] But Iwand disputes that the denial necessarily proceeds from God's invisibility. Rather, the change in conceptualizing the world, tracked by Comte and identified as positivism, dislodges the ability to account for that which is invisible.

The consequence is a running theme in Iwand's work: man placing himself in the position of God. At this point he formulates in terms of perspective. If God is no longer the all-encompassing being or force in the universe, and this non-existence can be definitively determined by the powers of observation of modern man, it must be concluded that man is the one whose reach knows no bounds.[15] In terms of the consequences of denying God's existence, this will be the connecting point to the other two denials to be discussed.

4.

Iwand's three denials of God's existence are closely related to one another, and almost appear to grow out of one another. But, in fact, each is its own denial

---

12. Iwand, "Glauben und Wissen," 135. "Hier gilt nur noch das für wirklich, was sich begrifflich erfassen und kontrollieren und was sich nach den Methoden der Naturwissenschaft untersuchen läßt."
13. Iwand, "Glauben und Wissen," 139.
14. Iwand, "Glauben und Wissen," 133.
15. Iwand, "Glauben und Wissen," 133.

and, although a certain escalation can be observed as he moves from positivism and God's invisibility to the other two denials, they can nevertheless be independently developed. In the second denial, like with the first, Comte's *Positive Philosophy* is at the basis. The denial bears the name sociology.[16]

In the *Positive Philosophy*, Comte recognizes five "fundamental sciences": astronomy, physics, chemistry, physiology, and social physics.[17] These are arranged in order of their relationship to one another, as well as in order of complexity. A consequence of the ordering is, according to Comte, that the latter sciences proceeded to their final positivist stage more recently than the beginning ones. This observation points to Comte's application of the *Law of Three Stages* in the task of organizing human knowledge. He contends that each fundamental science has undergone the development from the theological stage, through the metaphysical, before finally reaching the positivist stage. Demonstrating this in detail—and in so doing grounding the necessity of entering and fostering the positivist stage in each fundamental science—is a main goal of the *Positive Philosophy*.[18] It is a consequence of this intention that the individual parts contain subsections like astronomy ("when it became a science"), physics ("imperfect condition of the science"), chemistry ("great imperfection"), and biology ("its present imperfection").[19]

These criticisms of the "fundamental sciences," increasingly harsh, are finally outpaced by Comte's assessment of the condition of positivism in social physics:

> If we look with a philosophical eye upon the present state of social science, we cannot but recognize in it the combination of all the features of that theologico-metaphysical infancy which all the other sciences had to pass through. The present condition of political science revives before our eyes the analogy of what astrology was to astronomy, alchemy to chemistry, and the search for the universal panacea to the system of medical studies.[20]

Sociology, as the crown of Comte's foundational sciences, the most complex and the most important, is the "principal aim" of the *Positive*

---

16. Iwand, "Glauben und Wissen," 140. See footnote 5 above. Iwand is careful to distinguish sociology (socialism) in Comte's meaning as scientific socialism from "philanthropic" or "Christian" socialism, although he does not enter into a definition of either of these terms.
17. Comte, *Positive Philosophy*, 1:28.
18. Comte, *Positive Philosophy*, 1:8.
19. Comte, *Positive Philosophy*, 1:141, 215, 290, 357.
20. Comte, *Positive Philosophy*, 2:68.

Philosophy.[21] Its elucidation constitutes the content of the entire second volume of Comte's work, and it is the intersection of the culmination of two historical observations made by Comte: that every discipline has gone through three stages (sociology is, through his work, being brought into its own in the third, positivist stage), and that the foundational sciences proceed one from another, sociology being the final and most complex.

Iwand sees *Gerechtigkeit* at the center of Comte's sociology and therein its great challenge to the existence of God as well as—it will become clear why this must be added here—to the moral integrity of a society. To begin, a word must be said here about properly translating the German *Gerechtigkeit*.

Most theological usage of the word is safely translated with the English word "righteousness." The "righteousness of God" (Rom 1:17), for example, appears in the 2017 edition of the *Lutherbibel* (as in the 1912 edition, which Iwand would have read) as the "Gerechtigkeit, die vor Gott gilt." Article III of the *Formula of Concord*, bears the German heading "Von der Gerechtigkeit des Glaubens [vor] Gott" and in the English Kolb-Wengert edition "Concerning the Righteousness of Faith before God."[22] These contextually determined translations notwithstanding, the word may also, in other contexts, be legitimately translated as "justice."[23] Terms and phrases like "social justice," "to seek justice," and "injustice" often belong to proper renderings of usages of the German *Gerechtigkeit*.[24] Iwand's analysis moves in between the two meanings of the German word, thereby tying closely together the concepts of justice, as pursued by those who see its absence disproving the existence of God, and of righteousness, as it is freely provided by God to those who have faith.[25] With this in mind, it is a helpful reminder to the English-speaking reader of Iwand that in some places where he writes "*Gerechtigkeit*," "justice" may be a more apt translation than "righteousness."

The connection to sociology as the study of the laws that govern societal phenomena can now be made. The purpose of such study is the governing of society in a way that erects the greatest measure of

---

21. Comte, *Positive Philosophy*, 7.

22. See *BSLK* 1388–89; *BC* 562. The Latin version of article III in *FC SD* is titled *De iustitia fidei coram Deo*.

23. See Thyen and Clark, *Oxford-Duden German Dictionary*, 343.

24. Thyen and Clark, *Oxford-Duden German Dictionary*, 761.

25. The philosophical discussion of *Gerechtigkeit* in *RGG4* confirms this, noting that "die heute so prominente soziale Gerechtigkeit fehlt dagegen." Social justice is absent from classical conceptions of *Gerechtigkeit*. It further confirms the conceptual challenge in moving from German to English here, that the *Encyclopedia of Religion* and the *Encyclopedia of Philosophy* both index the word "justice," but neither the word "righteousness."

"*Gerechtigkeit auf Erden*"—"justice on earth."[26] Iwand extrapolates quickly beyond Comte's *Positive Philosophy* here, distinguishing types of Western from Marxist socialism but regarding as the common feature the human assumption of responsibility for this justice. The denial of God's existence enters here. If the benefactor of the previous social order was God, and one must now work to overthrow rampant injustices, then whatever invisible God might exist is one who either perpetuated injustice or was unable to end it. In either case, the denial quickly follows as part and parcel of the assumption of responsibility for justice.

Iwand becomes notably troubled in his description of the problem of justice, as he will again in approaching ethics. He describes an entirely binary situation, wherein a person chooses the path of Luther or Münzer, Alyosha or Ivan Karamazov, or most poignantly: the Crucified or communism. Characteristic of the second path is a "dissolution of all relations in the world into formulas, of all qualities into quantities."[27] He makes the choice most explicitly clear, however, in the short discussion of Dostoyevsky's *Brothers Karamazov*:

> The one and the other embody the love of man! But [Alyosha] in the engagement with the man himself, [Ivan] in the principle! Justice raised to the level of a principle and proclaimed as the love of man—this is the rejection of God.[28]

The second path, the dangerous one, sees only the big picture, remaining blind to the nearby consequences of its calculating action.[29] The French and Russian Revolutions are cited, and in an apparent reference to the "Great Leap Forward," a potential equivalent event in Asia. All three are rooted by Iwand in the Sermon on the Mount, and in so doing, he clarifies the nature of the danger. To receive the Sermon on the Mount without receiving the one who speaks it means—here the wordplay becomes important—to pursue justice (*Gerechtigkeit*) in the absence of the alien righteousness (*Gerechtigkeit*)

---

26. Iwand, "Glauben und Wissen," 140.
27. Iwand, "Glauben und Wissen," 143.
28. Iwand, "Glauben und Wissen," 144.
29. An editor's footnote in Iwand's lectures indicates that he read out of the chapter of *The Brothers Karamazov* entitled, in German translation, "Empörung." This would seem to be chapter 4 of part 1, book 5. Therein, Ivan Karamazov describes exactly the terror of a principle raised so high that its preservation legitimizes individual suffering, even torture. Iwand's description of several instances of severely mistreated children appears to be Dostoyevsky's argument against God's existence, but is given to Alyosha, whom it nearly crushes, but who at the end of the book, after all has been concluded, is found caring for children, seemingly a reminder that compassion in the midst of suffering can indeed be preserved.

freely given by Christ. This situation threatens a single-mindedness willing to set aside anything in the pursuit of its goal but ignorant of the truth that the trouble is in the person himself. The absence of forgiveness leaves as an alternative only the pursuit of perfection at all costs.

Iwand's estimation of this second motivation for the denial of the existence of God cannot be understood as a cry lamenting the consequences for Christianity—that Comte's social physics and subsequent efforts to establish social justice do so at the cost of the foundational Christian belief in God's existence. In other words, Iwand cannot be understood as lamenting merely a loss for the church and his own way of seeing the world. He is rather describing grave consequences for everyone involved: the denial of God's existence on account of the inexplicable and grave injustice at all levels of present-day society removes the ability of a person to interact with other people as fellow human beings. The pursuit of justice remains—in the absence of Christ's alien righteousness—as the only means to righteousness, and threatens to trod down much more than the downtrodden whom it would aim to help. In indicating this, Iwand is demonstrating that no new conceptual ground for understanding human history is won by this second denial of God. Instead, one set of conceptual problems (perennial injustice coexisting with the divinity) is exchanged for another (unchecked destruction in the name of the pursuit of justice).

4.

Iwand's third motivation for denial of the existence of God is bound up with the concept of human freedom and in an especially clear way with what is meant when one speaks of "God." To this concept "God" belongs the idea of an "ultimately effective finality of all things."[30] Put differently, if God exists, then everything that happens can be attributed to his power and judged as right because of his final authority. But this makes a mockery of human freedom, which presupposes consequence for decisions and actions. At risk, if God exists, is the person's potential to mold the world and even his own life. The drive to protect this freedom motivates the third denial. What flows from it, Iwand calls simply "ethics." By this, he means efforts to produce ethical systems on the basis of this freedom which, raised to the level of a first principle, necessitates the non-existence of God. For the majority of the parts of the lecture that deal with the third denial, Iwand reviews the work of scholars who have produced these kinds of ethical systems.

30. Iwand, "Glauben und Wissen," 142.

For Iwand's purposes, two German scholars represent this position in their writings: Nicolai Hartmann (1882–1950) and Max Scheler (1874–1928). It ought not be overlooked, however, that he also includes Jean Paul Sartre's *Being and Nothingness* among such writings. Hartmann's contribution, drawn from his 1926 *Ethik*, concerns the mutual exclusivity of human freedom and divine foresight. He provides the most explicit quotes representing the position Iwand categorizes as the third denial. These will be addressed below. At present, Scheler's work is of more interest, since Iwand chooses it first as a demonstration of the godlessness that can attend this elevation of human freedom in ethics.

Max Scheler's *Mensch und Geschichte* (just sixty pages long) is a survey of anthropological ideas as perspectives for understanding human history. Five ideas are considered and presented sequentially as they present themselves in the history of Western thought. The first is the *homo religiosus*, man caught up in the Judeo-Christian focus on sin, guilt, and fault. Although this is all myth, it is of great importance, since its influence on humanity is endlessly pervasive. Even those who have renounced religion remain infected by the fear it creates.[31] The second anthropological idea is the *homo sapiens*, which distinguishes man from animal through the postulation of a distinct and unique intellectual capacity called by the ancient Greeks the *logos*. As with the first idea, Scheler regards the *homo sapiens* as a deeply influential and extraordinarily persistent interpretation of what makes the human being.[32] The third idea is that of the *homo faber*. This conception of man regards people as qualitatively no different than animals. Instead, human beings simply expend more energy on the use of the brain. The result is the use of tools, a category to which already every kind of communication belongs.[33] Scheler lists many Enlightenment and modern thinkers who espouse a variant of this anthropology, including August Comte.

The somewhat more complex fourth position is named in opposition to these three and summarized by Scheler, quoting Theodor Lessing (1872–1933): "Man—a species of predatory ape that has slowly become megalomaniacal with regard to its so-called mind (*Geist*)."[34] In this anthropological conception, man is "the dead end of life,"[35] because the turn to relying on tools and faculties of reason in the struggle for existence has eliminated the

---

31. Scheler, *Mensch und Geschichte*, 18.
32. Scheler, *Mensch und Geschichte*, 24–25.
33. Scheler, *Mensch und Geschichte*, 31.
34. Scheler, *Mensch und Geschichte*, 41. "Der Mensch—d.h. eine auf ihren sogenannten 'Geist' langsam größenwahnsinnig gewordene Raubaffenspezies."
35. Scheler, *Mensch und Geschichte*, 42.

need to develop that which is more inherent to life: the organs of the body and the senses. The relation to the *homo faber* conception is clear, in that both refer to the use of instruments. But here, the expectation of a development is not seen as affirmed by that, but rather undermined: since man is driven by his mind (*logos*/*homo sapiens*) to use the instruments (*homo faber*) to develop, he is no longer developing his innate qualities.

The fifth and final position appears to be the one for which Scheler advocates, although he explicitly cautions the reader against assuming that any one of the positions is his.[36] The concept is the human being as a morally free being, as a person with responsibility, freedom, a sort of mandate. Freedom is the decisive matter: "But that predetermination of the future, arranged by a being outside of the man—destroys him as such."[37] It's the proper interpretation of a quote from Nietzsche that serves as the anchor for this position: "*Wenn es Götter gäbe, wie hielte ich es aus, kein Gott zu sein; also gibt es keine Götter* [If there were Gods, how could I endure it to be no God! Therefore there are no Gods]."[38] The sentence must be carefully read as a present unreal conditional: If there were gods (which is not the case) . . . but since Nietzsche endures, there must not be gods.

Iwand follows Scheler closely in explaining this "postulatory atheism," according to which the understanding of man precludes even the possibility of God's existence.[39] This is why freedom, in combination with the sort of ethical systems that can be constructed on its basis, form the final motivation for denial of God's existence: they quite forcefully demand it, in fact.

Among the conclusions drawn in connection with this third motivation, perhaps the theologically most dramatic has to do with redemption and the divine removal of human guilt. Turning once more to Nicolai Hartmann's *Ethik*, Iwand observes that the very concept of redemption is regarded as "ethically reprehensible."[40] The distance between this position and the freedom-necessitated denial of the existence of God is minimal. Just as the absence of freedom would prevent an individual from the assumption of responsibility,[41] so an authoritative action absolving a person of guilt would confirm that that person is, ethically speaking, still a child, incapable of and therefore not to be burdened with the decisions and consequences that attend

---

36. Scheler, *Mensch und Geschichte*, 14. A footnote directs the reader to his *Die Stellung des Menschen im Kosmos* (1928) for clarification.

37. Scheler, *Mensch und Geschichte*, 57.

38. Scheler, *Mensch und Geschichte*, 56; Nietzsche, *Also sprach Zarathustra*, 106.

39. Scheler, *Mensch und Geschichte*, 55; Iwand, "Glauben und Wissen," 150.

40. Iwand, "Glauben und Wissen," 152; cf. Hartmann, *Ethics*, 272.

41. Iwand, "Glauben und Wissen," 150.

a free individual in the world. The quite proper pursuit of self-determination is therefore grounds to oppose a doctrine of redemption.[42]

The elevation of this form of ethics—predicated on human freedom and at risk of being fundamentally undermined by the acceptance of any doctrine of redemption—appears to have its final consequence for Iwand not in the attitude toward the existence of God, but, rather, in the influence it has on individual morality:

> But [these] are such as have no more plan, make no sacrifice, do not allow themselves to be enraptured by the idea that they might discover the universal law that encompasses all phenomena and makes man able to rule as *res cogitans*; they are also untouched by the injustice and suffering around them, they are at the highest point, where no guilt troubles them and no loneliness drives them to seek God or the brother. This is the "free" man, the truly godless man, the actual opponent of Christ, [who is] the true man. This man is the incarnated *No* to God and he is his own idol, and his idolatry is called "ethics."[43]

On the one hand, Iwand is pointing here to a sharp contrast between what is and what is claimed. The very position that is founded on the pursuit of a truly human ethics leads in fact to the moral bankruptcy of a person, who as a consequence of it is instead not only bereft of any loftier goal but also unable to perceive the sorts of things that might motivate moral behavior, recognized suffering either in himself or in his fellow man. On the other hand, something even more fundamental is being identified, not just a methodical or logical error, but an unexpected yet seemingly unavoidable result. The pursuit of untethered human freedom, pushed so far as to willingly accept the cost of belief in God, actually undermines any ethical project, leaving the person and society worse off than they previously had been. At the end of the quote, Iwand hints at the final consequence. Man is not left then without a god, for he idolizes himself, usurping the place of the true God. Every idolatry has a name; this one is "ethics."[44]

Tied up with the kind of idolatry that replaces God not with an invented pantheon of wooden, stone, and painted gods, but with one's own rise to power, authority, and freedom, is inevitably not only a strictly speaking

---

42. Iwand, "Glauben und Wissen," 152.

43. Iwand, "Glauben und Wissen," 153.

44. This is far from the only place where Iwand's writings address the self-idolatry of desiring "for God to no longer be God and for man instead to be God." As mentioned above, this is a theme that runs through all types of denial of God. See also Iwand, "Freedom of the Christian," 7–15.

theological error, but also an anthropological one. Christian anthropology is capable of proceeding from the "true man, born of the virgin Mary."[45] Jesus Christ is the *True Man*, in whom all other human beings can begin to perceive who they are. This runs deeper than a legalism that positions the life of Christ as an example for Christians, but it does occur partly by means of a legal contrast—between the *True Man* Jesus Christ, and the *real man* living with the concupiscence and the bound will in all of their consequences for his relationship to himself, his fellow human beings, and God. But for the idolatry of ethics to arise, the *real man* must take a different turn, one perhaps more natural or even inevitable for him in the absence of the gospel. He must lay claim to a freedom he does not have, and in order to do this, he must proclaim the non-existence of the God whose very definition would show that freedom to be a sham and therefore undermine it in the moment it is postulated. Iwand calls this *real man* the "incarnated *antithesis* of God and of his redemption" and says that he, as such, "makes history."[46]

This observation concludes Iwand's discussion of the types of denial of the existence of God: the *real man* cannot coexist with the *True Man*. The man whose claim to freedom is the highest axiom of existence cannot endure the man Jesus Christ, who embodies a divinely operated redemption and with it the fullness of the problem of the lack of freedom (*De servo arbitrio*). The inability to coexist is not a logical inability, as though a reasonable person must conclude that one or the other, in fact, did not exist. Rather it is an inability seated in an "intellectual and practical world."[47] An ethics like that of Max Scheler, Nicolai Hartmann, or Jean-Paul Sartre cannot admit the proclamation of the gospel; and the proclamation of the gospel, where it is received, will undermine such an ethical standpoint. There is a tone of great discomfort or even fear in Iwand's lectures, and it would seem to arise in the context of this conclusion: to choose freedom as an ultimate principle is to reject, just as ultimately, redemption and forgiveness.

5.

Near the end of the portion of the *Believing and Knowing* lectures summarized in this article, Iwand correlates the three motivations for denying the existence of God with three conditions for (neutral) inquiry into God's

---

45. SC 17.

46. Iwand, "Glauben und Wissen," 154. One should recall here that Scheler's anthropological interest is in service of his interest in history.

47. Iwand, "Glauben und Wissen," 154.

existence that he had earlier posited.[48] The first denial, that based on God's invisibility (positivism), correlates to concupiscence, which is here, for Iwand, Augustine's idea of being chained to the things of this life and material world. The second motivation, that of the pursuit of justice/righteousness (sociology), is bound up in the failure to recognize that there is a righteousness of the law and a righteousness of the gospel, and that the free receipt of the latter must actually precede the pursuit of the former. Iwand ties this to Luther's problem of the *iustitia operum*, since the self-justification through works of the law assumes God's place as the one who justifies.[49] The third motivation, that of ethics, is the problem of life with one's neighbor, "the question of human beings living in a just relationship to one another."[50] It appears that it would be faithful to Iwand to summarize: This question presses and strives for an answer, and in the absence of the Christian concept that the love of God is found in Christian love, ethics, Scheler's "postulatory atheism," is the alternative answer. Concupiscence, the works of the law, and the isolation of the individual from his fellow human beings represent, therefore, the three kinds of atheism Iwand describes.[51]

That matter remains somewhat complicated. For each kind of atheism, Iwand identifies a modern source (positivism, sociology, ethics) and a legitimacy of the objection in view of the bondage of the will (God's invisibility, the need to assume God's work of justice, the inadmissible limitation of freedom necessitated by postulating God's existence). These three atheisms are then used as a lens to view the history of theology and see three major theological challenges that have arisen, essentially as a result of the persistence of the bondage of the will and its denial of God: Augustine's concupiscence, Luther's *iustitia operum*, and the present-day selfishness or love of the neighbor.

6.

It has been the main task of this article to reach the above conclusion. The *Glauben und Wissen* lectures are unsystematic in their structure, often repeating themselves (at least sometimes a clear sign of a new session beginning with review) and occasionally announcing a list of three matters only

---

48. Iwand, "Glauben und Wissen," 130–31.
49. Iwand, "Glauben und Wissen," 130.
50. Iwand, "Glauben und Wissen," 130. "Die Frage nach dem gerechten Zusammenleben von Mensch und Mensch."
51. Iwand, "Glauben und Wissen," 132.

to leave one or two unaddressed. Some things are clearly stated nowhere and must, instead, be cobbled together from the several places where the topic is mentioned. Even so, the lecture form provides something missing from carefully organized, systematic writing. The tone of Iwand's words is often an indicator in the lectures of where to pay particularly close attention. In particular, his concern about the consequences of the unchained pursuit of justice or preservation of the freedom postulate becomes clear in the way that he writes.

The real value of this study, however, is present already in the opening quote. Iwand expresses remarkable sympathy for the unbelieving skeptic, and this is based in his understanding of the bound will. Since the inevitable denial of God is not adequately characterized as an expression of belligerence, but better as the result of a blindness common to all and relieved only by the grace of God, he actually advocates for joining a person in their skepticism. Iwand models this in the lectures, showing convincingly how the dominant forms of atheism in Western culture today are actually entirely present in Christian thought. The response of the Gospel is an issue that remains. This article can only mention Iwand's remarks on this in passing, although there is some direct integration, as the ethical problem described above has very much to do with the *real man* and the *True Man*. At any rate, essential to grasping Iwand's response to these types of atheism is the conception of all forms of atheism as expressions of the bound will.

The problems that are addressed when Luther and the Lutheran reformers are treated as reliable guides in making theological statements are chiefly those of assuaging the troubled conscience. So emphasis is placed on the word of God as promises of God that are absolutely certain and sure; on the word of forgiveness being a decisive word, bearing divine authority even when spoken by a human being; and on the unshakeable foundation of baptism and the powerfully forgiving presence of the body and blood of Jesus Christ in the Lord's Supper. In as far as the gospel task is perceived as that of bringing the gospel to troubled, but nevertheless believing Christians, the Reformation approach seems to be quite appropriate. But Iwand's approach to the bound will introduces, in two ways, new dimensions to that way of thinking. On the one hand, he extends the community of people for whom the proclamation of the gospel certainty is relevant, by including those who skeptically question God's existence. Their inability to perceive God is not the expression of an unusually deep moral failure, but, instead, part of the problem of the bound will, which is common to all. On the other hand, he deepens the understanding of the "troubled, but believing Christian," so that unbelief supplants actual sin as the principal and foundational negative result of the bound will, for which the gospel is the proper medicine. The latter of these two moves is frequently and successfully pursued by those concerned with law and gospel as a preaching guide or with Luther's exposition of the First Commandment. The former, in contrast, lives on the edge of and confirms the continued necessity of Christian apologetics. Interestingly, it recommends that the person who expresses skepticism about God be seen not as having fallen below the supposed baseline of belief in God, but, rather, as having risen above the baseline of bound-will-induced atheism.

The coordination of the atheist denials to distinct demonstrations of the bondage of the will is the evidence that the question of the gracious God is the same as the question of God at all. For Iwand, the problem of the bondage of the will is only superficially grasped when it is described as a sort of irresistible inclination to violate the will and law of God. This inclination to sin is, for him, a secondary problem. The primary problem of the bondage of the will is not the denial of God's law, but the denial of God himself.

Bibliography

Audi, Robert, ed. *The Cambridge Dictionary of Philosophy*. Cambridge: Cambridge University Press, 1995.

Bayer, Oswald. *Living by Faith: Justification and Sanctification*. Translated by Geoffrey W. Bromiley. Grand Rapids: Eerdmans, 2003.

Comte, Auguste. *The Positive Philosophy of Auguste Comte*. Translated by Harriet Martineau. Vols. 1–2. Cambridge Library Collection—Religion. Cambridge: Cambridge University Press, 2009.

Edwards, Paul, ed. *The Encyclopedia of Philosophy*. 2nd ed. New York: Macmillan, 1996.

Hartmann, Nicolai, and Stanton Coit. *Ethics*. Vol. 3. London: George Allen & Unwin, 1932.

Iwand, Hans Joachim. "The Freedom of the Christian and the Bondage of the Will." Translated by Jacob Corzine. *Logia* 17.2 (2008) 7–15.

———. "Glauben und Wissen. Vorlesung." In *Nachgelassene Werke*, edited by Helmut Gollwitzer, 27–216. Vol. 1 of *Glauben und Wissen*. Munich: Kaiser, 1962.

Luther, Martin. *Luther's Small Catechism with Explanation*. St. Louis: Concordia, 2017.

Nietzsche. *Also Sprach Zarathustra*. Vol. 6.1 of *Nietzsche Werke Kritische Gesamtausgabe*. Edited by Giorgio Colli and Mazzino Montinari. Berlin: Walter de Gruyter, 1968.

Scheler, Max. *Mensch und Geschichte*. Zürich: Verlag der neuen Schweizer Rundschau, 1929.

Thyen, O., and M. Clark. *The Concise Oxford-Duden German Dictionary*. 3rd ed. Oxford: Oxford University Press, 2005.

2

Johann Georg Hamann, *Biblische Betrachtungen*

Roy A. Harrisville

In honor of my friend Oswald Bayer

Johann Georg Hamann (1730–1788), "Magus of the North," thinker, poet, pamphleteer, lifelong friend of Immanuel Kant, and intense critic of the Enlightenment, underwent a crisis leading to a life change while on a mission to London for the Riga firm of Berens. In the wake of what he called his *Anfechtung* (crisis of spirit), Hamann returned to his roots, and with the help of the English cleric and poet James Hervey,[1] began a renewed reading of the Bible, resulting in a volume-sized series of meditations entitled *Biblische Betrachtungen*, composed in March and April of 1758.

The *Betrachtungen* indicate use of the English Bible, as well as intensive concentration on the Hebrew and Greek texts. However, the linguistic investigations, philological and stylistic observations along with these texts clearly have the Luther Bible as their context. Additionally, Hamann's interest does not apply equally to all the biblical texts. There is intense concentration on Genesis, Psalms, Leviticus, Deuteronomy, Proverbs, Ecclesiastes, Isaiah, Jeremiah, Ezekiel, and Daniel of the Old Testament, and Matthew, John, Luke, Acts, and Romans of the New.[2]

---

1. James Hervey (1714–1758) was born near Northhampton, England, educated at Northhampton's grammar school and at Lincoln College, Oxford, where he came under the influence of John Wesley. Remaining in the Anglican Church, Hervey had lasting effect on English art through William Blake. His "Meditations among the Tombs" (German: *Betrachtungen bey den Gräbern*) led to his being included among the "Graveyard Poets" of the eighteenth century.

2. See Hamann, *Londoner Schriften*, 40–47, 48–53.

This discussion of the *Betrachtungen* will concentrate on particular, signal themes that stand out in the work, thus gathering under separate themes what is scattered or diffuse throughout. These themes include the Bible, translation and interpretation, reason, creation, fall and redemption, the new in the old and the old by the new, law and gospel, and, faith. All references to the *Betrachtungen* are taken from the *Londoner Schriften* edition of Hamann's writings which, together with Bernd Weissenborn, are edited by Oswald Bayer, responsible for the introduction of Johann Georg Hamann to the current theological world, and especially to readers in this country.

Bible, Translation, and Interpretation

God, writes Hamann, revealed himself to human beings in nature and in his word. These two revelations cannot contradict each other. For example, in the Bible precisely the same lack of order exists as can be detected in nature. In a tiny piece serving as introduction to the *Betrachtungen,* he exclaims, "God an author! The inspiration of this book is as great a humiliation and condescension of God as the creation of the Father and the humanity of the Son."[3] In his meditation on 1 Samuel 9:10, Hamann writes that God the Holy Spirit became a "history writer" of the smallest, most despised, most insignificant events on earth in order to reveal his counsels and mysteries to humankind in its own language, and its own history. In fact, Scripture can only speak in parables, since all human knowledge is sensuous, figurative. The revelation allowed to Job, for example, remained with physical curiosities, with beasts, with the Leviathan and the ants without seeing them to their core, to their relation to the invisible, the hidden and spiritual. Indeed, the Holy Ghost did not merely content himself with speaking and writing as a human being, but as "stupid, mad, raging," letting "his spit run down his beard."[4] And though this word was a revelation neither a Voltaire, a Bolingbroke, nor a Shaftesbury would find acceptable, since God had it in mind to reveal himself first to a single man, then to his race, to a particular people, and finally to the entire human family, it was folly to test it according to one's own taste and judgment.

At various points in the Pentateuch Hamann locates the *Rundgesang* (roundelay) of all of Scripture. He locates it in the narrative of the golden calf in Exodus 32:6: "They rose early the next day and offered burnt offerings

---

3. Hamann, *Londoner Schriften,* 59.
4. Hamann, *Londoner Schriften,* 160.

and brought sacrifices of wellbeing; and the people sat down to eat and drink and rose up to revel." Then in every chapter of 1 Samuel he sees a story of our redemption, including our sin, God's judgment on us and the tyrants whose enticements we followed, the story of our repentance, our faith, and all of religion, with ever new circumstances added in order to set the whole in a greater light. Or, he will write that the Holy Ghost was pleased to unveil himself in no history more than in David's.

"With what reverence," writes Hamann, "should we receive the Bible, the masterpieces of the divine wisdom, even treasure this book in which all the mysteries of the divine wisdom are contained, which for the simple should be a light on his way and a riddle for the angels of an unequally higher rank."[5] "How is it possible," he writes, "that a Christian, without the sin of idolatry, can set this book with indifference or irreverently among others?"[6]

With regard to Bible translation, Hamann writes that since the idioms of the ancient languages are nearest to the nature of ideas and experiences, translation should stay as close as possible to the language in which the Bible is written. The "emptiest, the most tasteless, the most sinful (*sündlichsten*)" words should be chosen since excellence requires cutting away whatever is unnecessary and expressing the thoughts in the least words and the most intense in the simplest. On occasion Hamann will admit to the inability of rendering the text in his own idiom. For example, he is in doubt whether the Hebrew text or the Septuagint translation of the word of the Lord to David during the battle with the Philistines ("when you hear the sound of marching in the tops of the balsam trees, then be on the alert") matches the tree on which Zacchaeus climbed to see Jesus, and decides to dispense with meditating on the book of Job since his ideas seem to deviate too widely from its meaning, the understanding of which is too difficult.[7]

As regards the Bible's interpretation, Hamann writes that the witness to Jesus is the test of exposition. "This rule," he writes, "serves in all of Holy Scripture as the cornerstone and must be the test of all expositors."[8] For this work the interpreter is encouraged to seek assistance:

> The need for us readers to situate ourselves
> within the perception of the author we have
> before us, to get as near as possible to
> his situation, which, by a fortunate power
> of imagination we are able to do, and

5. Hamann, *Londoner Schriften*, 113.
6. Hamann, *Londoner Schriften*, 180.
7. Hamann, *Londoner Schriften*, 172, 208.
8. Hamann, *Londoner Schriften*, 97 (on Genesis 33:19).

toward which a poet or historian seeks
to help us as much as possible, is a rule
which among its provisions is just as needful
as with other books.⁹

Hamann takes his own advice. In addition to citing James Hervey, in the *Betrachtungen* and other writings from this period he makes liberal use of Edward Young,¹⁰ translating individual portions of his work for his readers. He also cites the Greek rhetorician Longinus or Pseudo-Longinus, presumed author of the first-century treatise *On the Sublime* (Perì Hýpsous), with its accent on wonder and transport as required for the reading of great books.

Reason

Anyone acquainted with Hamann will recall his intense criticism of the Enlightenment and its insistence upon reason as the bar before which everything should be measured or judged. Throughout the *Betrachtungen* comments, critiques, and attacks respecting reason are attached to the various passages under investigation, thus appear diffuse, but which are gathered systematically in the author's later works. In the *Betrachtungen* Hamann writes that natural knowledge and history are the two pillars on which the true religion rests. Natural knowledge, however, has its limits. The nature of objects yields the material, and the laws according to which we experience it yields the form. For this reason natural knowledge is as old as nature, and since it remains unalterable, no novelty can occur in the experience of it. Accordingly, there is more to religion than the witness of the senses and of reason. For example, Hamann writes that reasons for the creation can no more be researched than the question why it pleased God to create in six days. Commenting on Genesis 2:3 and its reference to God's resting on the seventh day, he states that we must regard ourselves as those who are denied hearing at birth. In fact, reason should have been impregnated with the seed of the divine word, and the two should have lived under one roof as man and wife. But what God wanted joined together the Machiavellian enemy of God and man has rent asunder. Hamann likens the deception of the eyes in

---

9. Hamann, *Londoner Schriften*, 66.
10. Edward Young, son of the Dean of Salisbury, born at Upham, educated at Winchester, later at New College, Oxford, and from thence to Corpus Christi and All Souls, was nearly fifty when he took on holy orders. Young is best known for his poem *Night Thoughts*, enormously successful in Europe as a romantic classic.

the astronomy of Ptolemy to the deception of reason respecting Scripture. In the dark, Hamann writes, we have more faith in what closes our eyes to the light that would show us the nature and object of our desires. On Job 3:19 Hamann addresses his reader: "Don't you see in daily experience how you perish without his caring for you? Of what help is your reason when it dies in you without wisdom?"[11]

One after another the faults of reason are tallied up. The list is almost endless. The farther reason looks, Hamann writes, the greater the labyrinth in which it loses itself, and like Solomon begins to draw conclusions with which to support itself and not despair. There is so little coherence and propriety of conclusion in "blind reason." In fact our reason is of less use to us than a bird making use of only one wing. Reason is inclined to serve an unknown god, but at an infinite distance. It will not know him, and even more astonishing, when it does know him it ceases to serve him. Reason teaches us to hate and despise under the appearance of virtue. In the *Betrachtungen* on Acts and the Fourth Gospel, Hamann refers to the "excesses" of human reason, its explaining the workings of God through natural causes, such as the effects of sweet wine at the outpouring of the Spirit at Pentecost, or through miracles of lower rank, such as the voice of thunder or an angel at the voice of God in answer to Jesus's prayer.[12] In the wisdom of the world man has often wanted to oppose nature to its Creator. Hamann puts it simply: What is in us, our reason, our desires, our needs, our nature, our time, life itself, rise up against us. "Our times," he writes, "have produced a few fanatics of unbelief who have made of reason such as the papists have made only of Mary."[13] In fact, Hamann argues, "the instruction of God in sleep and dream makes us wiser and happier than the waking of reason and our natural powers and our best inclinations."[14]

Commenting on Romans 1:16 Hamann writes that one would expect reason to recognize and accept a teaching which before all others seems created for the imperfections of our nature, yet nothing is harder and more impossible for the natural man than this faith.[15] In his meditations on the Sermon on the Mount Hamann remarks on "how sour" Jesus's teaching office must have become for him. The disciples heard none of his words, and did not understand what he said. As for the Jews who awaited a universal monarchy, such persons as Jesus describes in the Beatitudes had to appear tasteless.

---

11. Hamann, *Londoner Schriften*, 208.
12. Hamann, *Londoner Schriften*, 282, 279.
13. Hamann, *Londoner Schriften*, 79.
14. Hamann, *Londoner Schriften*, 254.
15. Hamann, *Londoner Schriften*, 288.

Regarding the Pharisees' questioning Jesus's authority in Luke 20:1–8, Hamann writes that they use their reason, draw sly conclusions, deny their own ideas, pretend to an ignorance they do not have, all of it a consequence of appeasing "blind reason."[16] Regarding what the Jews lost with much and what the wise men saw with little, Hamann has this to say:

> So much that is extraordinary as could have made
> the Jews reflective was all lost. On the other hand,
> the sight of a child and his mother, after whom the
> wise men inquired as after a prince, and which they
> now found unknown and in circumstances one could
> regard as disadvantageous to their expectation
> and reason, could not make them err or insensible.[17]

The need, Hamann argues, is to get beyond reason to recognize the new and how it happens. It is beyond the course of nature and the circle of vision of reason and every rational creature that the new is encountered. God must alter that course, that vision, or must broaden it, if something more than the old is to be discovered and recognized. All this, Hamann argues, God ascribes expressly to himself in Holy Scripture.

Creation, Fall, Redemption

In the *Betrachtungen* on Genesis Hamann celebrates the coherence in Moses's narrative of the state of innocence and the fall. Both relate to each other as creation and redemption, or as the advantages of current society to their running to seed in its disadvantages. Remarking on the surest sign of the union of soul and body in Moses's description of it as the effect of the divine breath, Hamann proceeds to the narrative of the ruination of the image of God by "our first parents," caused by "one whom God did not even regard worth naming as its originator, but allows Moses to speak of the serpent."[18] The *Betrachtungen* are ripe with references to Satan, "the serpent's seed," to his portrait in contemporary art that needs no naming, to the root of his work as the divine word, to his tyranny, his blinding sense and reason, to what he does with God's wrath, misusing the freedom of his "sword," and to how that wily enemy uses redemption as a snare to entice us into his kingdom. God makes room for him, argues Hamann, allows him power

---

16. Hamann, *Londoner Schriften*, 107, 176.
17. Hamann, *Londoner Schriften*, 259.
18. Hamann, *Londoner Schriften*, 113.

over us. "Since Satan through his minions would happily swallow everything up, that much room God has made for him on earth and still makes room."[19] Our situation, our nature, and the condition of our existence make absolutely necessary the testing beneath which the first human was set. Without it, the lordship of the serpent would increase. On the other hand, there are limits to Satan's activity. In his reflection on Job Hamann writes that the devil took from Job everything belonging to flesh and blood and the weakness of our nature, but that the use of Job's wife was the only remedy, the only counsel the acceptance of which was available to him to ease the sufferer.[20] "This life," Hamann concludes, "is given [Satan] as a booty from God," but ultimately "he shall get to eat the dust from which man is made."[21] Nor is Satan himself beyond observing the amenities. Commenting on 1 Peter 3:4 ("let your adornment be the inner self with the lasting beauty of a gentle and quiet spirit") Hamann writes: "How ashamed must Satan be when he hears his own children mock and laugh at the works of God, about which he himself does not think without a shudder."[22]

Of the redemption Hamann writes that "God has come down," that this preeminent mark of his love for humankind is everywhere in Scripture. But God did not come down to "depend on his wife," but "shared her fate with her, shared her poverty, her sin and shame."[23] In this "wrestling" with humankind God confesses that he is "outmanned and conquered."[24] In this encounter, Hamann writes:

> God "forgets that he is God, forgets his omnipotence, cannot win out against man. He has given man so much power over his love that the whole creation itself views it almost jealously and as a weakness of the great God toward this perverted generation.[25]

All this cost God a call, that is, the calling of his Son, whereas the entire creation cost him only a word. More, all of God was involved in this call: "God the Father, as well as the other persons of the highly exalted Trinity, had to put up with seeing himself humiliated."[26] It was a humiliation

---

19. Hamann, *Londoner Schriften*, 121.
20. Hamann, *Londoner Schriften*, 206.
21. Hamann, *Londoner Schriften*, 245.
22. Hamann, *Londoner Schriften*, 304.
23. Hamann, *Londoner Schriften*, 272.
24. Hamann, *Londoner Schriften*, 272.
25. Hamann, *Londoner Schriften*, 144.
26. Hamann, *Londoner Schriften*, 103.

fulfilled in time, but in God's eyes already present at earth's first days. Describing the Redeemer as hiding himself in this miserable shape to make himself king of the world, Hamann writes that the intention of the Incarnation was to fulfill the law. Writing on Matthew 5:18 ("until heaven and earth pass away, not one letter, not one stroke of a letter, will pass from the law until all is accomplished"), he states that it rests with God to abolish the laws by which heaven and earth subsist, but a single letter, indeed, a jot from those laws founded on his holiness, is ineradicable.[27] To the question why God was so late in showing himself, Hamann answers, "because he knows that for man the knowledge of him is an offence, an irritation; that in their eyes he is foolishness and a thorn as soon as he wills to give himself to be revealed to them and to be known.[28]

Referring to Jesus's appearing as marking the midday of time or "the early rain," Hamann writes that in Matthew's record of his baptism the greatest event is told which earth or all of nature has ever seen, that it contains more than Moses's word, "In the beginning God created heaven and earth." There, at the baptism of Jesus, God in the shape of a poor human being, allows himself to be submerged for forgiveness at the hands of a sinner.[29] Stating that at the temptation Satan seemed to have been concerned only with knowing whether Jesus would be God's Son, Hamann asks:

> What would have been more human than to use the
> opportunity Satan gave to convince him that the
> Redeemer would be God's Son
> Then answers "No!" And again,
> Here was the moment in which a man would have to
> divest himself of divinity—in him not a robbery—
> to atone for the crime of Adam who to please the serpent
> lusted after being like God.

And again answers:

> No! God does not regard the prince of hell worth letting
> his omnipotence being seen.[30]

Moving to the Sermon on the Mount and its description of "the seven characteristics and marks of true Christianity," Hamann writes of its reflecting the two sides of Christ's truth, an odor of life for life or an odor of death to death, in either case the glorification of his Father and the doing of his

27. Hamann, *Londoner Schriften*, 263.
28. Hamann, *Londoner Schriften*, 286.
29. Hamann, *Londoner Schriften*, 256.
30. Hamann, *Londoner Schriften*, 260.

will. To the third Beatitude ("Blessed are the meek") Hamann writes that the history of Caesar and Augustus, then "a living example," furnishes the antithesis. Of the parables Hamann writes that nothing exalts the divinity of the Savior more than his continual appeal to observations of nature or common events.[31] Commenting on the parable of the Good Samaritan in Luke 10:25–37, Hamann asks, "Was not Jesus scolded as a Samaritan for your sake?" Construing Jesus's response in John 1:48 to Nathaniel's question, "Where did you get to know me?" as a parable ("I saw you under the fig tree"), Hamann comments that "our Savior seems to make use of the parable with so much pleasure since all three evangelists have collected it."[32] Finding extraordinary the contradiction of passions in the moods of Jesus's audiences at his miracles, he writes that the Redeemer gives himself to be known as a beneficent physician, that the sicknesses of the body belong to the ultimate purpose of his redemption, since they are parables and effects of sick souls. Of Jesus's summons to the lame man by the pool of Bethsaida, "See, you have been made well! Do not sin any more," Hamann first asks, "Was this remembrance necessary for a man who for so long had suffered the punishments for it?" then asks again, "was not this reminder itself based on the omniscience of the almighty physician?" He sees the miracle of the twelve baskets left from the seven loaves at Jesus's feeding of the four thousand a prophecy of the twelve apostles and the seven elders of the Jerusalem community. These numbers, he adds, enjoy a kind of solemnity in ordinary life, twelve the number of moons in a year, and seven the number of days in a week.[33]

Writing of the Passion Hamann remarks on the contrast between the wife of Potiphar, high officer of the Pharaoh, and the wife of Pontius Pilate. By a woman's hand Joseph's innocence serves to prove his crime, and by a woman's dream witness is paid the innocence of the accused. Just as there the wife lured the man to an unjust judgment, so here the man's wife vainly seeks to scare him to justice by her dream.[34] Reflecting on Jesus's word in Mark 9:49–50, "Have salt in yourselves, and be at peace with one another," and its intimations of sacrifice, Hamann writes that just as the Levitical sacrifices prefigured Christ and were accepted in his place by God, so "his sacrifice in our place" (*an unserer Statt*) was accepted by God. On the parable of the Good Samaritan in Luke 10 Hamann writes of Christ as our neighbor "whom we must love as ourselves, because he died in our place (*an unserer Statt*), lives in us, and we are buried and raised with him." And on John

---

31. Hamann, *Londoner Schriften*, 271.
32. Hamann, *Londoner Schriften*, 278.
33. Hamann, *Londoner Schriften*, 269.
34. Hamann, *Londoner Schriften*, 100.

10:17 ("For this reason the Father loves me, because I lay down my life in order to take it up again"), states that for our sake God loves his Son, for the love he has had for us, "for the death he died for us, in our place (*an unserer Statt*) and for our benefit.[35] In the *Betrachtungen* on 2 Samuel 1, Hamann writes that Christ's taking upon himself the wages of sin spelled a cruelty in God. The relevant sentences read:

> The innocence of Jesus was a suit of armor. . . . The deity was united with this innocence, this suit of armor, this unseamed garment, which totally sustained his life despite the wound Satan, sin and death dealt him. Thus God, our blessed Savior, could not take on the wages of sin without righteousness itself being changed to cruelty in God, indeed without petition being made for this cruelty as a grace, the only grace.[36]

Three fourths of the way through the *Betrachtungen* Hamann addresses his hypothetical reader:

> What man has done more good on earth as a mere man, and, were we to separate God from the great Mediator, what man is more despised, of whose name one is more ashamed than that of Jesus, while the wise Socrates and Plato are named with triumph and reverence?[37]

The New in the Old and the Old by the New

When in his introduction to the *Betrachtungen* Hamann writes that the history of Israel is of greater importance to our religion than that of any other people, or when toward their conclusion he writes that the greatest people on earth have served for nothing but to be prophets of invisible things, a "puppet show of the divine providence,"[38] he gives notice of the Augustinian thrust in his reflections on the relation between the Testaments. Again and again a person or event recorded in the Old Testament functions as a type or figure of those recorded in the New. The reason for the typology, or, as the case may be, for the allegory, is that creation and redemption belong together, everything in the Old Testament functioning as preparation for

---

35. Hamann, *Londoner Schriften*, 270, 274, 278.
36. Hamann, *Londoner Schriften*, 168.
37. Hamann, *Londoner Schriften*, 250.
38. Hamann, *Londoner Schriften*, 69, 238.

the Messiah. Thus, the life of the patriarchs is replete with allegory. Laban's harsh treatment of Jacob is "the most sensuous pattern" of the Jews against God.[39] Just as the story of Joseph is like a painting which appears directed at us, from whatever angle we view it, so we see glimpses of the Redeemer streaming out from his life.[40] Just as Abraham's grave was a pledge of the possession of the whole land, so the grave in which Christ was laid and from which he arose is a pledge of our resurrection and of heaven.[41] Of Moses's victory over King Sihon the Amorite, Hamann insists that "God would not have taken up this joy" if it had not been a figure of the great victory we all share, and of the burning bush and its piquing Moses's curiosity, writes that God was performing a test (*machte eine Probe*), all of it a mere figure of an infinitely greater redemption.[42] In the narrative of the conquest of Canaan, Hamann sees prefigured the founding of the Christian Church.[43] Hamann writes that in the discourse on the roof top between Saul and the "familiarity," as the Hebrew has it, we find the mystery of the Incarnation of God.[44] There is no end to the typology. The friendship of David and Jonathan is a figure of the unity of deity and humanity in Christ. Indeed, the Holy Spirit has not deigned to reveal himself in a history more than in David's.[45] The presumptive king's cutting the corner of Saul's cloak in the cave near Engedi suggests to Hamann that "God our Savior had God in his power, as it were. He did nothing more than to rob him of a tip of his coat, and with it cover men's nakedness and convince God he should forgive them."[46] In Nehemiah the spirit of the assembly gathered to hear Ezra's reading of the law was the Spirit of the Word, the Spirit of the cleansing and washing in Holy Baptism. The entire story of Balaam is a figure of the temptation of the Savior in the wilderness.[47] In order not to frighten men by its majesty the wisdom of Proverbs assumes a human appearance, an earthly majesty, is obedient unto death, even death on the cross.[48] In regard to Jonah's response to the Lord's summons, Hamann comments that it deserves comparison with

---

39. Hamann, *Londoner Schriften*, 96.
40. Hamann, *Londoner Schriften*, 100–101.
41. Hamann, *Londoner Schriften*, 102.
42. Hamann, *Londoner Schriften*, 121, 126.
43. Hamann, *Londoner Schriften*, 275.
44. Hamann, *Londoner Schriften*, 155.
45. Hamann, *Londoner Schriften*, 159, 162–63.
46. Hamann, *Londoner Schriften*, 162.
47. Hamann, *Londoner Schriften*, 199–200.
48. Hamann, *Londoner Schriften*, 214.

Peter's confession of faith in Christ.[49] Writing of Jesus's temptation in Matthew 4, Hamann states that it must be correlated with the story of Adam's fall. For example, the hunger of the Redeemer deserves comparison with the presumption that induced Adam to eat of the forbidden tree. Summing up Hamann writes as follows:

> The whole history of the life of our Savior and the
> Jewish people till the destruction of Jerusalem
> Is a prophecy which must be compared with the
> Revelation of John and the prophets of the Old
> Covenant. God repeats himself as in nature, in
> Scripture, in the governing of the world, in the
> founding of his Church, in the changing course
> of the times—at least it appears so to us, and it
> is necessary for us, that we see repetition—They
> are not the same fruits and yet are the same
> yielded every spring.[50]

Law and Gospel

Commenting on the cherubim and flaming sword at the entrance to the tree of life in Genesis 3, Hamann writes that the sword prefigures the nature of the law explained by Paul with so much depth of mind in his letter to the Romans.[51] In commenting on the blessing of Abraham by Melchizedek, Hamann states that "we should not think that in God's sight this law was the only condition necessary to please him"; that God had his true servants and worshippers in Japheth's as well as in Shem's line, an "order" to which, presumably, Melchizedek belonged.[52] Later, reflecting on Romans 1:16 Hamann would write that the law of the heathen was to God just as holy as that revealed to the Jews.[53] Nor was circumcision itself the covenant. In avenging their sister on the circumcised Shechemites, Simeon and Levi refute the advantage of circumcision.[54] Commenting on Leviticus 16, Hamann asks, "what can give us a greater concept of the holiness of God and the impossibility of easing it by the law than that the Holy Place itself, the altar, and

---

49. Hamann, *Londoner Schriften*, 247.
50. Hamann, *Londoner Schriften*, 299.
51. Hamann, *Londoner Schriften*, 78.
52. Hamann, *Londoner Schriften*, 91.
53. Hamann, *Londoner Schriften*, 291.
54. Hamann, *Londoner Schriften*, 97.

tabernacle needed reconciliation?"[55] The Jews, Hamann writes, should not disown the law by thinking their fathers and they themselves could have lived without it, yet not build so much on its perfection as though it would never cease.[56] In Nehemiah Hamann finds a foretaste of the evangelical spirit, not simply the spirit suppressed under the law in Ezra, but who in the cupbearer of God tastes the growth of the new covenant. Nehemiah, Hamann adds, is key to the entire history of Moses, the greatest miracle and core of the divine revelation in the Old Testament.[57] Seven days, Hamann writes on Job 2:13, God let us lie in the deep humiliation to which our sins had brought us before he gave us a most imperfect comfort through the revelation of the law, till he himself appeared and instructed and doubly blest us as he did Job.[58] On the other hand, in the old covenant, God, who would have been content with a single fulfillment of the law, ameliorated fulfillment of the law by instituting a sacrifice requiring the blood of men from beasts. And, adds Hamann, Christ ameliorated it even more. Reflecting on Jesus's injunction that one leave one's gift at the altar and be reconciled with whomever one has offended, Hamann writes:

> God will happily see the service delayed which
> you thought to give him.... Let God wait, hasten
> first to make friends with your brother, and toward
> you he will then likewise show himself to be a
> reconciled God, a reconciled brother.[59]

Reflecting on the parable of the Good Samaritan Hamann lyricizes:

> Neither priest nor Levite, neither Moses nor Samuel,
> neither law nor the prophets, neither the zeal of the
> Jews nor the wisdom of the Greeks—nothing could,
> nothing would help you. The priest appears to avoid
> the sight of you out of sympathy and gentility.
> The Levite examines you more closely—of what
> use to you is his curiosity. We are therefore dead to the
> law given through angels and managed by Levites.[60]

---

55. Hamann, *Londoner Schriften*, 110–11.
56. Hamann, *Londoner Schriften*, 111.
57. Hamann, *Londoner Schriften*, 199.
58. Hamann, *Londoner Schriften*, 206.
59. Hamann, *Londoner Schriften*, 263, 265.
60. Hamann, *Londoner Schriften*, 273.

✓ Faith

Commenting on the line in Hebrews 11 that reads, "by faith we understand the worlds were prepared by the word of God," Hamann asserts that without faith we cannot understand the creation and nature.[61] At the head of his exposition of the parable of the Good Samaritan he writes that its purpose is to indicate the nature of faith, free of all self-righteousness, and based solely on the love of a Redeemer. In what follows he identifies his hypothetical reader with the man who fell among robbers, and exclaims:

> Was he not a traveler for your sake—and with what
> inconveniences—did he not come where you were . . .
> had sympathy for you . . . not only came where you were
> but actually, came to you, to you—bound up your wounds . . .
> poured in oil and wine.

Then concludes:

> Did you have the powers to come to him on your own,
> and enter the free city, the guest-house which he sought
> out and prepared for you? No, he loans you his strength.[62]

In his *Betrachtungen* on Jesus's encounter with the woman of Samaria, Hamann asks, "What was the water that quenches the thirst of souls?" and answers, "faith in Jesus." We must deny the sham righteousness of the Pharisees and the superstition of human conceit that oppose this faith, our eyes opened to see the Savior more clearly, "in the beginning as a prophet, and gradually as the true and only God."[63] In his Comment on 1 John 2:20 ("you have been anointed by the Holy One, and all of you have knowledge"), Hamann writes that by faith we take such great share in the divine nature that we enjoy the omniscience and anointing of the heavenly kingdom, and on the parable of the Good Samaritan that we not only bear God's image in us, but also the Eradicator of sin. Hence, for the Christian "every foolishness, imperfection, weakness, sin on the part of our neighbor, is a nail to the cross, a drop of blood on Jesus's face, squeezing out from him the prayer: Father, forgive him [sic], they know not what they do."[64] In his comment on Genesis 31 he exclaims: "Can a greater exchange, a greater trade be conceived of?"[65] Thus, just as our Redeemer was the sacrifice for us, we owe ourselves as

---

61. Hamann, *Londoner Schriften*, 307.
62. Hamann, *Londoner Schriften*, 272.
63. Hamann, *Londoner Schriften*, 279.
64. Hamann, *Londoner Schriften*, 306, 274.
65. Hamann, *Londoner Schriften*, 103.

sacrifice to the Savior and Father, not as he was, but as were his patterns, his prototypes.[66] In this intercession for the other Hamann writes that all means are available to the Christian; all are hallowed. "In this connection," he states, "the poets are of help and the best specimens for disclosing to us the way of a person's and a people's thinking, as well as their inclinations."[67] It is by this faith that love for truth must be regulated, writes Hamann on 2 John 11, for such love is not to be extended to the enemies of God outside nor the secret enemies inside the Church. And continuing the same thought in connection with his reflection on 3 John 9-10 writes,

> Here in John we see an example that love for neighbor
> according to the intent of the Holy Ghost is not weak,
> no childish fear, nor inability; that when it forgives errors,
> it knows how to distinguish errors from malice; that it bears
> the first with patience and leniency, and seeks to
> help, but emphatically and zealously resists sacrilege.[68]

Reflections

The initial problem encountering the reader is Hamann's literary style, involving abbreviations, frequent omission of diacritical marks where needed, and, on occasion, the use of two verbs in tandem, forcing the reader to hunt for dual antecedents. Added to personal reference is the liberal use of the pronoun in the first or second person plural, and in a book not intended for publication. Some of the grandest passages in the *Betrachtungen* reflect this curious usage. To cite just one instance among hundreds, reflecting on a passage in the Song of Solomon Hamann writes:

> The more *we* veer off into pleasures, the nearer
> the approach to loud laughter; the more *we* feel
> *we* are in a sort of anger and fury that meets the
> eye of even a casual observer.[69]

With whom is Hamann sharing the experience? Are "we" friends and/or critics parading before his imagination? Or is use of the pronoun in the plural a mere editorial device? The bulk of the evidence points in the other direction: Intended for publication or no, Hamann has readers in mind.

66. Hamann, *Londoner Schriften*, 270.
67. Hamann, *Londoner Schriften*, 302.
68. Hamann, *Londoner Schriften*, 306.
69. Hamann, *Londoner Schriften*, 229.

Hamann has been labelled an irrationalist.[70] And in fact, his accent on reason as closed to novelty, penned in a labyrinth, inclined to serve an unknown god, teaching to hate under the guise of virtue, opposing nature to its Creator, appears to support the label. But his insistence on reason and the divine word as "meant for each other" despite their separation suggests that the reader take caution, and what he has to say of nature's thirst, its hunger, and its rumor of novelty challenges the allegation. In the introduction to the *Betrachtungen* he writes:

> Nature has put a salt in all bodies which the distillers (*Scheidekünstler*) know how to extract, and it seems that in midst of all the unpleasantness Providence has implanted a morally primal element which we need to analyze and separate, and can profitably use as an aid against the diseases of our nature and ill temper.[71]

Again, in the *Betrachtungen* on Deuteronomy 8:1–3, Hamann writes that we are earth, and that this earth is linked to an eternal God. By way of temporal benefits this God seeks to lure us (*versuchen*) to himself, to urge our temporal lack toward warnings of our spiritual hunger, and the poverty of our nature toward the riches and treasures of his love and grace.[72] Thus, a rumor of the novelty beyond nature and reason's circle of vision has been spread abroad, planted in us by God. It is a "thirst" which we feel, despite our sin of origin. For this reason, Hamann argues, the gospel is called "the good news of the kingdom of God," and Jesus the crucified the sole object for which that urge toward the new has been implanted.[73]

Hence, a certain double sidedness or communion of opposites is discernible in Hamann's reflections on reason. On the one hand, reason is an enemy, or, of less use to us than to a bird with only one wing. On the other, for Hamann himself, in midst of his "present condition," described as "the greatest solitude," "the bitterness of many an unhappy reflection on past idiocies," "the misuse of benefits," and "the prospect of a barren waste," he recognizes a loving Father.

From the section entitled "The New in the Old and the Old by the New," of which just some were farmed from myriad examples, it is clear that Hamann would have resisted the argument that the Old Testament must be interpreted for itself alone, without attention to its use at the hands of the

70. See Berlin, "Magus of the North."
71. Hamann, *Londoner Schriften*, 65.
72. Hamann, *Londoner Schriften*, 133.
73. Hamann, *Londoner Schriften*, 285.

New Testament authors or their interpreters. Who knows to what extent he was aware of the historical criticism of the Old Testament emerging with Jan Astruc (1684–1766) and J.G. Eichhorn (1752–1827), but it is hard to imagine that a man at home with the biblical languages, wrestling with translation problems, and conversant with the literary masters of the day and their reflections, would not have been aware of the activity of the critics. A century earlier Thomas Hobbes (1588–1679), Baruch Spinoza (1632–1677), and the Roman Catholic priest Richard Simon (1638–1712) had already subjected the biblical message to critical reinterpretation. Obviously, the Voltaires (1694–1778), Shaftesburys (1671–1713), and Bolingbrokes (1678–1751) did not escape him. Anyone who displayed such intimate acquaintance with the work of Immanuel Kant, his antecedents and followers, supporters and critics, must have known something of those eager to apply the principles of the Enlightenment to the biblical text. In any case, he had made up his mind: Typological exegesis of the Old Testament in light of the person and work of Jesus Christ was the single, sole and appropriate use of the same. The pages weigh heavy under this Augustinian rule.

One aspect of the critical approach Hamann could not have been aware of, that is, the attempt to solve the problem of the literary relationship between the Gospels. When he writes of Jesus's response to Nathaniel's question in John 1:48 ("Where did you get to know me?") as a parable ("I saw you under the fig tree"), Hamann comments that "our Savior seems to make use of the parable with so much pleasure since all three evangelists have collected it."[74] Not until 1838, when Christian Gottlob Wilke—born the year of Hamann's death (1788)—tracked the Gospels in parallel, would it be clear that such utterances as the fig tree "parable" had a single author on whom his co-evangelists depended.

In connection with his remarks on the Incarnation Hamann refers to the Savior's inability to take on the wages of sin "without righteousness itself being changed to cruelty in God."[75] Taken alone, the sentence appears to have all the earmarks of a cosmic child-abuse, God the Father subjecting the Son to a passion in which he is not involved, does not at all share. On occasion Hamann will allude to a separation between Father and Son in the event.[76] But when he writes that in the encounter with humankind God is outmanned and conquered, forgets that he is God, forgets his omnipotence,

---

74. See Hamann, *Londoner Schriften*, 278.

75. See Hamann, *Londoner Schriften*, 168.

76. See Hamann, *Londoner Schriften*, 270: "So [Christ's] sacrifice in our place (*an unserer Statt*) was accepted by God."

and cannot win out against man,[77] the suggestion is that the entire Trinity is involved in God's having "come down." If this suggestion should not suffice to convince, the comment on Genesis 31, according to which "God the Father, as well as the other persons of the highly exalted Trinity, had to put up with seeing himself humiliated,"[78] should certainly do so. Further, when Hamann refers to Christ's death as "in our stead" (*an unserer Statt*), he seems to imply the traditional Anselmian view of Christ's death as a substitutionary atonement.[79] Such may only seem so, since there is no emphasis on a "satisfaction" of penalty in Hamann's discussion of Christ's death, but rather on the love of God in assuming human flesh. Again: "Did not God leave heaven and everything to cleave to his wife? He shared her fate with her, shared her poverty, her sin and shame";[80] or again:

> God loves his Son for our sake, because
> of the love he has had for us, because of
> the death he died for us, in our place and for
> our benefit. God is love."[81]

As Johann Christian Konrad von Hofmann (1810–1877) years later would write, our view of the atonement must begin with the fact of God's originating love. The atonement was thus a "satisfaction," but "of [God's] love, the reason for it only in himself."[82] The twenty-eight-year-old Hamann was closer to a von Hofmann than to an Anselm.

Hamann may not be described as a patripassian, holding or intimating that God the Father was crucified together with the Son. Nevertheless, there are many references to God, absent the appositive "our Savior," as "coming down," "leaving heaven," giving humans such power over himself as to render creation jealous and himself suspect of weakness. And there is that stunning reference to God the Father, and the other persons of the Trinity as having to put up with seeing himself humiliated. At first sight, the reference suggests that Hamann does not share the traditional, orthodox view of the Father's impassibility over against the Son's humiliation. It rather implies that the Father was not unaffected by the suffering of Christ, that by this death something happened to the Father that had not happened to him before. On the other hand, when Hamann writes that the Incarnation was

---

77. Hamann, *Londoner Schriften*, 144.
78. Hamann, *Londoner Schriften*, 103.
79. Hamann, *Londoner Schriften*, 270, 274, 278.
80. Hamann, *Londoner Schriften*, 272.
81. Hamann, *Londoner Schriften*, 278.
82. Von Hofmann, *Schutzschriften*, 2:83, 99.

"already there with the first days of the earth,"[83] it is clear that he does not espouse a passivity in God according to which Christ's death took him by surprise. Hence, if the reference to the Trinity's having to put up with seeing himself humiliated spells a passivity in God, then not an involuntary passivity. And, if the reference to the Incarnation as being already there with the first days of the earth spells an impassibility in God, then an impassibility able to share in human pain and grief.

The double sidedness in Hamann's reflections on the Incarnation cannot be missed. On the one hand, the Incarnation involves the Father's separation from the Son (righteousness being changed to "cruelty in God"), but as already indicated, it involves the humiliation of all the persons of the Trinity. The same characteristic attaches to Hamann's reflections on redemption. On the one hand, the redemption implies an impassibility in God but an impassibility able to share human grief and pain, or it implies a passivity but a passivity that is voluntary.

On the surface, it appears that Hamann's description of the law as ameliorated by sacrifice, or as further ameliorated by Christ himself, reduces its demand, to say nothing of its existence. And indeed, Hamann can write that the law of Moses was not the only condition necessary to please God; that there is no greater concept of God's holiness and the impossibility of easing it by the law than that the Holy One himself needed reconciliation. Or when he speaks of the law's coming to an end, for which reason not so much should be built on its perfection.[84] But in his reflection on Jesus's word in Matthew 5:17 ("Do not think that I have come to abolish the law or the prophets; I have come not to abolish but to fulfill"), Hamann writes:

> In this regard our Savior declares to his disciples that
> the intention of his Incarnation is to fulfill the law. He
> discloses its mystery to them in its inalterability;
> he compares it with the law of creation and indicates
> the priority of the former over the will of God which
> produced nature, and by which it is sustained. It rests
> with God to abolish the laws by which heaven and earth
> exist, but a single letter, indeed, one stroke of those laws
> based on his holiness, is ineradicable.[85]

Thus, a certain double sidedness can also be noted in Hamann's description of the law. On the one hand, the law persists, is inalterable and

---

83. Hamann, *Londoner Schriften*, 156.
84. Hamann, *Londoner Schriften*, 91, 110–11.
85. Hamann, *Londoner Schriften*, 263.

ineradicable, but on the other its demand is reduced, ameliorated to the point that "we have died to the law given by angels and handed down by Levites."[86]

The same characteristic attaches to Hamann's reflections on faith. On the one hand, we are described as "loaned" the power to come to him and to enter the free city, but on the other we are to deny the Pharisaic pretense of righteousness and the superstition of human blindness, our eyes opened more closely to recognize the Savior, "in the beginning as a prophet." And in his *Betrachtungen* on Matthew 7:7 ("Ask, and it will be given you; search, and you will find; knock, and the door will be opened for you") Hamann writes that "a few things must merely be set before God and he thus be sought," while others must be sought "with more zeal, with the zeal a lost object of value deserves," and "still others with violence, as with Jacob: 'My God, I will not let you go.'"[87]

Years later, this young pamphleteer would rise to challenge the entire artifice of the Enlightenment, writing that the communion of the divine and human *idiomata*, or properties of the two natures of Christ is "a basic law and the master-key to all our knowledge."[88] Would it be incautious to describe this great and too lately acknowledged opponent of the Enlightenment as thinking altogether in terms of opposites, of embracing a method or approach at home in a double sidedness, and which began with a radical change, reflected in the *Biblische Betrachtungen*?

Bibliography

Berlin, Isaiah. *The Magus of the North*. New York: FSG, 1994.
Hamann, Johann Georg. *Londoner Schriften, Historisch-kritische Neuedition*. Edited by Oswald Bayer und Bernd Weissenborn. Munich: Beck, 1993.
Haynes, Kenneth. "The Last Will and Testament of the Knight of the Rose-Cross." In *Hamann: Writings on Philosophy and Language*, edited by Kenneth Haynes, 96–110. Cambridge: Cambridge University Press, 2007.
Hofmann, Johann Christian Konrad von. *Schutzschriften für eine neue Weise, alte Wahrheit zu lehren*. Nordlingen: Beck, 1857.

86. Hamann, *Londoner Schriften*, 291.
87. Hamann, *Londoner Schriften*, 259.
88. Haynes, *Hamann*, 99.

3

Through the Cross-Shattered Lens

A Cruciform Epistemology of Hope

John D. Koch

In his *Martin Luther's Theology: A Contemporary Interpretation,* Oswald Bayer observes that Luther had an "apocalyptic view about time . . . that rupture in the ages between the new and the old aeon that took place once for all on the cross of Jesus Christ."[1] With this observation, Bayer highlights a central tenet of Luther's theology, his so-called "theology of the cross," which was articulated shortly after his posting of the 95 theses and would remain a constitutive component of his work throughout his life. With this insight into the profundity of the cross, Luther saw a reformation not merely of how God chose to save, i.e., by faith, but a reformation of the very act of conceiving the relationship between God and humanity. This reformation of thought would have consequences on every aspect of his existence and would, accordingly, change the ways in which theological vocabulary—speech about God—would come to be understood. In what follows, we will examine the ways in which this new appreciation of the cross reordered his conception of human existence before God, established the cross as the epistemic center of his thought, and subsequently changed his way of understanding the work of God in the world. What will be seen is that Luther's "theology of the cross," based as it is on his revolutionary insight into the comprehensiveness of the doctrine of justification by faith and its corresponding distinction between law and gospel, establishes it not merely as one doctrine among many, but constitutive of an entirely new way of conceiving of oneself, God, and the world.

---

1. Bayer, *Martin Luther's Theology,* 10.

Reordering the Semantic Domain

October 31, 2017, marked the 500th anniversary of Martin Luther's posting of the 95 theses on the door of the *Schlosskirche* in Wittenberg, Germany. In his homily to an ecumenical service convened at the Lutheran Cathedral in Lund, Sweden, in 2016 Pope Francis stated:

> The spiritual experience of Martin Luther challenges us to remember that apart from God we can do nothing. "How can I get a propitious God?" This is the question that haunted Luther. In effect, the question of a just relationship with God is the decisive question for our lives. As we know, Luther encountered that propitious God in the good news of Jesus, incarnate, dead and risen. With the concept "by grace alone," he reminds us that God always takes the initiative, prior to any human response, even as he seeks to awaken that response. The doctrine of justification thus expresses the essence of human existence before God.[2]

With this statement, Francis highlights what would become the central tenet of the Reformation, i.e., justification by faith—the *articulus stantis et cadentis ecclesiae*—the article by which the church stands and falls. If, 500 years later, the leader of the Roman Catholic church can praise Martin Luther by pointing to a shared appreciation of the doctrine of justification, can the divide really be that significant? Although countless ink has been spilled on this question, Francis's predecessor Pope Benedict XVI saw its roots with unparalleled clarity and posed this very question. In a 1984 interview for *Communio: International Catholic Review*, entitled "Luther and the Unity of the Churches," then Cardinal Joseph Ratzinger asks the question, "How deep does the difference really go?" to which he answers:

> Luther himself was convinced that the separation of the teachings from the customs of the papal church—to which separation he felt obligated—struck at the very foundation of the act of faith. The act of faith as described by Catholic tradition appeared to Luther as centered and encapsulated in the law, while it should have been an expression of the acceptance of the gospel. In Luther's opinion, the act of faith was turned into the very opposite of what it was; for faith, to Luther, is tantamount to liberation from the law, but its Catholic version appeared to him as a subjugation under the law.[3]

---

2. Francis, "Common Ecumenical Prayer."

3. Ratzinger, "Luther," 217. While the topic of "love" and its relationship to the distinction between law and gospel are not within the precise bounds of this study, and despite his objections, Ratzinger again shows his grasp of the issue with a precision

He concludes:

> To sum up, Luther did indeed realize what he meant when he saw the actual point of separation in the teachings on justification which, to him, were identical with the "gospel" in contradistinction to the "law." To be sure, one has to view justification as radical and as deep as he did, that is, as a reduction of the entire anthropology—and thus also of all other matters of doctrine—to the dialectic of law and gospel.[4]

That Ratzinger sees the entire concept of "faith" in Luther redefined on account of his new appreciation of the doctrine of justification and the "dialectic of law and gospel," points to his understanding of how profoundly Luther's thinking had changed.[5] Indeed, what Ratzinger observes is that

---

sorely lacking from many protestant theologians. He writes, "It seems to me that the basic feature is the fear of God by which Luther's very existence was struck down, torn between God's calling and the realization of his own sinfulness, so much so that God appeared to him *sub contrario*, as the opposite of God himself, that is, as the devil who wants to destroy man. To break free of this fear of God became the real issue of redemption. Redemption was realized the moment faith appeared as the rescue from the demands of self-justification, that is, as a personal certainty of salvation. This 'axis' of the concept of faith is explained very clearly in Luther's Little Catechism: 'I believe that God created me. . . . I believe that Jesus Christ . . . is my Lord who saved me. . . . In order that I may be his . . . and serve him forever in justice and innocence forever.' Faith assures, above all, the certainty of one's own salvation. The personal certainty of redemption became the decisive center of Luther's ideas. Without it, there would be no salvation. Thus, the importance of the three divine virtues, faith, hope, and love, to a formula for Christian life underwent a significant change: the certainty of hope and the certainty of faith, though hitherto essentially different, became identical. To the Catholic, the certainty of faith refers to that which God has wrought, to which the church witnesses. The certainty of hope refers to the salvation of individuals and, among them, of oneself. Yet, to Luther, the latter represented the crux without which nothing else really mattered. That is why love, which lies at the center of the Catholic faith, is dropped from the concept of faith; Luther goes so far as to formulate this polemically in his large commentary on Saint Paul's Epistle to the Galatians: *maledicta sit caritas*, down with love! Luther's insistence on 'by faith alone' clearly and exactly excludes love from the question of salvation. Love belongs to the realm of 'works' and, thus, becomes 'profane'" (Ratzinger, "Luther," 218–19).

4. Ratzinger, "Luther," 220.

5. To this point, see Bayer, *Living by Faith*, xiii–xiv: "When the article on justification, as suggested in this tractate, is understood in a sense so broad and deep as to encompass even creation and the eschaton, then it does not suffice to speak of this article merely as the *articulus stantis et cadentis ecclesiae*, the article upon which the church stands or falls. It is the being of the world and its relation to God that hinge upon justification. *Creatio ex nihilo* (creation out of nothing), the basis of the Jewish and Christian doctrine of creation, is to be understood in terms of the theology of justification—and vice versa. . . . When this ontological significance of justification is grasped, then it becomes clear that justification is neither merely an event in the interior of the believer

Luther's objection to the received soteriology of the late medieval church was not a slight correction, but a reversal; it was a reformation of knowing—centered on the distinction between law and gospel—that upended his world through the word of the cross.[6]

At first glance, it may not seem obvious why the distinction between law and gospel would affect an understanding of faith to the extent cited by Ratzinger, but upon further reflection, we can observe in Luther's understanding of this distinction the reversal which precipitated the redefinition. In his description of his own "breakthrough" he recounts as to how:

> I made no distinction between the law and the gospel. I regarded both as the same thing and held that there was no difference between Christ and Moses except the times in which they lived and their degrees of perfection. But when I discovered the proper distinction—namely, that the law is one thing and the gospel is another—I made myself free.[7]

This freedom of which he speaks became synonymous with that which came through faith *alone* to the ungodly by the grace of God in Christ (cf. Rom 4:5). Accordingly, this newfound freedom by faith reoriented everything around God's action in history as personally "understood," i.e., appropriated by the believer as being *pro me*—for me.[8] In April 1518, less than a year after

---

nor one among many ways to express what Christian faith is about."

6. At this point, a footnote from Gerhard Forde's *On Being a Theologian of the Cross* will be instructive: "The word 'cross' here and in the entire treatise that follows is, of course, shorthand for the entire narrative of the crucified and risen Jesus. As such it includes the OT preparation (many of the foundational passages for the theology of the cross come from the OT!), the crucifixion and resurrection of Jesus, and his exaltation. It is important to include resurrection and exaltation because there is considerable confusion abroad about their place in a theology of the cross. It is often claimed, for instance, that a theology of glory is a theology of resurrection while a theology of the cross is 'only' concerned with crucifixion. Nothing could be further from the truth. As a matter of fact, a theology of the cross is impossible without resurrection. It is impossible to plumb the depths of the crucifixion without the resurrection" (Forde, *On Being a Theologian*, 1n1).

7. *LW* 54:442–43.

8. See Bayer, "Word of the Cross," 47–55, where he explains, "In understanding, there occurs a transformation. Inextricably bound up with the God-given understanding of the Word of the Cross (1 Cor 2:6–16) is a conversion—like that of Paul. He who seeks his salvation in fulfillment of the law and would take his footing on his own just actions, and thus be his own man, is thrown to the ground (Acts 9; 22; 26) and broken (Phil 3:1–11). His demand for identity which he endeavors to satisfy in a moral and metaphysical fashion is thoroughly contradicted, and his striving for wholeness is resisted. He is unable to establish any continuity across this divide, and in virtue of his experience, hitherto, of both world and self, he is not even able to recognize one. Rather, he is created anew and has his identity permanently outside himself, in another,

posting his 95 Theses, Luther had the opportunity to expound on his newfound theological insights in a series of theses given in Heidelberg that gave him the opportunity to elaborate and clarify the ways in which his breakthrough reordered his newfound appreciation of life in the "rupture."

The Epistemic Centrality of the Cross

In theses 19 and 20 he states:

19. That person does not deserve to be called a theologian who looks upon the invisible things of God as though they were clearly perceptible in those things which have actually happened [Rom 1:20].

20. He deserves to be called a theologian, however, who comprehends the visible and manifest things of God seen through suffering and the cross.[9]

With these theses, Luther articulates how this newly upended epistemology redefines his appreciation for how "the visible and manifest things of God" were to be ascertained. The cross has re-established and restored

---

a stranger: in one who has replaced him in a wondrous change and exchange of human sin and divine justice (Gal 2:19; cf. 2 Cor 5:21)."

9. *LW* 31:40. Luther defends these statements with appeals to Scripture, stating in his explanatory notes for thesis 19: "This is apparent in the example of those who were 'theologians' and still were called fools by the Apostle in Rom 1[:22]. Furthermore, the invisible things of God are virtue, godliness, wisdom, justice, goodness, and so forth. The recognition of all these things does not make one worthy or wise," and for thesis 20, "The 'back' and visible things of God are placed in opposition to the invisible, namely, his human nature, weakness, foolishness. The Apostle in 1 Cor 1[:25] calls them the weakness and folly of God. Because men misused the knowledge of God through works, God wished again to be recognized in suffering, and to condemn wisdom concerning invisible things by means of wisdom concerning visible things, so that those who did not honor God as manifested in his works should honor him as he is hidden in his suffering. As the Apostle says in 1 Cor 1[:21], 'For since, in the wisdom of God, the world did not know God through wisdom, it pleased God through the folly of what we preach to save those who believe.' Now it is not sufficient for anyone, and it does him no good to recognize God in his glory and majesty, unless he recognizes him in the humility and shame of the cross. Thus God destroys the wisdom of the wise, as Isa [45:15] says, 'Truly, thou art a God who hidest thyself.' So, also, in John 14[:8], where Philip spoke according to the theology of glory: 'Show us the Father.' Christ forthwith set aside his flighty thought about seeking God elsewhere and led him to himself, saying, 'Philip, he who has seen me has seen the Father' [John 14:9]. For this reason true theology and recognition of God are in the crucified Christ, as it is also stated in John 10 [John 14:6]: 'No one comes to the Father, but by me.' 'I am the door' [John 10:9], and so forth" (*LW* 31:52–53).

the now-corrupted communication of God to the world in a way that requires personal appropriation and contemplation, which forces a confession of culpability and, surprisingly (and simultaneously), redemption; it has clearly articulated and differentiated the law and the gospel. As Oswald Bayer observes:

> With the resurrection of the crucified took place the divine recognition of him that was despised and rejected of men, the justification of one who, in men's eyes, was cursed even by God (Gal 3:13)—a rehabilitation, which does not just refer to the ignominious death of Jesus as an isolated event, but includes everything that the crucified said and did in his earthly life. God vindicated and justified the one who had claimed to act in his name. In so doing he tied down and established himself—as the "Father" of this "Son": "This is my beloved Son" (Mark 9:7). The Son of God is our Lord. Whoever calls the crucified "Lord"—addresses him, in other words, with the divine name—acknowledges the intimate relationship between the death of Jesus on the cross and God's life.[10]

In other words, it is in the shame and ignominy of the cross where God exposes human need as well as the depth of his redemptive love. This counterintuitive method of God's redemption is central to the witness of the New Testament writers,[11] who, despite its "foolishness" (gk. μωρία, 1 Cor 1:18), continue to preach and thereby reset the communication from God to the world through the Son "ruling from the tree."[12] As Luther observed in his Heidelberg theses, those grasped by this counterintuitive reality are those deemed worthy of the moniker "theologian of the cross," and, therefore, (as articulated in thesis 21) is to be distinguished over and against a "theologian

---

10. Bayer, "Word of the Cross," 52. In another essay, Bayer further describes this "corrupted communication" to which the Gospel is directed: "The communication originally established by the triune God has now been corrupted. Hands opened to receive what is given and extended to pass on what has been received, are now clenched into fists. The search for identity, the search of the human who seeks his or her own in all things, leads inevitably to a terrifyingly perfect circle, in which the self is captive to itself. The circle constricts the self tightly, letting it suffocate; but simultaneously, the sickness is not unto death. In its self-captivity, the self tortures itself eternally" (Bayer, "Doctrine of Justification and Ontology," 48).

11. For a helpful exposition of how this remains the case today, see Newbingin, *Foolishness to the Greeks*.

12. Forde, "Atonement as Actual Event," 93. "There is indeed a cosmic dimension to the rule of the crucified and resurrected One," writes Forde, "But for the time being that is hidden—the seed growing secretly. It will be manifest in the end-times, in the eschaton. Now Christ is 'ruling from the tree.'"

of glory," because, as thesis 21 states, "a theologian of glory calls evil good and good evil. A theologian of the cross calls the thing what it actually is."[13] Being able to call something "what it actually is," requires a knowledge of how things actually are, which is what has been revealed about God and humanity through the cross.

As we have seen, Luther's "radical" appreciation of the ramifications of the doctrine of justification affected his entire perception of the relationship between humans and God as revealed through the "word of the cross" for the justification of the ungodly by the gracious action of God. This new appreciation of the breadth and scope of the doctrine of justification may not be immediately evident, but as one observes how it affects speech about God and humankind, the transformation in his thought will become clear. In the next section we will look at how "calling a thing what it is," when bounded by the epistemic reality of the "word of the cross" establishes the parameters of ontological speculation—from both a participationist and relational perspective—so as to ensure proper speech about God, humankind, and the interaction of the two this side of the eschaton, i.e., in our ruptured age.

What Is, What Ought, and What Will Be

In *The Theology of Martin Luther*, Paul Althaus writes that, for Luther, "Theology is concerned with the knowledge of God and of man. It is therefore both theology in the narrower sense—the doctrine of God—and anthropology. These two are inseparably joined together."[14] Accordingly, central to proper theological reflection is the right grasp of how to correctly characterize those involved, i.e., God and humans. For Luther, the distinction between law and gospel is woven directly into the very fabric of theological reflection on the nature of reality at precisely this point on account of how this distinction maintains the proper relationship. For Luther, the *subjectum theologiae*—subject of theology—is: *homo peccator et deus iustificans*—the sinner and the God who justifies that sinner. As Bayer explains the words "sinner," and God as "justifier," are not

> accidental and incidental, but rather as essential and determinative of the essence of the matter . . . when considered strictly

---

13. *LW* 31:40.
14. Althaus, *Theology of Martin Luther*, 9.

from a theological point of view, [because the human] is essentially the one accused and acquitted by God.[15]

In this way, the "theologian of the cross," is limited to seemingly intolerably narrow theological reflection by the parameters established by the doctrine of justification by faith, namely, that when speaking of God, one speaks of the "one who justifies" and when speaking of humanity, one speaks of sinners.[16]

While these descriptors do limit the breadth of theological reflection, confining as they do God and humanity in a definitive relation of subject and object, respectively, it opens a new depth of diagnosis that knows no limits because, as theses 22–25 will argue, the pursuit of self-justification before God is never exhausted, only extinguished.[17] In other words, calling a "thing what it is," is to point out the futility of human self-creation, i.e., justification, outside of the person and work of Christ. Theses 22–25 are as follows:

22. That wisdom which sees the invisible things of God in works as perceived by man is completely puffed up, blinded, and hardened.

---

15. Bayer, *Martin Luther's Theology*, 38.

16. This point is highlighted by an observation made by Reformed systematic theologian Kevin J. Vanhoozer: "When Lutherans speak of persons 'under the law,' they tend to have humans not as creatures but specifically as sinners in mind" (Vanhoozer, "Continuing the Conversation," 224). Indeed, Vanhoozer's observation is entirely correct, and highlights the enduring divide between the Reformed and Lutheran confessions. Bayer goes so far as to compare Luther and Calvin directly in Bayer, *Theologie*, 163–64, where he compares the two statements concerning the *subiectum theologiae*: Luther: "Et ita cognitio dei et hominis, ut referatur tandem ad deum iustificantem et hominem peccatorem, ut proprie sit subiectum Theologiae homo reus et perditus et deus iustificans vel salvator," (Luther, WA 40.2:327); Calvin: "Tota fere sapientiae nostrae summa, quae vera demum ac solida sapientia censeri debeat, duabus partibus constat, Dei cognitione et nostri" (Calvin, *Institutes* 1.1.1).

17. *LW* 31:40–41. "Because men do not know the cross and hate it, they necessarily love the opposite, namely, wisdom, glory, power, and so on. Therefore they become increasingly blinded and hardened by such love, for desire cannot be satisfied by the acquisition of those things which it desires. Just as the love of money grows in proportion to the increase of the money itself, so the dropsy of the soul becomes thirstier the more it drinks, as the poet says: 'The more water they drink, the more they thirst for it.' The same thought is expressed in Eccl 1[:8]: 'The eye is not satisfied with seeing, nor the ear filled with hearing.' This holds true of all desires. Thus also the desire for knowledge is not satisfied by the acquisition of wisdom but is stimulated that much more. Likewise the desire for glory is not satisfied by the acquisition of glory, nor is the desire to rule satisfied by power and authority, nor is the desire for praise satisfied by praise, and so on, as Christ shows in John 4[:13], where he says, 'Everyone who drinks of this water will thirst again.' *The remedy for curing desire does not lie in satisfying it, but in extinguishing it*" (*LW* 31:54 [emphasis added]).

23. The law brings the wrath of God, kills, reviles, accuses, judges, and condemns everything that is not in Christ [Rom 4:15].

24. Yet that wisdom is not of itself evil, nor is the law to be evaded; but without the theology of the cross man misuses the best in the worst manner.

25. He is not righteous who does much, but he who, without work, believes much in Christ.[18]

For Luther, the cross reveals not only how God is to be worshipped, i.e., in and through the work of the Son, but also how God allows wrath to be inflicted on people who "misuse the best in the worst manner," i.e., who continue to see in the law a way of salvation apart from faith in Christ alone.[19] This wrath takes the form, for humanity under the law, of unrelenting accusation—*lex semper accusat* (the law always accuses)[20]—which demands ceaseless defense. "Facing this tribunal," writes Bayer, "we are always called upon to legitimate our existence. We have to demonstrate each moment that we deserve to exist, to be noted, addressed, welcomed, and honored, even if it is by contradiction."[21] In other words, people are forced to hew out of their own existence purpose, meaning, and value, the very things God sent his Son to the cross to secure for them by faith alone. This is why all of creation is, properly understood, a "speech act," either one of humanity under wrath towards the heavens, or God's resurrecting word to the world through his Son.[22]

---

18. *LW* 31:40–41.

19. In his *Theology and Proclamaion,* Gerhard Ebeling reflects on the plight of humanity under the law outside of the security of the gospel. "Certainty (*Gewißheit*) confronts a man, when that which concerns him ultimately becomes that which he willingly affirms; it confronts him when his predicament becomes full of promise, when his inability to control his own destiny becomes the gift of his freedom, when his death becomes the arrival of life, his time the place of eternity. An integral part of the event, of such certainty is the conjunction of compulsion and freedom, law and grace. Now of course human life is continually full to the brim with both. As such, any time is an occasion for certainty, and any uncertainty is sin. Yet one comes to know certainty only as one comes to know the distinction which man in his uncertainty cannot make: namely between *tempus legis* and *tempus gratiae*, between *homo peccator* and *deus iustificans*" (Ebeling, *Theology and Proclamation*, 93).

20. For more on this concept, see Forde, "Lex semper Accusat," 33–52.

21. Bayer, *Living by Faith*, 10.

22. As Bayer explains, "With his trustworthy and loving Word God rules the world. Whoever responds to the Word and lives thereby, that person believes. Whoever closes himself to this word, that person's heart, mouth and hand shut themselves up; the entire world is too confining for him. He becomes fearful and experiences God's wrath. Then the world is no longer the medium that delivers on the promises to me, by which,

We've come to the point in our discussion now where we can look at the actions of humanity under wrath or promise, under law or gospel, by taking up briefly the concepts of "apocalypse" and "eschatology." Following Gerhard Forde, in his essay "The Apocalyptic 'No' and the Eschatological 'Yes,'" we observe with him:

> To get to the root of our problems with apocalyptic and eschatology, we have to go back almost to the beginning. To clarify matters, we need to make a distinction between apocalyptic and eschatology. Apocalyptic . . . for our purposes here, is the story of the beginning, the catastrophic misadventure, and coming cataclysmic end of this present age. . . . Eschatology, on the other hand, is more the story not so much of how we shall fare in the future cataclysmic end, but how the future will come to us in Jesus.[23]

In other words, the two future-oriented outlooks correspond to the distinction between law and gospel, because whereas the eschatological rests on the reception of a foregone conclusion, i.e., that Jesus will "come again to judge the living and the dead, and his kingdom will have no end," the apocalyptic necessitates the active participation of humanity in bringing about the promised end. Luther's insight articulated in thesis 24 is particularly apt in this regard, because what is the misuse of the "best in the worst manner," other than the lawful truth of humanity's predicament, i.e the final judgment (apocalypse) without the Gospel? In this way, penultimate realities are necessarily raised to ultimate levels and pursued, i.e., worshipped, as though they were God, in order to either bring about or avoid the coming apocalypse. One only has to flip through a newspaper or turn on the 24-hour news to see prophets of the coming doom pontificating alongside of those preaching a "gospel" of repentance from that which portends the coming apocalypse. Whether by moral, ecological, political, sociological, or philosophical means, there is no end to the ways in which the quest for glory will be pursued, because outside of the promise of the gospel it appears to be the only way. This quest, as it always has, will take the form of self-sacrifice on the altar of self-creation to the end of self-determination, until that self

---

having been addressed by God, I am installed into a place to live that is bestowed, with the bestowed rhythm of day and night, summer and winter, youth and age, and by which I am able to enjoy life and to relish it. If the world is not believed in as that which is promised, then it will be experienced as a 'fearful natural realm, as a relentlessly necessary, oppressive law, which says: you must squeeze some sense out of this chaos, this fearful natural realm in all its uncertainty; you have to be in charge of making sense in this and out of this chaotic world; you yourself have to establish its order!" (Bayer, *Martin Luther's Theology*, 102).

23. Forde, "More Radical Gospel," 21.

comes to an end in the "foolishness" of the cross, whereby "you have died, and your life is now hidden with Christ in God" (Col 3:3).

In the final analysis, it would seem that Pope Francis's statement on the 500th anniversary of the posting of the 95 Theses, that "The doctrine of justification thus expresses the essence of human existence before God," was more faithful to Luther's vision than many appreciate; however, as Ratzinger observed, it is only when understood in the context of the distinction between law and gospel that the genuine radicality of this statement can be fully appreciated. Thankfully, for over five hundred years, a faithful remnant has been held captive to the "word of the cross," which enlightens first the heart then the mind by its simple yet profound reordering of, well, simply everything. In and through the doctrine of justification, Luther discovered the meaning of Jesus's words in the Gospels, that "the Son of Man did not come to be served, but to serve, and lay down his life as a ransom for many" (Matt 20:28; Mark 10:45), and in that great and counterintuitive reversal, found the freedom of faith whereby he, and subsequently the world, was changed by the word of Christ, "ruling from the tree."

Bibliography

Althaus, Paul. *The Theology of Martin Luther*. Translated by Robert C. Schultz. Philadelphia: Fortress, 1966.

Bayer, Oswald. "The Doctrine of Justification and Ontology." Translated by Christine Helmer. *Neue Zeitschrift für systematische Theologie und Religionsphilosophie* 43.1 (2001) 4–53.

———. *Living by Faith: Justification and Sanctification*. Translated by Geoffrey W. Bromiley. Grand Rapids: Eerdmans, 2003.

———. *Martin Luther's Theology: A Contemporary Interpretation*. Translated by Thomas H. Trapp. Grand Rapids: Eerdmans, 2008.

———. *Theologie*. Gütersloh: Gütersloher, 1994.

———. *Theology the Lutheran Way*. Translated by Jeffrey G. Silcock and Mark C. Mattes. Grand Rapids: Eerdmans, 2007.

———. "The Word of the Cross." Translated by John R. Betz. *Lutheran Quarterly* 9.1 (1995) 47–55.

Ebeling, Gerhard. *Theology and Proclamation: Dialogue with Bultmann*. Translated by John Riches. Philadelphia: Fortress, 1966.

Forde, Gerhard O. "Atonement as Actual Event." In *Christian Dogmatics*, edited by Carl Braaten and Robert Jenson, vol. 2, 79–99. Philadelphia: Fortress, 1984.

———. "Lex semper Accusat." In *A More Radical Gospel: Essays on Eschatology, Authority, Atonement, and Ecumenism*, edited by Mark C. Mattes and Steven D. Paulson, 33–52. Grand Rapids: Eerdmans, 2004.

———. *On Being a Theologian of the Cross: Reflections on Luther's Heidelberg Disputation 1518*. Grand Rapids: Eerdmans, 1997.

Francis. "Common Ecumenical Prayer at the Lutheran Cathedral of Lund: Homily of His Holiness Pope Francis." *Libreria Editrice Vaticana*, October 31, 2016. https://w2.vatican.va/content/francesco/en/homilies/2016/documents/papa-francesco_20161031_omelia-svezia-lund.html.

Luther, Martin. *Luther's Works*. Edited by Jaroslav Pelikan and Helmut T. Lehmann. 56 vols. Philadelphia: Fortress, 1955–1986.

Ratzinger, Joseph. "Luther and the Unity of the Churches." *Communio* 11.3 (1984) 210–26.

Vanhoozer, Kevin J. "Continuing the Conversation: A Reformed Reflection." In *God's Two Words: Law and Gospel in the Lutheran and Reformed Traditions*, edited by Jonathan A. Linebaugh, 220–38. Grand Rapids: Eerdmans, 2018.

4

Practicing the Promises

Confession and Absolution in the Wittenberg Circle, 1530–1590

ROBERT KOLB

OSWALD BAYER EMPHASIZES THE critical role that the concept of "promise" played in Luther's coming to his evangelical convictions regarding the nature and function of the relationship that God establishes with sinners through Jesus Christ and through the action of the Holy Spirit in his Word.[1] Luther particularly developed this focal point of his proclamation in his discovery of the nature of *poenitentia* as he learned that the sacrament of penance was to be centered on the pronouncement of absolution, liberation from the burdens of sin through the expression of the promise of salvation in Christ.

The Wittenberg theologians made much of the resulting redefinition of the *Beichte*, confession and absolution, and the revision of its practice. Philip Melanchthon boasted in Augsburg Confession article XI, that "we have so explained and extolled the benefit of absolution and the power of the keys that many troubled consciences have received consolation from our teaching. They have heard that it is a command of God—indeed, the very voice of the gospel—so that we may believe the absolution and regard as certain that the forgiveness of sins is given to us freely on account of Christ and that we should maintain that we are truly reconciled to God by this faith. This approach has encouraged many devout minds, and in the beginning, it brought Luther the highest praise of all good people. For it discloses a certain and firm consolation for the conscience, whereas previously the entire power of absolution was smothered by teachings about works."[2]

1. Bayer, *Promissio*.
2. *BSLK* 428/429, 1–11; *BC* 186. On Melanchthon's concept of promise, see Bizer,

Luther himself offered readers a form for practicing confession and absolution in the second edition of his Small Catechism. This initial version reflects the medieval use of confession as a preparation or certification for receiving the Lord's Supper. It began with a confession of sins that concluded, "I really want to be freed of my sins. I ask you to strengthen my small faith and comfort my weak conscience with God's word and promise," to which the priest replies, "Why do you desire to receive the Lord's Supper?" The person responds, "Because I desire to strengthen my soul with God's Word and sign and to obtain grace." The priest asks, "But did you not find forgiveness in this confession and absolution?" The response comes, "So what! I want to add God's sign to the Word, for receiving God's Word in many ways is so much better."[3] Luther recognized that God is a multi-media communicator.

This encouragement to confess sin and receive absolution reflects the importance of the repetition of baptismal dying and rising that he expressed using Romans 6 in his Small Catechism: "The Old Adam in us with all sins and evil desires is to be drowned and die through daily contrition and repentance, and . . . daily a new person is to come forth and rise up to live before God in righteousness and purity forever."[4] He particularly urged and fostered receiving absolution from one's pastor although he encouraged its practice between individual Christians since his underlying concept of how God works ascribed saving power to the gospel itself (Rom 1:17), and he presumed a sometimes pressing need for verbal assurance of forgiveness in believers' lives.[5] As early as 1522, he had told his Wittenberg hearers, after explaining the necessity of the public office of the pastor, "But in private I may freely exercise the power to forgive sins. For instance, if my neighbor comes and says, 'Friend, I am burdened in my conscience, speak the absolution to me,' then I am free to do so, but I say it must be done privately. . . . This word, to forgive sins or to retain sins, concerns those who confess and receive absolution more than those who are to impart the absolution. We serve the neighbor by doing just that. For of all the ways to serve, the greatest is to release from sin, to deliver from the devil and hell."[6] Luther continued

---

Theologie.

3. WA 30.1:34, 1–12; *LW* 53:118.

4. *BSLK* 884/885, 14–18; *BC* 360.

5. As important as the nature of the presence of Christ in the Lord's Supper was for Luther, the nature of Baptism, the Lord's Supper, and Absolution as effective instruments that actually accomplish and effect the promise of new life in Christ was equally important for him.

6. WA 10.1.2:239,30–240,8.

to urge this practice in his preaching into the 1540s.[7] For Luther, the practicing of the promise of forgiveness of sin and liberation from Satan's domain formed a vital element of the life of both church and individual believer. Precisely the nature of the promise—not subject to proof but simply demanding and creating trust—made this concept so important.

How did the students of Luther and Melanchthon carry on this part of their vision of church living under the gospel? Several genre from the 1540s–1580s aid in constructing an image of the use of confession and absolution—*Beichte*—as church leaders envisaged it, also of the extent to which the concept of "promise" was used. Church ordinances of several lands, following Luther's and Melanchthon's *Instructions for Visitors* of 1528, reveal that the *Beichte* continued to be tied closely to the Lord's Supper as means of preparation of the pious and the prevention of spiritual damage to unrepentant sinners through unworthy reception of the sacrament.[8] Church ordinances often provided models for that confessional conversation, especially in the earliest years of the Reformation.[9] This study further employs more than thirty documents from nearly thirty authors in the Wittenberg circle from the 1530s to the 1580s. Manuals of pastoral care to guide pastors in the exercise of office began appearing mid-century, offering varying degrees of instruction, largely focused on proper carrying out of the task of hearing confession. Children continued to learn the content and practice of the faith from catechisms, mostly based on Luther's, and his treatment of the *Beichte* shaped how his students expanded on that topic (although some catechisms for children and youth treated only the five chief parts and ignored the *Beichte*).[10] Catechetical instruction took place not only in home and school but also in regular catechetical sermons, often prescribed for Sunday morning or afternoon in the church ordinances. Individual sermons as well as postil-like collections to model such sermons were published from the late 1530s on,[11] serving not only pastors but also parents in conducting family

---

7. WA 49:146, 5–14.

8. Sehling, *Kirchenordnungen*, 1,1:162; cf. the Hamburg *Kirchenordnungen*, 1529 (Sehling, *Kirchenordnungen*, 5:508); Mecklenburg, 1540/1545 (Sehling, *Kirchenordnungen*, 5:150–51); Lüneburg, 1564 (Sehling, *Kirchenordnungen*, 6,1:560); Braunschweig-Wolfenbüttel, 1569 (Sehling, *Kirchenordnungen*, 6,1:166–67).

9. E.g., the *Kirchenordnungen* for Albertine Saxony, 1539 (Sehling, *Kirchenordnungen*, 1,1:268–260); for Brandenburg, 1540 (Sehling, *Kirchenordnung*, 3:61–63); for Prussia, 1544 (Sehling, *Kirchenordnungen*, 4:68); for Lübeck (Sehling, *Kirchenordnungen*, 5:388–89); for Mecklenburg, 1552 (Sehling, *Kirchenordnungen*, 5:206–8); for Lüneburg, 1564 (Sehling, *Kirchenordnungen*, 6,1:560).

10. E.g., Baumgarten (1514–1578, pastor, Magdeburg), *Catechismi*; Fröschel (1496–1570, pastor, professor, Wittenberg and other places), *Catechismus*.

11. Cf. Haemig, "Living Voice."

devotions in the home. A related genre refashioned catechetical material into devotional works for family and individual use.

These works defined proper use of the *Beichte* over against papal abuses, particularly the necessity of sincere contrition to make sinners worthy of forgiveness, the insistence on specific enumeration of sins that could be forgiven, and the assignment of satisfactions to be performed in order to gain remission of temporal punishment in purgatory.[12] Objections to Schwenckfelder and others who regarded the *Beichte* with contempt because they failed to ascribe power to accomplish God's saving purposes to any form of his Word occur as well[13] though usually without any explicit critique of the root of the problem in their failure to acknowledge that God has selected certain elements of his created order, including forms of human language, to use as instruments that actually effect the forgiveness of sins and gift of new life.[14]

Confession and absolution is discussed under the term *Beichte*, often traced back to an earlier German usage for *bekennen*, to confess and specifically in this instance to confess sin. The rejection of the meritorious nature of contrition in no way excluded the expectation that sorrow over sin and heartfelt remorse-initiated repentance follows.[15] The term *absolutio* also appears frequently as a German word, synonymous with *lossprechen*, emphasizing the "unbinding" or liberating action accomplished by the "office of the keys" [*Schlüsselamt*] equated with "remission." *Absolutio* was also a standard topic under which the *Beichte* was presented.[16] Catechisms and catechetical sermons often placed "the office of the keys" or *Beichte*, with the topic "repentance," as the sixth or fifth chief part of Christian teaching in

12. E.g., Gallus (1516-1570, superintendent, Magdeburg, Regensburg), *Catechismvs*, B4a-b; Praetorius (1528-1588, pastor, Brandenburg), *Kleine Catechismus*, Q6b-Q7b; Cyriacus Spangenberg (1528-1604, pastor, Eisleben, Mansfeld), *Catechismvs*, Mm4b-MM5a; Gigas (1518-1581, rector and pastor, electoral Saxony), *Catechismus*, c4b-c5a. That these papal practices continued to be of concern is seen in the *Kirchenordnung* for electoral Saxony, 1580 (Sehling, *Kirchenordnungen*, 1.1:427-28); for Mecklenburg, 1552 (Sehling, *Kirchenordnungen*, 5:175-76).

13. E.g., Mörlin (1514-1571, pastor, superintendent, Arnstadt, Göttingen, Braunschweig, Königsberg), *Enchiridion*, H5a; Gigas, *Catechismus*, c2b-c3a, c6b-c8a.

14. On the association of rejection of absolution as a means of grace, in connection with rejection of the saving power of baptism and the Lord's Supper by those labeled "Schwärmer" by Luther, see Burnett, *Print and Authority*.

15. E.g., Lossius (1508-1582, rector, Lüneburg), *Qvaestivncvlae*, C4a-b; Cyriacus Spangenberg, *Catechismvs*, L8a; Gigas, *Catechismus*, c5a-c6a, where he explains that "repentance" can be understood as embracing both sorrow over sin and turning to God in faith, as did Johann Spangenberg (1484-1550, superintendent, Nordhausen, Mansfeld county), *Margarita*, 55-56.

16. E.g., Lossius, *Qvaestivncvlae*, C5b.

the catechism, reflecting either Luther's initial or his later placement of the subject.[17] The "crypto-Philippist" Wittenberg Catechism of 1571 situated it after the Lord's Prayer, before the sacraments, perhaps as an overview of the Christian life or perhaps to avoid sacramental associations.[18]

The question of whether to follow Luther in counting the *Beichte* as a sacrament, as he did in his treatment of it early in his *Babylonian Captivity of the Church*, or to accept his placing it together with baptism and numbering only two sacraments, as he did at the end of that work,[19] occupied several of his students. Erasmus Sarcerius posed the difficulty of labeling it a sacrament because it exhibited no outward sign but concluded that the laying on of hands could be counted as such a sign.[20]

No standard classification of types of confession and absolution emerged although the basic contours set by Luther remained. All his followers presumed that only those whose sorrow and remorse have filled them with fear and terror will seek the *Beichte*.[21] Simon Musaeus warned against pursuing one of two false paths, the path of arrogant security and presumption or the path of fear without comfort, in despair. Absolution combats both and permits neither the burdening of the innocent, as the papal party does, nor the antinomian absolution of the guilty.[22] All these authors agreed that faith in Christ required daily personal confession of sins directly to God, presuming that such prayer contained trust [*Vertrauen, Zuversicht*] that grasped the forgiveness Christ gives his own and continues to give as he is acting in every pronouncement of forgiveness. This Johann Spangenberg labeled the "*Beichte* of faith" since it flowed from faith in Christ, in contrast to two forms of confession that believers practice in relationships with each other. The "*Beichte* of love" is public and reconciles them to neighbors against whom they had sinned, whereas the "*Beichte* of assistance [*Radts*]" is private, taking place before the pastor or a fellow Christian when the conscience is

---

17. *BSLK* 886/887,1–888/889,9; as fifth, e.g., Musaeus (1521–1576, pastor Bremen, Coburg, etc., professor, Jena), *Handtbu[e]chlein*, C7b; Musaeus, *Catechistisch Examen*, P8b; as sixth, e.g., Rabus, *Predig*, c8b; Andreae, *Zehen*, Lxvb; Tetelbach, *Kleinot*, N3b.

18. *Catechesis continens explanationem*, I6a–K4b.

19. *WA* 7:543,4–549,19, 572,10–22; *LW* 36: 81–91, 124.

20. Sarcerius (1501–1559), *Hausbuch*, 47a, 267b, cf. 142a, on the sacraments in general, where he lists only Baptism and the Lord's Supper. Cyriacus Spangenberg, *Catechismvs*, Nn2a–b deems it a sacrament because it has the sign of the laying on of hands, as does Stöckel (1510–1560, rector, Bardejov/Slovakia), *Annotationes*, 128.

21. Johann Spangenberg, *Gros Catechismus*, 243a–b.

22. Musaeus, *Examen*, Q1a–b; Musaeus, *Catechismus*, X2b–X4b.

particularly plagued with sin against God.[23] All these authors provided for some form of receiving absolution in public or private forms.

Erasmus Sarcerius defined four forms of *confeßio*: (1) directly to God in prayer; (2) in public, presumably in the worship service in which those who had committed grievous sins came in repentance before the congregation; (3) private confession and absolution of such people following their public confession; and (4) other private confession to the pastor.[24] In Johann Tetelbach's widely-used catechism readers also encountered a four-fold array of forms of the *Beichte*: personal, in prayer to God; public repentance and forgiveness for sins committed in public; confession to and forgiveness from neighbors whom a person has offended; and private confession [*Ohrenbeicht*] "to the priest before reception of the sacrament." Tetelbach conceded that the fourth kind of *Beichte* is not commanded by God and that this "human institution and ordinance" is not necessary for salvation. Nonetheless, three reasons justify the continuing practice. The young and simple may be questioned and instructed so that they do not receive the sacrament unworthily. Those who are erring, troubled, and depressed can receive counsel and comfort in the absolution. Above all, absolution confirms hearts in the forgiveness of sins.[25] Nikolaus Gallus insisted that Christ had commanded that every Christian is obligated to receive private absolution; although Gallus cited no Bible passage at this point, he did point to examples of Jesus's pronouncing absolution to the paralytic (Matt 9:2–6), the sinful woman (Luke 7:41–50), the tax collector (Luke 18:9–14), and the thief on the cross (Luke 23:43). According to Gallus's reading, Paul had also pronounced individual absolution on the man who had committed adultery with his stepmother (1 Cor 5:1–5).[26]

The first, foundational confession and acceptance of forgiveness occurs privately in the believer's prayer. "Before you go to the priest, run to your room or find a little corner in the church and speak first with your dear God. Open your whole heart and freely pour it and your old skin out upon him. To make your groaning truly heartfelt, take the Ten Commandments.

---

23. Cf., e.g., Johann Spangenberg, *Catechismus*, 232b–35b; Cyriacus Spangenberg, *Catechismvs*, Mm1a–Mm3b; Fischer (1518–1598, pastor, superintendent, Schmalkalden, Lüneburg, Halberstadt), *Auslegung*, Bbbb4b–Cccc2b.

24. Sarcerius, *Noua methodus*, 584.

25. Tetelbach, *Kleinot*, N4a–N5a. Melissander (1540–1591, superintendent, Palatine-Neuburg, Altenburg), *Beicht vnd Betbüchlin*, 11–22, names three such forms, omitting Tetelbach's third. Melissander did repeat Tetelbach's three reasons for the practice of private confession without arguing that it has no explicit Biblical basis.

26. Gallus, *Catechismvs*, Cc2a–b. These examples were also used by, among others, Stöckel, *Annotationes*, 128.

They are your divorce papers [from your sin]. Go through them one at a time and think how horrible you have moved your dear God to justified wrath. Ask then that he be gracious to you for the sake of his dear Son. When that has happened, go then to the priest."[27]

Sarcerius had earlier contended that auricular or private confession is established only on human authority but that since God approves absolution in other forms, the church must retain this form of the *Beichte* as well.[28] This assertion is also found in church ordinances.[29] Nonetheless, a majority of these authors in the Wittenberg circle believed that Christ had indeed instituted private confession in Matthew 16:19; 18:15–20; John 20:21–23.[30] Caspar Melissander argued that because of the necessity of worthy reception of the Lord's Supper, the church has always viewed the private *Beichte* as necessary.[31]

Peter Praetorius listed five benefits gained from private absolution. It applies the promise of grace to the individual so that he might appropriate it and its comfort as his own. Second, this conversation gives opportunity to unload secret concerns and heartfelt burdens or particular spiritual struggles so that the necessary instruction and comfort can be given in a manner not possible in the sermon. Third, the practice preserves the understanding of the promise of grace that delivers the forgiveness of sins. Fourth, it gives the opportunity to ask the youth and the simple about the chief parts of Christian teaching and instruct them. Fifth, it gives a public witness that those who fall into sin can be restored to grace, against the heresy the Novatians and Cathari.[32]

The introduction of a general public absolution within worship services caused no small controversy in Nuremberg when in the late 1520s the city council promoted and then imposed this form of *Beichte* against the opposition of leading pastor Andreas Osiander. The Wittenberg faculty approved of this general absolution but expressed a cautionary word that private, individual *Beichte* dare not be neglected,[33] a warning repeated by Sarcerius in his *Pastorale* some two decades later.[34] Johannes Wigand and

27. Mörlin, *Enchiridion*, H5b–H6a; Sarcerius, *Noua Methodus*, 586–589; Fischer, *Heuptst[e]cke*, Bbbb4b–Ccccc1a.

28. Sarcerius, *Noua methodus*, 597–600.

29. E.g., that of Braunschweig-Wolfenbüttel, 1543 (Sehling, *Kirchenordnungen*, 6.1:64–65).

30. Cf., e.g., Cyriacus Spangenberg, *Catechismvs*, Nn1b–Nn2a.

31. Melissander, *Beicht vnd Betbüchlin*, 19–29.

32. Praetorius, *Catechismus*, Q8a–R2a.

33. Cf. Rittgers, *Reformation of the Keys*, esp. 114–92.

34. Sarcerius, *Pastorale*, C4a.

Matthäus Judex compared it to the general confessions of the Jerusalemites when they went to be baptized by John in the Jordan.[35] Conrad Porta attributed such use of the general absolution to the laziness of pastors, avoiding work and so pronouncing absolution on "ten, twenty, or more or fewer" at one time;[36] this may suggest a sort of semi-private absolution. Others took the general absolution in public worship for granted,[37] and some church ordinances included it in the regular order of the day.[38]

Members of the Wittenberg circle often followed Luther in emphasizing the pastoral use of confession and absolution, recognizing its value as an instrument of effecting both law and gospel in believers' lives through its two parts, confession of sins and reception of forgiveness.[39] The Holy Spirit makes the application of condemning law and life-restoring gospel in hearers' lives as the keys that bind or free are spoken.[40] However, in general, the chief use in the eyes of most of Luther's followers was proper preparation for the Lord's Supper, as had been the case in the Middle Ages and continued to be in the earliest years of the Reformation.[41]

In his pastoral theology of 1565 Danish professor Niels Hemmingsen clearly demonstrated that this continued to be true for some in the Wittenberg circle.[42] Luther's and Melanchthon's students found this preparation necessary for several reasons. It prevented the confessor, the *Beichtvater*, from failing to perform his office in the best interests of his *Beichtkind* since receiving the sacrament unworthily, while still stuck in unrepented sin, brought condemnation on this member of the congregation.[43] Furthermore, it allowed the *Beichtkind* to reflect on the Ten Commandments and to recognize his or her need for the forgiveness offered in the absolution. Enumeration of sins is not commanded in Scripture, and the *Beichte* should never

---

35. Wigand and Judex (1528–1564, editor, pastor, Magdeburg, Jena, Wismar), *Syntagma*, 312.

36. Porta (1541–1585, pastor, Eisleben), *Pastorale*, 258a–b.

37. E.g., Brenz (1499–1570, reformer, Schwäbisch Hall, Württemberg), *Catechismus*, 672; Andreae, *Zehen Predig*, lxxiija.

38. E.g., Mecklenburg, 1552 (Sehling, *Kirchenordnungen*, 5:197–98); Württemberg, 1553 (Sehling, *Kirchenordnungen*, 16:249–51).

39. E.g., Tetelbach, *Kleinot*, N4a, N5b; Gigas, *Catechismus*, c6b; Porta, *Pastorale*, 258a.

40. E.g., Gallus, *Catechismvs*, B4a, Cc1b–Cc2a; Brenz, *Catechismvs*, 680, 689; Wigand, *Methodvs*, Q3a–Q7a, Y7a–b; Andreae, *Zehen Predig*, lxxa; Musaeus, *Examen*, P8b; Porta, *Catechismi Nutz*, c1b–c2b.

41. Cf. Burnett, "Instructed."

42. Hemmingsen (1513–1600, professor, Copenhagen), *Pastor*, 175–90.

43. E.g., Musaeus, *Handtbu[e]chlein*, C6b–C7a; Musaeus, *Catechismus*, X5a.

become a "capital crimes court" or "criminal interrogation" searching for sins; but is a ministry, commanded by Christ as he commissioned the apostles and their successors to deliver forgiveness of sins.[44] Luther's formula for reflecting on one's several callings in life in light of the Decalogue was taken over[45] and even expanded[46] by catechists and preachers. This enhanced the appreciation for the benefits produced by reception of the sacrament. In addition, the dialogue afforded by the *Beichte* created an opportunity for the pastor to ascertain the level of the *Beichtkind's* knowledge—or ignorance, the chief concern—of the catechism and thus the occasion for teaching the fundamentals of the faith. Pastors could presume that if they displayed some comprehension of the doctrinal parts of Luther's catechism, they were prepared to receive the Lord's Supper.[47]

As important as the *Beichte* was for preparing to receive the Supper, however, Melissander admitted that it remained an adiaphoron, a good and useful ordinance, but not required for reception of Christ's body and blood.[48] Porta quoted Luther saying that the *Beichte* was not an absolute requirement for receiving the Supper.[49]

The practice of the *Beichte* brought the comfort of the forgiveness of sins and the basis of a new life of obedience in faith to believers, these authors taught. The accent on the use of the *Beichte* to comfort consciences, as a tool for general pastoral care, though not as prominent as its use as preparation for the Lord's Supper, certainly was recognized. Its value rested upon its bestowal of forgiveness leading to reconciliation with God and acceptance into eternal life, always based on Christ's death and resurrection.[50] "My only comfort and the firm foundation of my salvation is that Jesus Christ, as the only mediator and throne of grace, has fulfilled the Ten Commandments

---

44. Johann Spangenberg, *Catechismus*, 239b–40a; *Margarita*, 57–58.

45. BSLK 886/886,1–26; BC 360; Johann Spangenberg, *Catechismus*, 236b–38b; Lossius, *Qvaestivncvlae*, D3a–D5a; Mörlin, *Enchiridion*, H5b–H8a; Tetelbach, *Kleinot*, N6a–N8a.

46. E.g., Wigand, *Methodvs*, Y5a–Y7a; Tetelbach, *Kleinot*, N6b–N8. Cyriacus Spangenberg, *Catechismvs*, Mm4a, suggested that believers should think in terms of their callings in their daily walks of life and see if they have sufficiently fulfilled God's commands and live according to them, asking how their hearts stand in relation to God and his Word; how their thoughts, words, and deeds stand in relation to their neighbors, and how they have used their five senses, their reasoning, their property, health, strength, and appearance.

47. Porta, *Catechismi Nutz*, c1a.

48. Melissander, *Beicht vnd Betbüchlin*, 52–53. See also Sarcerius, *Pastorale*, 190; Fischer, *Heuptstu[e]cke*, Cccc3a–Dddd2b.

49. Porta, *Pastorale Lvtheri*, 258a–b.

50. Brenz, *Catechisvms*, 673–74.

for me with his perfect obedience in his actions and in his suffering. He has reconciled me with God and has gained for me grace and salvation, against the curse and condemnation," Musaeus affirmed.[51]

Sermons also deliver the promise of forgiveness, but several authors noted the advantage of hearing it individually delivered in private absolution.[52] Sarcerius admitted that "through the preaching of the gospel in public teaching, the people received an adequate account, but it does not benefit a person as much as being told face-to-face." Expressing one's sorrow over sin to another individual opens the way for receiving God's grace and mercy "as a deer being hunted in the heat longs for sweet, cool water."[53] Christoph Fischer found the *Beichte* more effective for pastoral care than twenty sermons.[54] In the kingdom of Hungary the advance of Calvinist arguments against the use of individual absolution in the *Beichte* caused Leonhard Stöckel to insist that if it is wrong to apply the promise of the gospel in this rite that Christ had instituted, it must also be wrong to administer Baptism and celebrate the Lord's Supper since they also are means by which God's grace and the forgiveness of sins are bestowed on individuals.[55]

Some mentioned the "promise(s)" [*Verheissung(en)*] as the vehicle that delivers forgiveness and peace of conscience,[56] but Luther's and Melanchthon's accent on the nature of this gospel as *promissio* is largely missing for these students' treatments of the *Beichte*. They presumed it as the instrument for delivering forgiveness but did not explore the verbal force of the promise in itself. These authors did emphasize that Christ is both the giver and the content of the promise. Jakob Andreae made much of the "keys" concept in describing that Jesus is both the key and the door. He is a wide door, as the door to the sheepfold (John 10:7–10), the door that is open because God has made him our wisdom, righteousness, holiness, and redemption (1 Cor 1:30). This door is wide open for all to come into heaven, and it is open at all times to the weary and heavily burdened (Matt 11:28). At the same time, he is a narrow door, for those who are carrying a sack or bundle of greed on their back will not fit through this door, nor will someone with a bottle full of wine—that is, one who carries drunkenness

51. Musaeus, *Handtbu[e]chlein*, D1a–b.

52. E.g., Porta, *Catechismi Nutz*, C2b; Pomeranian *Kirchenordnung*, 1542 (Sehling, *Kirchenordnungen*, 4:359).

53. Sarcerius, *Pastorale*, 187–88.

54. Fischer, *Heuptstu[e]cke*, Cccc4a.

55. Stöckel, *Annotationes*, 127–28.

56. E.g., Johann Spangenberg, *Margarita*, 62; Lossius, *Qvaestivncvlae*, C5b; Gallus, *Catechismvs*, B4a, Cc2b–Cc3a; Wigand, *Methodvs*, R1a; Cyriacus Spangenberg, *Catechismvs*, Nn2a; Eber, *Catechismuspredigten*, 146b.

and excess with him. This door permits none who practices the desires of the flesh to enter. Christ is, however, the key to open the door, in the proclamation of the gospel of the forgiveness of sins. This key God gave when Adam and Eve left Paradise, but it became rusty and had to be polished up to be given to Abraham. The same thing happened with Isaac, Jacob, and at Moses's time. Finally, Nicodemus was trying to open the door with the wrong keys, and Jesus had to show him in John 3 that, as Paul says, knowing Christ crucified is that which matters (1 Cor 2:2).[57]

Luther's students accentuated the necessity of faith as trust in both Christ's saving death and resurrection[58] and the word of absolution spoken by the pastor or other Christian. Part of many forms of absolution given in these works was the question, "do you believe that my forgiveness is God's forgiveness?"—always with the expectation of the answer "yes!"[59] Andreae explicitly criticized the papal practice that encouraged belief that simply receiving the priest's laying on of hands, apart from trust in Christ and his Word, can effect forgiveness.[60]

The reception of God's gift of righteousness in faith turns believers, these authors presumed, to improvement of their lives, to new obedience.[61] Several authors tied this new life in Christ closely together with Baptism and the Lord's Supper. Just as baptism is received individually, so absolution comes with the repetition of the Holy Spirit's promise to the individual, Gallus concluded.[62] Paul Eber emphasized the struggle of believers with Satan and their own desires and the aid given for that battle by baptism and its repetition in absolution.[63] Johannes Gigas argued in similar manner:

> we should diligently consider our baptismal gown of the covenant, which was established with us for Christ's sake, not forget it, and die to sin and live as children of God and the light, Romans 6, and our souls take hold of the cross with patience.... May our dear God help us exiled sons of Eve to remember our baptism as children and find comfort and encouragement in it and what we or our sponsors said in our place, namely that we hold fast to the articles of our Christian faith, not give place to the devil nor follow our fleshly lusts. When we are overtaken

---

57. Andreae, *Zehen Predig*, lxvjb–lxixb.
58. E.g., Wigand, *Methodvs*, Q7a.
59. E.g., Mörlin, *Enchiridion*, H7b–H8a.
60. Andreae, *Zehen Predig*, lxxijb.
61. E.g., Johann Spangenberg, *Catechismus*, 234a; *Margarita*, 65.
62. Gallus, *Catechismvs*, Cc2b.
63. Eber (1511–1569, professor, Wittenberg), *Catechismuspredigten*, 141a–42a, 145b–46a. Cf. Bode, "Preaching," 401–423.

and surprised in this clever world by the devious and crafty trapper of birds and we foul our baptismal garment, we [must] quickly turn to the heavenly Father in true repentance, seek gracious forgiveness of our sins for Christ's sake, and quickly go to the comforting absolution and to the Holy Supper; and then practice with diligence our Christian knightly nature, and only because of Jesus Christ await a settled and quiet hour [of death], such as Simeon experienced.[64]

Musaeus wrote that the foundation of the Christian life springs from the "irrevocable covenant of grace and [joyous] exchange that took from me all that was evil and damnable in me, namely, sin and death, and bestowed on me what he gained for me, the good and the blessed, namely righteousness and salvation." Absolution renews the covenant of grace and overcomes the troubled, repentant heart, as a "noble and powerful seal, not of wax or lead, like the papal bulls, and also not of mere bread and wine, as the Sacramentarians deceptively say." Indeed, God has given Christ's body and blood, to which the absolution leads believers, to strengthen them against the devil.[65]

Luther's and Melanchthon's students did not discuss the efficacy of God's Word in either condemnation or restoration of righteousness and life to any significant extent in the works considered here, but they made it clear that the power of the keys lay with the entire church and in the Word, not only in the office of the public ministry. Precisely in that Word believers found forgiveness and comfort.[66] God has humbled himself in order to place this holy Word in human mouths in order to address his people directly.[67] That meant in no way that these authors diminished the necessity and significance of the pastoral office, but their repeated designation of pastors as "ministers of the Word" reinforced their view that the Word is the Holy Spirit's instrument in the mouths and hands of his people. Andreae explained that Christ had made his disciples his doorkeepers on earth in John 20, and that they passed that office on to other learned servants of the Word. However, Christ's setting the pastoral office in place does not preclude that "in time of need, for every Christian, whether man or women, can call this key to mind for the sick and

---

64. Gigas, *Catechismus*, b7a–b8a, c1b–c2a; cf. Sarcerius, *Pastorale*, 193–94.

65. Musaeus, *Handtbu[e]chlein*, D1b–D3b.

66. E.g., Wigand, *Methodvs*, Q3a.

67. Porta, *Catechismi Nutz*, c3b; cf. Eber, *Catechismuspredigten*, 147a; Fischer, *Heuptstu[e]cke*, Dddd3a.

comfort them with it. For Christ has promised his entire church that what they loose on earth shall be loosed in heaven."[68]

The surveyed documents occasionally offer glimpses of the circumstances of hearing confession in the sixteenth century. The church ordinances of electoral Saxony of 1580 strongly suggest that it not occur in the pastor's or deacon's house, nor in the sacristy, but at the front of the church. The *Beichte* should be administered Saturday late afternoon, not on other days, although exception should be made for the aged, the sick, and pregnant women, who might receive absolution on the morning of the communion service, especially in winter.[69] The church ordinances of Goslar (1528) and the Pomeranian agenda provided for the *Beichte* required for communion attendance to be conducted after Saturday evening vespers.[70] The congregation in Mansfeld held a Saturday evening service of confession and absolution at which instruction, confession, and absolution took place.[71]

The authors shaped by Luther's and Melanchthon's teaching were trained to take practical problems in the perception of the people seriously. Thus, some treated specific issues that laity might raise on occasion. Johann Spangenberg posed the question whether it is not shameful to confess sins to one's pastor and responded that this shame is nothing compared to that on Judgment Day when one's sins will be exposed to God, the whole world, and even the devils.[72] Joachim Mörlin constructed a dialogue with readers that began with the concern that many do not care whether they have been absolved or not. The office of the keys, the proclamation of the gospel, is necessary for giving the gift of faith, Mörlin insisted. "Must all be absolved then who come to the *Beichte*?" The binding or freeing from sin lies with discretion of the preacher, the author posited. "May a preacher do anything he wants to? Certainly not!" He is sent by the Father and is bound by what God wishes (John 7:16–18; 8:14–16; 12:44–45).[73] Others might question whether pastors or any human being has the right to forgive, but Andreae assured readers that Christ had appointed his servants to forgive sins in John 20:19–23.[74] To the question of whether impious holders of the pastoral

---

68. Andreae, *Zehen Predig*, lxxja–lxxijb. See also Melissander, *Beicht vnd Betbüchlin*, 46–47, who said that all Christians could absolve "in time of necessity."

69. Sehling, *Kirchenordnungen*, 1,1:428.

70. Sehling, *Kirchenordnung*, 7,2,2: 241; 4:436.

71. Cyriacus Spangenberg, *Catechismvs*, Mm3b.

72. Johann Spangenberg, *Catechismus*, 241a–b.

73. Mörlin, *Enchiridion*, inserted into the 1564 edition, 7a–J8a.

74. *Zehen Predig*, lxxb–lxxja. The Brandenburg *Kirchenordnung*, 1540, prescribes special instruction for the people assuring them that Christ has commissioned pastors to forgive sins in his stead (Sehling, *Kirchenordnungen*, 3:50).

office can validly forgive sins, Andreae answered with an analogy. If a municipal judge makes a judgment, it is valid on the basis of his execution of office, as that is appraised by an appeals judge. God remains the appeals judge over all use of his keys.[75]

Porta used chiefly citations from Luther to construct his pastoral theology and posed several questions that pastors needed answered. "How should the confessor deal with persons whom he suspects are still stuck in their sin?" On the basis of Jesus's communing of Judas, Luther had said that the confessor's suspicions should yield to the sinner's denial of sin. "May a servant of the Word give public testimony regarding what he has heard in confession? Absolutely not!" Nor should the secular judge take the pastor's absolution into account when passing sentence. A series of questions on the use of excommunication followed, reproducing largely the Wittenberg consistory's rules for its procedure.[76]

Several authors reminded readers that Jesus had told Peter to forgive seventy times seven times (Matt 18:21–22) and Paul urged correcting those who fall with a spirit of gentleness (Gal 6:1).[77] How frequently should believers make use of private confession? Melissander answered: "this precious and noble treasure is bound to no time or place, but however often a Christian needs this special comfort for the strengthening of his weak faith, he may and should find absolution even if he is not at that time to receive the holy sacrament."[78]

Some specifically rejected the Novatians and Cathari for teaching the impossibility of a return to grace after a believer's fall into sin, treating in this connection the interpretation of Hebrews 6:4–6; 10:26–31, usually by defining "falling away" and "sinning deliberately" to persistence in blasphemy or rejection of God.[79]

Without providing a complete picture of the state of confession and absolution in the Late Reformation, these works demonstrate that the *Beichte* continued in Lutheran hands to find its primary purpose in preparation for receiving the Lord's Supper. Despite their failure to employ Luther's and Melanchthon's concept of promise prominently, these works did accentuate the utility of confession and absolution as an instrument of pastoral care for direct application of law and gospel, calling to repentance and delivering the comfort of the forgiveness of sins. These authors left no doubt that

---

75. Andreae, *Zehen Predig*, lxxjb.
76. Porta, *Pastorale Lvtheri*, 267a–76b.
77. E.g., Johann Spangenberg, *Margarita theologica*, 62.
78. Melissander, *Beicht vnd Betbüchlin*, 51.
79. E.g., Johann Spangenberg, *Margarita*, 63–64.

absolution naturally leads to a new life as God's child, obediently carrying out his commands. These Wittenberg school theologians also exhibited their native character in their concern for the practical details of how to execute this aspect of pastoral care. Repentance and the forgiveness of sins remained at the heart of the Wittenberg way of practicing the faith.

Bibliography

Andreae, Jakob. *Zehen Predig von den sechs Hauptstucken Christlicher Lehr (Catechismus genannt)*. Tübingen: Ulrich Morhart's widow, 1562.

Baumgarten, Johann. *Der Catechismi / Christliche vnnd Heilige Kinderleer / sie die fragweiss in der Alten Stadt Magdeburgk auffgericht gebetet / Bekent vnd Christliche gehalten wird*. Magdeburg: Pangratz Kempff, 1552.

Bayer, Oswald. *Promissio: Geschichte der reformatorischen Wende in Luthers Theologie*. 2nd ed. Göttingen: Vandenhoeck & Ruprecht, 1989.

Bizer, Ernst. *Theologie der Verheißung. Studien zur theologischen Entwicklung des jungen Melanchthon, (1519–1524)*. Neukirchen-Vluyn: Neukirchner, 1964.

Bode, Gerhard. "Preaching Luther's Small Catechism. Paul Eber's *Catechismuspredigten* (1562)." In *Paul Eber (1511–1569): Humanist und Theologe der zweiten Generation der Wittenberger Reformation*, edited by Daniel Gehrt and Volker Leppin, 401–23. Leipzig: Evangelische Verlagsanstalt, 2014.

Brenz, Johannes. *Catechismvs pia et vtili explicatione illvstratvs*. Frankfurt: Peter Brubach, 1551.

Burnett, Amy Nelson. *Debating the Sacraments. Print and Authority in the Early Reformation*. Oxford: Oxford University Press, 2018.

———. "'Instructed with the Greatest Diligence Concerning the Holy Sacrament.' Communion Preparation in the Early Years of the Reformation." In *From Wittenberg to the World*, edited by Charles P. Arand, et al., 47–66. Göttingen: Vandenhoeck & Ruprecht, 2018.

Catechesis continens explanationem simplicem & breuem, Decalogi, Symboli Apostolici, Orationis Dominicae, Doctrina de Poenitentia & de Sacramentis. Wittenberg: Johann Schwertel, 1571.

Dingel, Irene, ed. *Die Bekenntnisschrften der Evangelisch-Lutherischen Kirche*. Göttingen: Vandenhoeck & Ruprecht, 2014.

Eber, Paul. *Catechismuspredigten*. Edited by Theophil Feuerlin. Nuremberg: Katharina Gerlach and Johann von Berg's heirs, 1578.

Fischer, Christoph. *Auslegung der Fu[e]nff Heuptstu[e]cke des Heiligen Catechismi*. Leipzig: Rhambau, 1573.

Fröschel, Sebastian. *Catechismus wie der in der Kirchen zu Witteberg nu viel jar / auch bey leben D. Martini Lutheri ist gepredigt worden*. n.p., 1559.

Gallus, Nikolaus. *Catechismvs predigsweise gestelt*. Regensburg: Kohl, 1554.

Gigas, Johannes. *Catechismus Gepredigt zur Schweidnitz Elysiorum veterum*. Frankfurt: Eichorn, 1578.

Haemig, Mary Jane. "The Living Voice of the Catechism: German Lutheran Catechetical Preaching 1530–1580." ThD diss., Harvard University, 1996.

Hemmingsen, Nils. *Pastor sive pastoris optimvs vivendi agendiave modvs.* Leipzig: Vögelin, 1565.
Kolb, Robert, and Timothy J. Wengert, eds. *The Book of Concord.* Minneapolis: Fortress, 2000.
Lossius, Lucas. *Qvaestivncvlae methodicae de Christiano Catechismo, in formam dialogi* Wittenberg: Rhau, 1545.
Luther, Martin. *D. Martin Luthers Werke.* Weimar: Böhlau, 1883–1993.
———. *Luther's Works.* Philadelphia: Fortress, 1955–1986.
Melissander, Caspar. *Beicht vnd Betbüchlin Für andechtige Communicanten. Mit Christlichen Vnterricht von der Beichte / Absolution / vnd Abendmal.* Leipzig: Beyer, 1583.
Mörlin, Joachim. *Enchiridion. Der kleine Catechismus Doct. Martini Lutheri/sampt der Haustaffel / in mehr Fragest[e]ck vorfasst.* Magdeburg: Lotter, 1554.
Musaeus, Simon. *Catechismus / Mit kurtzen Fragen vnnd Antworten / von den aller notwendigsten vnd wichtigesten Artickeln Christlicher Lehre.* Frankfurt, 1580.
———. *Catechistisch Examen mit kurtzen fragen vnnd antwort / von den aller notwendigsten vnd wichtigsten Artickeln Christlicher Lehre.* Ursel: Nicholas Heinrich, 1568.
———. *Handtbu[e]chlein Von Zweyerley Nu[e]tzlichem Gebrauch vnd vbung des Catechismi: der Erste fu[e]r die warhafftige Beter gegen Gott: der Ander fu[e]r die Busfertige Beichtkinder gegen den Priester.* Magdeburg: Gehen, n.d.
Porta, Conrad. *Des Heiligenn Catechismi / oder Leyen Bibel / Nutz vnd Hoheit. Aus den geistreichen Bu[e]chern D. Martini Lutheri des Mans Gottes / vnd anderen Furtrefflicher Theologen.* Halle: Gaubisch, 1578.
———. *Pastorale Lvtheri. Das ist: Nützlicher vnd notiger Vnterricht von den fu[e]rnemlichsten stu[e]cken zum heiligen Ministerio geho[e]rig.* Eisleben: Petri, 1586.
Praetorius, Peter. *Der Kleine Catechismus Doctoris Martini Luther. Fu[e]r die Jugent vnd Einfeltigen der Christlichen Gemeine / in ko[e]nigsbergk einfeltig erklert.* Wittenberg: n.p., 1563.
Rabus, Ludwig. *Ein Kurtze vnd Christliche Predig von notwendigem vnnd einfaltigem verstand der Sechs Hauptstuck vnsers Christlichen Catechismi.* Ulm: Varnier, 1560.
Rittgers, Ronald K. *The Reformation of the Keys.* Cambridge: Harvard University Press, 2004.
Sarcerius, Erasmus. *Hausbuch Fur die Einfeltigen Hausueter / von den vornemesten Artickeln der Christlichen Religion.* 2nd ed. Leipzig: Bärwald, 1555.
———. *Noua methodus in praecipvos Scripturae divinae locos.* Basel: n.p., 1546.
———. *Pastorale, Oder Hirtenbuch / Darinn das Gantz Ampt aller trewer Pastorn / Lehrer / vnnd Diener beschrieben wird.* Frankfurt: n.p., 1565.
Sehling, Emil, et al., eds. *Die evangelischen Kirchenordnungen des XVI. Jahrhunderts.* Leipzig: Reisland: Mohr/Siebeck, 1902–2018.
Spangenberg, Cyriakus. *Catechismvs. Die Fünff Heuptstu[e]ck der Christlichen Lere.* Smalcald: Schmuck, 1566.
Spangenberg, Johannes. *Der Gros Catechismus vnd Kinder Lere: Mart. Luth.* Wittenberg: Rhau, 1541.
———. *Margarita theologica, continens praecipvos locos doctrinae Christianae.* Leipzig: Blum, 1540.
Stöckel, Leonhard. *Annotationes Locorum communium doctrinae Christianae Philippi Melanchthonis.* Basel: Operinus, 1561.

Tetelbach, Johann. *Das gu[e]ldene Kleinot. D. Mart. Lutheri Catechismus / In kurtze Frage vnd Antwort gefasset.* Frankfurt: Bassaeus, 1584.

Wigand, Johannes. *Methodvs Oder Heubtartickel Christlicher lere / wie sie in der Kirchen zu Magdeburg furgehalten vnd gelert werden.* Magdeburg: Kirchner, 1558.

Wigand, Johannes, and Matthäus Judex. *Syntagma, seu Corpus doctrinae Christi, ex novo testament tantum.* 3rd ed. Basel: Fabricius, 1563.

5

Sanctification as Divine Order or Divine Gift?

Simon Pauli (1531–1591) and Simon Musaeus (1521–1576) on New Obedience

JASON D. LANE

Introduction

LEADING UP TO THE Formula of Concord (1577), Lutherans attempted in their preaching and teaching to sort out how sanctification and justification relate to one another. After the legalistic and antinomian errors were identified and condemned, all Lutherans agreed that justification was a monergistic act of God alone, who graciously forgives sins for Christ's sake, and that sanctification was not properly part of justification. But it was still not entirely clear in practice how sanctification and the increase of holiness ought to be taught. Is sanctification, like justification, a monergistic act? If so, does this not lead to a kind of enthusiasm, in which sanctification happens automatically without any human effort to live and to love according to God's will? Or if we are to live and love according to God's will, would not the many admonitions and exhortations in the New Testament suggest that sanctification depends on our obedient response to God's word? If sanctification is not part of justification, does not sanctification fall under the category of good works, and therefore require human cooperation with divine grace to carry out this new obedience? All these questions led to an ongoing struggle to interpret sanctification. Was sanctification a locus under the law that required a response of thankfulness to the gospel and response of obedience to God's law? Or was sanctification a locus under the gospel, a divine gift granted by the Holy Spirit that depended solely on his means of grace rather than human obedience?

Herr Bayer has firmly denied the notion that justification and sanctification are two separate acts in which sanctification must follow justification as a response of obedience or of obligation.[1] Our sanctification, he argues, is not a result of a categorical imperative, but of a categorical gift, through which God the Holy Spirit enlightens, sanctifies, and keeps us in the holy faith, even while we rejoice and suffer, fail and hope.[2] Bayer identifies two pitfalls in the Lutheran treatment of sanctification since the Reformation. Either we are drawn into pietistic or rationalistic streams with the constant desire to see a manifest moral change, or else we tend toward a kind of enthusiasm, with the expectation that works take place automatically without means and without a willing spirit.

Two names are famously associated with these two errors: George Major (1502–1574) who taught that good works are necessary for salvation and Andreas Osiander (1498–1552) who taught that the mystical union with the divine nature of Christ is the basis for both our justification and sanctification. Major assumed that the freedom of the gospel would lead to laziness and lawlessness among Christians, because the sinful flesh still clings to them. Therefore, he emphasized the abiding power of the law and the responsibility of Christians to do the good works that the law demanded. For Major, sanctification fell under the divine imperative that made human obedience necessary for salvation. It was perceived by many that Major relied on the law to produce these works rather than the gospel, and therefore his views were regarded as synergistic, even though he denied that he taught anything synergistic in the article of justification.[3]

Johann Agricola (1494–1566), who denied that Christians need the preaching of the law, is typically associated with enthusiasm and antinomianism, but Andreas Osiander is a more appropriate target for the controversies leading up to the Formula of Concord concerning new obedience. The controversy over the righteousness of faith in the Formula, Article III, concerned Osiander, who claimed that the essential righteousness of God, who is Christ, "dwells in the elect through faith and impels them

---

1. Bayer, *Aus Glauben Leben*, 65. "Rechtfertigung und Heiligung sind nicht zwei Akte, die zu unterscheiden wären, etwa so, daß die Heiligung auf die Rechtfertigung folgte oder gar folgen müßte."

2. Bayer, *Freedom in Response*, 16. Sanctification, for Bayer, is located in the *communio sanctorum* or the fellowship of the altar. "That is why the whole area of ethics does not arise from the quality of categorical imperative, but rather from that of categorical gift. It is not primarily in the realm of imposed fellowship, but of fellowship granted as a gift, that we are to live, acting and suffering, failing and hoping."

3. *BOC* 192.

to do what is right and is therefore their righteousness."[4] The danger of Osiander's position was not only that he divided up the person of Christ, so that Christ is our righteousness only according to his divine nature, but also that he made the righteousness of faith dependent on the outward manifestation of Christ's righteousness through works. Although he was heavily criticized by the Gnesio-Lutherans for his teaching on justification, Osiander's fusion of sanctification and justification was, in reality, an attempt to preserve sanctification as an entirely divine act. Thus, in an effort to preserve sanctification as monergistic, Osiander made justification dependent on an effectual change in the Christian and, in his own way, made justification synergistic. Whatever the case, both Major and Osiander were deeply concerned about how sanctification occurs and both were adamant that is does occur. One saw sanctification as a human response, the other saw it as an act of Christ dwelling in us.

With these two debates in the background, two other views of sanctification emerged in the Lutheran Church side by side and within orthodox camps in the 1570s. Both argued that justification is by faith alone without works, but both expressed sanctification in different ways. One view, represented by Simon Pauli (1531–1591), saw sanctification as part of God's eternal order for man's salvation. In this divine order of salvation, sanctification and good works follow faith, because it is God's will that a good tree produce good fruit. Although he maintained that salvation was God's doing alone, he describes sanctification as a response of the regenerate will to God's word. The response of the renewed will belongs to God's order of salvation for man. According to this view, there are two distinct steps: God creates faith through the gospel and the Holy Spirit renews the individual to act in accord with God's will. The first step is solely the Holy Spirit's work through the gospel. The second step appears to be a response to God's law. In response to God's grace, the new man obeys God's will and does what the law commands. The order may sound chronological, but as we will see, it is for Pauli a logical order. How this new obedience takes place, whether monergistically or synergistically still needs further exploration.

Another view, represented by Simon Musaeus (1521–1576), was concerned almost entirely on how new obedience or sanctification takes place. Musaeus did not emphasize sanctification as part of the divine order wherein faith produces sanctification. Musaeus, seemingly at every turn in his preaching, hesitated to speak of faith as a power unto itself, even as many others had used the term "faith" by way of synecdoche to describe the entire saving work of God. He also avoided speaking of the law as the

---

4. *FC* 3.2.

final goal of the Christian life, as if the gospel freed us only to return us in obedience to the law. For Musaeus, sanctification like justification is a divine work through the word alone. By the gospel, the Holy Spirit creates faith and sustains faith to live and to suffer in conformity to Christ's image. Thus, faith is not an agent to produce good works, but faith receives the gospel that is the power of the Holy Spirit to justify and to sanctify. For Musaeus, the gospel creates faith and the same gospel produces new and holy impulses in us, although often greatly hindered by sin. Moreover, the law still is in effect after faith, but only to kill and bring to nothing the sinful flesh. Whatever growth takes place in this life takes place through the Holy Spirit killing the flesh and making alive in the Spirit. Growth is passive. God, however, is active, forming us in Christ and conforming us to Christ by speaking. Sanctification is thus monergistic through and through. Lutherans who took up either position determined to distinguish sanctification from justification, so that our righteousness was not confused with the righteousness of faith. Furthermore, both Pauli and Musaeus taught that law and gospel are to be preached to Christians until they fall asleep in Christ. Yet I hope to show how Pauli and Musaeus differed in preaching sanctification and suggest why that matters for our preaching and teaching today.

Bayer has demonstrated in his writings that justification by faith never leads to sanctification by works. Rather, the life of a Christian is lived by faith in God's word from start to finish, by faith in the law that kills and by faith in the gospel that makes alive. It seems to me that sanctification, an often-misunderstood locus in Lutheran theology, is an appropriate place to engage Lutheran theology in his honor. In presenting both Pauli and Musaeus on sanctification, I intend to suggest that Bayer's view of sanctification aligns most closely with that of Simon Musaeus, whose views appear prominently in the Formula of Concord as the orthodox position on sanctification, though not by name. Simon Pauli's view of sanctification as divine order appears in the Formula as well,[5] and it certainly has dogmatic merit, since there is a divine order to the Christian life. Sanctification cannot precede justifying faith. Yet Pauli's insistence that one must respond to God's grace with obedience inevitably moves sanctification into the realm of the law, works, and human will.

The diverging approaches of Simon Musaeus and Simon Pauli on the locus of new obedience first came to my attention in my study of Lutheran preaching on the Epistle of St. James.[6] James 1:16–27—since it appeared twice

---

5. *FC SD* 3.40–41.

6. The following portion of this essay draws from that research. Lane, *Luther's Epistle of Straw*, 128–57.

in the lectionary during Eastertide and was included in the postil sermon collections—became fertile ground for Lutherans to stake out their position in the controversies leading up to the Formula of Concord. The controversial loci abound in James 1: original sin, temptation, and the origin of evil (1:13–15), the nature of God, the illumination of the Spirit, and the means of grace (1:17), regeneration, the image of God, and new obedience (1:18), the right reception of the word (1:21), the necessity of good works (1:22–25), and the right worship of God (1:26–27). In their preaching on James 1, both Pauli and Musaeus seek to account for the *necessitas* of good works in the Christian life and the apostolic exhortations to good works. But each preaches sanctification with distinctly different emphases on this point.

Simon Pauli (1531–1591)

Pauli matriculated at Wittenberg in 1552, studied several years with Melanchthon, and received his master's degree in 1555.[7] Following in the footsteps of Formula writer David Chytraeus (1530–1600), he was called to Rostock to serve both as cathedral preacher and professor of theology at the university. He received his doctorate in Rostock on the same day as Chytraeus, 29 April 1561.[8] Pauli worked alongside Chytraeus and served at different times as rector of the University (1566, 1570, 1582, and 1588). He may have been inferior to Chytraeus in intellectual rigor but he made up for it with his gifts for preaching and pastoral care.[9] Although a student of Melanchthon, Pauli states in his preface to the postils (1572, Part II) that he intentionally sought to speak in the way of Luther and uphold

---

7. Krause, "Pauli," 273–74.
8. Krause, "Pauli," 273–74.
9. Krause notes that Pauli was a gifted theological counterpart to Chytraeus (Krause, "Pauli," 273). "Ein treuer Schildknappe des David Chyträus, dem er in Gelehrsamkeit nachstand, an Predigtgabe und praktischem Sinn aber überlegen war, hat er seitdem bis zu seinem Tode mit jenem gemeinsam alle Gutachten der theologischen Facultät verfaßt und vertreten, als eifriger, wortgetreuester Halter an Luther's Ausdruck."

the doctrine as the Reformer taught it.[10] This is especially the case in the doctrine of the Lord's Supper.[11]

Seeking out a middle road between Georg Major and Nikolaus von Amsdorf in the controversy concerning the necessity of good works for salvation, Pauli insists that Luther's teaching concerning good works, particularly his explanation of faith in his *Preface to Romans*, is the proper interpretation of Article VI of the Augsburg Confession concerning new obedience.[12] Faith, Luther argues, is a living, active thing, from which works spontaneously flow. For Luther, the word to which faith clings is creative, delivers the Holy Spirit, and spontaneously brings forth good fruits. Works are a necessary consequence of faith in Christ by the working of the Holy Spirit through the word. Yet in contrast to Luther, at least in Pauli's preface to his epistle postil sermons, he does not link the necessary cause of good works with faith, word, and Spirit, but rather with the necessity of God's created order. Pauli writes:

---

10. See Kaufmann, *Universität und lutherische Konfessionalisierung*, 508–38 (esp. 510–11). In his preface, Pauli pledges his allegiance to the doctrine of the Augsburg Confession as it was taught by Luther. "Also sind bald nach des seligen Luthers tode / Gottlose enderungen vnd verfelschungen der waren Religion (von jme geleutert vnd ernewert) vnd vielfeltige jrthume vnd Secten / auch vnter der Auspurgischen Confession namen / in vnsere Kirchen eingedrungen / Das also der Teufel vnter dem falschen schein vnd namen der Ausburgischen Confession / nichts anders suchet / denn das er die ware Confession / vnd reine Göttliche Lehr / so in der selben Confession begriffen / sich vnterstanden hat. Denn die Auspurgische Confession vnd Apologia / wie zu ersehen / wenn die alten vnd newen Exemplaria gegeneinander gehalten vnd gelesen werden / in den newlichsten Drücken vielfeltig geändert vnd gemehret / vnd offt gefehrlich etliche wort ausgelassen / auch etliche hochwichtige Artickel also geändert vnd gestellet sind / das auch diese Secten / welche D. Luther auffs ernstlichste verdampt / vnd von vnsern Kirche abgesondert hat / jtzund die Augspurgische Confession / zu jrer jrthumb Schanddecke brauchen können" (Pauli, *Postilla*, A2r–A2v).

11. Pauli gives the most attention in his preface to the controversies over the Sacrament of the Altar and Christology, in which he shows his commitment to Luther's teaching (Pauli, *Postilla*, 166r). See also on this point Kaufmann, *Universität und lutherische Konfessionalisierung*, 534–35.

12. Pauli, *Postilla*, A4r. "Es hat aber Doctor Luther den jtzt gedachten sechsten Artickel der Augspurgischen Confession / das der Glaube sol gute früchte bringen / vnd das man müsse gute Wercke thun / die Gott befohlen hat / also erkleret / Das der Glaube / dieweil er nicht ein blosser vnd loser Wohn oder Dünkel des Hertzens ist (wie die falschgleubigen haben) sondern ein krefftiges newes lebendiges wesen / so bringe er viel frücht / thu jmmer guts: gegen Gott mit loben / dancken / beten / predigen / vnd lehren: Gegen dem nehesten / mit lieben / dienen / helffen / raten / geben / leihen / vnd leiden allerley vbels bis in den tod." See also Luther's *Preface to the Epistle to the Romans* (WA DB 7.8.30–12.4) and the exegesis of James 2:19–24 (*Ap* 4.244–52; *BOC* 157–59). Both passages guided later Lutheran interpreters of James, especially 2:19 and the matter of *fides historica*.

[Because faith is a living thing] good works that God commands must necessarily follow faith in all the converted, not out of compulsion, but because the divine wisdom and righteousness has made this arrangement that all reasonable creatures should be obedient to God their Creator, and all those who have been freed from sin out of grace for Christ's sake should no longer sin but live in righteousness and holiness. But these statements, "one must do good works to be saved" or "good works are necessary for salvation" or "it is impossible to be saved without good works," Luther expressly rejected, because, as they stand in their genuine and natural sense, they are completely contrary to the central statements concerning our salvation.[13]

Pauli, like Luther, denies that works are salvific, but he differs from Luther when he argues that the arrangement of the Creator and his creatures is the cause of a human being's good works. Whereas Luther speaks about the spontaneity of good works that flow from the gospel, Pauli points to an overarching order (*Ordnung*) of divine wisdom and righteousness.[14] The distinction here between Luther and Pauli is one of emphasis. Pauli's dogmatic expressions about the necessity and cause of good works can be regarded as standard Lutheran fare, since the language of order appears in the Formula.[15] Yet these dogmatic expressions should be read in

13. Pauli, *Postilla*, A4r. "Derhalben müssen die guten Werck / die Gott gebotten hat / notwendig / in allen bekerten dem Glauben folgen / nicht aus zwang / sondern dieweil Göttliche weisheit vnd gerechtigkeit die ordnung gemacht hat / das alle vernünfftige Creaturen / Gotte jrem Schöpffer sollen gehorsam sein / vnd alle so aus gnaden vmb Christi willen von den Sünden erlediget sind / nicht mehr sündigen / sondern in gerechtigkeit vnd heiligkeit leben sollen. Aber diese Reden: Das man mus gute Wercke thun / die Seligkeit dadurch zu erlangen / Das gute Wercke zur Seligkeit vonnöten sein: Das vnmüglich sey / ohn gute Wercke selig zu werden. Hat D. Luther ausdrücklich verworffen / dieweil sie in jrem eigentlichen / natürlichen verstande / wie sie lauten / diesen Heuptsprüchen von vnser seligkeit / gantz zu wider sind."

14. It is true that the *Formula* writers would later use God's order of the planetary circuits to describe the new life of a Christian (*BSLK* 964; *FC SD* 6:6), but this serves as an illustration of continuity in the Christian life, rather than as the sole cause of good works.

15. *FC SD* 3:41. "Therefore, the proper order between faith and good works, and likewise the proper order between justification and renewal or sanctification, must be preserved and maintained. For good works do not precede faith, nor does sanctification precede justification. Instead, first of all, in conversion, the Holy Spirit kindles faith in us through the hearing of the gospel. This faith lays hold of God's grace in Christ, and through it a person is justified. Thereafter, once people are justified, the Holy Spirit also renews and sanctifies them. From this renewal and sanctification the fruits of good works follow. This is not to be understood as if justification and sanctification are separated from each other in such a way that a true faith can exist for a while along with an evil intention, but rather this only indicates the order in which the one thing precedes

consultation with his exegesis to see how Pauli understands the relationship between faith, works, and the word of God. In his sermons on James 1, a passage that is clearly about the need for good works in the Christian life, we will look especially at Pauli's explanation of the cause of good works. Is it law or is it gospel?

Pauli's postils from the early 1570's become something of a gold standard in the Lutheran postil tradition.[16] All later postil writers in one way or another try to match Pauli's thoroughness and rhetorical strategy. They may not have copied his every insight, and in some instances they seek to correct him, but they did aspire to his ability to draw from the pericopes clear doctrine and present that doctrine as winsomely in their expositions as he had done. One may argue that some of them, especially Simon Musaeus (1573, a year after Pauli), succeeded. We look now to Pauli's treatment of two pericopes from James 1 and then compare them to two sermons from Simon Musaeus on the same texts.

Pauli on James 1:13–21 (Cantate Sunday)

Pauli argues that this pericope was placed in the lectionary to complement the gospel lesson for *Cantate* from John 16:5–15 and the teaching that the Holy Spirit will accuse the world of sin.[17] His *Cantate* sermon on James is peculiar in that it extends the pericope to include 1:13–15, to treat temptation and the origin of evil. The inclusion allows him to play the two images of birth against each other, the birth of original sin and the new birth of the gospel. In good rhetorical fashion, Pauli gives a summary of the main doctrines from the text.

> Therefore, the Epistle for today is a teaching concerning original sin or the evil works that people do, where this sin originates, and what kind of fruit it produces. The Epistle also teaches concerning good works of godly and pious Christians and where these originate. It teaches concerning the word of GOD through

---

or follows the other."

16. As far as structure, Robert Kolb's presentation of Georg Major's preaching (Kolb, "Georg Major as Preacher," 93–121) overlaps in many ways with what I have found in Pauli's sermons. However, there are also similarities it seems in content, especially concerning the life of new obedience.

17. Pauli made a habit of drawing together the gospel and epistle lessons for each Sunday. Kaufmann, *Universität und lutherische Konfessionalisierung*, 515. "Wo es sinnvoll erscheint, versucht er in einer Epistel—oder Evangelienpredigt auch auf den jeweiligen Evangelien—und Episteltext desselben Sonntags einzugehen und so die Predigten der beiden Hauptgottesdienste aufeinander zu beziehen."

which children of wrath and of the devil are born again and become children of grace and of God.[18]

Pauli separates the sermon into three parts: (1) concerning sin, (2) concerning good works, and (3) concerning new birth through the word and the new life that follows. Although Pauli is adamant that the full disclosure of the doctrine of original sin is the only way to show the sweetness and incomprehensible character of the doctrine of grace, rebirth, and the new life of faith, he nevertheless seems to safeguard the gospel with the doctrine of the law. It is unclear if this is his intention. As mentioned, Pauli does not state clearly that works flow from the power of the gospel. Rather he suggests that works necessarily follow faith due to God's *Ordnung*, an overarching divine law to which creation must submit to its Creator. Therefore, in his exposition of James 1:16–21, we look more closely at Pauli's understanding of the cause of good works.

In his second part of the sermon, he moves from the origin of evil into a discussion of the origin of good works.[19] Tying together James 1:18, 21, and 1 Peter 1:23, Pauli writes, "Therefore out of the pure, incorruptible seed of the divine word, we are born again as new people, who live and can live a new pure life, just as God's word is pure and without sin."[20] The word is the source of the new birth, and the Holy Spirit is active in the word. Clearly Pauli upholds a monergistic view of justification.[21] What is unclear, however, is how he relates the regeneration and justification through the word and Spirit to the new obedience and sanctification that necessarily follow the new birth. In this sermon, Pauli presents two realities. First, God creates a new creature through the word of truth. Second, the new creature must do good works. But the relationship between these two realities lacks the clarity of his discussion of original sin and its fruits. Rather than emphasize the cause of the good fruits, Pauli describes what works (virtues) Christians should cultivate, using the five examples of James: (1) be quick to listen, (2) quick to hear, (3) slow to wrath, (4) put away all filthiness and wickedness, and (5) flee

---

18. Pauli, *Postilla*, 82r. "Jst demnach die heutige Epistel eine Lehr von der Sünde / oder bösen Wercken / so die Menschen thun / Woher sie sind / vnd Was für früchte sie geberen. Von den guten Wercken der Gottseligen fromen Christen / Woher die sind / Vnd von dem Wort GOTTES / dadurch die Kinder des Zorns vnd des Teuffels zu Kindern der gnaden / vnd Gottes widergeborn werden."

19. Pauli, *Postilla*, 86v.

20. Pauli, *Postilla*, 86v. "Also werden aus dem reinen vnuergenglichem Samen des Gottlichen worts / durch den heiligen Geist widergeborn newe Menschen / die ein new rein leben füren / vnd füren können / wie Gottes wort rein vnd ohn Sünde ist."

21. Pauli, *Postilla*, 87r. "Das ein Christ eine newe Creatur Gottes wird / darzu thut er nichts / sondern Gott thuts allein / nach seinem willen."

all actual sins that flow from the well of sin, namely, the old nature. These are the works that James expects will follow regeneration.[22]

The only place where Pauli connects the works of the new creature with the word of God is at 1:21: "He gave birth to us by the word of truth." But even here, Pauli does not spell out the power and effect of the word on the Christian life. Instead he concentrates on the hearer's reception of the word that must take place according to the virtue of humility, for it is the nature of the word to interpose the cross on the Christian life:

> Wherever God's word is, there is also the cross, as St. Paul says in 1 Corinthians. The gospel is a word of the cross, not only because it preaches the crucified Christ but also because the gospel brings with it the cross. Therefore, it must be received and kept with meekness. It can save your souls.[23]

Although Pauli sees a connection between the word and the cross, by which he interprets the Christian life as conformity to Christ in suffering and preservation by the saving word, he attempts to make clear two sets of responsibilities: God's responsibility to save and the Christian's responsibility to pursue actively the virtuous life that God's law commands in his word.

In his *Cantate* sermon, the division between the saving word and the responsibility of each Christian to respond with good works becomes especially clear:

> This, then, is the sense of St. James in today's Epistle: our Lord is not the cause of sin or evil. All actual sin is conceived and born of evil desire or original sin, as from a mother. God, however, is the only source of all good and perfect gifts. We are reborn by God through his word, so that we would do good works, namely, that we would be quick to hear, slow to speak, and slow to anger, that we would put aside all filthiness and wickedness, and with meekness or patience in suffering receive the word of God, which is the power of God that saves our souls.[24]

---

22. Pauli, *Postilla*, 87r. "MJt diesen vnd den folgenden worten redet er von etlichen Früchten / so auff die Widergeburt erfolgen sollen."

23. Pauli, *Postilla*, 88r. "Wo Gottes wort ist / da ist das Creutze mit / wie Sanct Paulus Corinth. 1. das Euangelium ein wort des Creutzes heisset / nicht allein darumb / das es den gecreutzigten Christum prediget / sondern auch das es das Creutze mitbringet. Derhalben mus es mit Sanfftmut vnd mit gedult angenomen vnd behalten werden. Welches kan ewre Seelen selig machen."

24. Pauli, *Postilla*, 88r. "Jst demnach S. Jacobs meinung (in der heutigen Epistel verfasset) diese / das vnser HERR Gott nicht eine Vrsach der Sünde vnd des bösen sey / sondern das alle wirckliche Sünde / von der bösen Lust / oder Erbsünde / wie von einer Mutter / empfangen vnd geborn werden. Hiergegen aber / das alle gute / vnd vollkome

While upholding the all-sufficiency of the gospel to give new life and save the soul, Pauli struggles to leave the production of good works to the power of God's saving word and the indwelling of the Holy Spirit. One expects Pauli to express the fruits of faith and new birth as he had done with original sin and its fruits, namely, that from this new birth flow the new life with good works of both the first and second table of the law. In this sermon, however, Pauli appeals to Christians to act in accord with God's will, and he does not preach the gospel as the means to fulfill God's will.

Pauli on James 1:21–27 (Rogate Sunday)

Pauli recognizes a continuity between James 1:17–21 and the *Rogate* lesson from James 1:22–27. His sermon on James 1:22–27 begins with a rehearsal of the arguments of James 1:13–21. He describes the Christian life born of the word of truth and then offers a summary of the *Rogate* pericope:

> This Epistle is an admonition to new obedience or a new life which is guided by the divine word. The summary of the Epistle in short is this: "I admonish you to cleanse and wash the stains and filth of sin that you see in the mirror of the divine word, and that you adorn yourselves according to the image of the new man."[25]

Pauli is the first Lutheran postil writer to declare that the mirror is two-sided: one mirror is law; the other is the gospel.[26] This motif of two mirrors becomes permanently fixed in the Luther postil tradition starting with Pauli. All interpreters hereafter take up the image to teach both law and gospel.

In this sermon Pauli also gives the most extensive description of the law and its catechetical application.[27] He suggests five different uses of the law. First, the law proves that God exists and that he is good and wise, since the law and what it commands is good and wise. Second, and similar to the first, the law reveals that God is merciful, long-suffering, honest, and chaste,

---

gaben / allein von Gott sind / Vnd das wir hiezu von Gott durch sein wort widergeborn sind / das wir sollen gute wercke thun / schnel sein zu Hören / langsam aber zu Reden vnd zu Zorn: alle vnsauberkeit / vnd bosheit ablegen / vnd mit Sanfftmut oder gedult im Leiden annemen das wort Gottes / welches ist die krafft Gottes / dadurch vnsere Seelen selig werden."

25. Pauli, *Postilla*, 96r.

26. Pauli, *Postilla*, 97v. "WJe aber zwey Heubtstück sind der Göttlichen Lehr / nemlich das Gesetz / vnd Euangelium / also sind auch zween Spiegel / darinne wir vns beschawen. Der eine Spiegel ist des Gesetzes / der Andere des Euangelij."

27. Pauli, *Postilla*, 97v.

because the laws reveal the nature of the lawgiver.[28] Third, the law is a mirror in which we see the image of God, as God intended us to have it in the beginning; thus the law teaches us a pre-lapsarian anthropology.[29] Fourth, the law is also a mirror to show the corruption of sin (*usus elenchticus*).[30] Finally, he says, after we have washed and been cleansed, the law becomes a mirror in which we see how to adorn ourselves, so that the image of God in us will constantly be renewed.[31] The final description of the mirror is clearly an attempt to articulate the third use of the law (*usus didacticus*), as the Formula writers would later call it,[32] and to teach according to the Ten Commandments which works Christians should do. The Christian who sees in the law's reflection the pre-lapsarian image of God and the reflection of the restored *imago Dei* in Christ will learn to be adorned with divine virtues.[33] Pauli thus maintains a positive use of the law (even where there is no sin), to guide and to instruct Christians in doing good works.

Like the mirror of the law, the mirror of the gospel, according to Pauli, reveals more than one reflection. The mirror of the gospel reveals by special revelation what the law could not. First, Pauli argues, the gospel reveals that God is triune and that this one God is worthy of praise and

---

28. Pauli, *Postilla*, 97v. "Denn weil Gottes Gesetze diese erzehlete vnd dergleichen Tugenden von vns erfoddert / müssen für allen dingen sie in jm selbst sein."

29. Pauli, *Postilla*, 97v. "Zum dritten siehestu in dem Spiegel des Gesetzes / was das bildnis Gottes / vor dem Fall Adam gewesen ist / wie herrlich vnd schön die Menschliche natur damit ist geschmücket gewesen / vnd wie herrlich noch die Engel Gottes im Himel / mit diesem bilde gezieret vnd gescmücket sind. Das siehestu wie in der Menschlichen natur gewesen für dem fall / vnd in den Engeln noch ist / ware erkentnis vnd anruffung Gottes / ware furcht Gottes / ware liebe Gottes / warer gehorsam gegen Gott / ware hertzliche Barmhertzigkeit / ohn Zorn vnd Bitterkeit / ware Keuscheit / vnd dergleichen herrliche Tugenden."

30. Pauli, *Postilla*, 97v. "Jn diesem Spiegel siehestu mit was schwartzen / scheuslichen Flecken der Finsternis vnd Blindheit / so Gott nicht recht erkennet / vnd der bösen Lüsten."

31. Pauli, *Postilla*, 97v. "Zum Fünfften siehstu in diesem Spiegel / wie du / nachdem du die Klicke vnd Flecken der Sünde abgewischet vnd abgewaschen hast / dich wider zieren vnd schmücken solt / auff das das Bildnis Gottes in dir ernewer werde / vnd du Gott wolgefallen mögest."

32. It is also noteworthy that Pauli does not offer any specific teaching of the law that correlates to the first use of the law (*usus politicus*).

33. Pauli, *Postilla*, 98r. "Wer also geschmücket ist / der gefelt Gott wol / vnd mit diesen Tugenden werden wir gezieret vnd geschmücket sein im ewigen Leben. Derhalben / wer da wil wissen / wie herrlich vnd schön er mit allen Göttlichen Tugenden ohn flecken vnd runtzeln wird gezieret sein im Himelreich / der trete für den Spiegel des Göttlichen Gesetzes / vnd sehe darinnen das Bilde seiner künfftigen herrlichen vnschuld vnd schönen schmucks."

requires praiseworthy virtues.[34] Second, the gospel reflects the will of God in Christ, so that we may believe in him.[35] And finally we see in the mirror of the gospel how to wash the stain of sin through holy baptism and the blood of Christ.[36]

Pauli's description of the Christian life appears in many ways colored by the law. He is careful not to add works into justification, but his description of new obedience is often cast within a legal framework of divine command and human response. This apparent weakness is overcome in part by his clear exposition of the mirror of James 1:23 as both law and gospel, since it allows him to teach the reception of the word as a matter of repentance and faith in the forgiveness of sins.[37] Furthermore, his assertion that the mirror of God's word reveals the *imago Dei* is indicative of the efforts of Luther's theological heirs to articulate a distinctly Lutheran anthropology.[38] In this sermon, Pauli presents in Augustinian fashion the entire *Heilsgeschichte* according to the four conditions of the *imago Dei*: the image God originally gave in Eden, the image man lost in the fall into sin, the image God has begun to restore in Christ, and the image that God will bring to completion on the day of resurrection. His discussion of the law of liberty at 1:25 follows the same pattern as his interpretation of the mirror; it is both law and gospel. Although he clearly states that a good tree produces good fruit and therefore faith produces good works as evidence that faith is genuine,[39]

34. Pauli, *Postilla*, 98r.
35. Pauli, *Postilla*, 98r.
36. Pauli, *Postilla*, 98r.
37. Pauli, *Postilla*, 98r–98v. "DEmnach müssen wir beide Spiegel / des Gesetzes vnd des Euangeln / allezeit für vns haben / auff das wir vns / darinne beschawen / vnd erkennen was für vnfletige Flecken wir an vns haben / vnd wie / vnd wo durch sie zu reinigen vnd abzuwaschen sind. Da müssen wir zu erst ansehen den Spiegel des Gesetzes / darinnen befinden wir die Flecken der Sünde die an vns sind. Darnach im Spiegel des Euangelij sehen wir / das wir in vnser Tauffe gereinigt sind / vnd teglich vns weiter von den Sünden reinigen sollen vnd müssen / durchs Blut Jhesu Christi / zur vergebung für vnsere Sünde vergossen. Jn das Blut Jhesu Christi müssen wir eintauchen den Püschel Jsopen / vnsers Glaubens / oder Busse / so im Glauben geschiehet / vnd vns damit Besprengen vnd reinigen / wie Dauid im 51. Psalm spricht."

38. For a helpful discussion of Lutheran anthropology and the fallen and restored image of God in the sixteenth and seventeenth centuries, see Hägglund, "Was ist der Mensch?" 159–173.

39. Pauli, *Postilla*, 99r. "AUff diesen Glauben durch das vollnkomene Gesetz der Freyheit / das Euanglium / erlanget / folgen die guten Wercke / welche von dem Glauben / dadurch man Gerecht vnd Selig wird / vnd zu gleich / mit von der Seligkeit / zeugen / als die guten Früchte zeugen / vnd die erklerung thuen / das der Baum gut ist. Denn Sanct Jacob wil nicht hie lehren / das wir durch die Werck gerecht werden / sondern das die Werck von der Seligkeit / die allein durch den Glauben an Jhesum Christum erlanget wird / zeugen / oder den jenigen der aus dem Glauben gute Wercke

Pauli, at least in these sermons, does not describe sanctification or new obedience as an ongoing divine work of the Holy Spirit through his word. Pauli concentrates primarily on the human responsibility of hearing the word and doing it. This certainly means washing away sins by daily contrition and repentance, but ultimately the doing of the word is interpreted as obedience to God's law, by which we maintain and adorn the restored image of God in us.[40] To see how Musaeus's preaching of sanctification differs in emphasis from Pauli's, and in many respects reflects Bayer's teaching of living by faith, we now turn to his sermons on James 1:16–27.

Simon Musaeus (1521–1576)

Simon Musaeus, a gifted theologian who wrote many exegetical, dogmatic, pastoral, and catechetical works, studied in Frankfurt an der Oder and in Wittenberg.[41] However his Gnesio-Lutheran sensibilities caused him to be pushed from one post to another, and he was often in transition. He served as preacher or professor in over ten different cities in his career and never stayed in one place for more than three years. Part of his enduring legacy in Lutheranism is his theological influence through family connections. His oldest daughter Barbara married Tilemann Heshusius (February 4, 1566). His younger daughter, Marie, married Daniel Hoffman, later prominent Lutheran dogmatician from Helmstedt. Musaeus's postils on the epistle lessons were published first in 1573, a year after Pauli's went on the market, and appeared in the following years in various formats.[42]

---

thut / erkleren das er recht gleube / vnd durch den Glauben selig ist."

40. Pauli, *Postilla*, 101v. "DEmnach / wollen wir aus dem Spiegel des Göttlichen worts / nicht allein erkennen lernen / die flecken vnd klicke vnserer Sünde / sondern wollen sie auch abwischen vnd abwaschen mit dem Blut Jhesu Christi / vnd vns widerumb schmücken vnd zieren nach den Tugenden des bildnis Gottes / darzu wir erschaffen sind / vnd in diesem Schmuck feste vnd bestendig bleiben."

41. *RGG4* 5:1591. Outside of the standard German bibliographical articles, little research has been done on Musaeus. For a more detailed biographical sketch and a sample of his preaching, see Beste, *Die bedeutendsten nachreformatorischen Kanzelredner*, 192–201. J. A. Steiger has given an analysis of Musaeus's holistic pastoral care for those suffering from depression (*melancholia*). See Steiger, *Melancholie, Diätetik und Trost*, 20–29. He also offers a critical edition and brief commentary on Musaeus's tract, *Melancholischer Teufel* (1572), in Steiger, *Medizinische Theologie*, 210–46.

42. Reprints of his epistle postil appeared in 1574, 1575, and 1589. By 1590 his epistle sermons went through a total of 12 printings. See Frymire, *Primacy of the Postils*, 495n149. I used a complete edition of his postils, published in 1583, for the sermon on James, but refer to the preface from the 1573 edition (see Musaeus, *Postilla*).

In his preface and dedication to the Duke Johann Wilhelm (1530–1573),[43] Musaeus begins with a laud of God's kingdom and his spiritual governance in Christ. His preface reveals theological convictions that conform to the message of James 1, especially concerning the power of the word. Musaeus declares that God "has secured in this life his complete reign and spiritual governance among us through his oral and written word and in the preaching office of law and gospel [*Predigampt deß Gesetzes vnd Euangelij*]."[44] Christ's royal scepter is the law and the gospel by which he rules from his hidden throne, to gather his sheep who wander through this valley of sorrow.[45] Musaeus's description of God's revelation in his word is frequently expressed as a revelation of God's character and will (*wesen vnd willen*). Echoing a theme that reoccurs in Lutheran expositions of James 1:17, Musaeus teaches that to know God's word is to know God and his will, and nothing can be known of God outside of his word.[46] It is significant that the human reception of God's word is not central to Musaeus's preface, although for someone preparing to receive the word of God through his postils, such an emphasis would have been appropriate. Instead, Musaeus concentrates on God's active delivery of the word through the preaching office of law and gospel.

Musaeus describes that the purpose of his postils is to deliver the word of God in a tangible way to Christians in every walk of life, to teach them the articles of the faith, urge and edify them toward holy living, and especially to prepare them to die.[47] Characteristic for the genre, his postils were intended to serve as devotional material that communicated the sum of the Christian faith and should be read as the living voice of God among his people. Musaeus's pastoral care can be detected in his evangelical consolation to his hearers and readers concerning the reception of the word. He does not place the responsibility of receiving the word on the individual as an exercise of the intellect or will. Instead, Musaeus, like Luther, describes the reception of the word in the context of *tentatio*. Christians are in the midst of a cosmic battle over the word of God, in which Satan, the world, and the sinful flesh seek to

---

43. Around the time that Musaeus finished his preface (*Laetare* 1573) Duke Johann Wilhelm died (2 March 1573).

44. Musaeus, *Postilla*, A2r. As far as I can tell, this claim that preaching is the office of law and gospel is unique to Musaeus among the "postillers." The term is telling of Musaeus's theology of the word and understanding of the pastoral office.

45. Musaeus, *Postilla*, A2r.

46. Musaeus, *Postilla*, A2r. "Also / daß er ausser solchem wort mit keinem Menschen auff Erden in güte vnd gnaden wil zuschaffen haben / sondern es sollen stracks seyn vnd heissen / Leute ohne Gott / die ohne sein reines Wort wandeln vnd fahren."

47. Musaeus, *Postilla*, A4v.

obscure and belittle the word and rob it from the heart. God is not unaware of the struggle. "Now God sees," writes Musaeus,

> how we poor people, through the devil's deception and enticement, regard nothing so little and get bored with nothing so much as with his precious word, and throw away eternal life for the cares and concerns of this dying maggot sack. With unbridled desire and energy we go off to satisfy and comfort ourselves with all the things in this fleeing life that we already have and have never lacked.[48]

Knowing that human beings would fall into sin and sorrow were it not for God's gracious preservation, Musaeus vividly describes God as the doorkeeper of damnation and destruction, who mercifully shuts the door at every turn and guards and protects his people from every evil of body and soul.[49] For Musaeus, human nature is so corrupt and so inclined to despise God's word that there is nothing in us, in our reason, will, or understanding, that could receive the word. It must be a miracle that comes only through prayer for divine assistance. Therefore, the bridge between the word delivered and the word received, according to Musaeus, is not a human response to the word, as in a leap powered by the human will or understanding. That is to say, the word of God does not appeal to any power in the individual; the word is of itself powerful. As Musaeus explains, earnest prayer (*oratio*) is a bridge between proclamation and reception, not on its own merit, but insofar as it seeks to flee from the destructive nature of the sinful heart and receive the life-giving power of the divine word (*meditatio*). Therefore, it says in Psalm 119:36, "Lord, incline my heart to your word and not to selfish gain."[50] He also describes the reception of the word by fruitfully taking up Luther's analogy of the blessed exchange:

> This is how God portrays [*vorbilden*] his saving word for us in the Bible. He fashions the word as though it were a special workshop, a treasure chamber, and door through which we come to him with our poverty and he comes to us with his heavenly riches, to take us to himself and to make souls rich and save them eternally.[51]

Already in his introduction, Musaeus presents the themes of preaching and the reception of the word of God that appear again in his exposition of the

48. Musaeus, *Postilla*, A2r.
49. Musaeus, *Postilla*, A2r–A2v.
50. Musaeus, *Postilla*, A2v.
51. Musaeus, *Postilla*, A2v.

gift of the word that comes down from above (Jas 1:17–18). He then moves to the effective power of the eternal word to save and likens it to a medicine for the soul. Musaeus writes,

> We search endlessly for temporal supplies and medical treatments, when our bodies get weak or sick, so that we don't die of hunger, nakedness, or plague. But why don't we search all the more for the word of God as the richest of all treasure chests, the costliest of all medicines, and the heavenly pantry, so that with our daily bread for the body we may also fill our soul and keep it strong and well against all spiritual sickness and spiritual death? Just as the Son of God says in Matthew 4[:4], "that man does not live on bread alone, but on every word that comes from the mouth of God."[52]

Musaeus develops the themes here to include not only the word's power to save (*salvatio*), but, also with his allegory of food and medicine for the soul, he illustrates the word's power to keep and to preserve Christians in the faith (*preservatio fidei*). Musaeus combines God's preservation of the faithful to St. Paul's image in Ephesians 6 of the full armor of God and word of God as the sword. The word of God defends the Christian from all the attacks of the devil, the world, and the sinful flesh, just as Christ defended himself from Satan (Matt 4:1–11; Luke 4:1–13) with the words "it is written . . . it is written."[53]

To describe God's plan of salvation, Musaeus uses the simile of a splendid castle, surrounded by a deep moat and towering walls, impenetrable to all those standing outside.[54] No one can enter into the safety of the castle unless the king mercifully extends the bridge. And this God did in Christ, the only mediator between God and man. The Father mercifully sends Christ to open up the way to paradise and Christ himself is the light of the Father. However, it is difficult to distinguish between the light of Christ who is the light of the Father, and the light of the gospel. Musaeus simply lets Christ and his word coalesce through the image of light. He moves from the incarnation, death, resurrection, and ascension of Christ, by which God made for us a way, to the preaching office and the gift of the Holy Spirit, who lights the way of Christ. Musaeus seeks to resolve some of the tension between Christ as the light and the word (*externum verbum*) as the light. After Christ ascended, Musaeus says, "He became our heavenly sun and light through the institution of the preaching office of the gospel and through the sending

---

52. Musaeus, *Postilla*, A2v.
53. Musaeus, *Postilla*, A3r.
54. Musaeus, *Postilla*, A3r–A3v.

of the Holy Spirit in our hearts, and he opened to us the Father's heart and his merciful will concerning our salvation."[55] Now that the light of God's saving word shines, Christians ought to take advantage of the time of God's grace and not waste it on the invented religion of the papists and Jesuits and on the deceptive teaching of all the enthusiasts and sects.[56] The light of the Father is therefore Christ, his word, and the Holy Spirit's pure distribution of that word through the preaching office and means of grace.

Musaeus on James 1:16–21 (Cantate Sunday)

Musaeus[57] follows his own advice and arranges the *Cantate* pericope into three lessons from the Catechism: the First Article of the Creed, the Third Article of the Creed, and the Third Commandment. His division, however, influences the exposition itself. Musaeus interprets James 1:16–17 and the preceding context of 1:13–15, as an exposition of the First Article of the Creed concerning God the Father and his nature, will, and work.[58] The second part of the sermon, which begins with James 1:18, belongs to the Third Article of the Creed, and the powerful working of God to recreate those who are spiritually dead and make them members of his church and heirs of eternal life.[59] Here Musaeus explains that James leads us from the First Article of the faith to the Third, from the first bodily creation to the second spiritual creation, or sanctification (*Heiligung*).[60] Drawing on early church motifs of the *Heilsgeschichte* (Irenaeus), Musaeus, not unlike Pauli, interprets the new creation and sanctification as a recapitulation of the first. "James sets the first creation against the new creature, and shows that God, who is the Father of light and the Spring of all good things, indeed created us in the beginning as the most lovely of all creatures after his own image, and adorned us with good and perfect gifts."[61] Through the fall the

55. Musaeus, *Postilla*, A3v.
56. Musaeus, *Postilla*, A4r.
57. I now refer to a quarto edition: Musaeus, *Postilla* (1583).
58. Musaeus, *Postilla* (1583), 44. "1. Von Gottes natur / willen vnd werck / nach dem ersten Artickel vnsers glaubens / wie nichts denn alles gutes von jm kommen / derhalben jm niemand die Sünde / noch etwas böses sol zumessen."
59. Musaeus, *Postilla* (1583), 44–45. "2. Von dem sonderlichen hohen werck vnd wolthat Gottes an vns / nach dem dritten Artickel vnsers Christlichen glaubens / daß er vns verdorbene vnd Geistlich todte Weltkinder vmb Christi deß Mittlers willen / zu Gliedern seiner Kirchen geheiliget / vnd zu newen Creaturen vnd Erben deß ewigen Lebens gemacht."
60. Musaeus, *Postilla* (1583), 48.
61. Musaeus, *Postilla* (1583), 48.

image was lost; man "cast his endowed wisdom, righteousness, and life from the light and into the horrid darkness of foolishness, unrighteousness, and death."[62] God's restoration of the image takes place, according to Musaeus, not only by sending his Son for our redemption, but also by creating us anew as his creatures.[63] Musaeus makes the first explicit comparison of the original creation of man and the new creation of man from these verses. He maintains from the context in James that the new creation is a greater work of God, "for in the first creation, God made man from the clay of the earth and breathed into him a life-giving breath [*Seele*], as Moses describes in Genesis 1–2. But here James says that he begot us or (in his way of speaking) God ἀπεκύησεν, that is, he gave birth as a mother births a child into the world from her own body."[64] Musaeus draws strongly from James on the birth analogy:

> In order for this new birth to take place, the word of truth (he says) is needed, namely, the gospel through which God truly works in us with his Spirit and forms us into his image, giving us again his heavenly wisdom, righteousness, and life, as St. Paul says in Romans 1: "The gospel is the power of God that saves everyone who believes it." So the gospel is the power of God for salvation, as St. Paul clearly says and the gospel is the word of truth, as James testifies, through which God, like a mother who gives birth anew, makes us spiritually alive.[65]

---

62. Musaeus, *Postilla* (1583), 48.

63. Musaeus, *Postilla* (1583), 48. "Aber dieweil wir jm vmbgeschlagen / vnd auß dem Liecht seiner mit getheilten Weißheit / Gerechtigkeit vnnd Lebens / in die schräckliche Finsterniß aller thorheit / vngerechtigkeit vnd Todsgefallen / hat er vns durch seinen Son / den Mittler / nit allein lassen erlösen / sondern vns auch auffs new zu seinen Creaturen zu schaffen."

64. Musaeus, *Postilla* (1583), 48. "Wie S. Jacobus allhie solche neuwe schaffung nach allerley vmbständen also abmahlet / dz sich Gott hie viel mehr kosten leßt / denn in der ersten Schöpffung / da er schlechts den Menschen aussem Erdenkloß gemacht / vnd jm einelebendige Seele eyngeblasen / wie Moses / Gen. 1. vnd 2. schreibet / Hie aber sagt S. Jacobus / habe er vns gezeuget / oder (wie es in seiner sprach lautet) ἀπεκύησεν / dz ist / geboren / wie ein Mutter ein kind auß jrem leibe an die Welt bringt."

65. Musaeus, *Postilla* (1583), 48. "Vnd brauchet darzu deß Worts der Warheit (spricht er) das ist / deß Euangelij / dadurch Gott warhafftig mit seinem Geist in vns wircket / vnnd vns zu seinem Bild formieret / vnnd seine Himmlische Weißheit / Gerechtigkeit vnd leben / wider gibt / wie auch S. Paulus Rom. 1. sagt: Das Euangelium ist ein krafft Gottes / die da selig machet alle die dran gläuben. Jst nu das Euangelium eine krafft Gottes zur seligkeit / wie S. Paulus hie deutlich sagt: Vnd ein Wort der Warheit / wie S. Jacobus zeuget / dadurch vns Gott / wie eine Mutter auffs neuw gebieret / vnd geistlich lebendig macht."

God, like a mother, gives birth to us through the gospel and makes us spiritually alive. The conception of the new creation through the gospel stands, for Musaeus, in direct contrast to the teaching of Caspar Schwenkfeld and other spiritualists who deny the power of the external word to convert and regenerate.[66]

The power of the word creates and sustains the new life. Musaeus does not address, as Pauli had, new obedience in terms of human responsibility. According to Musaeus, God has made us his first fruits, so that, as Luther put it in his explanation to the Second Article of the Creed, "we might be his own and live under him in his kingdom and serve him in everlasting righteousness, innocence, and blessedness."[67] Musaeus, quoting Ephesians 1:3–12, describes the new life according to God's adoption and promise of the eternal inheritance. Rather than placing a new demand of obedience on the new creature, Musaeus says that being new creatures and the first fruits of God's creation is a great comfort for us Christians: "We are the most dear children, the next in line for the inheritance, those who will sit at his breast for all eternity and be his glory and joy."[68]

In the final section of the sermon on James 1:19–21, Musaeus applies these verses to the Third Commandment. Here he does not speak of our obedience (*Gehorsam*), but instead describes how God trains us through his word (*von fruchtbarlicher vbung Göttliches worts*).[69] According to Musaeus, James gives three characteristics (*eigenschafften*) belonging to every newborn child of God, so that as good disciples and hearers of the word we steadily grow and are saved.[70] First, he warns at 1:19—just as Luther had against the enthusiasts—that one should not quickly become a master of the word and burst out with whatever comes into their head: "That is a wretched plague that corrupts every preacher and hearer."[71] Musaeus, therefore, admonishes preachers with a summary of St. Paul's words to Timothy: "Stick to reading, so that everyone can see your progress" (1 Tim 4:12).[72] The second characteristic of a good disciple is humility and patience. Musaeus applies this especially to hearers of the word who should be ready humbly to receive correction and discipline from the preaching of repentance and

---

66. Musaeus, *Postilla* (1583), 48. "So muß der Schwenckfelt liegen / als ein verzweiffelter Ketzer / der es für einen todten Buchstaben / vnkrässtig vnd vnnötig zu vnser bekehrung vnd erleuchtung lestert."

67. *BSLK* 511; *SC* 2:2.

68. Musaeus, *Postilla* (1583), 49.

69. Musaeus, *Postilla* (1583), 49.

70. Musaeus, *Postilla* (1583), 49.

71. Musaeus, *Postilla* (1583), 50.

72. Musaeus, *Postilla* (1583), 50.

from the cross.[73] The last characteristic of a true disciple of the word is true repentance. That is, true disciples will flee from the sins against their conscience (Jas 1:20). Musaeus laments that many hear the preaching of repentance and are struck by the words, but then refuse to flee from their sin. They "remain in the same filth as before and are not sorry for their sins and do not pray to improve their life."[74]

Musaeus made it a practice to end each of his sermons with a prayer that summarized the lesson. This sermon ends with a prayer of praise to God the Father for both the first creation and the new creation through the word of truth. He adds this final petition: "Incline our hearts to your word, so that throughout all our days we may hear it with humility, without wrath, putting aside all wickedness, so that we grow and remain in this new birth that you have begun in us."[75]

What stands out in Musaeus's exposition is the birth imagery and the restoration of the *imago Dei*. His sermon on James 1:16–21 is thoroughly grounded in God's gracious activity through his word and Spirit. Now that the new creation has come in Christ and through his word, Christians must put aside the old self with all its desires and grow from day to day by receiving the word that can save and keep their souls eternally.

Musaeus on James 1:22–27 (Rogate Sunday)

Musaeus differs from Pauli's treatment of these verses and offers an ecclesiological interpretation of James 1:22–27. The message, he says, belongs to the Third Article of the Creed, particularly the phrase, "the communion of saints" and the distinction between the visible and hidden church. Drawing on the parables of the wheat and the tares (Matt 13:24–30) and the sheep and the goats (Matt 25:31–46), Musaeus applies James's message both to preachers and members of the church, who

---

73. Musaeus, *Postilla* (1583), 50.

74. Musaeus, *Postilla* (1583), 50.

75. Musaeus, *Postilla* (1583), 52. "Summa dieser Epistel ins Gebett verfasset. WJr dancken dir HERR Gott Himmlischen Vatter / daß du vns nicht allein anfänglich an vnsern aller ersten Eltern / als ein Vatter alles liechts / nach deinem Göttlichen Bild geschaffen / vnd mit guten vnd volkömmlichen Gaben gezieret / sondern auch nach dem Fall vmb Christi vnsers einigen Mittlers willen wider zu Gnaden angenommen / vnd durch das wort der Warheit zu gliedern deiner Kirchen gemacht / vnd geheiligt zum Erstlingen deiner Creaturen / neige vnsere Hertzen zu deinem Wort / daß wirs vnser lebenlang ohn zorn / mit sanfftmut vnnd ablegung aller boßheit hören / vnd in angefangener neuwen geburt wachsen vnnd verharren / der du mit deinem lieben Son vnd heiligen Geist lebest vnd regierest ein warer Gott jmmer vnd ewiglich / AMEN."

with various discernible signs are set apart from the hypocrites and posing Christians, who serve the devil in the Christian name, until, on the day of judgment, they are eternally separated as tares from the good wheat, as goats from obedient sheep, or even as ulcers from a healthy body, and thrown into the abyss of hell with the devils.[76]

He then ties the Epistle in with the theme of *Rogate* (pray!), to teach that we must learn to sing faithfully in prayer to God. Musaeus uses the example of the nightingale, who does not screech like the owl or boom like the great bittern, causing a hideous and unbearable sound, but sings a beautiful tune that pleases God in heaven and moves him graciously to hear our prayer.[77]

Musaeus draws together the major themes of James 1, including prayer and true faith, and sees the lesson for *Rogate* as an unbroken continuation of the previous Sunday.[78] After James has explained how God recreates his fallen creatures through the word, he now offers several tests (*Proben und Werckzeichen*), "so that by these one can examine and perceive both in himself and in others whether he is a true Christian or a hypocrite, as St. Paul teaches us in 2 Corinthians 3 [13:5]: 'Test [*versuchet* / πειράζετε] yourselves to see if you are in faith. Test yourselves [*prüfet euch selbs* / ἑαυτοὺς δοκιμάζετε]. Or do you not realize that Christ is in you?'"[79]

As just mentioned, Musaeus places the *Rogate* pericope in the locus of the Third Article of the Creed. However, his division of the sermon places the three major parts under one or more of the Commandments, to test whether one is a true Christian. Musaeus formulates the text's major parts negatively,

---

76. Musaeus, *Postilla* (1583), 53.

77. Musaeus, *Postilla* (1583), 53. Musaeus draws attention to an important aspect of Lutheran theology that also plays a significant role in Lutheran exegesis, namely, that God can through prayer be moved to mercifully change His mind toward His creatures. J. A. Steiger has shown the importance of prayer in the Lutheran exegesis of Jonah, that even in the depths of hell a prayer that lays hold of the *promissio* can overcome the power of hell: "Noch in der Hölle, in der Gott nicht gelobt wird (Jes 38,18), ja gar nicht ist, ist und bleibt die göttliche promissio gültig, daß der Glaube die Macht hat, Gott herbeizuzitieren und durch das Gebet (und sei es nur ein Stoßgebet) die Hölle zu überwinden. Insofern ist Jona exemplum fidei: Weil er die Allmacht des Glaubens vorexerziert, Gott dazu zwingt, seine Verheißung wahrzumachen, das Schreien des Beters nicht ungehört zu lassen, und dadurch die Hölle in einen Ort ungeahnter Gottesnähe verwandelt" (Steiger, "Jonas Hölle," 67). See Steiger, "Jonas Hölle," 55–77. There is further study that could be done on the Lutheran theology of prayer as drawn from James (1:6–8; 3:3; 5:13–20). It is not by chance that in his commentary on Jonah (1526), Luther turns on several occasions to James, in order to teach about faith and prayer.

78. Musaeus, *Postilla* (1583), 53–54. "Es hengt aber diese heutige Epistel an der vergangenen heute acht tage / als einerley vngetrennete Predigt."

79. Musaeus, *Postilla* (1583), 54.

according to the unsavory characteristics of those who preach and hear the word. One must test oneself and others against the Commandments to make plain whether one is true or not. The first part, and the one to which Musaeus gives the most attention in his exposition (Jas 1:22–25), is an examination of the Third Commandment, to show that not everyone hears and receives the word in the same way. The second part (Jas 1:26) is an examination from the Second and Eighth Commandments, to discern who holds their mouth in check before God and the world. And the final section (Jas 1:27) is an examination of all the Commandments in general.[80]

Musaeus remarks that James is not dealing with blatant rejection of God's word.

> For St. James is not speaking here of the gross hypocrites, such as the papists who seek and establish the church and salvation outside of God's word in purely human arrangements. He is speaking of the subtlest and finest hypocrites, who confess the pure teaching with true Christians and let themselves be berated as evangelical.[81]

The danger with this sort of inspection of faith, of course, is that it can turn into a witch hunt. Musaeus avoids this insofar as he does not attempt to deal programmatically with an evaluation of true Christianity, to rid the church of all hypocrites, as would later be the case in radical pietism. Instead he acknowledges the subtleties of a good pastoral application of the law and the need for self-inspection in light of God's word. The issue for James, as he sees it, is not that lazy Christians are deceiving others and corrupting the fellowship of the church, but rather that by having outward fellowship in the true church and not internally in their own hearts they only deceive themselves, and the Day of Judgment will make it plain. God already knows the heart.

> God does not look at outward appearances, to see whether you hear his word in the congregation and blabber on about it. God looks at the foundation of the heart, to see whether his word has taken root through faith and has blossomed through good

---

80. Musaeus, *Postilla* (1583), 54.

81. Musaeus, *Postilla* (1583), 55. "Denn S. Jacobus redet hie nicht von den groben heuchlern / wie die Papisten sind / welche die Kirche vnd Seligkeit / ausser Gottes Wort / in lautern Menschenstand suchen vnd setzen / sondern von den aller subtilsten vnd besten / die sich mit den rechten Christen zu der reinen lehre bekennen / vnd für Euangelisch schelten lassen."

works. If he does not find it so, he will surely damn you as a hypocrite.[82]

God will judge the genuineness of the inward being and not the appearance of godliness. Yet the Christian life is not merely inward. Musaeus states:

> True Christians . . . have both internal and external communion with the Christian church and hear the word not only externally with the ear, but receive it with the heart through the working of the Holy Spirit, and are made holy and converted, so that, if they were secure in their sins, they start to fear them by the preaching of the law. Or if they were despairing, they begin to be comforted by the preaching of the gospel, through faith in Christ, and show forth their faith through new obedience and guard themselves from intentional sins against conscience. This is just what the Third Article of our Christian faith says, that true Christians are a communion of saints, who have the forgiveness of sins and life everlasting.[83]

What is most striking in this passage and telling of Musaeus's exegesis of this pericope as a whole is his application of the mirror as law and gospel. Musaeus picked up on this interpretive strategy from Pauli and developed it further. Pauli used the mirror to give a rather elaborate anthropology of pre-lapsarian humanity. Musaeus, however, says simply that:

> God's law and gospel is a bright mirror of our nature and the essence and will (*wesen vnd willen*) of God that is placed before all people to reflect back and expose them even down to their pores. . . . But those who look in the mirror are not at all the same; there are two kinds.[84]

Musaeus lists the expectations of those who are faithful hearers, and develops here something of an *ordo salutis*. When true Christians look into the mirror of the law, they see their sins, repent and wash. And when true Christians look into the law of liberty (gospel), they believe and trust it, give thanks for it, fight against sin, and contemplate further the word that has been preached to them. This is the Christian whom James says "will be blessed in his doing" (Jas 1:25).

82. Musaeus, *Postilla* (1583), 56. "Gott fraget nichts nach dem eusserlichen schein / ob du vnderm hauffen sein Wort hörest / vnd mit dem Maul viel davon plauderst / sondern nach deß hertzens grundt / ob sein Wort darinn durch den Glauben eyn wurtzle / vnd durch gute Werck herauß wachse / findet er das nicht / so verdammt er dich gewiß als einen Heuchler."

83. Musaeus, *Postilla* (1583), 56.

84. Musaeus, *Postilla* (1583), 57.

Musaeus is aware of misinterpretations on this point. If the true Christian is the one who studies the word and is blessed for his perseverance, is not the study of the word and the perseverance of the saints a human work? Musaeus not only explains the passage but seeks to lay out a hermeneutic for the whole Epistle:

> For in no way does he ascribe salvation to one's own doing and work. Rather, he distinguishes throughout his entire Epistle between a true, living faith and hypocrisy, and says: "A true, living faith could not and must not be without works and fruits, even though one is certainly justified and saved without works. But if a man is without works, he is completely dead, that is, he is full of useless hypocrisy." That is therefore the first point of this Epistle concerning the testing of faith, to distinguish between true Christians and hypocrites.[85]

In summary, the entire pericope concerns the testing of true Christians, so that their faith would be genuine and distinguished in this world from that of the hypocrites. Although works and the fruits of faith do not justify or save a person, a true Christian is never without them, as the examples of Abraham, Rahab, Job, Elijah, and the prophets demonstrate.

As a final note on Musaeus, his summary prayer shows how by reading the passages with the Catechism, he steers clear of the difficulty Pauli had with the responsibility of the hearers. Whereas Pauli left little room for the powerful working of the word and Spirit, and instead emphasized the believer's necessary response to the word in obedience to the *norma legis*, Musaeus places the whole life of the Christian under the work of the Holy Spirit and his word.

Summary of this Epistle in prayer form:

> We give You thanks, Lord God, heavenly Father, that you have revealed to us your saving word and have called us into the communion of your holy, Christian church. Renew our evil nature through your Holy Spirit with every passing day, so that we may not decay with the great masses of hypocrites and dead members of your church. As true Christians, make us both hearers and doers of your word who unceasingly examine themselves

---

85. Musaeus, *Postilla* (1583), 57–58. "Denn er mit nichte einiger that vnd Werck die Seeligkeit zuschreibt / sondern in seiner gantzen Epistel durchauß den rechten lebendigen Glauben vnderscheidet von Heucheley / vnd sagt: Ein rechter lebendiger Glaub könne vnd müsse ohne Werck vnnd früchte kurtzumb nicht seyn / ob er wol ohn alle Werck gerecht vnd selig machet. Jst er aber ohn Werck / so ist er gantz todt / das ist / nichtig vnd lauter heucheley / das ist nun der erst Punct dieser Epistel von der ersten Probe vnnd vnderschiede der rechten Christen vnnd Heuchler."

with the same, as our mirror, that we would wash the dirt and filth of our sin from us, control our tongues, and keep ourselves unstained from the vileness of the world, through Jesus Christ, your dear Son, our eternal Mediator and Savior. Amen.[86]

Conclusion

At table, sometime in the spring of 1532, Martin Luther lamented that the righteousness of faith was hardly ever taught and that Christians so easily trust in their own righteousness: "For our righteousness or the righteousness of works brings only sorrow. Sin harms us less than our own righteousness."[87] One of the great challenges facing every preacher is how to preach sanctification in such a way that does not lead to idolatry. The proper distinction between law and gospel is a difficult art. And living by faith, Luther suggests, easily turns into living by sight. We look for results. Pauli, in his sermon on James 1, attempted to promote very God-pleasing activity of Christian obedience for those who had been freed by the gospel, but still struggle with sin. But preaching sanctification as obedience to the law inevitably turns into more preaching on the law. Not only should Christians avoid laziness, but they should also avoid looking at their progress as grounds for self-justification in the world. Whenever preachers use the law to produce righteousness, they will always need more law.

Pauli and Musaeus both recognized that this outward life of holiness and good works ought to follow faith, not only because God commands it but also that he has promised to bring the work he has begun in us to completion (Phil 1:6). One cannot be justified and reject the new life. Justification and sanctification belong together, just as faith and good works fit

---

86. Musaeus, *Postilla* (1583), 61. "Summa dieser Epistel ins Gebett verfasset. WJr dancken dir HERR Gott Himmlischer Vatter / daß du vns dein seligmachendes wort geoffanbaret / vnd zu der gemeinschafft deiner heyligen Christlichen Kirchen beruffen. Verneuwe vnser böse natur durch deinen heiligen Geist je lenger je mehr / daß wir nicht mit dem grossen hauffen der heuchler vnnd todter Glieder deiner Kirchen verderben / sondern als warhafftige Christen / deines Worts beyde Hörer vnd Thäter seyen / vnd dasselbige als vnsern Spiegel on vnterlaß also anschauwen / daß wir vnser heßliche mahlen vnnd schandtflechen drauß abwischen / vnser Zunge zämen / vnnd vns von der schnöden Welt vnbefleckt halten / durch Jesum Christum deinen lieben Son vnsern ewigen Mittler vnnd Heyland / Amen."

87. WA TR 1.106.9–10; *LW* 54:34. "Quia die iustitia nostra seu operum iustitia hat das hertzleyd. Peccatum thut vns nit so wehe als iustitia propria."

beautifully together and belong together.[88] Therefore, one must venture to live, to do, and to act in the world, knowing full well that acting rightly can be more dangerous to faith than sin itself. In doing righteous deeds, idolatry is always close at hand, and nothing could appear godlier than to do God's will according to his law.

The danger of idolatry in the preaching and living of sanctification looms. It is for this reason that the different approaches to sanctification by Pauli and Musaeus are so illustrative for our own day. The temptation to turn to the law or to appeal to the regenerate will to produce noticeable change—tendencies we can observe in Pauli's sermon on James 1—quickly turns into forms of idolatry, because the *peccator* in all of us will always find a way to live by sight rather than faith and trust in some progress in us. To preach sanctification monergistically, to have Christ as our righteousness and our sanctification, is to live by faith, to hope in that which is not yet seen in us. To preach sanctification the Lutheran way is not to steer us to the word as if it required a response, but to deliver the word that has the power to save our souls (Jas 1:18) and keep them safe, hidden with Christ in God until the end.

Bibliography

Bayer, Oswald. *Aus Glauben Leben: Über Rechtfertigung und Heiligung*. 2nd ed. Stuttgart: Calwer, 1990.

———. *Freedom in Response: Lutheran Ethics: Sources and Controversies*. Translated by Jeffrey F. Cayzer. Oxford Studies in Theological Ethics. Oxford: Oxford University Press, 2007.

Benz, Hans, et al., eds. *Religion in Geschichte und Gegenwart*. 8 vols. 4th ed. Berlin: de Gruyter, 1998–2007.

Beste, Wilhelm. *Die bedeutendsten nachreformatorischen Kanzelredner der älteren lutherischen Kirche des Reformationszeitalters in Biographien und einer Auswahl ihrer Predigten*. Leipzig: Meyer, 1858.

Frymire, John M. *Primacy of the Postils: Catholics, Protestants, and the Dissemination of Ideas in Early Modern Germany*. Leiden: Brill, 2010.

Hägglund, Bengt. "Was ist der Mensch?" In *Chemnitz—Gerhard—Arndt—Rudbeckius: Aufsätze zum Studium der altlutherischen Theologie*, edited by Alexander Bitzel and Johann Anselm Steiger, 159–74. Waltrop: Spenner, 2003.

Kaufmann, Thomas. *Universität und lutherische Konfessionalisierung. Die Rostocker Theologieprofessoren und ihr Beitrag zur theologischen Bildung und kirchlichen Gestaltung im Herzogtum Mecklenburg zwischen 1550 und 1675*. Gütersloh: Gütersloher, 1997.

---

88. *FC* 3.41

Kolb, Robert. "Georg Major as Preacher." In *Georg Major (1502–1574): Ein Theologe Der Wittenberger Reformation, Leucoreastudien zur Geschichte der Reformation und der Lutherischen Orthodoxie*, edited by Irene Dingel and Günther Wartenberg, 93–121. Leipzig: Evangelische Verlagsanstalt, 2005.

Kolb, Robert, and Timothy J. Wengert, eds. *The Book of Concord: The Confessions of the Evangelical Lutheran Church*. Translated by Charles Arand, et al. Minneapolis: Fortress, 2000.

Krause, K. E. H. "Pauli, Simon." In *Allgemeine Deutsche Biographie*. 56 volumes. Leipzig: n.p., 1875–1912.

Lane, Jason D. *Luther's Epistle of Straw: The Voice of St. James in Reformation Preaching*. Historia Hermeneutica Series Studia. Berlin: de Gruyter, 2018.

Musaeus, Simon. *Postilla Das ist Außlegung der Episteln und Evangelien, welche durchs gantze Jahr, an allen Sontagen, und ander namhafften Festen, in d. Kirchen ublich und bräuchlich sind, 2. Teil: Ostern bis auffs Advent*. Frankfurt: Basseus, 1583.

———. *Postilla Das ist Außlegung aller Episteln / so durchs gantze Jar an Sontagen vnd namhafftigen Feyertagen / in der Kirchen vblich vnd gebreuchlich sind / in drey Theil gefasset vnd gestellet*. Jena: Hüter, 1573.

Pauli, Simon. *Postilla Das ist / Außlegung der Episteln vnd Euangelien / an Sontagen vnd fürnemesten Festen / ordentlich vnd richtig / nach der RHETORICA gefasset: Neben einer kurtzen erkklerung des Textes. Gepredigt zur Rostock: Das ander Teil / von Ostern / bis auf Advent*. Magdeburg: Kirchner, 1572.

Steiger, Johann Anselm. "Jonas Hölle: Ein auslegungsgeschichtlicher Beitrag zu Luthers Interpretation des Alten Testaments." In *Innovation durch Wissenstransfer in der Frühen Neuzeit: Kultur- und geistesgeschichtliche Studien zu Austauschprozessen in Mitteleuropa*, edited by J. A. Steiger, et al., 55–77. Chloe 41. Leiden: Brill, 2016.

———. *Medizinische Theologie: Christus Medicus und Theologia Medicinalis bei Martin Luther und im Luthertum der Barockzeit*. Leiden: Brill, 2005.

———. *Melancholie, Diätetik und Trost: Konzepte der Melancholie-Therapie im 16. und 17. Jahrhunderts*. Heidelberg: Manutius, 1996.

6

The Psalm from which We Never Graduate

Luther's Exposition of Psalm 51 1532/38

Naomichi Masaki

Introduction

"The Psalm from which We Never Graduate" is a paraphrase of Dr. Luther's own words in his *Lectures on Psalm 51*.[1] I take these words to mean Luther's way of teaching his students that we Christians never graduate from Jesus! Along with his *Great Lectures on Galatians*, this short exposition on Psalm 51 remains one of my dearest treasures. It is eye opening every time I read it. It is comforting and encouraging. It always brings me back to the chief doctrine of the Christian faith and invites me to the utmost certain place where our Lord Jesus extends his pastoral care.

I was first introduced to this important writing when I attended my *Doktorvater* Professor Norman Nagel's graduate seminar on Luther Studies. Following his lead, as soon as I started to teach at Concordia Theological Seminary in Fort Wayne in 2001, I assigned the *Lectures on Psalm 51* regularly in the required courses in systematic theology. The response from my students has been overwhelming. They all fell in love with it. Professor Oswald Bayer had already articulated from these lectures that for Luther the *proprium* of the subject of all theology was sinning man and justifying Jesus.[2] It was a profound joy to know that I shared with him the same conviction of Luther's theological vitality.

---

1. "This is the teaching of this Psalm and our perpetual school, from which we never graduate as perfect masters, neither we nor the apostles nor the prophets" (*LW* 12:331; WA 40:357.31-33).

2. *LW* 12:311; WA 40:328.17-18. "Nam Theologiae proprium subiectum est homo peccati reus ac perditus et Deus iustificans ac salvator hominis peccatoris." Cf., WA 40

Known as one of the seven penitential psalms since the sixth century,[3] Psalm 51 had occupied a vital part of the liturgical life of the church. At the Augustinian monastery in Erfurt, Luther had learned the entire Psalter by heart, including this Psalm 51, as he recited fifty Psalms a day during seven prayer offices from 3 a.m. to 9 p.m. every three hours. We too recite part of this Psalm habitually in our communion services ("create in me a clean heart, O God") and prayer offices ("O Lord, open my lips," "and my mouth will declare your praise").[4]

Luther lectured on this Psalm in June to August of 1532.[5] He gave eleven lectures in all. Having been convinced that the Holy Spirit was the author of this Psalm, as of the entire Scripture, Luther's posture toward Psalm 51 remained that of a humble student who was eager to receive "whatever he [the Holy Spirit] gives."[6] It is rather astonishing to read such a modest comment, when we acknowledge that he was thoroughly familiar with this Psalm. Rather than stating that he had mastered it, he expressed his honesty that there was still much to learn from it. He had a good reason for saying this, of course.

The aim of this essay is unpretentious. Although scholarly investigations *about* these lectures are both interesting and important, we would rather get into the content. We want to hear Luther speak, just as his students at the University of Wittenberg sat at the feet of Dr. Luther. In doing so, I would like to reflect how Luther's exposition of Psalm 51 resembles one of the confessional documents that came from his own pen, the Smalcald Articles, particularly in its Part III. We know that Melanchthon followed the outline of the book of Romans when he drafted the first edition of his *Loci Communes*. Similarly, in composing Part III of the Smalcald Articles, it appears as though Luther had utilized Psalm 51 as his outline. The point of departure in both was the fact of our sinfulness. Then, Luther moved on to the doctrine of the law, repentance, the gospel, the means of grace, the office of the holy ministry, the church, good works and Christian vocation in this sequence.

1:406.24–25, *LW* 26:259: "Cum tamen iustificare peccatorem sit solius Christi proprium officium." See also Bayer, *Theology the Lutheran Way*, 17–21, 49–50, idem.; Bayer, *Martin Luther's Theology*, 37–42.

3. Along with Ps 6; 32; 38; 102; 130; 143. *LW* 12:304; WA 40:316.25.

4. *LW* 12:393; WA 40:446.17–19.

5. WA 40:315–470; *LW* 12:301–410. Luther's lectures on Psalm 51 at an earlier time are also recorded in *LW* 10:235–43; 14:165–75; WA 3:286–93; 18:499–507.

6. *LW* 12:303; WA 40:315.26.

I dedicate this brief essay in my humble acknowledgement and profound gratitude for Professor Bayer's immeasurable theological contribution as a Luther scholar.

Understanding Sin as the Key Difference between Luther and His Opponents

According to Dr. Luther, the doctrine of repentance is the chief doctrine this Psalm teaches.[7] Now that he had gained a deeper understanding of repentance than at the time of his Ninety-five Theses, we hear Luther expound on the doctrine in a much more profound and more evangelical way. To discuss the doctrine of repentance is to articulate the doctrine of justification, as Luther explained it, especially later in this work.[8] For example, in his Smalcald Articles, there is no specific article on the doctrine of justification. Whereas the *chief article* in Part II, Article 1 may be a strong candidate, it is subtitled "the office and work of Christ," not "justification." The fact is that the article on the doctrine of justification is hidden in the article on repentance.[9] Such a presentation resembles the way Dr. Luther lectured in his *Lectures on Psalm 51*.

The mandate of the crucified and risen Lord to the apostles included the preaching of repentance (Luke 24:47). The apostles faithfully carried this out, beginning on the day of Pentecost. The book of Acts gives us an account that their preaching of repentance was followed by the teaching of the Lord's doctrine, holy baptism, and the bestowal of the forgiveness of sins. It culminated in the breaking of the bread, the κοινωνία, the administration of the body and the blood of the Lord for the baptized to eat and to drink (Acts 2:37–42). Luther's theological diagnosis of his day was that his opponents, both the papacy and the sects, did not know this fundamental doctrine of repentance.[10] Why so? Because, as Luther was convinced, they did not understand sin. A lack of understanding of sin corresponds to a lack of proper understanding of Christ and his grace.[11] Luther went on to unpack this enormous problem of his opponents by pointing out that where sin is not

---

7. *LW* 12:303; WA 40:315.19–26.

8. *LW* 12:331, 367; WA 40:356.34, 357.35, 408.33–36.

9. SA 3, 3.

10. *LW* 12:304; WA 40:316.27–36; *LW* 12:311; WA 40:328.18–20; *LW* 12:317; WA 40:336.30; *LW* 12:329; WA 40:354.28–29; *LW* 12:330; WA 40:355.28–33; *LW* 12:375; WA 40:419.15–21.

11. Cf. SA III, I, 11.

known and understood correctly, there we find Scripture not understood,[12] new liturgy and new Divine Service invented,[13] and baptism, the Lord's Supper, new obedience, and the entire Christian life falsely comprehended as mere ideas.[14] Luther advocated that the doctrine of sin is the most necessary doctrine that must be taught in the church.[15] A denial of sin is a denial of God.[16] Moreover, it is not only a denial of God, but it is also our persecution and condemnation of God.[17]

In the present day, we often debate what the place of the law should be in the Christian life. We ask questions concerning the so-called Third Use of the law. We continue to struggle over the question of the proper distinction between law and gospel.[18] Yet, in hearing Luther in these lectures, although the questions regarding the law remain crucial, we cannot help but recognize that the even more fundamental question is sin, the fact in our life and a condition from which nobody can escape.

Our resistance to talk about sin at the present time is nothing new when we glance at the history of humanity. It is true that the church is facing new challenges today, such as the breakdown of the family, the rise of so-called same-sex marriage and the gender revolution, the advent of postmodernism, a radical secularism, and physical isolation from each other in cyber-age culture. In addition, the liturgical movement from the twentieth century still affects many of our churches today. Many Lutherans unfortunately had come to agree with its Roman Catholic and Anglican proponents that the theme of sin and forgiveness should be carefully avoided.[19] "We need to warm up our services," they claimed, "because our Lutheran liturgy has been too pessimistic, focusing too much on such negative notions as sin and forgiveness. Let's make our services become brighter and more entertaining and celebratory. The 'eucharistic hospitality' is the way to go. Let's ignore our doctrinal differences with other traditions. We should seek a visible unity of the church."

The church faces new challenges in every era. Although they may appear in different forms, most seem to have a common root, that is, our unwillingness and indeed inability to admit that we are sinners in need of

12. *LW* 12:351; WA 40:385.27–29.
13. *LW* 12:315; WA 40:334.17–20.
14. *LW* 12:375; WA 40:419.13–21.
15. *LW* 12:351; WA 40:384.30–31.
16. *LW* 12:341; WA 40:371.23–25.
17. *LW* 12:341; WA 40:371.38–40.
18. See a recent contribution of the subject in Collver et al., *Necessary Distinction*.
19. See Masaki, *He Alone Is Worthy!*, 343–61.

help. Reading another of Luther's legendary works, *Lectures on Genesis*, will only help us understand this ageless problem persisting since the creation of the world.

Sin and Major Religions in Asia

Before we get into details of Luther's insight on our sinfulness, it may be worth broadening our scope, for when Luther observed that a denial of sin is a denial of God, he did not have in mind only the papacy and various kinds of sectarians. He also included "the Turks," "the Jews," and the "Gentiles."[20] How about other religions? Does Buddhism deny sin? Does Confucianism know what sin is? What about Shintoism? Does Luther's general statement on the religions still hold true?

Buddhism is a religion that teaches not only about Buddha, but also about how to become a Buddha, an enlightened one. Buddhism does not profess creator God. There is no divine revelation such as God's word or Scripture. The pursuit for becoming a Buddha is therefore by doing something that is carefully prescribed by teachers. By denying a way of hedonism (快楽主義) and also rejecting the opposite option of following strict rules with the extreme kinds of self-training (苦行主義), Buddhism pursues a middle way (中道). This Indian version of *via media* consists of mastering four unwavering truths of life (四聖諦).

The first truth is on suffering (苦聖諦). To be born is a suffering. To get old is a suffering. To become sick is a suffering. To die is a suffering. In addition to these four fundamental sufferings of basic experiences of all human beings (生老病死), there are four incidental or supplemental sufferings as well, making eight human sufferings in all (四苦八苦). To have to be separated from the loved one (愛別離苦). To have to live together with the hated one (怨憎会苦). To have to be satisfied when you do not get what you desired (求不得苦). And to have to come finally to acknowledge that everything in life is a suffering (五陰盛苦).

When one has fully grasped this first unchanging truth of life as suffering, not superficially as mere concepts but truly as experiences, he is ready to move on to the next level. The second truth is that all sufferings have particular causes and origins (集諦). There is no suffering that comes from nowhere. Every suffering has a chain of events and causes, but they go all the way back to the fundamental human desire and the passion for survival (根本的生存欲).

20. *LW* 12:341; WA 40:371.39–40; *LW* 12:310; WA 40:326.20–21.

Once this truth is learned, the next door is opened. The third truth of life is that if one cuts himself off from this fundamental desire for survival, his sufferings will disappear (滅諦). One does not need to suffer any more. At least, he does not feel everything as suffering.

The fourth truth teaches you how to attain to this third truth (道諦), that is, to master the Eight Ways (八正道). When one completes those eight self-training points, he then will be able to successfully withdraw from the vicious cycle of unending sufferings (解脱) of both of this world and at his death from other five (地獄、餓鬼、畜生、修羅、人、天の六道). He becomes a Buddha. Now, those Eight Ways of self-discipline are to have the right view (正見), to have the right thought (正思), to use the right words (正語), to do the right things (正業), to live the right life (正命), to make the right efforts (正精進), to have the right awareness (正念), and to do the right meditation (正定).

Obviously, what we presented here is a simplified way of describing the basic teaching of Buddhism. But it may be sufficient to give us an answer to our question. Where is sin in Buddhism? Nowhere. How can Buddhism know sin when there is no God? Buddhism is not concerned about sin and forgiveness, but only about how one may be liberated from this world of suffering.

How about Confucianism? Like Buddhism, there is no creator God, no sin, and so no forgiveness. However, unlike Buddhism, whose worldview is so pessimistic that life is considered as unending sufferings, Confucianism maintains a much more positive worldview. For Confucians, this world is an enjoyable place to exist. In fact, Confucianism knows of no other worlds apart from this world. There is no heaven and no hell. Confucianism is not interested in a metaphysical explanation of the origin of life or the destination of life after death. Rather, it limits its scope to life that is observable. Confucianism teaches that the life that is lived out is a gift from the past generation. The task of the present is to pass over this gift of life to the next generation. Thus same-sex marriage is unconceivable for Confucianism because in marriage the most important thing is to guarantee the prosperity of descendants rather than to enjoy selfish pleasure. Respect for elders, a famous teaching of Confucianism, derives from its high value in the continuation of life from one generation to another. The goal of Confucianism is for one to become like a saint. A saint in Confucianism is the one who lives his life according to the highest morality. Even when he follows his natural instinct, he lives uprightly without internal or external struggles. Obviously, this goal is not easily attainable.

Confucianism views man as a union of soul and body. In Chinese characters, soul is written as 魂 and body as 魄. On the right hand side of both characters, we find the same character, 鬼, which means a dead person. However, on the left hand side, different characters are used. 云 means a cloud (from 雲), and 白 means a white (bone). Thus, soul is a dead person in a cloud, while body is a dead person in white bones. As long as man is alive, there is a union of body and soul. But when he dies, his soul will float about in the air like a cloud, while his body will go down to earth and end up becoming white bones. What this means is that, according to Confucianism, even after one dies, his soul and body still stay somewhere in this world. When ancestor worship, another characteristic in Confucianism, is conducted, it reunites the deceased man's soul in the air and his body on the ground at a memorial tablet (位牌) located on an altar within a household. Children, especially the eldest son, must perform this rite or prayer, because only then, the *spirit* of the children and the *spirit* of the deceased father or mother may be able to respond to each other. The reunification of body and soul of the deceased is then accomplished. When friends or strangers offer prayers, such vivifying correspondence will not happen.

Confucianism teaches both good order in society and high morality of the individuals. Those teachings have their basis in Confucianism's understanding of life and death. That the deceased loved one, such as mother or father, still watches over you from somewhere, "from behind the grass or from behind this or that tree," to follow a popular notion, gives a profound comfort to the surviving family. Where is sin? Does Confucianism talk about forgiveness? By no means.

Finally, what about Shintoism? Is there at least a concept of sin in it? The answer is, surprisingly, yes, but a very different kind. Like Buddhism and Confucianism, there is no creator in Shintoism. There is no Scripture as revelation. There is no stated doctrinal standard. There is not even a concept of afterlife. What, then, does Shintoism teach? It teaches how people may live together in harmony as a community and how to secure peace and prosperity there. When Shintoism talks about sin, it is a sin against this most important element in life, the community. Anything that man does to disturb unity and tranquility of a community is considered sin.

Basic to Shintoism is participation in festivals and rituals, rather than obedience to certain rules and guidelines. Festivals in Shintoism are the time when a community comes together to welcome and entertain their ancestor gods. There are many kinds of gods in Shintoism. In fact, according to Shinto, a god is one who has done something extraordinary, either great things or the worst kind of things. A man or a woman can become a god. However, the most important gods are the deceased family members or the members of the community who have gone through a purification process of thirty-three years. Now they periodically visit their homes and their original communities. From the side of a community, gods are their guests. If the community treats them disrespectfully, gods are there to harm it with their wrath. For fear of this, the community prepares gods' visitation by cleaning up their houses and by preparing the best Japanese cuisine. When gods do arrive, the community entertains them with singing and traditional dancing. The highest point of gods' visitation takes place at the meal table. There gods and people eat together and drink together (神人共食). This is the reason why at these festivals special chopsticks are used. Both ends of chopsticks are narrowed, so that when one eats by using one end, gods also eat with them by using the other end of the same chopsticks. If the ancestor worship in Confucianism is comparable with the so-called "real presence," then, we may find in Shintoism something analogous to the meal itself. This is "eucharistic hospitality" for gods! The *Religionsgeschichtliche Schule* or comparative religion scholars would enjoy connecting those religious practices with the Lord's Supper. Such a view is possible only when one denies the Lord's mandate and institution of his Supper.

Does Shintoism know sin as it is revealed in the Scripture? The answer is obvious. Luther was right when he said that no Gentiles know what sin is.

What It Means to *Know* Sin

Luther's understanding of sin goes beyond most of our imaginations. Even he was not capable of grasping the full depth of his sinfulness, as he also uses an expression "bottomless [*grundlos*]" in the Smalcald Articles.[21] His basic critique of his opponents was that they minimize the magnitude of sin.[22] He says: "Human nature is more seriously infected and corrupted by sin than I could ever have suspected."[23]

What is Luther's grounding? One of his arguments is that for his opponents sin is only external[24] and actual,[25] such as, in David's case, adultery, murder, covering up of this murder, and the blaspheming of the name of God.[26] What they did not arrive at was that out of those external sins David had come to a knowledge of "the whole sin [*totius peccati*],"[27] as Luther

21. *SA* III, II, 4.
22. *LW* 12:305; WA 40:316.31–34; *LW* 12:331; WA 40:357.22–24.
23. *LW* 12:337; WA 40:365.24–25.
24. *LW* 12:305; WA 40:319.21–22.
25. *LW* 12:319; WA 40:339.34.
26. *LW* 12:306; WA 40:319.26–320.19.
27. *LW* 12:307; WA 40:322.15.

called it. Sin is not merely what "the law can recognize,"[28] which the scholastic distinction of the merit of condignity and the merit of congruity could help.[29] The root of sin is much deeper.[30] Our whole nature is corrupted by sin and subject to eternal death.[31] "We are nothing but sin,"[32] says Luther. "We are born and conceived in sin."[33] As a result of the original sin,[34] man has lost a correct knowledge of God, and so he flees from God, hates him, supposing that he is not merciful God but a judge and a tyrant. From this fountain, endless other sins follow.[35]

Another argument by Luther against his opponents' lack of understanding of sin is that they are ignorant of what it means to *know* sin. Here Luther simply expounds on a Hebrew word עֲדִי in verse 3.[36] The knowledge of sin is not a speculation [*speculatio*] or an idea [*cogitatio*], but a true sense/feeling [*verus sensus*] and true experience [*vera experientia*], indeed, the weightiest struggle of the heart [*gravissimum certamen cordis*].[37] It is to feel [*sentire*] and to experience [*experiri*] the intolerable burden of the wrath of God [*intolerabile onus irae Dei*].[38] In his Smalcald Articles, Luther uses similar language to express the same thing: "the true heartache, suffering, and the feeling/sensation of death [*das recht Herzeleid, Leiden und Fuhlen des Todes*]. The Latin translation is even stronger: "torment of conscience, true passion of heart, and feeling of death [*conscientiae cruciatus, vera cordis passio et sensus mortis*].[39]

Luther articulates such knowledge of man when he compares it with other kinds of knowledge of man. A philosopher knows man as a rational animal; a lawyer knows man as a master of property; a physician knows man as healthy or sick, but a theologian knows man as a SINNER. Luther must have stressed this point in his lecture, because the printed version puts the word "sinner" in all capital letters [*PECCATORE*].[40]

---

28. *LW* 12:308; WA 40:322.25–27.
29. Cf. *LW* 12:321; WA 40:341.26–27.
30. *LW* 12:304; WA 40:316.32–34.
31. *LW* 12:307–8; WA 40:322.24–25, *LW* 12:321; WA 40:341.21–22.
32. *LW* 12:307; WA 40:322.18.
33. *LW* 12:310; WA 40:325.32.
34. *LW* 12:319; WA 40:339.35, *LW* 12:350; WA 40:383.34.
35. *LW* 12:309; WA 40:324.19–20.
36. *LW* 12:310; WA 40:36, *LW* 12:333; WA 40:360.21–28.
37. *LW* 12:310; WA 40:326.34–36.
38. *LW* 12:310; WA 40:327.13–14.
39. SA III, III, 2.
40. *LW* 12:310; WA 40:327.17–21.

Luther is aware that not everyone senses his sin in the same manner. Indeed, sin is sin whether one knows it or not.[41] Yet, it is necessary to know sin theologically.[42] The fact is, a sinner is *answerable* and *guilty* before God. Here Luther uses the same term, *reus* (answerable/guilty),[43] as in 1 Corinthians 11:27 (or Matt 26:26; Jas 2:22), a Latin translation the Greek word ἔνοχος. Paul wrote: "It goes from the foregoing that whoever eats the bread or drinks the cup of the Lord unworthily will be *answerable/guilty* [ἔνοχος, *reus*] of the body and the blood of the Lord." When Luther articulated the twofold subject of theology as sinning man and justifying Jesus, what he actually said was "sinning man" as "answerable/guilty and ruined/lost [*homo peccati reus ac perditus*]."[44] To such a man both sinful and guilty, Jesus comes as justifier and savior!

Two Kinds of Sinners

Luther observes that there are two kinds of sinners: the sinner who *feels* his sin and the sinner who does *not feel* his sin.[45] The sinner who feels his sin has hard and bitter battles. "I dare not lift my eyes to heaven. I am afraid of the sight of God. I know I am a sinner. But I also know God hates sins."[46] The natural instinct of him who dwells "in the midst of sins," and in fact, "in the very sea of his sins," is that he thinks, "I must delay praying until I become worthy to pray." Yet, Luther sees David pray: "Have mercy on me." According to Luther, prayer is the most difficult of almost all good works. "God hears your prayer not because of your worthiness but because of his mercy!"[47] Because our whole life is sin, and man is continually in sin, he must continuously pray. Luther recommends that when one is under *tentatio*, the moment when he is least prepared to pray, he should go off into a solitary place (Matt 6:6) to pray the Lord's Prayer.[48]

When a sinner feels his sin, having been crushed by the hammer of the law, the wrath and judgment of God, Luther says that that is the exact time and place to grasp God's wisdom. God is wrathful only against those who

41. *LW* 12:333; WA 359.39.
42. *LW* 12:372; WA 40:415.16–20.
43. *LW* 12:311; WA 40:328.17–18, 30–33.
44. *LW* 12:311; WA 40:328.17–18.
45. *LW* 12:315; WA 40:333.31–32.
46. *LW* 12:314; WA 40:332.29–32.
47. *LW* 12:314–15; WA 40:333.18–29.
48. *LW* 12:318–20; WA 40:338.9–340.12.

are hard and unfeeling. However, to those who do feel the burden of their sins, God says: "The Lord takes pleasure in those who fear him" (Ps 147:11). God does not despise a contrite and humble heart (Ps 51:17).[49] Luther's thorough familiarity of the Psalter navigates him to quote one passage from the Psalms to another (such as Ps 10:17; 113:7, etc.). Luther cannot stop in rejoicing in the Lord's mercy.[50] If it is true that our whole life is sin, it is also true that our whole life is enclosed in the bosom of the mercy of God. It is at this point where he speaks of the "laughing God,"[51] although *Deum ridentem* may be more accurately translated as "the smiling, or cheerful God." Luther also expresses his joy by using the words from *Gloria in Excelsis*, "only God is holy, as the church chants." Luther exhorts, "Let all men chant this verse (Ps 51:1) with David and acknowledge that they are sinners but that God is righteous, that is, merciful. This confession is a sacrifice acceptable and pleasing to God, and David invites us to it."[52] If Luther had known the Swedish liturgy of the nineteenth century, which Hermann Sasse regarded as the most beautiful among Lutheran liturgies, he would have urged all men to chant, "*Alena Han är värdig tack och lof!*"[53] The church sings not to the naked God, but God clothed in his word and promises, God in Christ, the God we can grasp for sure.[54]

The sinner who does not feel his sin has another story. He may still pray, "Have mercy on me," but God does not listen. To this sinner he announces no forgiveness. Does Luther deny the universal atonement of Christ here? Of course, not! "God does not want the prayer of a sinner who does not feel his sins, because he neither understands nor wants what he is praying for."[55] Luther is not cheated by mere recitation of syllables or by those who pray for forgiveness while still trusting in their pious works. To Luther, such is an open mockery of God. Luther says that against such secure sinners the preacher should set forth examples of God's wrath in the Scripture, such as the destruction of Sodom and the coming of the Flood over all flesh.[56]

---

49. *LW* 12:316; WA 40:334.31–335.24.
50. *LW* 12:320; WA 40:340.15–16.
51. *LW* 12:321; WA 40:341.35–342.19.
52. *LW* 12:325; WA 40:348.35–37.
53. Masaki, *He Alone Is Worthy!*
54. *LW* 12:312; WA 40:329.17–330.21.
55. *LW* 12:315; WA 40:333.32–34. Cf., *LW* 12:333; WA 40:360.13–15.
56. *LW* 12:315; WA 40:334.26–30.

Two Kinds of Sins in the Christian

Luther's distinction between two kinds of sinners is not about a distinction between a pagan and a Christian. Luther is speaking about the baptized in both. "No Christian has sin." Yet, "every Christian has sin." For Luther, both statements are true.[57] A Christian lives in the midst of this conflict. We know it by experience. Christ has forgiven all the sins of all sinners in the world. A Christian is a man fully forgiven as a baptized child of God.[58] Yet, because of our weakness of the flesh, the old fruits still sprout within our flesh to make us feel as secure, thankless, and ignorant of God as we used to be. It may not be an exaggeration to say that every sermon of Dr. Luther was an address to the Christians concerning this problem, and every lecture was his occasion to approach his students pastorally, in his effort to shape future pastors. To those who engage in a daily, bitter, and unceasing battle against their sinful flesh, the devil, and the world, Luther kept on proclaiming the unchanging Gospel to comfort them, using every occasion he had.

Theologically speaking, understanding and handling this Christian conflict was what separated Luther, once again, from the papacy and all the sects.[59] Just as he did it in his *Great Galatians Lectures* only a year before, and just as he would do it later in his *Antinomian Disputations*, Luther borrowed an Aristotelian distinction of "formal" and "relational" to explain the biblical doctrine of *simul iustus et peccator*.[60] In the *Lectures on Galatians*, Luther said that the Christian righteousness is not within the saint in a formal sense [*formaliter*] but outside of him in God's imputation.[61] In the fifth set of theses in the *Antinomian Disputations*, in thesis 48, Luther spoke against the antinomians: "For sin is eliminated, law abolished, and death destroyed *relatively* [*relative*], not *formally* [*non formaliter*] or substantially [*substantialiter*]."[62] In our *Lectures on Psalm 51*, Luther writes:

> Therefore the Christian is not formally righteous [*formaliter iustus*], he is not righteous according to substance or quality [*secundum substantiam aut qualitatem*]—I use these words for instructions' sake. He is righteous according to his relation to something [*secundum praedicamentum ad aliquid*]: namely, only in respect to divine grace and the free forgiveness of sins,

---

57. *LW* 12:328; WA 40:352.24–25.
58. *LW* 12:329; WA 40:354.33–355.21.
59. *LW* 12:329; WA 40:353.36–354.32.
60. *LW* 26:285; WA 40 1:445.16–18; *LW* 27:85; WA 40 2:106.34–107.21. See Masaki, "Luther on Law and Gospel," 135–67.
61. *LW* 26:234; WA 40 I:370.28–32.
62. WA 39 I:356.27–32.

which comes to those who acknowledge their sin and believe that God is gracious and forgiving for Christ's sake, who was delivered for our sin (Rom 4:25) and is believed in by us.[63]

As the choice of the word *praedicamentum* shows, Luther may have included in his mind *preaching*! David rejoices in God's mercy, but he still asks for what remains: "wash me," and "cleanse me from my sin." Luther's diagnosis was that the sects did not understand this relational point. The papacy did not either.[64] Such a situation still remains today in the theology of the western Christendom at large, both Rome and the Reformed.

This theological problem manifests concretely in the daily life of a Christian. Our problem is that it may be easy to say, "I believe in Jesus," but it is so hard to keep this faith fixed and sure and permanent in our heart.[65] The doctrine of justification is "the kind of thing that can never be learned completely," says Luther.[66] The Christian does not graduate from Christ at the point of baptism.[67] Rather, as he matures as a Christian, he will increasingly discover the fact that he is indeed more deeply sinful than he has ever realized before. The battle between flesh and spirit, between old and new Adams, between *iustus* and *peccator* continues. In the Lectures on Galatians Luther commented: "In fact, the godlier one is, the more he feels this battle."[68] In our *Psalm 51 Lectures*, he mentions: "A godly man feels sin more than grace, wrath more than favor, judgment more than redemption. An ungodly man feels almost no wrath, but is smug as though there were no wrath anywhere, as though there were no God anywhere who vindicates his righteousness."[69] The more a godly man feels his weakness, the more earnest he is in prayer. The godly man always talks as if he were a sinner, and indeed, he is. The feeling of grace is weaker because of the flesh. He has forgiveness. But he still prays and sighs for forgiveness. Luther speaks of two men who went to the temple to pray in Luke 18.[70] The *Lutheran Service Book* captures this point by putting the words of the sinner of Luke

---

63. *LW* 12:329; WA 40:353.36–354.19.

64. *LW* 12:376–77; WA 40:421.22–24. "It belongs to the category of relationship [*Pertinet autem ad praedicamentum relationis*], which the dialecticians say has a minimum of entity and a maximum of power. So you should not think it is a quality, as the scholastics dreamed [*Ne putetis esse qualitatem, sicut Sophistae somniarunt*]."

65. *LW* 12:330; WA 40:355.28–29.

66. *LW* 12:375; WA 40:419.25–31.

67. *LW* 12:331; WA 40:357.31–32; cf. SA III, III, 40.

68. *LW* 27:74; WA 40 2:94.14–15.

69. *LW* 12:358; WA 40:395.27–30.

70. *LW* 12:358–59; WA 40:395.35–396.25.

18:11 at the beginning of the Divine Service, Setting Four, in Confession and Absolution: "God, be merciful to me, a sinner."[71]

Hidden Sin Revealed

Part of the reason why a Christian faces a constant battle against the remnants of sin has to do with his pride. Like David, even when we acknowledge our sinfulness, we still do not want to be known as sinners. Luther's attention to a Pharisee in Luke 18 was an illustration of that point.

The problem is that our sin is hidden in our nature, so that it cannot be fully recognized unless and until it is revealed by the Word of God.[72] But what word of God? The word of the law is self-evident, as David came to know his sinfulness when he heard the words of Nathan. The law kills! Yet, Luther seems to include the Word of the gospel also in the work of revealing our hidden sin. Luther says: "The revelation of sin takes place through the law and through the gospel, or promise. Both teachings denounce sins." James Nestingen focuses on this point in one of his essays.[73] The Formula of Concord echoes in Solid Declaration Article V. After having articulated the distinction between law and gospel as the preaching of the law and the preaching of the gospel, that is, "everything that preaches something about our sin and God's wrath is the preaching of the law, however and whenever it may take place. On the other hand, the gospel is the kind of preaching that points to and gives nothing other than grace and forgiveness in Christ," a little later the confessors continued: "Indeed, what could be a more sobering and terrifying demonstration and proclamation of the wrath of God against sin than the suffering and death of Christ, his Son?"[74] In other words, the preaching of Good Friday is the sweetest gospel to be sure, but, at the same time, it can be heard as the proclamation of the law. Luther remarks: "If God promises life, it follows that we are under death. If he promises forgiveness of sins, it follows that sins dominate and possess us. . . . Both the threats and the promises all show the same thing."[75]

---

71. *LSB* 203.

72. Cf. *SA* III, I, 3.

73. Nestingen, "Luther on Psalm 51," 201–212. Dennis Ngien has recently published *Fruit for the Soul: Luther on the Lament Psalms*, in which he also includes a treatment of Luther's Psalm 51 (Ngien, *Fruit for the Soul*, 25–83).

74. SD 5.12.

75. *LW* 12:340; *WA* 40:370.28–31.

Grace and Gifts: Continuing Justification

Against all medieval scholastic theology before him, against all the prevailing sectarian theologies of the day, and in contradiction to the default position of the human heart, Luther proclaimed the freedom of the gospel. The law is not ultimate any longer. Christ is the end of the law (Rom 10:4). The accusing voice of the law in our conscience is no more for the baptized.[76] Christ is the *telos*: he is not only the fulfilment of the law, but also its end. Yet, how may a Christian be kept in Christ? As Luther continues this subject in his lectures, he was delighted to read a distinction between grace and gifts. Grace is about justification, and the gifts of the Holy Spirit are that which follow the forgiveness. Luther confesses that it is the gifts of the Holy Spirit that keep the Christian in his baptismal living. We are reminded of Luther's explanation of the Third Article in the Small Catechism.

> I believe that I cannot by my own reason [*Vernunft, rationis*] or strength believe in Jesus Christ, my Lord, or come to him; but *the Holy Spirit* has called me by the gospel, *enlightened me with his gifts* [*mit seinen Gaben erleuchtet*], sanctified and *kept me in the true faith* [*im rechten Glauben geheiliget und erhalten*]. In the same way he calls, gathers, *enlightens*, and sanctifies *the whole Christian Church* on earth, and *keeps it with Jesus Christ in the one true faith* [*und bei Jesu Christo erhält im rechten einigen Glauben*]. *In this Christian church he daily and richly forgives all my sins and the sins of all believers* [*in welcher Christenheit Er mir und allen Gläubigen täglich alle Sünde reichlich vergibt*]. On the Last Day he will raise me and all the dead, and give eternal life to me and all believers in Christ. This is most certainly true.[77]

It is the gifts of the Holy Spirit that keep the Christian in Christ and his forgiveness. It is the gifts of the Holy Spirit through which the doctrine of repentance is preserved in the church.[78] One of the most astonishing phrases in Luther's Small Catechism, "I believe that I cannot . . . believe," comes here with a direct rejection of his most learned opponent Erasmus, concerning free will, as Luther uses the term *ratio* that Erasmus called the *liberum arbitrium*.

When the Holy Spirit comes (John 14:23), he dwells in the baptized, and always does something.[79] Luther says: "He (the Holy Spirit) does not

---

76. *LW* 12:331; WA 40:357.35–358.19.
77. Emphasis added.
78. *LW* 12:365; WA 40:405.21–27.
79. *LW* 12:377–78; WA 40:422.18–20, 27–423.17.

give his gifts in such a way that he is somewhere else or asleep; but he is there with his gifts."[80] The gift that the Holy Spirit gives is not a quality hidden in man's heart, so that he may cooperate with grace in his free will, or so that he may declare, "once saved, always saved." Rather, Luther says that when David prayed, "create in me a clean heart, O God, and renew a right spirit within me" (Ps 51:10), he was not talking about some momentary operation of the Holy Spirit but the continuous and perpetual operation. Luther was free from synergism and mechanical monergism.

"Our Time Is Better!"

How does the Holy Spirit give his gifts to keep the baptized in the one true faith in Christ? Luther answers by expounding on "sprinkling with hyssop" in verse 7 and "joy and gladness in hearing" in verse 8. Just as he said frequently in his *Lectures on Genesis* later on, here Luther speaks that our time is better than the time of the Old Testament. "Many kings and prophets desired to see what you see" (Matt 13:17; Luke 10:24).[81]

What do we get to see which the Old Testament people did not? Luther speaks of preaching, baptism, holy absolution, and the Lord's Supper. They are more a splendid sprinkling than the blood sprinkled over priests and the tabernacle in Exodus 29 and the water in Numbers 19. The New Testament hyssop comes in more than one way.[82] The mouth of the preacher of the gospel is the hyssop and the sprinkler. He also says: "In baptism we are baptized into the death of Christ, and in the Lord's Supper the body and blood of Christ are distributed to the church."[83] While presenting all the means of grace as better gifts than the old, Luther never loses sight of the uniqueness of each gift. Baptism is not the same as the Lord's Supper. Neither baptism nor the Lord's Supper is merely another form of the Word.[84] Staying with the *proprium* of each gift is Luther's faithful confession, which we find also in the Smalcald Articles and everywhere.

"Troubled consciences are like geese," Luther comments. "When the hawks pursue them, they try to escape by flying, though they could do it better by running. On the other hand, when the wolves threaten them, they

---

80. *LW* 12:377; WA 40:421.37–38.
81. *LW* 12:365–66; WA 40:402; *LW* 3:165–66.
82. Cf. *SA* III, III, 8; III, IV–VIII.
83. *LW* 12:363; WA 40:402.33–35, 37–403.17.
84. *LW* 12:367; WA 40:407.22–29.

try to escape by running, though they could do it safely by flying."[85] With this illustration, Luther portrays both our stupidity and the importance of *externum verbum*. His emphasis is on our passivity,[86] because "only hearing brings joy." Luther knows that "everything else . . . leaves doubt in the mind."[87] Luther finds such hearing of the voice of Jesus (cf. *ipsa vox Dei*)[88] extended in all the means of grace. In baptism, we hear: "I baptize you in the name of the Father and of the Son and of the Holy Spirit" (Matt 28:20). In the Lord's Supper we hear: "This is my body, which is given for you" (Luke 22:19). In holy absolution we hear: "Have faith. Your sins are forgiven you through the death of Christ."[89]

The result of such hearing is our confidence. Luther speaks of our solid confession: "I am baptized." "I have received the body handed over for me on the cross," and "I have heard the voice of God from the minister."[90] Luther rejoices in the *externum verbum* and the office of the holy ministry that was also instituted by the Lord for serving each one of them.

Threefold Gift of the Holy Spirit

As Luther continues to discuss the gifts of the Holy Spirit for the life of the justified, he adds two more gifts to the one we already observed above, joy and sure confidence. The second gift of the Holy Spirit is the daily growth of the hearers in new obedience.[91] And the third gift that Luther enumerates is the confession of the Justifier before the world.[92]

Luther's words on the third gift are to our comfort and encouragement. Luther knows by experience that to confess Jesus before the world [*coram mundo*] requires "a courageous and strong mind" which will not let itself be driven away by any dangers."[93] As the one who confessed Christ against the will of the emperor, pope, princes, kings, and almost the whole world, Luther exhorts his pastoral students that "the office of teaching in the

---

85. *LW* 12:368; WA 40:409.31–35.
86. *LW* 12:368; WA 40.410.14. "Tota enim ratio iustificandi quoad nos passiva est."
87. *LW* 12:368; WA 40:409.25–26.
88. *LW* 12:370; WA 40:411.33–34.
89. *LW* 12:369; WA 40:411.23–32.
90. *LW* 12:371; WA 40:413.32–34.
91. *LW* 12:381; WA 40:427.30–471.15; *LW* 12:384; WA 40:432.30–35.
92. *LW* 12:382; WA 40:429.22–28.
93. *LW* 12:382; WA 40:429.26–30.

church requires such a mind that despises all dangers."[94] To all the baptized also he says: "In general, all the devout should prepare themselves so that they are not afraid of becoming martyrs, that is, confessors or witnesses of God. Christ does not want to hide in the world, but he wants to be preached, 'not between four walls but from the roof' (Matt 10:27), so that the Gospel shines in the world like a torch on a high mountain or on a watchtower."[95] Doesn't Luther speak to us in our time? However, Luther did not forget to add the comforting words when he said: "the outcome of the ministry is not with the will of men, but with the will of God."[96]

"Our Theology"

As Luther comes to the end of his lecture series, he once again exhibits his tender heart to his students whom he calls "future doctors of the church" [*future Doctores Ecclesiae*]. Just as in his *Lectures on Galatians*, he repeats the phrase, "our theology" [*Theologia nostra*] to say that "our theology" is not for the stubborn and the secure; "our theology" is only for the consolation of the afflicted, miserable, and despairing.[97]

> Thus we see that our theology is a word of life and righteousness [*verbum vitae et iusticiae*], because it battles and strengthens against sin and death, and cannot be exercised except in sin and weakness. It is also a word of joy [*verbum laeticiae*], whose power cannot be seen except in sadness and afflictions. But this is the way we are. We want to have the word of life and joy, [*verbum vitae et laeticiae*] but we want the temptations of death and sadness to go away. Fine and pleasing theologians! We have to learn that a Christian should walk in the midst of death, in the remorse and trembling of his conscience, in the midst of the devil's teeth and of hell, and yet should keep the word of grace, so that in such trembling we say, "Thou, O Lord, dost look on me with favor."[98]

"Our theology" is only for the afflicted and miserable. Luther articulates that the contrite and humble heart which *knows* sin and which confesses Christ the Savior is the primary sacrifice to the Lord. Such

---

94. *LW* 12:383; WA 40:431.17–18.
95. *LW* 12:383–84; WA 40:431.18–22.
96. *LW* 12:388; WA 40:438.22–23.
97. *LW* 12:405; WA 40:460.33–461.4.
98. *LW* 12:405; WA 40:461.33–462.17.

passiveness or empty-handedness of living in the Lord's mercy, Luther says, produces another sacrifice from the heart: "a sacrifice of thanksgiving for the gift you have received."[99]

Toward the end of his *Lectures on Psalm 51*, Luther confesses the church, just as he placed an article on the church toward the end of his Smalcald Articles.[100] Luther confesses an article on good works of the justified immediately following the article on the church in the Smalcald Articles.[101] This resembles the way *Lectures on Psalm 51* ends, as Luther prays that "the Lord might build his church," because then the sacrifices that are pleasing and acceptable to God follow.[102]

Conclusion

Luther does not let us treat theology as a mere science in which researchers may stay in a safe place where no dangers are experienced. Rather than being a spectator and commentator of a game, he guides us to acknowledge that we are all players on the field. God and we are in relationship with each other whether we know it or not, and whether we like it or not. Theology belongs to the church. Theology belongs to the liturgy. Our Lord is delighted in our *knowing* our sin and our *hearing* of the voice of the gospel.

The proper response to the voice of the gospel is our acclamation of such a Lord! Affected by the liturgical thinking of Theodor Kliefoth, an acclamation of "*Alena han är värdig tack och lof!*" that is, "He Alone Is Worthy of Thanks and Praise!" emerged in the Preface of the liturgy of the Lord's Supper of the Church of Sweden in the nineteenth century. This acclamation restores the original sense of ἄξιον καὶ δίκαιον. He alone, the Lord alone! It is the office of Jesus alone to justify and to keep justifying the sinner. "He alone is worthy!" is a faith speaking to the Savior as "everything is from the Lord." The gifts that come only from the Lord prompt to create and enliven faith into the living of all our life toward him in the life of the service to our neighbor.

Indeed, we can never graduate from Psalm 51 and from Jesus. Precisely because of our sinfulness, Jesus wills to care for us with the sweet gospel. The tense of the verbs of the gospel ever remain *present* in preaching, baptism, holy absolution, and the Lord's Supper. He wants to dwell among

---

99. *LW* 12:409; WA 40:469.16–27.
100. *SA* III, III, XII.
101. *SA* III, III, XIII.
102. WA 12:410; WA 40:470.34–35.

us in his church, to work among us, and to continue to give his gifts to us and for us.[103] Luther's *Lectures on Psalm 51* is an invitation to such ongoing pastoral care of Jesus in his church.

Bibliography

Bayer, Oswald. *Martin Luther's Theology: A Contemporary Interpretation*. Translated by Thomas H. Trapp. Grand Rapids: Eerdmans, 2008.

———. *Theology the Lutheran Way*. Translated by Jeffrey G. Silcock and Mark C. Mattes. Grand Rapids: Eerdmans, 2007.

Collver, Albert B., III, et al., eds. *The Necessary Distinction: A Continuing Conversation on Law & Gospel*. St. Louis: Concordia, 2017.

Masaki, Naomichi. *He Alone Is Worthy!: The Vitality of the Lord's Supper in Theodor Kliefoth and in the Swedish Liturgy of the Nineteenth Century*. Gothenburg: Församlingsförlaget, 2013.

———."Luther on Law and Gospel in His *Lectures on Galatians 1531/1535*." In *The Necessary Distinction: A Continuing Conversation on Law & Gospel*, edited by Albert B. Collver III, et al., 135–67. St. Louis: Concordia, 2017.

Nestingen, James Arne. "Luther on Psalm 51." *Lutheran Theological Journal* 50 (2016).

Ngien, Dennis. *Fruit for the Soul: Luther on the Lament Psalms*. Minneapolis: Fortress, 2015.

---

103. *FC SD* 8.79.

7

The Holy Spirit in Luther's Catechisms

Mark C. Mattes

IN PRINCIPLE, A DISTINCTION between the person and the work of the Holy Spirit can be made. It is akin to the distinction made between the person and work of Christ or between the inner-trinitarian relations within the Godhead and the missions of each triune person in the world. This distinction, however, is to be found neither in the Scriptures nor in either of Luther's Catechisms. In each Catechism, the person and the work of the Holy Spirit are intertwined as a figure eight, seamlessly flowing from person to work and vice versa. As is evident in both Catechisms, the Reformer maintained that while God's actions in the world are indivisible, in that all three persons of the Trinity are involved with the other persons in creation, redemption, and sanctification; nevertheless, creation is appropriated to the Father, redemption to the Son, and sanctification to the Spirit.

We cannot then abstractly consider the person of the Holy Spirit apart from his sanctifying work by means of the daily forgiveness of sins through the ministry of the church. In the Catechisms, the Spirit is the agent who makes sinners holy precisely by bringing them to Christ and forgiving their sins. God's mercy is a gift, and the Holy Spirit is himself a gift empowering believers to serve as Christs in the world. In addition to exploring the relationship between Christ's redemptive work and sanctification, we must also attend to current theological interest in gift exchange, as opposed to economic exchanges, for an adequate portrayal of the Spirit.

A Western Pneumatology with a Twist

With respect to the ancient church's teachings about the person of the Spirit, Luther made no innovations.[1] He affirmed with the Council of Constantinople (381) that the Spirit, like the Son, was of one substance with the Father. Hence, along with the Father and the Son, the Holy Spirit is truly divine. Following Augustine, he taught the *filioque*, that the Spirit proceeds both from the Father and the Son. He also acknowledged the distinction between the Spirit as person (*persona*) and gift (*donum*).[2] As we will see, it is pivotal for Luther to understand the triune God through the category of gift. In his core, God is ever-generous self-giving love. The Father gives himself in the blessings of creation, the Son in the gift of redemption, and the Spirit by applying Christ's redemption to us, to create and sustain faith, thus helping us to "use"[3] it for our welfare and to share it with others. Apart from the Spirit's giving Christ's merciful goodness of forgiveness and new life, Christ's salvation would not be made available to humans. This is because the Spirit's giving comes through the means of word and sacrament, the office of preaching, and thereby creates saving faith.

Where Luther became innovative in his teachings about the Spirit is when he challenged his opponents, both Roman Catholic and other Protestants, especially the "Enthusiasts" (*Schwärmer*). Luther called those theologians "Enthusiasts" who seek the counsel of the Spirit directly or immediately apart from God's Word, whether in intuition or experience or some inner voice not demarcated and narrated by the Word. Luther revised the medieval tradition's beliefs about words which regarded words as descriptive of realities or directives for ethical behavior. While Luther did not deny this, he understood that words can also be performative, that is, they can transform reality by giving what they declare.[4] The Spirit is active precisely through the gospel, that is, in word and sacrament, a promise which not only describes the forgiveness that Christ brings but actually brings this forgiveness home to believers. Likewise, he objected to the Enthusiasts

---

1. See Nelson and Hinlicky, *Oxford Encyclopedia of Martin Luther*, 618–36; Wengert et al., *Dictionary of Luther*, 338–40; Lamport, *Encyclopedia of Martin Luther*, 342–45.

2. "When the Holy Spirit writes the law with his finger on Moses's stone tablets, then he is in his majesty and assuredly accuses sins and terrifies the hearts. But when he is 'swaddled' in tongues and spiritual gifts, then he is called 'gift,' then he sanctifies and makes alive. Without this Holy Spirit who is 'gift,' the law points to sin, because the law is not a 'gift,' but the word of the eternal and almighty God, to consciences a consuming fire." See *Disputatio gegen die Antinomer* (WA 39 1, 370, 18–371, 1). Translation from Lohse, *Martin Luther's Theology*, 217.

3. For a discussion of "use" in Luther, see Zahl, "Tradition and its 'Use.'"

4. See Bayer, *Theology the Lutheran Way*, 128–34.

because they failed to see that God only works through tangible, material means, such as the sacraments of baptism (with the material sign of water) and the Lord's Supper (with the material signs of bread and wine), and the oral, preached word, since sinners need a way to grasp or apprehend God's promise in a specific way.[5]

The Holy Spirit as Sanctifying Agent

Given the importance that Luther accorded the article of justification by grace alone through faith alone ("without this article the world is nothing but death and darkness,"[6] and even that this article defines what it means to be human),[7] it is striking that neither Catechism explicitly refers to or spells out justification. After all, the word "catechism" is a description of appropriate instruction in the Christian faith.[8] One would think that the word "justification" would then appear in each. The roots of the Large Catechism lie in an earlier series of didactic sermons, indicating that Luther's homiletical commitment was not solely to the gospel as proclamation, but also as instruction in wholesome behavior and true doctrine. Luther was concerned that a regular rhythm of spiritual practices, the threefold *oratio, meditatio, tentatio,* as well as sound teaching in the faith should be honored within evangelical communities. Luther insisted that believers read a page or two from the catechism each day, as well as from his Personal Prayer Book (1522), and the Bible.[9] Luther was committed to what we today call discipleship.[10] He insisted that we need to put the Catechism into "practice,"[11] and this could not be done apart from regular familiarity with it as well as the Scriptures and prayer.

Although not specified, justification is, of course, implicit in both Catechisms. Strikingly, Luther developed the doctrine of creation in the First Article of the Creed in the Small Catechism through the lens of justification by faith alone: "all this is done out of pure, fatherly, and divine goodness and

---

5. Paulson, "Graspable God," 51–62.
6. WA 39/1, 205, 5. See Bayer, *Martin Luther's Theology,* 98.
7. *LW* 34:139 (WA 39/1, 176, 33–35): "Paul in Romans 3[:28], 'We hold that a man is justified by faith apart from works,' briefly sums up the definition of man, saying, 'man is justified by faith.'"
8. See the editor's introduction to the Large Catechism (*BoC* 377–79).
9. *BoC* 380:3.
10. Mattes, "Discipleship in Lutheran Perspective," 142–63.
11. *BoC* 383:19.

mercy, without any merit or worthiness of mine at all!"[12] As Oswald Bayer has indicated, the reference to "merit" here targets the works righteousness of late medieval piety while "worthiness" implies the acceptable admittance to the sacrament.[13] In a word, Luther's doctrine of creation as *creatio ex nihilo* is crafted with reference to the article of justification in which God re-creates humanity anew out of the nothingness of sin and death. While justification is not directly spelled out per se, clearly the Second Article, "On Redemption," in the Small Catechism, as well as the Second Article in the Large Catechism, highlight the work of Jesus Christ to bring sinners to God. In the well-known words of the Small Catechism:

> He has purchased and freed me from all sins, from death, and from the power of the devil, not with gold or silver but with his holy, precious blood and with his innocent suffering and death. He has done all this in order that I may belong to him, live under him in his kingdom, and serve him in eternal righteousness, innocence, and blessedness, just as he is risen from the dead and lives and rules eternally.[14]

It is the Spirit's work to install this language on one's tongue. Luther's inclusion of this truth in the Catechism *is* the Spirit's doing what the Spirit does: calling, gathering, enlightening, and sanctifying.

The link between redemption and justification is specified later in the Smalcald Articles (1537): Jesus Christ "was handed over to death for our trespasses and was raised for our justification (Rom 4[:25])."[15] For Luther, it is clear that the article of justification by grace alone through faith alone gets at the core of what the gospel is all about in spite of the fact that it is accorded no headline or section in either Catechism. He assumes this throughout as the way to articulate God's generosity in giving temporal life as well as new birth. But it is remarkable that "sanctification" is highlighted in the Third Article. That should clue us in right away that Luther does not separate justification and sanctification as later Lutheran orthodoxy would do in the *ordo salutis*. As Steve Paulson and Paul Koch note,

> Justification and sanctification are of the same cloth, and a person must be careful not to make too great a distinction between the two. The notion of a momentary justification followed by a progress in sanctification is foreign to Scripture. Acts 26:18

---

12. *BoC* 354:2.
13. Bayer, *Martin Luther's Theology*, 96.
14. *BoC* 355:4.
15. *BoC* 301:1.

speaks of being sanctified by faith. Paul speaks of sanctification as a completed event alongside justification (1 Cor 6:11), and Hebrews 10:14 speaks of the sanctified as already perfected. Gerhard Forde . . . described sanctification as getting used to one's justification. One must never treat progress in sanctification as though one gradually needed less and less of Christ's forgiveness.[16]

Surprisingly, Risto Saarinen, working out of the Mannermaa school, an approach quite different from that of Forde, speaks of sanctification markedly similar to Forde as a "prolongation of justification," albeit one that evokes "secondary cooperation between God's agency and that of the believer's."[17] Surely Forde would have had no qualms with that latter assertion since it is found in Luther's *De Servo Arbitrio*.[18]

For Luther, the agent in sanctifying humans is the Holy Spirit. While creation, redemption, and sanctification can be logically distinguished, they come as a three-some. Sanctifying work is an expression of the Spirit's creative *dynamis*. This creative agency has been acknowledged in the church throughout the ages in the hymn *Veni Creator Spiritus*. As Scripture attests throughout, the Holy Spirit creates all things, sustains all things out of nothing, and renews creation by providing humans new birth through the word and sacraments administered in the church. The Spirit is the agent of this new life, since we are unable to cooperate in either our creation or re-creation. So, we read in the Small Catechism: "I believe that by my own understanding or strength I cannot," that is through various metaphysical or moral exercises, "believe in Jesus Christ my LORD or come to him, but instead the Holy Spirit has called me through the gospel, enlightened me with his gifts, made me holy and kept me in the true faith."[19] In other words, if I have come to Christ, it is not something for which I can take credit. Indebted to Paul, Augustine, and Tauler, Luther rules out all versions

---

16. Wengert et al., *Dictionary of Luther*, 659–60.

17. Saarinen, *Luther and the Gift*, 270.

18. "What I assert and maintain is this: that where God works apart from the grace of his Spirit, he works all things in all men, even in the ungodly; for he alone moves, makes to act, and impels by the motion of his omnipotence, all those things which he alone created; they can neither avoid nor alter this movement, but necessarily follow and obey it, each thing according to the measure of its God-given power. Thus all things, even the ungodly, co-operate with God. And when God acts by the Spirit of his grace in those whom he has justified, that is, in his own kingdom, he moves and carries them along in like manner; and they, being a new creation, follow and *co-operate* with him, or rather, as Paul says, are made to act by him (Rom 8:14)" (Luther, *Bondage of the Will*, 267–68 [emphasis added]).

19. *BoC* 355:6.

of Pelagianism in which one seeks to take some credit for one's salvation. For Luther, such self-acknowledgement is incompatible with the receptive humility in which God fashions us.

The Corporate Dimension of the Spirit's Agency

Significantly, the work of the Holy Spirit in bringing Christ to us and us to Christ is thoroughly social, not individual, in that the Holy Spirit "calls, gathers, enlightens, and makes holy the whole Christian church on earth and keeps it with Jesus Christ in the one common, true faith."[20] Acknowledging the inherently corporal dimension of redemption through the church, the Third Article of the Creed parallels the social dimension to the creation of temporal reality specified in the first article: we are created "together with all creatures."[21] The creatures which God creates or re-creates are bound together in a network of fellow creatures and fellow believers.

For Luther the social dimension of human experience is not a construct or add-on but foundational. While Luther sees government as a third "estate" added to the church and the family in order to maintain order and security as a response to the fall, he could never agree to the individualism of Thomas Hobbes or other modern political theorists.[22] For Hobbes, humans are primordially individuals who artificially covenant to organize a government. In a state of nature, with no government, individuals are completely free, but ever insecure, vulnerable to abuse and violence by others, and so let go of their total freedom by covenanting with one another to establish a government. Here the social dimension is a human creation generated by individuals' rational self-interest. For Luther, the individual is an abstraction of the family, even the tribe, and not a pre-existing building block of society. Nor, for Luther, does the world begin in a primordial chaos, the threat of war of all against all, as Hobbes maintained, but instead original righteousness and social peace and harmony in Eden.

20. *BoC* 355:6.
21. *BoC* 354:2. Translation altered.
22. For further discussion of the three estates, see Bayer, "Nature and Institution," 90–118.

A Non-Legalistic Approach to Sanctification

If by sanctification one intends a program of moral or religious self-improvement, a measurable progress in personal or social holiness that can be judged to be either successful or unsuccessful through some common rubric or metric, equipping one to judge others as well, then we can indeed affirm that Lutherans are "weak on sanctification." In fact, to be more precise, if this definition of sanctification holds, we can say that Lutherans do not believe in sanctification at all. Luther's vision of reform challenged the ancient affirmation of the "evangelical counsels," that is, poverty, chastity, and obedience as leading to a "perfect" life. In this earlier way of thinking, the Christian faith is construed as two-tiered: (1) those following a "secular" life of service in the world and (2) those following a "religious" life above the hubbub of temporal, earthly affairs and seeking as much as possible to accord with eternal, heavenly matters. Not only have many medieval and contemporary Catholics followed this path, but various strands of Protestantism, to one degree or another, have improvised on it. In contrast, for Luther, even as Christ came down to earth in order to serve the neighbor, so we too ought to live lives of service. Thus, we do not live in seclusion from this rough and ready world, but instead within the cacophony and hurly-burly of life, a world marked by a crack in it, as the late Kierkegaard translator Edna Hong reminded us.[23] Due to this "crack" of sin, God re-creates the world, to be consummated in a new heavens and earth.

In Luther's view, sanctification is not a program leading to empirically quantifiable growth in godliness but instead is an abundant life arising from God's disempowering the old being and re-creating new people of faith. Undoubtedly, human behavior grows out of or manifests one's character. But, for Luther, one's character is established in the identity one receives from Christ. In this light, it makes no sense to separate or even distinguish forensic justification from effective justification.[24] God's imputative word which claims sinners for Jesus's sake makes them to be people of faith. That justification, understood as participating in Christ's death and resurrection, is one with sanctification as illustrated thoroughly in Luther's doctrine of the sacrament of baptism outlined in the Large Catechism:

> Thus a Christian life is nothing else than a daily baptism, begun once and continuing ever after. For we must keep at it without ceasing, always purging whatever pertains to the old Adam,

---

23. Hong, *Bright Valley of Love*, 60–61.

24. Forde, *Justification by Faith*, 21–38; Kolb, "God Kills to Make Alive," 33–56; Wengert et al., *Dictionary of Luther*, 385–89.

so that whatever belongs to the new creature may come forth. What is the old creature? It is what is born in us from Adam, irascible, spiteful, envious, unchaste, greedy, lazy, proud—yes—and unbelieving; it is beset with all vice and by nature has nothing good in it. Now, when we enter Christ's kingdom, this corruption must daily decrease so that the longer we live the more gentle, patient, and meet we become, and the more we break away from greed, hatred, envy, and pride.[25]

Hence, we should not agree with Karl Holl (1866–1926) who saw imputed righteousness as an analytic judgment. In that view, righteousness is a temporary loan given to cover the lack of our own personal capital until we have earned enough goodness to offer God. So, the more capital we accrue, God's imputation of righteousness is less significant. Sinners are declared righteous because God knows that eventually they will become so. Instead, for Luther, imputed righteousness is a synthetic judgment. It is a judgment which "synthesizes" what it declares.[26] Not only is the old being daily condemned to death, but the new being called forth by the gospel is given a new, clean heart, a new identity which opens one up to live freely by trusting God's promises, and so assist the neighbor and tend to the earth (Eph 2:8–9). In the absolution, God forgives sins and thereby makes believers holy. This allows the church to serve as a communal leaven in the world, empowering mission so that, as Wilhelm Loehe (1808–1872) put it, the one church of God is in motion in the world.[27]

Out of this faith good works come, just as good fruit comes from good trees. As Paulson and Koch note, "Where Luther does speak about the good works associated with sanctification, he insists that they are the fruit of holiness, not the building blocks."[28] It is simply not the case that Lutherans "shout justification but whisper sanctification." Those who make such a charge buy into a spirituality which sees Christian progress as greater degrees of spiritual perfection on a ladder moving sinners upward to the eternal. But, such a view distorts the nature of goodness itself since it fails to love God for his own sake or neighbors for their own sakes. It simply uses both God and neighbor for one's own spiritual advancement, not for the spread of charity.

---

25. *BoC* 465:65–67.
26. Lindberg, "Do Lutherans Shout Justification?," 11.
27. Loehe, *Three Books about the Church*, 152.
28. Wengert et al., *Dictionary of Luther*, 660.

The Spirit's Sanctification as a Gift

The Holy Spirit seeks to alter human existence completely. In the Large Catechism, Luther uses the word "heart" to get to the core of human spirituality: "Therefore, to have a god is nothing else than to trust and believe in that one with your whole heart. As I have often said, it is the trust and faith of the heart alone that make both God and an idol."[29] "Heart" describes the center of human existence but is also a clue to who God is. Luther defines deity as "something in which the heart trusts completely."[30] In order to get at the core of what anyone's deity is, as Gerhard Forde explained, the question, "what captivates you?" must be asked. In a way, to be human is to be enchanted, captivated, and held by something. Idols fashioned by humans as ways to symbolize their greed or lust to dominate are not benign, but instead abusive to devotees and their recipients. To highlight the heart as the core of the human is to acknowledge that we fundamentally live outside ourselves and want to give ourselves to something far greater than ourselves. We seek a "joyful surrender into the keeping of another."[31] As Luther puts it, "to cling to him [God] with your heart is nothing else than to entrust yourself to him completely."[32] In this light, "the critical questions of human life become clear: Who is trustworthy? What is our good and what is our evil?"[33] The old being insists on the impossibility of a free lunch and insists on taking credit for the life which God wishes to give, and so is, thereby, out of touch with the reality of both God and the core of its own being.

Luther's vision of God draws on a tradition which highlights divine goodness over being.[34] Undoubtedly, his attraction to German mysticism brings the transcendental of goodness to the fore over that of being.[35] The image of God which Luther portrays in the Large Catechism is that God is generous. God is the "One, eternal good" who wants to "lavish all good things upon you richly."[36] God is an "eternal fountain" overflowing.[37] God sustains all creatures in their being out of nothingness, provides for their

---

29. *BoC* 386:2 (*BSLK* 930:13).
30. *BoC* 387:10 (*BSLK* 932:23—934:2).
31. Wengert et al., *Dictionary of Luther*, 24.
32. *BoC* 388:15 (*BSLK* 934:19).
33. Hinlicky, "Anthropology," 24.
34. See Mattes, *Luther's Theology of Beauty*, 43–67.
35. With respect to Luther's grounding in mysticism, see Leppin, *Die fremde Reformation*.
36. *BoC* 388:15 (*BSLK* 934:15)
37. *BoC* 389:25 (*BSLK* 938:15).

needs, and protects them in danger. In familiar words, Luther itemizes all these gifts, heaps them upon each other:

> God has given me and still preserves my body and soul: eyes, ears, and all limbs and senses; reason and all mental faculties. In addition, God daily and abundantly provides shoes and clothing, food and drink, house and farm, spouse and children, fields, livestock, and all property—along with all the necessities and nourishment for this body and life. God protects me against all danger and shields and preserves me from all evil. And all this is done out of pure, fatherly, and divine goodness and mercy, without any merit or worthiness of mine at all![38]

Luther echoes Paul in 1 Corinthians 4:7: "What do you have that you did not receive?" Here we have a critique of legalistic approaches not only to sanctification but also to secular notions of self-creation. Nothing in Luther could ever support contemporary notions of *autopoiesis*. Our experiences and the sense of self with which we experiment all presuppose the creative power of God to sustain us. Not only is human agency upheld and sustained out of nothingness by God, but God is our true good from which everything in our lives should be ordered. This is not primarily to express our entelechy, as Aristotelian approaches to theology would have it, but because we are creatures who have our good only by receiving it from God in faith.

That said, we do Luther's anti-Pelagianism no favors by employing a logic of disjunction in which the value of human agency is downplayed or even degraded for the sake of acknowledging God's unsurpassable mercy. The fact that the quest for merit before God (*coram deo*) is ruled out is not done to squelch human agency but instead to establish its goodness by liberating it from the quest for merit. Human agency in relation to others, ourselves, other creatures, and the earth is established in God's grace. We are, after all, called to cooperate with God in the ongoing work of creation.[39]

This all ties into the Holy Spirit's work to sanctify us. As I mentioned earlier, the dominant medieval theory endorsed the "evangelical counsels" of poverty, chastity, and obedience as works of supererogation. Luther sees this as an insult to God's generosity. To maintain the evangelical counsels is to desire to earn merit instead of receiving and enjoying God's gifts. For Luther, the evangelical counsels contribute to a self-righteousness in those who observe them. Likewise, they let "secular" Christians not following the "religious" life off the hook, as if they need not be Christs in the world.

---

38. *BoC* 354:2.
39. Luther, *Bondage of the Will*, 267–68 (WA 18, 753, 21).

Tying the matter of human righteousness before God back into the question of desire or captivation which is at the core of the human heart, Luther asks this crucial question: "what more could you want or desire than God's gracious promise that he wants to be yours with every blessing, to protect you, and to help you in every need?"[40] The Holy Spirit sanctifies us over and over by forgiving us for Jesus's sake, bringing Christ as a treasure to our conscience. The fact that we insist on earning instead of receiving bears upon Luther's understanding of the heart as corrupt. Of such corruption, Luther notes that the human is a "rational being with a fabricating heart."[41] And Bayer remarks:

> As such it is continually producing images in the mind, in other words, idols. Concepts of metaphysics in particular can become idols. Even a theological doctrine of the divine attributes produces idols if in speaking of God's attributes—his power, wisdom, goodness, and righteousness—it bypasses the cross of Jesus Christ.[42]

It is the refashioning, indeed re-creating, of the human heart which characterizes the sanctifying work of the Holy Spirit. The Spirit does this by preaching to us, bringing us to Christ. In his redeeming work which liberates us from sin and death, Christ has won a treasure for us: the forgiveness of sins. This treasure should not be "buried," but instead appropriated or used and enjoyed.[43] Likewise, this treasure of forgiveness—which makes us to be holy—is offered without our merits. After all, if it were something that we could earn, then it would be invalidated as a gift.

Triune Life as Gift

Behind all this language of salvation as a gift is the fact that God is himself a continuous and eternal event of triune self-giving. In the words of the Large Catechism, the Father "has given himself completely to us," while the Son offers "gifts beyond temporal goods" having restored us to the Father's favor and grace.[44] By doing this, the Son, as our Lord, possesses us and protects

---

40. *BoC* 391:41.
41. *LW* 2:123 (WA 42, 348, 37–40).
42. Bayer, *Theology the Lutheran Way*, 26.
43. *BoC* 436:38.
44. *BoC* 434:26 (*BSLK* 1054:25).

us. The Holy Spirit effectuates the treasure of the Son through the Christian church and its ministry.

In *Concerning Christ's Supper*, written in 1528, the same year the Catechisms were written, Luther outlines how gift is at the core of the triune life:

> These are the three persons and one God, who has given himself to us wholly and completely, with all that he is and has. The Father gives himself to us, with heaven and earth and all the creatures, in order that they can serve us and benefit us. But this gift has become obscured and useless through Adam's fall. Therefore the Son himself subsequently gave himself and bestowed all his works, sufferings, wisdom and righteousness, and reconciled us with the Father, in order that restored to life and righteousness, we might know and have the Father with his gifts.[45]

In the next paragraph, Luther specifies the Holy Spirit as a divine gift present in individual believers:

> But because this grace would benefit no one if it remained so profoundly hidden and could not come to us, the Holy Spirit comes and gives himself to us also, wholly and completely. He teaches us to understand this deed of Christ which has been manifested to us, helps us receive and preserve it, use it to our advantage and impart it to others, increase and extend it. He does this for us both inwardly and outwardly—inwardly by means of faith and other spiritual gifts, outwardly through the gospel, baptism, and the sacrament of the altar, through which as through three means or methods he comes to us and inculcates the sufferings of Christ for the benefit of our salvation.[46]

In this light, Luther even said that there were two parts to justification, grace as God's favor given to sinners but also the conferring of the Holy Spirit as a resident in the heart.[47]

It would seem that for Luther the chief way in which God captivates us is through the gospel, which not only outlines all the ways in which God gives to us, but also by actually delivering these goods, giving them with a tangible sacramental element, precisely to capture our hearts. The new being is captivated by and bound to Jesus Christ who is a generous, even faithful, and forgiving Lord. We have not only a clean heart but are empowered by the Holy Spirit so that Christ-like behaviors, giving to others

---

45. *LW* 37:366 (WA 26, 505, 38–506, 3).
46. *LW* 37:366 (WA 26, 506, 3–12).
47. *LW* 12:331 (WA 40/2, 357, 35ff).

in their needs, are evoked. "Outside this Christian community, however, where there is no gospel, there is also no forgiveness, and hence there also can be no holiness. Therefore, all who would seek to merit holiness through their works rather than through the gospel and the forgiveness of sin have expelled and separated themselves from this community."[48]

Duplex Gratia?

Properly speaking, holiness does not reside in works whatsoever but instead in God's word that forgives. No doubt, this is the basis for the discomfort Lutherans feel when evaluating John Calvin's contention of a two-fold grace or *duplex gratia*.[49] In Calvin's view this double grace means that the Father is not a judge and that we are to cultivate a pure life. It issues in a rule of faith and a rule of love. For Lutherans to have misgivings with this formulation raises the charge that Lutherans are quietists. But that is hardly the case—in spite of Max Weber's (1864–1920) reduction of Protestant ethics to the Reformed perspective. For Lutherans, holiness resides in divine forgiveness. Such forgiveness breaks human incurvation—allows the human a genuine alternative not focused solely on self-serving behaviors. The metaphor which describes the energizing power of the *Creator Spiritus* is "flow":

> The good that flowed from Christ flows into us. Christ has "put on" us and acted for us as if he had been what we are. The good we receive from Christ flows from us toward those who have need of it. As a result, I should lay before God my faith and righteousness so that they may cover and intercede for the sins of my neighbor. I take these sins upon myself, and labor and serve in them, as if they were my very own. This is exactly what Christ did for us. This is true and sincere love and the rule of a Christian life.[50]

Luther is concerned that we trust that, in the ups and downs of life, God purifies our motives, and our behavior spontaneously flows out of that. The reduction to nothingness experienced through encountering the accusations of the law, the "mystical smelting furnace," as Luther once put it,[51]

---

48. *BoC* 438:56.
49. Calvin, *Institutes*, 37.
50. Luther, *Freedom of a Christian*, 88 (WA 7, 69, 4–10).
51. "The kingdom of Christ is a mystical smelting furnace [*mysticus caminus*] that purges out the impurity of the old Adam" (*LW* 18:410 [WA 13, 694, 23–24]).

serves to create a receptive heart that is willing to cling to God's promise. It can trust no other alternative since all of its own potentialities are exposed as cul-de-sacs. As Wade Johnston puts it:

> The Spirit is not in this for a quick buck. He does not come in and flip a house. No, he renews it and makes it his own temple, his own eternal dwelling place. This is not a matter of some paint and new floors. The Holy Spirit kills and makes alive, drowns and raises. Transformation, as we understand it, is often measured in law. Baptism is measured in crosses, Christ's cross traced upon our head and our heart and the crosses we bear from Him.[52]

For Luther, when good works are done simply to achieve a higher status with God and not for the actual well-being of others, goodness is undermined. It is not good to leap frog over others in their need simply to achieve a higher status with God. Instead, Luther is interested that genuine love be evoked in the heart. He thinks that such love is evoked when we understand just how privileged we are in the excess of constant mercy and love heaped upon us, not only in our preservation out of nothingness but especially in the daily forgiveness of our sins declared in the church. In that way, "our trust in him [Christ] means that we are Christs to one another and act toward our neighbors as Christ has acted toward us." This is said in opposition to "a very human way of teaching" which claims that "the life of faith involves the seeking of merits and rewards. The result is that Christ is seen simply as a task master who is far harsher than Moses."[53]

Again, Lutherans are far more apt to see the Christian life as hidden, not open to measurement. It is not that faith does not bear on public life or that one concedes to the regnant secularistic worldview. Lutherans seek neither "exile" from public life (like Mennonites) nor "conquest" of public life (like the Reformed). Instead, as Charles Arand and Joel Biermann indicate, "The Lutheran stress on active righteousness widens our vision regarding the left-hand realm and seeks to identify the common ground for moral reflection between Christians and non-Christians"[54] insofar as such common ground can be established. Lutherans are apt to be whistleblowers but never utopians.[55] The gospel restores us to creation, not social engineering of the politics of either the right or left. Lutherans advocating traditional stances on abortion

---

52. Johnston, *Uncompromising Gospel*, 83.

53. Luther, *Freedom of a Christian*, 84.

54. Arand and Biermann, "Two Kinds of Righteousness?," 131.

55. See, for example, the case of resistance with the Magdeburg Confession of 1550 in Whitford, *Tyranny and Resistance*.

and marriage in the public realm do so because these stances accord with natural law, not the quest for an America as a "city shining on a hill." In a sense, if we use Charles Taylor's criteria of reform, Lutheranism fails as a reform movement—and confessional Lutherans are good with that.

No Free Gift?

Interestingly enough, the category of gift, so central for Luther in his opposition to a theology of merit, has received much attention of late.[56] Oswald Bayer speaks of it as "categorical gift" in opposition to Kant's Categorical Imperative.[57] Years ago, sociologist Marcel Mauss (1872–1950) noticed that all gifts are reciprocal and assume activity and self-interest from all parties. In ancient times, as well as in most cultures, the giving of gifts is not free of expectations on the part of the recipient. British New Testament scholar John M. G. Barclay points out that, for Paul, God's gift of mercy is indeed unconditioned; that is, not based on what sinners can return to God, or on their worthiness or prior status, but is nevertheless not unconditional, that is, totally free of expectations.[58] God expects gratitude and living in accord with his mercy, a kind of witness or "living billboard" of the Christ-gift. Luther agrees. In the Small Catechism, Luther indicates the appropriate response to God's grace: "Therefore we surely ought to thank and praise, serve and obey him [God]."[59]

Does that reality undermine the graciousness of God's gifts of forgiveness and the Holy Spirit? Many readers of Mauss highlight the awareness that gift exchanges, which tend to be reciprocal, altruistic, and achieve strong bonds between givers and recipients, are to be distinguished from commercial exchanges which optimize the utility of both parties and lead to impersonal bonds. The gift is a reciprocity in which there is an obligation to give, to receive, and to return the gift. In a word, gifts provoke counter gifts which, while not legally required, seem to be the appropriate response to a gift. As Risto Saarinen notes, the meaning of "give" entails both a personal giver and also a "living recipient."[60] Hence, for Saarinen, recipients are not merely passive or, if they are rendered passive in some way, it must

---

56. For a summary of "gift" in Luther Studies, see Nelson and Hinlicky, *Oxford Encyclopedia of Martin Luther*, 558–73.
57. See Bayer, *Freedom in Response*, 13–20.
58. Barclay, *Paul and the Gift*, 526.
59. *BoC* 355:2 (*BSLK* 870:16).
60 Saarinen, *Luther and the Gift*, 3.

be a passivity of a special kind. Naturally the question arises for Lutherans: does the expectation of counter gifts undermine the purity of God's grace which is neither earned nor deserved? Does God still expect something of us which somehow aids our redemption?

To attempt to respond to that question, we need to acknowledge that God's grace as a gift is analogical. Analogies honor differences as much as similarities. When, for example, God's gift is seen as a rescue operation and not like a favor offered at a dinner party, a somewhat different spin is put on the notion of gift. When redemption is seen as rescuing sinners from sin and death, God does not merely give a gift where a return favor is easy or even remotely reciprocal. If God delivers sinners from life-threatening circumstances, sin, death, and the power of the devil, similar to throwing a life preserver to a drowning person, we deal not just with the social bonding activated by, say, a holiday gift exchange, but instead lives that are actually saved. Not only is there an element of drama in such rescuing, but there is also an asymmetry that heightens both the gratuity of and inability to repay the gift. Seen in those terms, divine gifting conveys the fact that none of us are self-sustaining moment by moment in the face of nothingness, but instead are constantly preserved. Nor can we raise ourselves from death.

That said, the fact that gifts trigger counter gifts, in distinction to economic exchanges based on payment, seems to reinforce the spontaneity of good works that are paid forward and that Luther is convinced will flow forth from those who receive mercy from Jesus Christ. It would seem that Luther's ruling out of merit and worthiness is his way of refocusing grace away from any Pelagian-inspired economic exchange. Indeed, being reduced to nothing through the law's accusations takes away any ability to claim merit or worthiness, and so any kind of spiritual *superbia* that one may wish to establish even in one's spirituality. The point of God's grace is not to give sinners a choice, but instead a whole new will, new desires, and new convictions.[61] Sinners might think that they are free, but they are no freer than alcoholics for whom choice means either gin, beer, wine, or vodka, but not sobriety. In order to claim sobriety alcoholics must let go of the illusion that they have control over their drug of choice.

---

61. "Thus a new creation is a work of the Holy Spirit, who implants anew intellect and will and confers the power to curb the flesh and to flee the righteousness and wisdom of the world. This is not a sham or merely a new outward appearance, but something really happens. A new attitude and a new judgment, namely, a spiritual one, actually come into being, and they now detest what they once admired. Our minds were once so captivated by the monastic life that we thought of it as the only way to salvation; now we think of it quite differently. What we used to adore, before this new creation, as the ultimate in holiness now makes us blush when we remember it" (*LW* 27:140 [WA 40/2, 178, 21–29]).

Any response to God's grace is such because it is evoked. This response is not for an instrumental, calculative purpose designed to elicit further divine gifts. In fact, if the above discussion of "flow" makes sense at all, the point is to liberate incurvated selves so that they stop seeking merit and actually do good works in the world as Christs to the neighbor. Such reciprocity is echoed by John M. G. Barclay: believers act out of love for God, not from self-concern. Helpfully, Barclay itemizes six traits indicating the "purity" of gifts: (1) *superabundance*, that is, how excessive the gift is, (2) *singularity*, that the giver's sole and exclusive mode of operation is benevolence, (3) *priority*, that is, the gift's timing as prior to the initiative of the recipient, (4) *incongruity*, that the giver gives generously even though selectively, (5) *efficacy*, that the gift fully achieves what it was designed to do, and finally (6) *noncircularity*, no return can be demanded but not detached from every notion of exchange.[62] Without going into detail, it is fair to say that Luther's view of grace scores high according to all these metrics.

Saarinen notes that, for Luther, the reception of the gospel is of course not an exercise of the free will (which, after all, God alone possesses), but even so it is a personal reception of gifts. The human has a capacity for receiving (*aptitudo naturalis*).[63] No doubt, the agency of the law to mortify sinners, the reduction to nothingness, is precisely to bring humans to that point so that through the work of the Spirit humans can grasp Christ. For Saarinen, the personal being of the subject is not completely eradicated.[64] The old being which claims it can understand the grounds for God's mercy through metaphysics, or accrue sufficient merit through ethics, is eradicated, thereby leaving a purified subject who can receive God's mercy and so can be reborn. But this stance is not so dissimilar to that of German theologian, Ingolf Dalferth. For Dalferth, the gift itself transforms the addressee into a recipient: God's law annihilates human resistance to grace. The passivity worked by the Holy Spirit through the law uproots the old incurvated self, allows one to be renewed by God's grace, and gives the Holy

---

62. Barclay, *Paul and the Gift*, 70–75.

63. Saarinen, *Luther and the Gift*, 35. "Note, however, that if we meant by 'the power of free-will' the power which makes human beings fit subjects to be caught up by the Spirit and touched by God's grace, as creatures made for eternal life or eternal death, we should have a proper definition. And I certainly acknowledge the existence of this power, this fitness, or 'dispositional quality' and 'passive aptitude' (as the Sophists call it), which, as everyone knows, is not given to plants or animals. As the proverb says, God did not make heaven for geese!" See Luther, *Bondage of the Will*, 105 (WA 18, 636, 16–22).

64. Saarinen, *Luther and the Gift*, 36.

Spirit who awakens genuine concern for the neighbor. Dalferth calls this "passivity-rooted activity" (*Passivitätsaktivität*).[65]

In sum, Luther's problem is not with human agency per se, but instead with humans' misplaced faith in their own agency. It is not that we need to pit the human against the divine; humans already do a good job of that when they insist on being their own divinities for themselves. No doubt, at the metaphysical level, the being of the human along with all other creatures is that of being upheld out of nothing. But at the level of personal identity and ethical agency, the human is addressed by its Creator who calls forth new life for it by claiming it as its own, forgiving sin, and implanting the Holy Spirit right in its heart.

The Newness of the New Life

What shape, form, or contour can we expect from this new life evoked by the Spirit? Is it amorphous, shapeless, or readying itself to be shaped through conspicuous consumption or consumerism? Remember, for the Reformer, the human is characterized by the heart and that upon which it trusts. Trusting in a generous God whose grace on account of Christ is excessively rich, free from entrapment to various idols, such as mammon or even the "self," free from concupiscence which, as the Heidelberg Disputation tells us, is being extinguished, free of incurvation, we have new impulses and directions in life. No longer defined by covetous, controlling desire, or uncontrolled will, we have a new desire awakened within us. Indeed, for Luther, it is the Holy Spirit that makes us burn with desire (*flammen ins Hertz*) for God.[66] Indeed, the Holy Spirit enlivens the heart to believe (*spiritus vivificans*).[67] Thereby, Christians do make "some progress in that which shall be perfected in the future life."[68] But such progress never removes us from the starting point. As Roger Trigg explains:

> Luther's understanding of justification by faith removes all the evidence of human spiritual progress from sight. By the same token, it imparts a certain circularity to the Christian life. There is

---

65. Dalferth, *Creatures of Possibility*, 66.
66. WA 21, 440, 8.
67. WA 11, 53, 10.
68. *LW* 31:358 (WA 7, 59, 31).

no possibility of progress away from the start point, or from the need for *conversio*; rather a continual return to that beginning.[69]

The late Robert Jenson agrees: "Short of the End, the believer does not go on to anything after baptism, for baptism is initiation into the gate-community after which there is only the kingdom. Short of the End, the believer never advances beyond his or her baptism but instead falls behind it and must catch up to it."[70]

Naturally, given this view of the Christian walk as a continual return to mercy, the question arises, what becomes of ethics? Is there no ethical progress for believers? As Oswald Bayer explains:

> Ethical progress is only possible by returning to Baptism. That progress which will promise us good things, and not just good things but the very best, is a converting and returning to Baptism, and therefore to a new perception of the world in which we no longer have to choose between optimism and pessimism, between shrill anxiety about the future and euphoric hope regarding the further evolution of the cosmos and the enhancement of its possibilities; all the same it remains true that God the Creator unceasingly does new things.[71]

Hence, with respect to our spirituality, we have no progress in measurable, demonstrable, or quantifiable outcomes; that is, longer, more intense hours in prayer or meditation—as important as prayer and meditation are—do not translate into a holier life. Instead, as Christians what we have is a progress *from* faith in Christ *to* faith in Christ.[72] Again, this is not to rule out ethical development, but such ethical development has no bearing on righteousness *coram deo*. As the adage goes, God does not need your good works, but your neighbor does.

We have joy and comfort trusting in God's promise. We receive forgiveness of sins in the church. We are empowered by the Holy Spirit to love God and to serve our neighbor. All this goodness is offered together

---

69. Trigg, *Baptism*, 169.
70. Jenson, *Systematic Theology*, 2:297.
71. Bayer, *Living by Faith*, 66.

72. "For this life is a constant progress from faith to faith, from love to love, from patience to patience, and from affliction to affliction. It is not righteousness, but justification; not purity, but purification; we have not yet arrived at our destination, but we are all on the road, and some are farther advanced than others. God is satisfied to find us busy at work and full of determination. When he is ready he will come quickly, strengthen faith and love, and in an instant take us from this life to heaven. But while we live on earth we must bear with one another, as Christ also bore with us, seeing that none of us is perfect" (Luther, *Complete Sermons*, 1.1:212).

with the fact that through cross and trial God is ever shaping us to trust solely in him and not in ourselves. As Roy Harrisville noted, "But unless the message of justification is apprehended as the good news that God not merely acquits but heaps on the sinner undeserved riches in abundance, indeed, hammers the sinner into the shape of the One who died and rose, it lies amputated."[73] Through baptism we participate both in Christ's death and resurrection: we live ever from a faith that uncorks joy in God's abundant mercy but also faces trials with courage. Living in prayer, meditation on the Scriptures, and facing spiritual attack, our discipleship in Christ is that of a discipleship with the Crucified. Again, Harrisville wrote: "the event which establishes such existence, renders it hidden in contrast to the apocalyptic vision, or in contrast to the ideal visibly achieved and wanting to be applauded, is the cross of Jesus Christ."[74] Hence, the purpose of exhortation when preaching is not to summon believers to become what they already are but instead to charge them live in accord with both their death and resurrection in Christ.[75]

Conclusion

In a nutshell, earlier than the Catechisms Luther had summed up the person and work of the Holy Spirit as the One who calls, enlightens, gathers, and sanctifies in his 1524 catechetical Pentecost hymn "Come, Holy Ghost, God and Lord":

> Come, Holy Ghost, God and Lord,
>
> With all your graces now outpoured
>
> On each believer's mind and heart;
>
> Your fervent love to them impart.
>
> Lord, by the brightness of your light
>
> In holy faith your Church unite;
>
> From ev'ry land and ev'ry tongue,
>
> This to your praise,
>
> O Lord, our God be sung:
>
> Alleluia! Alleluia!

73. Harrisville, *Romans*, 77.
74. Harrisville, *Romans*, 79.
75. Harrisville, *Romans*, 95.

In the second stanza we request the Holy Spirit to "teach us to know our God aright," while in the third we ask, "grant us the will your work to do and in your service to abide."[76] This hymn is an apt, albeit brief, description of Luther's beliefs about the Holy Spirit. As we have seen, in the Catechisms, Luther richly and succinctly elaborates on the person and work of the Spirit outlined in this hymn.

That the Spirit sanctifies means that everything in our lives is upheld in the palm of God's hand and that even in the face of the old sinful nature, with which we wrestle, we are wholly and completely God's workmanship. The Spirit builds community and works through preachers to build congregations through administrating word and sacrament. The church is an oasis of truth and beacon of hope in a world which increasingly buys into an individualism where each seeks to be one's own divinity for oneself. The Spirit is the guarantee that God will bring all the faithful to their fulfillment in the life of the world to come.

Bibliography

Allen, Michael. *Sanctification*. Grand Rapids: Zondervan, 2017.
Arand, Charles P., and Joel Biermann. "Why the Two Kinds of Righteousness?" *Concordia Journal* 33 (2007).
Barclay, John M. G. *Paul and the Gift*. Grand Rapids: Eerdmans, 2015.
Bayer, Oswald. *Freedom in Response; Lutheran Ethics: Sources and Controversies*. Translated by Jeffrey F. Cayzer. Oxford: Oxford University Press, 2007.
———. *Living by Faith: Justification and Sanctification*. Grand Rapids: Eerdmans, 2003.
———. *Martin Luther's Theology*. Translated by Thomas Trapp. Grand Rapids: Eerdmans, 2008.
———. *Theology the Lutheran Way*. Edited and translated by Jeffrey G. Silcock and Mark C. Mattes. Grand Rapids: Eerdmans, 2007.
Calvin, John. *Institutes of the Christian Religion*. Edited by John T. McNeill. Translated by Ford Lewis Battles. Louisville: Westminster John Knox, 2004.
Dalferth, Ingolf. *Creatures of Possibility: The Theological Basis of Human Freedom*. Translated by Jo Bennett. Grand Rapids: Baker Academic, 2016.
Wengert, Timothy J., et al., eds. *Dictionary of Luther and the Lutheran Traditions*. Grand Rapids: Baker, 2017.
Forde, Gerhard. *Justification by Faith: A Matter of Death and Life*. Philadelphia: Fortress, 1982. Reprint, Eugene, OR: Wipf & Stock, 2012.
Harrisville, Roy A. *Romans*. Augsburg Commentary on the New Testament. Minneapolis: Augsburg, 1980.
Hong, Edna Hatlestad. *Bright Valley of Love*. Minneapolis: Augsburg, 1976.
Jenson, Robert. *Systematic Theology*. Vol. 2. New York: Oxford University Press, 1999.

---

76. *Lutheran Book of Worship*, s.v. "163." See also *LW* 53:265–67.

Johnston, Wade. *An Uncompromising Gospel: Lutheranism's First Identity Crisis and Lessons for Today*. Irvine, CA: New Reformation, 2016.

Kolb, Robert. "God Kills to Make Alive: Romans 6 and Luther's Understanding of Justification (1535)." *Lutheran Quarterly* 12 (1998) 33–56.

Lamport, Mark A., ed. *A–L*. Vol. 1 of *Encyclopedia of Martin Luther and the Reformation*. Lanham, MD: Rowman & Littlefield, 2017.

Leppin, Volker. *Die fremde Reformation: Luthers mystische Wurzeln*. München: Beck, 2016.

Lindberg, Carter. "Do Lutherans Shout Justification but Whisper Sanctification?" *Lutheran Quarterly* 13 (1999) 11.

Loehe, Wilhelm. *Three Books about the Church*. Translated by James Schaaf. Philadelphia: Fortress, 1969.

Lohse, Bernhard. *Martin Luther's Theology: Its Historical and Systematic Development*. Translated by Roy A. Harrisville. Minneapolis: Fortress, 1999.

Luther, Martin. *The Bondage of the Will*. Translated by J. I. Packer and O. R. Johnston. New York: Fleming Revell, 1957.

———. *Complete Sermons of Martin Luther*. Edited and translated by John Nicholas Lenker. Grand Rapids: Baker, 2000.

———. *The Freedom of a Christian*. Translated by Mark D. Tranvik. Minneapolis: Fortress, 2008.

Mattes, Mark. *Luther's Theology of Beauty: A Reappraisal*. Grand Rapids: Baker Academic, 2017.

Nelson, Derek R., and Paul R. Hinlicky, eds. *The Oxford Encyclopedia of Martin Luther*. New York: Oxford University Press, 2017.

Paulson, Steven. "Graspable God." *Word & World* 32 (2012) 51–62.

Saarinen, Risto. *Luther and the Gift*. Tübingen: Mohr/Siebeck, 2017.

Trigg, Jonathan D. *Baptism in the Theology of Martin Luther*. Boston: Brill, 2001.

Whitford, David Mark. *Tyranny and Resistance: The Magdeburg Confession and the Lutheran Tradition*. St. Louis: Concordia, 2001.

Zahl, Simeon. "Tradition and its 'Use': The Ethics of Theological Retrieval." *Scottish Journal of Theology* (forthcoming).

8

"With Those Who Weep"

Towards a Theology of Solidarity in Lament

Joshua C. Miller

Since Old Testament times, God's people have engaged in the practice of lament in response to the experience of evil and suffering. The Bible is full of examples of believers who, when faced with these experiences, called out to God on the basis of a promise given to them by him. Oswald Bayer has brought the theme of lament to the forefront in his theology. In his contemporary Lutheran approach to this theme, Bayer identifies the cry of believers to God to honor his justifying and creation-opening promise in the midst of the experience of the contradiction of that promise. Bayer describes lament as the "*Sitz im Leben*" of believers who live in the "rupture of the ages—between the old age of sin and death and the new age of forgiveness and new life, inaugurated by Jesus Christ—to be fulfilled eschatologically."[1]

Bayer's work on lament presents a helpful way forward for those who seek to do theology in a categorically Lutheran way, being faithful to the evangelical proclamation of God's effectual word of promise in Jesus Christ, but also taking seriously the realities of evil and suffering that are experienced by believers as the contradiction of that promise. One of the aspects Bayer highlights in his theology of lament is that believers do not lament alone but are joined by Christ and all creation in crying out to God.[2] In this essay, I will explore the theme of solidarity in lament, identifying how lament emerges in the Christian life, how Christ joins believers in lament,

---

1. Bayer, *Martin Luther's Theology*, 11; *Gott als Autor*, 157; *Living by Faith*, 69, 71; cf. Miller, *Hanging by a Promise*, 244–54.

2. Bayer, *Gott als Autor*, 187–88; *Schöpfung als Anrede*, 177–78; *Martin Luther's Theology*, 113–14.

how creation joins in this solidarity in lament, and how the church is the community marked by solidarity in lament.

Lament in the Christian Life

Lament is our *modus vivendi* as believers in the time between Christ's first and second advent, we who have been grasped in faith by the promise of Jesus Christ, which is a word that does what it says. Bayer identifies that this effective word of God's promise forgives and justifies the sinner before God.[3] In liberating us from the domain of sin, death, and the power of the devil, the promise creates a new relationship of peace and communion between us now-forgiven sinners and God, a relationship called "faith."[4] This relationship is established by the promise, the active word of God that comes through the preaching of the gospel and the handing over of the gracious promise of Christ in the sacraments.[5]

In liberating and opening us up to God, the promise also opens us to our neighbors, and God's creation anew.[6] By freeing us from God's wrath, sin, and the powers of evil, says Bayer, God's word of promise re-establishes us in a new relationship with our fellow humans and the creation itself.[7] Drawing from a sermon preached by Luther in 1538, Bayer proclaims that God's promise embodied in Jesus's performative word "*Ephphatha!*" reopens creation itself and heralds the dawning of a new age, the new creation that is reconciled to God.[8]

Yet, this is not what we as believers experience all around. Instead of experiencing creation as the scene of God's reconciliation with all that he has made and restoration of it to the state in which he intended it to be, we continue to live in a broken world in which we undergo tragedy, death, suffering, and evils both of our own human making and those that encounter

---

3. Bayer, *Martin Luther's Theology*, 46–47, 52–53, 107–8; *Gott als Autor*, 2; *Zugesagte Gegenwart*, 196.

4. Bayer, *Theology the Lutheran Way*, 127–28; *Martin Luther's Theology*, 50–51; "Preaching the Word," 255; *Zugesagte Gegenwart*, 392–93; Miller, *Hanging by a Promise*, 155–56.

5. Bayer, *Theology the Lutheran Way*, 130.

6. Bayer, *Martin Luther's Theology*, 54–55; "Justification as the Basis and Boundary," 286; *Leibliches Wort*, 33; Miller, *Hanging by a Promise*, 159–60.

7. Bayer, *Martin Luther's Theology*, 108–11; cf. WA 46:493–95; Miller, *Hanging by a Promise*, 164.

8. WA 46:493–95; Bayer, *Martin Luther's Theology*, 106–19; cf. Mark 7:34–35; Bayer, *Schöpfung als Anrede*, 62; Miller, *Hanging by a Promise*, 164.

us through nature and disease. Our ongoing experience of evil and suffering is not merely the subject of intellectual theodicy, it is a real-life encounter of what Bayer calls "the rupture of the ages," wherein we are caught between the promise of a new creation and its complete eschatological fulfillment.[9]

Bayer highlights that we experience evil and suffering in this ruptured time as a contradiction of God's promise in Christ. The problem of evil, as theology has often termed it, thus forms part of our experience of *Anfechtung*, the attack upon our faith in the promise of the God revealed to us in the promise of Christ. This attack comes not only from the world, the devil, and our own sinful nature. It also comes from the hidden God.[10]

Bayer utilizes the distinction made by Luther in *The Bondage of the Will* between God as he is revealed and preached in Christ through word and sacrament on the one hand, and God hidden and unpreached on the other hand. Whereas in Christ through the word God reveals himself as a God of grace, mercy, and love, God hidden outside of revelation exists as a God of wrath, who wills the death and damnation of sinners and all things that come to pass.[11] Bayer adopts Luther's doctrine of the hidden God and utilizes it in his theology, juxtaposing the activity of the hidden God with God's justifying, liberating, and creation-opening promise in Jesus Christ. Bayer defines the hiddenness of God as the believer's experience of the contradiction of God's promise, a contradiction existentially evident through the reality of the problem of evil. *Anfechtung* thus becomes an agonizing struggle of existential proportions, a struggle for faith to hold on to the promise of justification and a renewed creation in the midst of experiencing the contradiction of that promise.[12] The struggle of *Anfechtung* is not simply some form of a generic human angst but the experience of believers addressed by God's word. *Anfechtung*, says Bayer, is the experience of the contradiction of God's word of promise; it is the contradiction apparent in reality against what God says in the word. It is the touchstone of being believers.[13]

---

9. Bayer, *Martin Luther's Theology*, 11, 113; *Gott als Autor*, 158–59.

10. Bayer, *Martin Luther's Theology*, 213; *Theology the Lutheran Way*, 95–96, 102–5; Miller, *Hanging by a Promise*, 210–17.

11. *BoW*, 169–71; WA 18:684–86.

12. Cf. Kittelson, *Luther the Reformer*, 56–57; LW 34:285–87; WA 50:659–61. Although *Anfechtung* and its Latin translation, *tentatio*, could be translated—and indeed has been, by Mark Mattes—as "temptation," I have followed Thomas Trapp's translation "agonizing struggle," which I believe fits better with Luther's idea of *Anfechtung* that Bayer is seeking to employ here.

13. Bayer, *Theology the Lutheran Way*, 63–64; *Martin Luther's Theology*, 20–21, 35–37.

Bayer describes the hidden God's attack on faith coming via the creation through theodicy or "the problem of evil."[14] Although all people experience this work of the hidden God to some extent, the situation is more acute for believers who experience it as *Anfechtung*, as the hidden God's attack on the promise.[15] God's work of justification includes not only God's forgiveness and declaring righteous of the individual believer but also the opening of creation itself and its ultimate reconciliation and restoration. Bayer states that God's justification of the sinner has ontological and cosmic dimensions and that justification and creation should be addressed together and not divided from one another. Bayer consequently understands God's work of justification to entail God's work of opening a new creation, which is actually a return of creation to its original state. The problem arises that such transformation is not presently visible to believers who still see the world full of suffering, pain, and evil. This reality of the "problem of evil" evident in the world, which is at odds with the trust that God is opening a new creation, and constitutes the believer's experience of *Anfechtung*.[16]

All human and natural evils are experienced by us believers as *Anfechtung*[17] and place us in a context where good and evil are intertwined with one another, with the suspicion constantly in our minds that it is God who is responsible for all of this.[18] We then become keenly aware that, in some hidden and completely incomprehensible way, God is responsible for large-scale evils of hurricanes, tornadoes, earthquakes, tsunamis, famines, wars, pandemics, and even the existence and the threat of the use of thermonuclear weapons. Yet perhaps, what is even more difficult for faith is that God's hiddenness becomes evident in the more personal tragedies of life. The contradiction of God's promise in *Anfechtung* does not just come to us through the global events we see portrayed in the media, it also comes to us through the illnesses and deaths of the people we love. It comes to us through the broken lives and relationships that we see all around us and in which we find ourselves.[19] In this way, the experience of the contradiction

---

14. Bayer, *Martin Luther's Theology*, 198–99; "Plurality of the One God," 345; *Zugesagte Gegenwart*, 102.

15. Bayer, "Plurality of the One God," 349–50; *Zugesagte Gegenwart*, 106.

16. Bayer, *Martin Luther's Theology*, 199; "What is Evangelical?," 10; *Zugesagte Gegenwart*, 31. It is not as if there is a specific and necessary order to these two forms of the hidden God's contradiction of the promise in *Anfechtung*, which is a spiritual attack or struggle that comes ultimately from God.

17. Bayer, *Zugesagte Gegenwart*, 31, 105; "Plurality of the One God," 349.

18. Bayer, *Martin Luther's Theology*, 202; "Creation as History," 261; "God's Omnipotence," 92–93; *Zugesagte Gegenwart*, 119, 229.

19. Bayer, *Schöpfung als Anrede*, 161; *Zugesagte Gegenwart*, 244–45; "Der Glanze

of God's promise drives us to question why God is causing or allowing evil and suffering, forming the cry of lament that arises from faith in the midst of this experience of *Anfechtung*.

According to Bayer, lament is the response of faith to the experience of *Anfechtung* through the problem of evil. When faced with the contradiction of God's promise that we are forgiven and that creation will be restored, we often begin to ask the inevitable question of "why?"

While at first glance this question may seem impious or even blasphemous, the opposite is true. The question of why forms the beginning of lament, which, as Bayer identifies, is the response of authentic faith to the contradiction of God's promise via evil and suffering. Whether it flows from humanly caused evil or the suffering caused by the natural evils of disease and disaster, crying out to God through lament forms the setting in life for us as believers as we find ourselves stuck between the eschatological fulfillment of God's promise and its present contradiction.[20]

In this rupture of the ages, lament is a cry out to God from us as believers for God to put an end to the contradiction. This cry is based on that same promise. Thus, lament is an appeal to God to keep his promise. This cry of appeal has three distinct parts: identifying the real problem, leveling an accusation against God, and confessing faith in the promise of God.[21]

In identifying the real problem, lament dispenses with false questions about vague notions of God's attributes and the metaphysics of evil through theodicy. Instead of speculating philosophically, lament addresses the problems of evil and suffering for what they are: *Anfechtung*, an attack on faith in God's promise. Lament realizes that evil and suffering are real problems, not philosophical ones. Our cry of lament realizes that these problems present a matter of trust in what God has said in the midst of life and are not components of equations to be speculated about in ivory towers.

When it recognizes the real problem, our cry of lament then moves to address God directly. Instead of arguing about God, lament argues with God. It presents God with the promise and accuses him on the basis of that promise. In this way, lament is what I like to call "faithful backtalk."[22] It is backtalk because it presumes to enter God's presence like Moses, Job, David, and Habakkuk all did, questioning God directly; asking whether

---

der Gnade," 80; *Gott als Autor*, 272; Chan and Miller, "Prayer that Prevails," 36–37; cf. Golden, "Responding to Evil," 47.

20. Bayer, *Martin Luther's Theology*, 11; *Gott als Autor*, 157; *Living by Faith*, 71; cf. Miller, *Hanging by a Promise*, 244.

21. Miller, "Between Openness and Hiddenness," 29–30; *Zugesagte Gegenwart*, 64, 116–17; *Martin Luther's Theology*, 213; *Gott als Autor*, 16–17, 147–48.

22. Miller, "Between Openness and Hiddenness," 29.

he remembers and will keep his promise and challenging him to do so.[23] At the same time, lament is faithful, because it flows from a deep trust in God's promise despite all the evidence in life and in the world that this promise is not trustworthy, affirming that God made a good creation, and indicting the present state of affairs as being contrary to how he originally intended and created it.[24]

In the midst of this accusation lament thus moves to confession of God's promise. We can observe this transition from accusation to confession in Psalm 22. David begins his Psalm with the accusation that God has forsaken him, explains the real situation of what that forsakenness looks like, appeals to God to keep his promise, then moves to confession and doxology (Ps 22:19–23).

Perhaps the most colorful biblical scene that illustrates how the faithful backtalk of lament moves to confession is the wrestling match between God and Jacob on the banks of the Jabbok. Taking his cue from Luther, Bayer encourages us to wrestle with God in lament. Drawing from Luther's *Lectures on Genesis*, Bayer compares our crying out in lament to God in the midst of *Anfechtung* with Jacob's struggle with God on the banks of the Jabbok. According to Luther, this struggle was not just a wrestling match, it was Jacob's fight to cling to God's promise for him in the midst of God's contradicting it by ambushing him in the middle of the night.[25] Jacob fights with his whole being, struggling to gain the upper hand by using God's own promise against God, and it works.[26]

Like Jacob, says Bayer, we cannot really distinguish what is going on in our experience of evil and suffering. All we know for sure is that God's word of promise is being contradicted and that the only thing we have to defend ourselves against this attack is that same word of promise.[27] By crying out in lament we struggle with God, holding him to his promise to renew creation, confessing him to be a God *for us* in Christ.

In the Christian life, lament is the response of faith that identifies the real problem of suffering and evil as a problem of trust. Lament then confronts God, accusing him of not keeping his promise and holding him to his word. Yet, lament is also a confession. Suffering and evil are only a problem for faith, not unbelief. Lament is not an impious rejection of the promise

---

23. See Exod 32:11–14; Job 23–31; Ps 6; 22; 77; 90; 94; 118; Heb 1:12–17.

24. Golden, "Responding to Evil," 54–55.

25. *LW* 6:135–40.

26. *LW* 6:135–36.

27. Bayer, *Theology the Lutheran Way*, 18–19; *Martin Luther's Theology*, 2–4, 40, 204; *Zugesagte Gegenwart*, 77; "Rupture of Times," 37–38; *Gott als Autor*, 150–52.

but is, rather, the greatest expression of ultimate trust in God's promise right in the middle of the experience of its contradiction. Lament is our setting in life as believers who find ourselves in the midst of evil, suffering, and a fallen creation, rejecting the state of affairs as contrary to God's promise and entrusting our entire being to the God who has promised that he will one day restore the entire order of things.

Solidarity in Lament: The Fallen Creation and the Creator Christ

Far from being simply an individualist and existential experience, lament is the reality that marks the time between Christ's first and second advents, the rupture of the ages.[28] When we do cry out to God in the struggle of lament, we do not cry alone. We are joined by all creation and by Jesus Christ himself. In this way, lament takes on cosmic and christological dimensions.

St. Paul tell us that the whole of creation cries out with us, groaning "in labor pains" for its promised renewal in God's final, eschatological act of redemption (Rom 8:22, NJB). All creatures join us in lamenting the brokenness of this world. As Bo Giertz states in his commentary on Romans, even though they are not at fault, all creatures have suffered from sin and death brought into the world by Adam and long for their share in the redemption of God's children and the renewal of all creation (Rom 8:19–22).[29] While we may from time to time give into the solipsistic desire to look upon our personal experiences of evil and suffering as unique, the apostle reminds us that we are not alone in undergoing this contradiction of the gospel. All humans, all creatures, even the cosmos itself, are marked by the curse of spoiled Eden. Human sin has brought what Paul terms "the bondage of decay" (Rom 8:21, ESV).

While Christ's word "*Ephphatha!*" is a performative declaration that has effectively proclaimed the renewal of creation, the creation around us does not yet fully enjoy the benefits of that renewal. We and all creatures with us still live under the pall of death. We still suffer the effects of decay brought on by the sin of our first parents whose rebellion against God mired the entirety of creation with them in a cursed brokenness. All creation is stuck between the effective proclamation of Christ's "*Ephphatha!*" and the complete reversal of all of the effects of sin and death that will one day be

---

28. Bayer, *Martin Luther's Theology*, 11, 113; *Gott als Autor*, 158–59.
29. Giertz, *Romans*, 49–50.

heralded with his effective proclamation of "Come, for everything is now ready!" (Luke 14:17b, ESV).

Lament is the setting that marks the Christian life between Christ's first and second comings, but we as Christians are not alone in our lament. Creation itself, along with us, is a recipient of the promise that it will be renewed by God's ultimate eschatological act of salvation. It awaits the renewal foretold by Isaiah, wherein "the wolf will lie down with the lamb," all hostility within nature will cease, and death itself will be undone (Isa 11). The complete fulfillment of this prophecy by John the Revelator still lies in the future (Rev 21–22), but creation has been given a foretaste of that fulfillment in the resurrection of Jesus, standing as an indictment of evil, a death sentence on death itself. Until such a time when the dwelling of God ultimately is with us, when "he shall wipe away every tear," creation joins us in lament, groaning and praying with us, "*Maranatha!*" (Rev 21:3–4, ESV).

Yet, it is not only creation that laments with us. As Bayer also points out, God himself joins us in lament. For God has not abandoned us or his creation. Instead, God has become a part of creation as a creature, as God incarnate *for us* in Jesus Christ. Bayer maintains that God's incarnation in Christ is given to us as the direct answer to our lament and the sighing of creation in what he calls a "Christology of answered lament."[30]

In answer to our lament—in what Bo Giertz terms the "great intervention"—Christ has come among us as one of us in answer to our lament over the brokenness brought into our lives and into creation by sin.[31] Christ has become incarnate for us not only to take away the stain, guilt, and punishment of our sin—though he unequivocally has come for that—but also as the herald and guarantor of a renewed creation. He is, as St. Paul proclaims to us, the second Adam, and his resurrection is the first fruits of the resurrection of all the dead and the restoration of all creation (Rom 5:12–21; 1 Cor 15:20–28).

The Christology of answered lament preaches Christ as the one who stands in solidarity with us and the broken creation as he answers our lament. This solidarity becomes audible in the "*Ephphatha!*" text, as Christ joins his own expression of weariness over sin and brokenness to the groaning of all creation. As Bayer reminds us, when Christ healed the deaf-mute, he first looked up to heaven and sighed (Mark 7:34).[32] With the Christology of answered lament in mind, says Bayer, we begin to grasp the meaning in

---

30. Bayer, "Toward a Theology of Lament," 211; *Martin Luther's Theology*, 113; *Zugesagte Gegenwart*, 61.

31. Giertz, *Romans*, 34.

32. Bayer, *Martin Luther's Theology*, 113.

Jesus's word *"Ephphatha!"* By his sighing, Jesus placed himself in solidarity with the groaning, fallen creation that so desperately needs the renewal he has promised and with us who trust that promise.[33]

Perhaps the starkest image of Christ's solidarity with us and with the broken creation in lament, however, is the scene of his crucifixion. As Christ hangs upon the cross for our sins and the sins of the whole world, as the justice of the law and God's wrath are satisfied, as he hangs there in our place, he utters the greatest words of contradiction that have ever been said: "My God, my God, why have you forsaken me?" (Matt 27:46, ESV). Knowing the full story of how in the atonement Christ became a sinner for us, taking our place on the cross, and giving us his righteousness in return, we cannot relegate the cry of dereliction to a mere recitation of Psalm 22. Here, on the cross, the Creator God has become a judged, condemned creature who suffers for his creatures. Here, the God of the universe not only joins in solidarity with the lamenting creation and condemned humans, but actually takes away condemnation and answers lament. For in the crucified Christ we are met by both the true human who laments with us and the God who answers that lament. In the cross, the Christ who finds us is the God who stands in solidarity with us in lament, and the God-man who alone is the answer to our lament. There could be no greater act of both solidarity and answering lament.

The same Christ who sighed and opened creation to renewal with his *"Ephphatha!"* who rendered the ultimate act of solidarity with his death and the cross, and who pronounced the death of death with his resurrection stands in solidarity with us, lamenting with us today. The same Christ who came into the world in answer to the lament of Israel comes to answer our lament, as he comes to us through his word of promise in Scripture, preaching, and the sacraments. This solidarity of God *with us* in Jesus becomes tangible *for us* in the here and now through his word of promise as it is preached to us and given to us through created means of bread and wine. In these means of grace, Jesus Christ comes to us today as true God to identify with us his fallen creatures. Jesus comes to us in the sacrament as the crucified and risen God who sustains us in the midst of lament, as he gives us his word of promise and his very self as God *for us*.[34]

Thus strengthened by the Lord who laments with us, our cry of lament is a call for God to act, in which we join our voices with the groaning of creation, crying for God to put an end to evil and suffering. With all creation

---

33. Bayer, *Martin Luther's Theology*, 113.

34. Bayer, "Rupture of Times," 47; *Gott als Autor*, 159–60; *Martin Luther's Theology*, 11–12, 113–14; "Tod Gottes und Herrenmahl," 353–54; *Leibliches Wort*, 296–97.

we cry to God, "*Maranatha!*" (Oh, Lord, come!), by which we petition him to fulfill the promise given to his disciples in the first chapter of Acts that he will return (Acts 1:11; cf. John 14:1–3).[35] When we lament, we pray for Christ's second coming, whereby he will wipe away all tears, put an end to evil and suffering forever, and renew all of creation. The faith in Christ's promise that he will return is the real power behind lament, and it is the only real answer to the problem of evil and suffering.

Far from being abandoned to our fate, in lament Christ comes to us as a true human who becomes one of us and identifies with us in every sense, including our lament. At the same time, however, Christ is the revealed God who comes in answer to our lament. He is the God-man who stood and rebuked the storm on the lake of Galilee and still stands and rebukes the storms of *Anfechtung* in our lives. He is the God-man who took God's wrath on the cross. He is the God-man of promise who comes to us with his righteousness and his very self in the preached word and with his own body and blood in the Sacrament of the Altar, creating faith in our hearts with his active word of promise. Ultimately, he is also the God-man who will definitively answer our lament and the groaning of all creation eschatologically by fulfilling his promise and ending evil and suffering forever. In Christ, we have a fully human and fully divine Jesus who both identifies with our lament and answers it.

The Church as the Community of Solidarity in Lament

Christ's solidarity with us in lament is not simply an historical event but is living and active today through his body, the church. The church is the place where God in Christ lives and gives his gifts in word and sacrament for the life of the world, where he is confessed by the faithful in the liturgy, and where Christ's solidarity with us in lament is preached, given, and lived out. Christ works in and through the means of grace, the ministers of his church, and her laity to bring his saving promise to forgive sinners and comfort the hurting. The church as the body of Christ lives out his solidarity in lament through the vocation of her members, through the pastoral office, and through corporate acts of mercy.

One way in which the church lives out solidarity in lament is through her corporate confession of faith in God's promise in the midst of its contradiction. The church is the pilgrim people of God who trust

---

35. Bayer, "Mercy from the Heart," 31; "Toward a Theology of Lament," 212; *Zugesagte Gegenwart*, 57, 63; *Leibliches Wort*, 223.

in an eschatological promise that God will fix everything wrong, heal all wounds, and restore creation. The church trusts in and claims the coming of God's kingdom.

While we in the church may not see that promise at work and that kingdom present, it does come in the present when the congregation is gathered around the preached, sacramental promise who is Christ himself. Worship is thus truly Divine Service in the deepest sense, because it entails a doxological response to what God has given through the preached word and sacraments, which engender faith. In the midst of life, which contradicts the promise received here, the doxological response forms a corporate expression of lament's deep trust in the promise.[36]

In what is perhaps the most well-known Psalm of lament, David expresses this corporate confession of faith in the promise in the midst of its contradiction. "In the midst of the congregation I will praise you" (Ps 22:22b, ESV). The same David, who so recently expressed his feeling of God-forsakenness and who challenged God to act on his behalf in the face of his enemies, now moves to leading the corporate praise of God in the assembly of believers. Far from being a merely individualistic concern, David's lament moves from the feeling of being abandoned by God to corporate confession and doxology. In the context of liturgy, lament thus becomes a defiant expression of hope and complete trust in God's promise in spite of the lived experience of contradiction.

The same attitude of defiant hope marks the corporate lament of the pilgrim assembly of believers today, we who are gathered by the Holy Spirit around the word and sacraments as we eagerly await the final eschatological act of God's salvation. This hope becomes manifest liturgically in the kyrie, "Lord, have mercy," and in the second petition of the Lord's Prayer, "Thy kingdom come." As Bayer reminds us, these aspects of the liturgy form the cry of the church that has marked it since the first century: "*Maranatha!*" In this cry, the Church's corporate lament evidences both the hope that God will keep his promise and the collective longing for the ending of evil and healing of all brokenness for all eternity.[37]

In addition to the liturgy, a second way in which the church lives out solidarity in lament is through the vocation of all believers. The Christian's joining in the solidarity of lament is nothing less than the living out of the call to serve the neighbor. In *The Freedom of a Christian*, Luther identifies loving service to one's neighbors as the proper role for good works and the

---

36. Bayer, "Plurality of the One God," 352–53; *Zugesagte Gegenwart*, 108–9; Miller, *Hanging by a Promise*, 242.

37. Bayer, "Erhörte Klage," 270–71; *Leibliches Wort*, 346–47; Miller, *Hanging by a Promise*, 251.

activity that forms the content of the Christian life. Service is the natural product of faith and a demonstration of kenotic discipleship.[38] As God in Christ emptied himself, became a servant, took upon himself our humanity and the sins of all humankind, we too empty ourselves, taking upon ourselves the needs of the neighbor and living for the neighbor rather than just for ourselves.[39] Luther says that we as believers are to "put on the neighbor," acting as if we were in their place, even as Christ has put on our own flesh and taken upon himself all of our human frailty and sinfulness.[40] Serving the neighbor is not simply following the Golden Rule, but a radical call that flows from faith in an incarnational God who created and redeemed humans.

Mark Tranvik connects such incarnational service to the experience of human suffering. In seeking to serve the neighbor, says Tranvik, we often encounter suffering and even enter into it. While he cautions that we should be careful not to seek out suffering through some misguided sense of asceticism, Tranvik argues that as Christians, like Christ, we are called to go where the suffering is.[41]

If the call to serve the neighbor is a call to go where the suffering is, then it is a call to solidarity in lament. What greater service, what greater Christian love can be shown to the neighbor than coming alongside them as they are suffering and sharing with them in bearing their burdens of pain and grief? Vocation means being Christ to the neighbor through entering into solidarity in lament with the neighbor, as Christ has done for us all.

Matthew Harrison describes how our call to serve the suffering flows from God's promise to us in Christ. Harrison highlights Luther's sermon on Holy Communion from 1519, wherein the Reformer explicitly connects the reception of Christ's benefits in the Sacrament of the Altar to bearing the burdens of our brothers and sisters. Drawing from Luther, Harrison states that "at the Sacrament, you come to the altar, you kneel and you lay your burdens upon Christ and the gathered community. When you leave the altar, you take up the burden of others."[42]

By his incarnation, death, and resurrection Christ took upon himself our sins, our death, the curse of the law, God's wrath and the brokenness of

---

38. Luther says, "I will therefore give myself as a Christ to my neighbor, just as Christ offered himself to me. I will do nothing in this life except what is profitable, necessary, and life-giving for my neighbor, since through faith I have an abundance of all good things in Christ" (FC 82).

39. FC 79, 82.

40. FC 88.

41. Tranvik, *Martin Luther*, 72.

42. Harrison, "Being Active in Mercy," 39; LW 35:54–55.

creation and gave us instead his righteousness, eternal life, freedom from condemnation, peace with God, and the promise of a restored creation. Christian vocation lived out through solidarity in lament means that we take upon ourselves the trials, contradiction, and suffering of our neighbor and give them our love and presence. Yet we give them something else as well. We give the promise on which lament itself depends. This promise says that, despite all the evidence to the contrary, they are at peace with God. This promise says that Christ will return to judge evil, end suffering, and renew all creation, undoing sin and death forever. The Christian vocation of solidarity in lament means both presence with the neighbor and the pastoral care of preaching the promise into the situation of its contradiction.

The Christian vocation of solidarity in lament, thus, leads directly to proclamation. While it is the duty of all Christians to preach the gospel (Matt 28:19–20), the public call to the public proclamation of God's saving promise in Christ rests with the pastoral office in the church.[43] It naturally follows that the pastor should play a unique role in solidarity in lament. Thus it follows that a third way in which the church lives out Christ's solidarity in lament is preaching and pastoral care enacted through the pastoral office. In the context of solidarity in lament with the hurting, there is both a priestly aspect and a prophetic one to this responsibility of the one who fulfills the pastoral office of ministry.

The priestly aspect of the pastor's solidarity in lament may be termed "presence." Often it is said that a pastor sometimes just needs to "be there" or "be present" with a hurting believer. This in and of itself is insufficient, but it is an important aspect of a ministry of solidarity in lament. In the midst of the situation of lament, the pastor is what Luther called a "mask of God," that through which God comes to humans.[44] The pastor is the one who stands between the people and God, bringing God's presence to the people.

The pastor should realize that the cry of lament flows from the wellspring of faith in God's promise, and give the assurance for which such faith looks. The problems of evil and suffering are problems of faith, because they contradict God's promise. As Steven Paulson puts it, "Lament is only possible when you have a promise."[45] The accusatory question of lament takes God's promise so seriously, that it cannot accept false solutions. The pastor can exercise presence by giving room and giving voice to the believer's cry of lament but also must say something as well.

---

43. *BoC* 46–47.
44. *LW* 45:331; cf. Wingren, *Luther on Vocation*, 140.
45. Paulson, *Lutheran Theology*, 211.

Presence is an imperative in times of suffering, but presence does not mean silence. Being present through solidarity in lament entails not only standing between God and the people of the community of faith, but also between the people and God. Lament is a cry out to God, and the pastor not only should hear and give voice to such a cry but also join in with it.

Whether it is literally before the altar, where he faces God on behalf of the people gathered for Divine Service, or privately with those to whom he is giving pastoral care in a situation of suffering and grief, the pastor brings the prayers of the people to God on their behalf. Solidarity in lament entails crying out together to God, and part of the task of being present in pastoral care when faced with evil and suffering is to lead the people in doing so. Such leadership in the situation of lament is bold, but it is also absolutely vital to the life of faith in the midst of contradiction.[46]

Beyond presence and prayer, the pastor who stands in solidarity in lament is also called to preach.[47] Faith depends for its very existence upon the preaching of the promise that created it in the first place. As Bayer emphasizes, *Anfechtung* is the touchstone of the Christian life, and thus the Christian life is always a struggle to hold onto faith.[48] It is not, however, as if God leaves Christians alone in this struggle. He has sent Christ, and he sends preachers to them who bring Christ through the proclaimed word and sacrament.

Through the priestly and prophetic aspect of solidarity, the pastor has a public role in lament. Pastor Jeremiah Johnson has described this well in his essay "Learning to Lament." He says, "Lament is how the preacher, fulfilling both the prophetic and priestly offices of Christ, stands between the suffering of the present age and the restoration of the age to come without neglecting either one."[49]

Yet Christian vocation and pastoral care are not the only ways through which the church embodies solidarity in lament. These practices of solidarity in lament mainly have to do with personal experiences of suffering by

46. Jeremiah Johnson's essay, "Learning to Lament," provides an invaluable essay to pastors and lay Christians alike in considering why and how both private and corporate lament should take place in the life of the church. See Johnson, "Learning to Lament," 225–40.

47. In his essay, "Answering the 'Why' Questions," John Pless rebukes a model of ministry that purports that presence alone is sufficient for pastoral care in the midst of suffering. Pless explains well how pastoral care must move beyond presence to proclamation in the situation of lament and what it is that the pastors must proclaim. See Pless, "Answering the 'Why,'" 51.

48. David Scaer has also defined the Christian life through the experience of *Anfechtung* and explores this at length. See Scaer, "Concept of *Anfechtung*."

49. Johnson, "Learning to Lament," 239.

particular believers or families or even a shared tragedy within a local church community. The call to follow Christ in serving the neighbor also takes on a corporate dimension, however, when tragedies and disasters strike.

The corporate practice of Christian mercy thus forms a fourth way in which the church lives out solidarity in lament. Such mercy is defined as an attitude of pity or compassion exercised by believers who are moved by the suffering in the world around them to action on behalf of all of their neighbors and their world.[50] Mercy is the natural outgrowth of pilgrim faith in God's promise and a practical way in which solidarity in lament demonstrates itself in loving service in difficult times.

Often when these times come and when tragedies strike, people look for a reason as to why such things are happening. As John Pless points out, reasons for why such events take place are ultimately elusive, because they belong to the realm of the hidden God.[51] Ultimately, the answer to lament is an eschatological one. This does not mean, however, that we as believers are allowed to retreat into an eschatological quietism in which we sit on our hands and await Christ's return. Instead, we are called to serve our neighbors. This service takes on bodily form as solidarity. We may not be able to figure out why tragedies take place, but that does not mean we cannot do anything. We are called to serve through our labor and giving on behalf of those in the midst of tragedies and loss.

As Harrison highlights, serving our neighbors who are hurting is a furtherance of the mercy that God shows to the world in Jesus Christ. It is the giving of diakonic love as God in Christ has given himself to us, through which the church literally acts as the body of Christ to and for the neighbor and the life of the world.[52] God's solidarity in Christ with those who are suffering in lament is not an abstract idea but a concrete reality in the world through the church that exists to serve others in the midst of a world full of suffering, brokenness, and death.[53]

When disasters strike, the church is found where the hurting is. Instead of looking for a reason "why," the church is called to be the helpers in tragedies.[54] Just as God in Christ identified with us in our sin and death,

---

50. I adopt this definition of "mercy" from Matthew Harrison, president of the Lutheran Church—Missouri Synod in his introduction of the volume entitled *Mercy in Action*. See Harrison, "Introduction," 11.

51. Pless, "Answering the 'Why,'" 48–49.

52. Harrison, "Theology for Mercy," 27. Harrison defines "diakonic love" as "love care and concern for those in need . . . actions motivated by the gospel."

53. Harrison, "Theology for Mercy," 28.

54. Fred Rogers said that when he was a boy and was troubled by the coming of tragedies, his mother would tell him "Look for the helpers. You can always find people

taking it away, we are called to identify with those who are undergoing suffering in the brokenness of our fallen world. As God in Christ comes to us in our lament today, we as believers are called to go where the hurting is—to Christians and unbelievers alike—and render service both by preaching the good news of God's coming kingdom when all sorrow will end and by helping our hurting neighbors in their temporal needs.[55] In so doing, we act as the hands and feet of Christ in this present rupture of the ages.

We as believers live between the times, with our feet standing in the present, firmly on the promise to whose fulfillment our eyes of faith look. Knowing how the story will end, we are called to stand in solidarity with the hurting by rendering mercy in word and deed. We can practice solidarity through mercy with confidence, because we are given the promise that the groaning of the natural order will be answered when God puts an end to suffering forever and heals the rupture of the ages.

Conclusion

Oswald Bayer has correctly identified that lament is our setting in life as believers in the rupture of the ages, between Christ's first and second comings. Bayer defines lament as the cry out of the depths that flows from faith and challenges God to keep his promise to renew creation in the midst of the contradiction of that promise experienced all around us. Bayer reminds us that we do not lament alone, but that all creation groans with us for renewal and that God himself in Christ stands in solidarity with us in lament.

A robust theology of lament is absolutely essential for the life of the church in the world today. Lament is no *a priori* abstraction of philosophical theodicy. It flows, instead, from the real experience of faith lived in the midst of contradiction. Lament is the cry of authentic faith to the God of promise in a fallen world and a ruptured age.

The individual believer is not alone in lament but is joined by the groaning creation, the God incarnate in Christ who takes our suffering and death upon himself, and the church that is the body of Christ lived out in solidarity in lament. That solidarity takes the form of corporate confession,

---

who are helping." Often in the midst of tragedies those who are helping are Christians motivated by a deep faith to love and serve their neighbors as God in Christ has loved them. See Schulten, "Look for the Helpers." Schulten contributed this piece as a photo essay commending those rendering aid in the aftermath of Hurricane Harvey, a tragedy to which many Lutherans responded with gifts of time, talents, and treasures.

55. Harrison, "Theology for Mercy," 28.

praise, and petition in the liturgy; of service that believers render to their neighbors; of the proclamation of the promised answer to lament through the pastoral office; and through corporate acts of mercy the church renders in times of chaos and tragedy.

In the midst of lament, it may be tempting to give up on the fulfillment of God's promised renewal of creation, the end of all suffering, and the complete undoing of death. We as God's people in Christ are still pilgrims and live in a world wracked by brokenness and death. We do not, however, wait alone. For the one who has conquered corruption and death stands with us, giving us his promise and his very self to us to sustain us.

Still, living by a promise in a broken world where the contradiction of that promise is everywhere may seem laughable, as it did when Jesus spoke it at the death of Jairus's daughter. In a sermon I recently heard on the raising of Jairus's daughter, entitled "Laughing at Jesus," Pastor Steven Bielenberg explained how the solidarity of God in Christ meets our lament in the present and answers it with the reaffirmation of his promise that we trust while the world laughs.

> Here on earth, you and I must take comfort in the words of Jesus as he put his arm around Jairus's shoulder and wiped away his tears: *Do not fear, only believe.* Until the Resurrection, we can't afford to laugh at his promise. . . . As we go through our own difficulty or grief or temptation, Jesus is the one who stands next to us in the crowd. We may feel like we can't move either, but Jesus is the one who says, *Do not fear, only believe.* He knows when we are afraid, and he knows he's given us something we can believe in. He has given us himself.[56]

As Pastor Bielenberg proclaims to us, the same Jesus who stood with his arm around Jairus at his daughter's death stands in solidarity with us in our lament. Yet, this same Jesus, who is true God and true man, also defeated death and while he laments with us in this age, he also gives us the very substance of the age to come: his very self. For there could be no greater sustenance for us pilgrims who live by faith on this side of the eschaton than what he gives us: "Take, eat; this is my body, broken for you. Take, drink; this is my blood, shed for you." Here we find the ultimate comfort and solidarity on this side of eternity. Here, at the Sacrament of the Altar, we find our fellow brothers and sisters, the re-opened creation, and Christ himself all in solidarity with us in our lament. Here the almighty God calls us together as his lamenting children and knits us together as one body as he re-opens the creation again with his "*Ephphatha!*" forgiving our sins, defeating our death,

---

56. Bielenberg, "Laughing at Jesus," 4–5.

and giving us the substance of the eternal life that he has won for us. In this vale of tears, this gift, this promise is worth holding onto as we stand in the solidarity of lament with those who weep.

I wish to express my congratulations to Oswald Bayer on his eightieth birthday and my heartfelt gratitude for the kindness that he has shown to me.

Bibliography

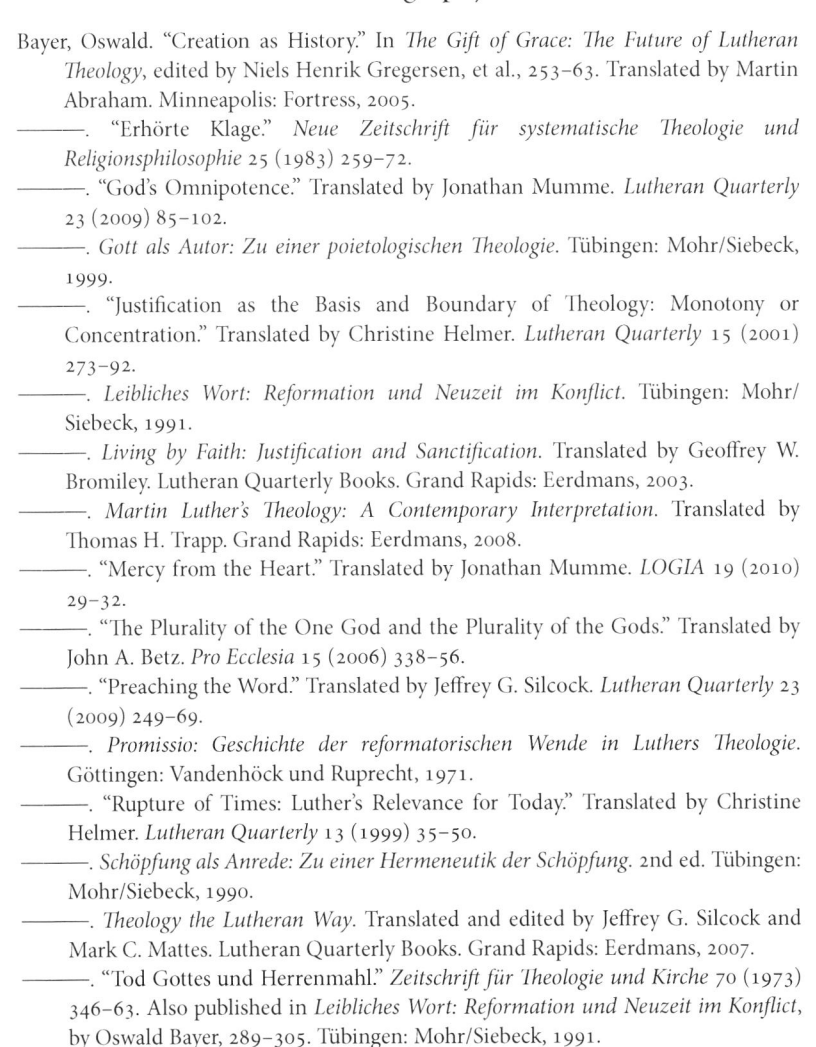

Bayer, Oswald. "Creation as History." In *The Gift of Grace: The Future of Lutheran Theology*, edited by Niels Henrik Gregersen, et al., 253–63. Translated by Martin Abraham. Minneapolis: Fortress, 2005.

———. "Erhörte Klage." *Neue Zeitschrift für systematische Theologie und Religionsphilosophie* 25 (1983) 259–72.

———. "God's Omnipotence." Translated by Jonathan Mumme. *Lutheran Quarterly* 23 (2009) 85–102.

———. *Gott als Autor: Zu einer poietologischen Theologie*. Tübingen: Mohr/Siebeck, 1999.

———. "Justification as the Basis and Boundary of Theology: Monotony or Concentration." Translated by Christine Helmer. *Lutheran Quarterly* 15 (2001) 273–92.

———. *Leibliches Wort: Reformation und Neuzeit im Konflikt*. Tübingen: Mohr/Siebeck, 1991.

———. *Living by Faith: Justification and Sanctification*. Translated by Geoffrey W. Bromiley. Lutheran Quarterly Books. Grand Rapids: Eerdmans, 2003.

———. *Martin Luther's Theology: A Contemporary Interpretation*. Translated by Thomas H. Trapp. Grand Rapids: Eerdmans, 2008.

———. "Mercy from the Heart." Translated by Jonathan Mumme. *LOGIA* 19 (2010) 29–32.

———. "The Plurality of the One God and the Plurality of the Gods." Translated by John A. Betz. *Pro Ecclesia* 15 (2006) 338–56.

———. "Preaching the Word." Translated by Jeffrey G. Silcock. *Lutheran Quarterly* 23 (2009) 249–69.

———. *Promissio: Geschichte der reformatorischen Wende in Luthers Theologie*. Göttingen: Vandenhöck und Ruprecht, 1971.

———. "Rupture of Times: Luther's Relevance for Today." Translated by Christine Helmer. *Lutheran Quarterly* 13 (1999) 35–50.

———. *Schöpfung als Anrede: Zu einer Hermeneutik der Schöpfung*. 2nd ed. Tübingen: Mohr/Siebeck, 1990.

———. *Theology the Lutheran Way*. Translated and edited by Jeffrey G. Silcock and Mark C. Mattes. Lutheran Quarterly Books. Grand Rapids: Eerdmans, 2007.

———. "Tod Gottes und Herrenmahl." *Zeitschrift für Theologie und Kirche* 70 (1973) 346–63. Also published in *Leibliches Wort: Reformation und Neuzeit im Konflikt*, by Oswald Bayer, 289–305. Tübingen: Mohr/Siebeck, 1991.

———. "Toward a Theology of Lament." In *Caritas et Reformatio*, edited by Carter Lindberg and David Whitford, 211–20. Translated by Matthias Gockel. St. Louis: Concordia, 2002.

———. "What Is Evangelical? The Continuing Validity of the Reformation." Translated by Jeffrey G. Silcock. *Lutheran Quarterly* 25 (2011) 1–15.

———. *Zugesagte Gegenwart*. Tübingen: Mohr/Siebeck, 2007.

Bielenberg, Steven. "Laughing at Jesus: Mark 5:21, ff." Sermon delivered at King of Kings Lutheran Church, Roseville, MN, July 1, 2018.

Chan, Michael J., and Joshua C. Miller. "Prayer that Prevails." *Word and World* 35 (2015) 31–39.

Giertz, Bo. *Romans: A Devotional Commentary*. Translated by Bror Erickson. Irvine, CA: Fifteen-Seventeen, NRP, 2018.

Golden, Kevin. "Responding to Evil within God's Good Creation." In *The Mercy of God in the Cross of Christ: Essays in Honor of Glenn Merritt*, edited by Ross Edward Johnson and John T. Pless, 47–55. St. Louis, MO: Lutheran Church—Missouri Synod, 2016.

Harrison, Matthew C. "Being Active in Mercy." In *Mercy in Action: Essays on Mercy, Human Care, and Disaster Response*, edited by Ross Edward Johnson, 37–43. St. Louis: Lutheran Church—Missouri Synod, 2015.

———. "Introduction." In *Mercy in Action: Essays on Mercy, Human Care, and Disaster Response*, edited by Ross Edward Johnson, 11–12. St. Louis, MO: Lutheran Church—Missouri Synod, 2015.

———. "Theology for Mercy." In *Mercy in Action: Essays on Mercy, Human Care, and Disaster Response*, edited by Ross Edward Johnson, 27–30. St. Louis, MO: Lutheran Church—Missouri Synod, 2015.

Johnson, Jeremiah. "Learning to Lament: Preaching to Suffering the Lament Psalms." In *Feasting in a Famine of the Word: Lutheran Preaching in the Twenty-First Century*, edited by Mark W. Birkholz, et al., 225–40. Eugene, OR: Pickwick, 2016.

Kittleson, James. *Luther the Reformer: The Story of the Man and His Career*. Minneapolis: Fortress, 2003.

Miller, Joshua C. "Between Openness and Hiddenness: The *Simul* of the Sighing Creation." *Logia* 25 (2016) 27–31.

———. *Hanging by a Promise: The Hidden God in the Theology of Oswald Bayer*. Eugene, OR: Pickwick, 2015.

Paulson, Steven D. *Lutheran Theology*. London: T. & T. Clark, 2011.

Pless, John T. "Answering the 'Why' Question: Martin Luther on Human Suffering and God's Mercy." In *Mercy in Action: Essays on Mercy, Human Care, and Disaster Response*, edited by Ross Edward Johnson, 45–55. St. Louis, MO: Lutheran Church—Missouri Synod, 2015.

Scaer, David P. "The Concept of *Anfechtung* in Luther's Thought." *Concordia Theological Quarterly* 47 (1983) 15–30.

Schuluten, Katherine. "Look for the Helpers." *New York Times*, August 30, 2017. www.nytimes.com/2017/08/30/learning/look-for-the-helpers.html.

Tranvik, Mark D. *Martin Luther and the Called Life*. Minneapolis: Fortress, 2016.

Wingren, Gustaf. *Luther on Vocation*. Translated by Carl C. Rasmussen. 1957. Reprint, Eugene, OR: Wipf & Stock, 2004.

9

The Eschatology of Forgiveness

James Arne Nestingen

In John 20:19–23, John's account of Jesus's first appearance to his disciples following his crucifixion, Jesus correlates forgiveness with the resurrection. Suddenly appearing among them where they have hidden themselves, he bids the disciples present a double measure of peace, breathes on them the breath of the new creation, and sends them with the authority to forgive and retain sins.

The traditional associations of forgiveness are altogether absent. There are no references to guilt or moral failing; repentance goes unmentioned; the authority of absolution is released untethered to any established office. Risen from the dead, Jesus urgently moves to commission his fear-driven disciples in the power of the Holy Spirit, in the power of this word, to bring in all and sundry.

It is possible on the basis of this reading of John 20 to see a different dimension of the forgiveness. Usually, it is spoken of therapeutically. Whether in ignorance or passion, a sinner has lost himself or herself and so stands under indictment, either privately within the self or publicly, in the community. As therapy, forgiveness offers a way, accompanied by repentance and resolution to improvement, to restoration. In John 20, in relation to the resurrection itself, forgiveness has an eschatological character. Absolution declares the inbreaking power of Christ and asserts his power over the new creation as complete unto itself.

The purpose of this paper, written in thanksgiving to Oswald Bayer for his penetrating studies of Luther, is to explore the eschatological character of forgiveness in the theology of the Reformer. The contention is that when forgiveness breaks out of its therapeutic dimensions into its eschatological connections, the absolution can be declared as the present expression of the resurrection.

Further Notes on John 20:19–23

The disciples are not subjected to the same scrutiny in John's Gospel that they receive in the Synoptics. Peter's three-fold betrayal is recounted; Jesus entrusts his mother to the beloved disciple, a peculiarity of John. But there is no sweeping indictment, as in Mark: "They all forsook him and fled" (Mark 14:50). Mark's description provides no basis in John's narrative for ascribing guilt to the disciples.

John does, however, mention the fears of the disciples. Given the unfolding of the passion account, these fears would have undoubtedly found a serious basis. Indicting Jesus as an insurgent, the authorities would have had solid basis for sweeping up his companions and putting them to the same fate. There was reason to be afraid.

But the contrast is striking: while Jesus was being called forth from his grave, the disciples were burying themselves behind whatever protections they could find. Jesus doesn't stop to consider the irony. Instead, he knows exactly where to look, appears there and, without a moment's hesitation, goes right through the wall to get them. This may have been more practical than miraculous—knocking on the door of a roomful of frightened men would have been more likely to produce blockade than welcome. Clearly, bearing the fruit of the resurrection, Jesus wasn't going to be stopped.

Jesus's greeting, the twice stated "peace be with you," could be taken as a statement of the absolution in a traditional formulation. But it appears in this context to have been stated, and repeated, to calm the apprehensions raised by his appearance from the grave. Predicted or not, that would have compounded the terror already present.

Confronting the disciples, Jesus tips their heads back and breathes life into them, just as God breathed life into the dust that became Adam in the first creation. Jesus breathes the breath of life into disciples so that he can authorize them, call and commission them to the declaration of his life-giving word.

It is fundamental to note here that this word is not guilt-dependent. Neither does it require a sensitive conscience, real or imagined. Its reference is not to the past but to the future Christ is creating. In this, the word is sufficient unto itself, bestowing what it declares. Blown on the breath of God, as

Article V of the Augsburg Confession states, this word creates faith "when and where he pleases in those who hear the gospel."[1]

The forgiveness granted is eschatological in a double sense. To begin with, it declares Christ's intervention in the chains of cause and effect, resolution and disappointment, planning and failure that bind the self to itself. In the sacred absolution, the self is no longer its own project, swept up in tides of resentment and retribution, resolution and withdrawal. God's life-giving word creates it anew in the freedom of the gospel.

This forgiveness is eschatological further in that it gives the believer a place in God's redemption of the creation. The resurrection was not merely revivification. It is manifestation of the authority invested in Christ Jesus to make all things new. Raised from the dead, Jesus goes on to overturn his enemies and to bring in a new heaven and a new earth. His beneficiaries are in Paul's word, "the first fruits of them that have fallen asleep" (1 Cor 15:20.)

Therapeutic Forgiveness

In the Smalcald Articles, Luther describes elements of the movement from attrition to contrition to confession of actual sin that can be put together as follows. Attrition is an inchoate suspicion in relation to other people, to life as a whole or to God, that something has gone wrong. Just about anything—a wisp of memory, frustration at work or in the family, apprehension about current conditions—can raise this suspicion. But at the level of attrition, it remains vague, with no specific focus. Something is out of whack, out of place, not quite right. Asked about the problem, people in attrition have trouble identifying it. "What's wrong? Oh, nothing, I'm not sure, but I don't feel right for some reason."

Attrition becomes contrition when the law enters to confirm the difficulty. This is the chief purpose or office of the law, as Luther calls it, to identify sin. *Lex semper accusat*—"the foremost office or purpose of the law is that it reveals inherited sin and its fruit."[2] The accusation may come from one of the commandments. But it can also spring from a disappointment in relationships or, commonly, out of conflict with someone close. Whereas attrition remains vague, contrition develops out of the specifics when the law, like a doctor, makes a diagnosis: "here is the trouble." Luther distinguishes this from active contrition, which the self works within itself when it knows

---

1. *BOC* 40.
2. *BOC* 312.

it should feel bad. Passive contrition, in contrast, is worked in the self by the law. It is a "true affliction, suffering and the pain of death."[3]

This is the hallmark of self-loss. Attrition leaves the sense that there is something that can be done, some as-of-yet unrealized possibility. Under the force of the law, contrition closes down exposing the plight-there is no way out. This is the law's driving, as Luther calls it, in which the sinner gets stripped of alternatives. As the sinner under the accusation of the law sees it, there is literally no further possibility. Having lost its perceived alternatives, the sinner dies to himself/herself. Something, someone external is needed, namely, Christ Jesus.

Neither attrition nor contrition necessarily leads to the gospel. A self under the accusation of the law tries anything or everything, sorting through false absolutions that momentarily relieve the pressure while leaving the troubling circumstances in place. If the law is going to lead to the gospel, the gospel has to overlap the law, confirming the indictment while declaring it, in Christ, without standing.

This happens classically in the absolution: "Your sins are forgiven for Jesus's sake." The first words, "your sins," confirm the law's accusation, underscoring the sinner's predicament. The gospel is not an illusion—it offers no cheap alternatives. Only sinners are forgiven—the accusation has to be registered. This is the gospel's bite.

But the accusation confirmed, the very next words declare it to be without standing: "Your sins are forgiven for Jesus sake." Christ Jesus takes the accusation upon himself, soaking it up in his blood, to free the sinner from the self. For the believer, atonement happens in and through the word.

In this way as Luther says, the gospel "offers help in many ways." It bursts open, like a cornucopia of grace, pouring out its blessings. Often, as Gustaf Wingren after Gustaf Aulen emphasized, the gospel describes the victory Christ has won over sin, death, and the power of the devil. Becoming incarnate in the flesh and blood of a man, Christ took on humanity to break into the thrall, where sinners have been bound. But unlike Adam, he kept the faith even as death obliterated him on the cross. The resurrection vindicates his death, manifesting him as Lord of all. He is the victor. In word and sacrament, he shares the fruits of victory—deliverance from sin, death, and the devil. In the explanation of the second article of the Apostles Creed in the Small Catechism, Luther uses the New Testament language of substitution or ransom. "He has redeemed me, a lost and condemned person, delivered and freed me from all sins, from death and the power of the devil, not with silver and gold but with his holy and precious blood and

---

3. *BOC* 312.

his innocent sufferings and death, in order that I may be his, live under him in his kingdom and serve him."

As Luther's explanation makes clear, substitutionary atonement is not a theological abstraction which takes place far away, in heaven, but Christ's down to earth deliverance of the sinner, as real as his bloody death.

Freed from himself and its grasping dreads, the sinner under the power of the word can go back to the point where things have broken down to make amends and begin anew. The Holy Spirit does not leave the self hanging in inactivity, suspended between death and life. Slaying, he simultaneously raises, bringing forth the new self which delights in Creator, creation and creatures. The lost is found.

It is in this sense that forgiveness can be spoken of as therapeutic or remedial. The original problem is what Luther calls "actual sin." Trouble has erupted in defining relationships, leaving people out of sorts with creature and Creator. The law exposes the fault, moving the sinner with the support of the gospel to repentance that in turn creates faith and renewal.

Eschatological Forgiveness

In his explanation of the Lord's Supper in the Small Catechism, Luther poses the question of gifts, "What are the benefits of such eating and drinking?" He answers by describing forgiveness eschatologically. "The words 'given for you' and 'shed for you for the forgiveness of sin' show us that forgiveness of sin, life and salvation are given to us in the sacrament through these words, because where there is forgiveness of sin there is also life and salvation."[4]

Eschatologically, forgiveness turns the sinner from the past to the future. Adam and Eve can breathe again. What they so desperately sought, attempting to become their own creators, blows out of Christ's nostrils in the means of grace as he goes ahead to bring in a new future. Likewise, salvation is bestowed—sin, death, and the devil have lost the final word. In Christ, the future opens in grace, new each day in the power of the resurrection.

Thus, there are no references in Luther's explanation to the old conflicts, penance, or new resolves. Christ has taken, is taking care of all of that. Even the *simul*, which describes the necessary conflicts of life in faith, is left unmarked. A new future has dawned in which Christ Jesus unfolds the future out of his hands.

Though there are no conditions stated, forgiveness in its eschatological character certainly does not eliminate repentance. Rather, in the light of

4. *BOC* 362.

grace, under the power of the gospel, the sinner can finally see what he or she is being delivered from—the utter power and corruption of original sin. So, Psalm 51, traditionally ascribed to David: "I was born guilty and in sin did my mother conceive me" (Ps 51:5).

To be sure, the powers that have been so decisively broken in the cross and the resurrection will not surrender so easily. They have lost their finality but there is still enough left in them to keep faith in contention. Theologically, it will have to be said that faith lives under the sign of the cross, amidst humiliations and defeats, contradictions and uncertainties.

Yet, sustained by Christ, faith stands in the hope of a new future promised for the whole creation. Luther saved some of his most beautiful imagery to speak of the justification that is the contemporary equivalent of the forgiveness of sins. In Christ, God makes us what Adam and Eve were meant to be, only better—the better not referring to a moral quality but to faith. In Christ, God brings us back to the point from which Adam and Eve fell. We become now the joyful and content creatures of the earth which Adam and Eve were meant to be.

Sounding the background of such great words comes the beat of an even greater promise: a new heaven and a new earth where the tears that inevitably accompany sin and death no longer flow. He will dwell in us then, Creator and creatures joined in the bond of faith on its way to sight. What has now begun will be eschatologically complete.

10

On Swearing and Certainty

STEVEN PAULSON

At the apex of his appeal to Erasmus in *The Bondage of the Will* Luther diagnosed the ailment of his adversary: "For uncertainty is the most miserable thing in the world."[1] But as miserable as uncertainty is, Luther found that it ends in "five little letters" (F-A-I-T-H). This absolute trust was unknown both to his and Erasmus's teachers.[2] The logicians were preoccupied with certainty in the form of the syllogism; monastics were preoccupied with the experience of humility. Both lost sight of faith as anything other than the antechamber of truth or love. Once Luther understood Paul's (and the Johannine) meaning of πληροφορία faith ceased being the poor whipping boy of reason or humility, since certainty was not inside, but outside the thinking person, and of all things, in a promise. Whenever God makes a promise he necessarily and indubitably keeps it since he cannot lie. So F-A-I-T-H conjoins W-O-R-D to tell us what is certain—and what certainty is.

Peter blurted out the matter of faith's certainty after the apparent debacle of Jesus's "I am the bread" speech at Capernaum that horrified its earnest hearers and left Jesus with only a handful of disciples. Jesus then asked the despondent remnant: "Do you want to go away as well?" What were they to do? Peter was constrained to confess faith once all possibilities were removed: "Lord, to whom shall we go?" Just so, the misery of uncertainty ceases once necessity excludes choices and gives the one certain thing: "You have the words of eternal life, and we have believed, and have come to know, that you are the Holy One of God" (John 6:67–69). Belief and knowledge

---

1. *LW* 33:23; WA 18:605.

2. Luther's later reference to the "five letters" F-A-I-T-H is the same as his initial discovery of *fides specialis* used in opposition to Cajetan at Augsburg in 1518, and reported in Bayer, *Promissio*, 194–97.

merge as faith and promise (words of eternal life) once laws of logic or humility (the words of death) are removed.

Faith Seeking Understanding

This explains why the common theological way of interpreting Peter's simple conjunction ("we have believed *and* come to know") is opposite Luther's. The "and" normally accords with the scholastic teaching that had sprung from Anselm's *faith seeks understanding*; "so to my mind it appears a neglect if, after we are established in the faith, we do not seek to understand what we believe."[3] Anselm's conjunction assumes there is something missing in faith that only thinking can supply. He assumes faith requires a free will that constantly encounters God's law, but whose outcomes are uncertain. While knowledge must be certain, faith operates in the lower, conflicted realm of "possibilities" for its own good. Likewise, a monk's praying requires free possibilities to enable the choice of abject humility. Thus, in order to preserve its freedom, faith's primary feature is uncertainty. Contrariwise, reason's integrity is preserved only when uncertainty is removed because reason describes the nature of God's unchanging law. Luther and Erasmus were both steeped in this teaching at the schools and monasteries. Reason is definite, settled, positive and fixed; faith is indefinite, unsure, unknown, and variable. Reason lays down the law and the free will associated with faith determines to obey or disobey that law.

This assumption produces the opposite of Peter's "faith and knowledge" so that as long as philosophy operates without Luther's special F-A-I-T-H, the misery of uncertainty keeps recurring. Over a century later this was evidenced in the letters on certainty passed between the Bishop of Worcester and John Locke (1696), along with summary of the exchange from Leibniz (1699). More recently, the matter of certainty was raised by G.E. Moore's reply to Kant (1939): "I know for certain this is my hand," followed by Wittgenstein's (1950–51) response to Moore that denies the possibility of private language.

In the earlier case, Leibniz agreed with the Bishop of Worcester's complaint: every time people think they have something like a "clear and distinct" idea (Descartes)—including whether or not the soul is eternal or that God exists—they end up referring to their own insides for assurance—the inner assurance.[4] Wittgenstein later parodied this conundrum as an impos-

---

3. Anselm, *Cur Deus Homo*, 1.2.

4. "Appealing (even in philosophy and especially as regards ideas) to their own

sible "private language," and the inevitable acceptance or rejection of any proposition on the basis of the proposer's own faithfulness.[5]

In one way we would disagree with Wittgenstein by saying that private language is not only possible, but common since people routinely talk to themselves in a functioning language as an "other" (as my own teacher Paul Ricoeur must conclude in his *Oneself as Other*), and derive their greatest assurances by what seem to them like clear ideas—and perhaps even distinct ones. However, the broader point is definitely the case—that knowledge's certainty always ends up inside the self in just the way Luther encountered enthusiasts. Leibniz's favorite example of this private language, which is necessarily always consigned to uncertainty, is Descartes's proposition that body as "extension" is at least clear, if not distinct—but only as a self-reference: "I perceive or think." But as the good Bishop of Worcester had observed to Locke, this way of verifying ideas (certainty) always devolves into taking Descartes's word for it, and the philosopher never seems as trustworthy to others as he does to himself.

Something similar to Descartes's private language recurred in the reply to the Bishop based on Locke's (admittedly shaky) "lay" exegesis of the King James translation of Hebrews 10:22: "Let us draw near with a true heart in *full assurance* of faith." Assuming that this English translation had as much "spiritual testimony" as the original Greek πληροφορία (as human beings are fallible liars, English or Greek), Locke was willing to say that faith has *assurance* but only knowledge has certainty: "I find my Bible speaks of the assurance of faith, but nowhere, that I can remember, of the certainty of faith, though in many places it speaks of the certainty of knowledge."[6] Locke figured that faith needed nothing more to "do its good works" than "evidently strong probability."[7] So the Greek word πληροφορία must refer to faith's practical end in good works (the mode of probability), while knowing concerns "demonstration" or necessity of absolute law.

Luther had earlier seen that such efforts were vain. They obscured the real issue of what God is doing outside the law to make both faith and

---

inner testimony and resting their judgements on what they say they experience in themselves" (Leibniz, "Reflections," 29).

5. "If I don't know whether someone has two hands (say, whether they have been amputated or not) I shall believe his assurance that he has two hands, if he is trustworthy. And if he says he knows it, that can only signify to me that he has been able to make sure, and hence that his arms are, e.g., not still concealed by coverings and bandages, etc. etc. My believing the trustworthy man stems from my admitting that it is possible for him to make sure" (Wittgenstein, *On Certainty,* 5).

6. Locke, *Works of John Locke*, 275.

7. Locke, *Works of John Locke*, 299.

knowledge. But few are the ears who have listened to him. Instead, the struggle for certainty ends by binding a fanatic in the inward misery of his uncertainty as it did G. E. Moore arguing that "this is in fact my hand, I am certain that this is my hand." Waving one's hand was to answer Kant's plea in *Critique of Pure Reason*: "It still remains a scandal to philosophy . . . that the existence of things outside of us . . . must be accepted merely on faith, and that, if anyone thinks good to doubt their existence, we are unable to counter his doubts by any satisfactory proof."[8] But this external proof only led to a deeper "skeptical paradox" in Wittgenstein that "when I respond in one way rather than another to such a problem as '68 + 57,' I can have no justification for one response rather than another."[9] Simple addition has no assurance of the token ("+"), even if there were an omniscient God up in heaven counting all the finite computations done from Adam and Eve to the present. In the end, this skeptical paradox concludes that "there can be no such thing as meaning anything by any word."[10]

How does one move from inner, spiritual certainty "accepted only by faith," to something that others can assert with equal certainty at the same time? How do we escape from knowledge itself being fanatic? How can certainty ever become external, since what is external—the word or "token"—cannot by definition have meaning? For Luther this has to do with the difference between an *idea* (Leibniz's "modern" notion arising in the seventeenth century), "term," "token" (like "+") or a proposition (like Moore's "this is my hand") and a *word*.

Kripke must be correct that if we had an omniscient, but silent, God in heaven counting up all the finite computations ever made by human beings, God could himself never be sure about the next computation. All-knowing only means God is a bean counter in heaven who knows how things have gone up to now, but knows nothing of the future. The only thing worse to contemplate than the radical, skeptical paradox is divine necessity. And the only thing worse than divine necessity is something other than a "sleeping God" merely counting computations on earth. But in fact, Luther discovered a most active God who does not wait for humans to add meaning to words, but makes language with external meaning merely by speaking, "For he spoke, and it came to be; he commanded, and it stood firm" (Ps 33:9).

But without a preacher, Wittgenstein is correct that knowing has rules—laws—and knowing is trying to escape the internal fanaticism of an

8. Moore, "Proof," 147.
9. Kripke, *Wittgenstein*, 21.
10. Kripke, *Wittgenstein*, 55.

individual "game." But the only way out of inner certainty is by determining what, if anything, God is bound to by our knowledge: "One is often bewitched by a word. For example, by the word "know." Is God bound by our knowledge? Are a lot of our statements incapable of falsehood? For that is what we want to say. "[11] What we really want by "certainty" of knowledge and "assurance" of faith is to find something that God is bound to by our knowledge. But God is not bound by our knowledge; he is bound, strangely, by faith: "They have neither knowledge nor understanding, they walk about in darkness; all the foundations of the earth are shaken" (Ps 82:5). Indeed, knowledge is certain about only one thing in the inner self: "since through the law comes knowledge of sin" (Rom 3:20).

Knowing is supposedly reserved for whatever is sure, certain, and proved by what God is bound to, and what God cannot possibly escape is law. The super-human attempt to know for certain then binds God not only to the present, but the eternal future by means of this law. Luther found this effort not only futile (a skeptical paradox), but blasphemous.[12] It is not blasphemous that humans rise like Icarus beyond our stations in wanting to know God. It is blasphemous that inner certainty attempts to secure itself externally by binding God to the unchanging law and thereby words are made merely into signs pointing to that law. However, Luther knew this attempt at transcendence not only shackled God—it bound humans to misery. Such knowledge means they are deaf to any word from God that is not law. Meanwhile, faith is more certain than a rigorous proof—even of the certainty of things external to us like an arm or body. It frees the mind rather than binds God by giving faith the one sure, external thing to believe in.

Faith as certainty

Certainty is the primary subject of knowing, while uncertainty is its universal outcome because words themselves appear to be secondary to Locke's "idea." Luther cut his teeth on the powerful examples of Ockham in protecting speech from two ontological mistakes, (1) saying more than we can know about universals, and (2) saying more than we know by means of a proposition—especially non-modal, present tense properties that assert something indicative like, "this is an angel," or "this is my hand." But Luther saw that the simple desire for truth in propositions hid its underlying bound God. If Scripture gives a command, "You are to have no other gods," surely the old

11. Kripke, *Wittgenstein*, 35.
12. *LW* 33:44; WA 18:620.

assumption was correct that faith must doubt in order to secure the future for free will. Yet, Luther saw that the command did not open the future; it closed it once and for all in regard to this very free will. The command said nothing certain about the future. But when Scripture uttered a promise—"I forgive you"—it opened the future to something other than free will.

Not least in Luther's step beyond propositions was the concern of the nominalists as to whether the term "law" is an extra-mental reference to a real, existing "universal," or whether this term "law" referred to a secondary intention—a *sign*—that inevitably points to individuals in nature (and so ultimately to God). Eventually Luther asked what happened to the law/God when the keys to the kingdom were applied. What, or who, is "God" in the strange utterance of absolution? That word of forgiveness did not seem to bind God and our future to law, but loosened both God and law. That led Luther to discover that the misery of uncertainty was not resolved, as expected, by knowing—but by faith. Unexpectedly, faith lived in the mode of necessity—knowledge in the mode of possibility. Everything had been turned around. It is one thing to determine "I know this is my hand," but another to say, "I believe Christ when he says to me, 'This is my body given for you.'" The heart of Scripture is not a proposition, but a promise, "the just shall live by faith alone" (Rom 1:17), or more basically, "I am the Lord Your God" (Exod 20:2).

At first it seems strange that Christians would agree with the frightening conclusion that simple propositions like "this is my hand," are not sure—but then turn around to say, "I forgive you," is necessarily true without any doubt. Faith is then more certain, not less, than thought or feeling.

God's Oath (Genesis 22:16)

In faith, God ceases being the external existence of the law as either an individual or an extra-mental universal. He is not apprehended by means of a logical proposition, but "as he has revealed himself and condescended to speak and deal with us in human fashion."[13] How does God speak and deal with us? One of the most dramatic stories in Scripture, Abraham's (near) sacrifice of Isaac, became infinitely more dramatic when God made a promise followed by an astonishing oath: "by Myself, I have sworn, says the Lord" (Gen 22:16). Earlier lectures on Hebrews helped Luther focus on faith, but he failed to understand the impact of this divine oath until his Genesis lectures. There Luther recollected how he had escaped the misery

13. *LW* 4:144; WA 43:240.

of uncertainty, and taught his students how to end the misery of others in "these five letters—F-A-I-T-H." Faith's certainty refuses to bind God to the law, while God shockingly binds himself to his own promise.[14]

God swears to his own word only this once, and Scripture recognized the import by reiterating the phenomenon repeatedly. His single oath guaranteed all future promises, especially those made to David: "The Lord has sworn and will not change his mind," (Ps 110:4); "The Lord swore to David a sure oath from which he will not turn back" (Ps 134:11); "Once for all I have sworn by my holiness; I will not lie to David (Ps 89:35). Other prophets used the guarantee as well: "The Lord of hosts has sworn: 'As I have planned, so shall it be, and as I have purposed, so shall it stand'" (Isa 14:24)—up to the very end of the prophets in Zechariah's Psalm: "the oath which he swore to our father Abraham, to grant us that we, being delivered from the hand of our enemies, might serve him without fear" (Luke 1:73). The full exegesis of the oath is given in Hebrews: "So when God desired to show more convincingly to the heirs of the promise the unchangeable character of his purpose, he interposed with an oath, so that through two unchangeable things, in which it is impossible that God would prove false, we who have fled for refuge might have strong encouragement to seize the hope set before us" (Heb 6:13–20).

The vital words of this exegesis jump off the page—"unchangeable" and "impossible." So, what exactly was this oath uttered by God to Abraham and what has been its effect? In Genesis 22, God had just finished contradicting himself in a most terrifying and glorious way in the sacrifice of Isaac. When Abraham's excruciating preparations for the sacrifice were complete and the sacrifice began, the angel's voice interrupted with: "Do no lay your hand on the boy." Instead, a ram was provided and so the place was called "the Lord will see" (which is the more likely meaning than the "Lord will be seen" [Gen 22:14]), since from that moment God intended one thing only—to fulfill his own promise. So the angel/preacher called to Abraham a "second time from heaven and said: 'By Myself I have sworn,' says the Lord" (Gen 22:15–16). In this single moment, God directly swore to his own promise: "By your Seed shall all the nations of the earth be blessed" (Gen 18).

Why swear? The oath, Luther recognized, answers the question of who God is, or his person (systematically, the doctrine of God). But further, it explains what this God does. He rescues sinners from the misery of uncertainty—and so the majestic article of God's being is united with the chief article of justification, or "these five letters—F-A-I-T-H."[15] Yet faith

---

14. *LW* 4:142–43; WA 43:238.
15. *LW* 4:149; WA 43:243.

can remain five letters on a page unless the words are preached off the page so that faith is made. That is the first point of Paul's: "the letter kills, the Spirit gives life" (2 Cor 3:6). The other point is exactly how the Spirit gives life in the down-to-earth, incarnate, external words—in this case through God's irrevocable swearing. Thus, these two things, God's swearing and Abraham's faith, teach us what we mean by our two key words: certain and certainty. What is certain, if anything? Where and how does the misery of my own uncertainty end?

Swearing's common usage

For a moment, ordinary language re-emerged from obscurity with figures like Wittgenstein, Ryle, Austin, and Moore as a way of disentangling scholastic attempts to create an ideal language using sure and certain syllogisms. Unfortunately, it fell out of favor as quickly as it rose, but Luther remains always interested in our common use of the word "swear." At crucial moments in life people swear or take an oath, like when they are about to provide testimony in a court trial: "I swear that I will tell the truth, the whole truth, and nothing but the truth, so help me God" (with the sign of laying the hand on the Bible). To a promise is added a vow, pledge, bond, or guarantee that makes one's future act/word a solemn, sober, grave matter—indeed a matter of life and death. More than this, swearing turns the promise of a future act into a sacred confession; the momentary matter is reckoned in relation to the conscience's final judgment before God. Luther observed, "Our people have the custom to swear 'by their troth,' and 'upon their soul.'"[16] In so swearing, people transfer their earthly cause to the eternal effect it has on their *souls*. Suddenly, when we swear, our words are not trivial. We are no longer merely observing or offering an opinion, but making a promise that determines the soul's eternal future.

That means this speech is none other than swearing *by God*. It is *transcendence*, and so theology proper. Oaths implicate God in our utterance, whether one says "as God is my witness," or "on my mother's grave." At the crucial moment, we reach for our highest authority and proffer our own eternal judgment to ensure that our promise is backed by everything we have—including the eternal soul, and God too. All chips are in on this bet. The oath is thus really a sublime prayer, especially by those who have no notion of talking to God when they make it, and our best human attempt to secure the future.

16. *LW* 4:142; WA 43:238.

By the same token, our common practice of swearing is a self-imprecation—the turning of one's prayer inward, or invocation, offering the whole self and its eternal future as collateral for this single moment's promise. I curse myself if I lie in order to seal the promise; I offer myself as collateral for the promise that I hereby make. This is philosophy's "existential" moment, or bottom line: I am hereby making the ultimate sacrifice—myself. There isn't anything more I can say, do, give or offer; the buck stops here—you can be certain. Once one swears, there is nothing more to say.

It is no surprise, then, that swearing becomes a legal issue with all sorts of consequences for falsehood. Swearing is also tied to one's justification before God, and so became a bone of contention among the fanatics who departed from Luther on this very point. They refused to take an earthly oath because they could not differentiate their own oath from God's in the form of the gospel promise. It is common language's limitation to think of swearing or oaths only as a legal act, and so when God makes an oath it must be an act of fulfilling God's law. Jesus explained the matter in the Sermon on the Mount: "But I say to you: do not swear at all, either by heaven, for it is the throne of God, or by the earth. And do not swear by your head, for you cannot make one hair white or black" (Matt 5:35–36). Yet this is simply stating the truth of the law itself as it has been given to humans. The law always accuses because taking an oath "by the hairs, by heaven or by earth," means the creature has taken an oath for the future precisely "by something that is not ours, by what is not in our power."[17] The creature is not God, and so every creature's promise fails—along with his swearing. Jesus is not explaining how Christians can successfully fulfill the law—by not swearing. He is presenting the necessary contrast between human promises and divine. When you swear by your soul or by God, your self-imprecation necessarily fails.

God's Uncommon Usage

Yet in direct disregard for this common rule, God utters his own oath to seal his *promise*, not a command. God proceeds to do exactly what we cannot—swearing by himself—and providing the sacrifice that he momentarily demanded of Abraham. Only this time, the swearing actually works. Human swearing intends to be truthful, but lies because swearing on one's soul or a mother's grave ends with one's own death. We cannot control the future even by swearing. For that reason, swearing has a bad reputation and

17. *LW* 4:142; WA 43:238.

comes to mean the opposite of a guarantee or assurance. Swearing becomes cursing, or vulgarizing, our own statements and diminishes the object of our oath by shock and offence. Children are taught not to swear since oaths vulgarize rather than valorize a promise. In common language, swearing and cursing do not mean "I'm guaranteeing something," but "I am blaspheming it," as in, "he is swearing like a sailor." Oaths are thus discredited in the misery of uncertainty.

But when God swears he swears by himself. Who else is higher upon whom one can base the oath? If God were merely one more human swearing by himself it would defeat the purpose. Like us, God would then be utterly sincere but unable to bring about his promise, since he sleeps while the future is both unknown and uncontrollable. Yet, when God swears by himself to Abraham, he achieves the purpose of the oath and does not blaspheme. God's promise is his, and entirely within his power, since the future is God's proper domain. In contrast to common language, "the fact that God swears by himself is something great and wonderful,"[18] because it reveals his heart and what he is determined to attain. This was what the author of Hebrews noted in his exegesis of the oath when he determined to forsake "milk" for "solid food" by taking up the *two unchangeable things* of God's promise and oath to Abraham. Human oaths reveal one's deepest desire. Just so, God's oath opens his otherwise hidden heart in its burning, inexpressible love, and to our astonishment God burns for our salvation. Human love wants to possess its object, but God's love burns until it makes justice where there was none, and so we see that God is not only giving a promise to Abraham, but declares that he is here "offering Myself as a pledge."[19] God's heart is not merely a self-expression, a "revelation" to the outside world; it is the Holy Spirit's power to create what is not there. God's Spirit uses his word to make the future rather than simply fall into it. Paul makes the same point with the same words: "that is why it depends on faith, in order that the promise may rest on grace and be guaranteed . . . who gives life to the dead and calls into existence the things that do not exist" (Rom 4:16–17).

By offering himself as pledge, God accomplishes two things at once. First, he speaks directly to Abraham to produce the faith Abraham cannot. Second, that faith needs something to believe in, and so outside of Abraham's inner trust God makes a promise from nothing—outside any rule, law or order. One cannot get more external or more certain. Thus, God self-authorizes this same promise from nothing. There is no greater assurance to offer, no higher step to take, than to give himself as both promise and

---

18. *LW* 4:142; WA 43:238.
19. *LW* 4:143; WA 43:238.

pledge. In swearing, God has reached the nadir and end—"there is nothing greater than I." He gives himself as promise, then seals it by pledging himself as the only final pledge, loan, collateral, indemnity, backing and guarantee that such a promise could ever afford.

Of course, pledging like this depends upon whether God's relation to the future is changeable or unchangeable. Joining pledge to promise is much more than a natural event in history or the capstone of an official arrangement between trading parties; it is God expressing his "heart burning with inexpressible love."[20] Here God is in *extremis*, not because he has reached the end of his powers but because we are seeing those powers' apogee. Revelation is too small a word for what God is doing here. The common expression in theology that grace is God's *self-giving gift* undershoots his burning love because the gift is precisely for sinners. There is nothing God desires more than to make his promise to the unworthy—and keep it himself, "as though God were saying: 'I desire so greatly to be believed and long so intensely to have My words trusted that I am not only making a promise but am offering Myself as a pledge. I have nothing greater to give as a pledge, because as surely as I am God there is nothing greater than I. If I do not keep My promises, *I shall no longer be He who I am*."[21]

This is simply astounding. God makes a promise, then pledges himself—since there is nothing greater to pin his promise upon than himself. This is the only proper meaning of Anselm's *that than which nothing greater can be thought*. God's love operates outside the boundary of the law altogether, which makes it burn, and so pledges his own existence/essence in the deeply personal and down-to-earth, love/pledge: "If I do not keep My promises, I will—in the future—no longer be who I am." In this oath, God lays out the proper exegesis for the later encounter with Moses at the burning bush: "I am" and "I will be who I will be" (Exod 3:14).

God is not speaking as an unchanging essence or being, but saying he will not abandon his word in any possible future. God could have sworn on the basis of something else—even of all creation or the cosmos itself: "I shall sooner let heaven, the earth, the sun, the moon, and the very beautiful structure of the entire world [that is the eternal law] perish than permit My promise to become of no effect."[22] But in this pledge, God proves he is not bound to the law because he is not legal in essence. The unfaithful naturally believe that God could not swear to anything higher than the good order of the world, or the law itself. What more could he, or we, possibly lose than

20. *LW* 4:143; WA 43:238.
21. *LW* 4:143; WA 43:238 (emphasis added).
22. *LW* 4:143; WA 43:238.

the rules of any language game, or the substance and order of the universe? But beauty and order are not what God offers as the highest assurance of his fealty. It is not creation, but the Creator who is the ground—in himself, by himself, for himself—but even more, *as he speaks to us*.

God has put himself on the line, having no greater collateral on which to enter his bet for the future than this: *If I do not keep my promises*. What then? What consequence shall follow this utterance? What is the penalty for not keeping the promise he himself made? His own life! *I shall no longer be He who I am*. God will not only give up the future, but the future will no longer have him. God is saying it is not his eternal law that makes him who he is, but the astounding fact that I am not, or will not be myself without giving this promise and keeping the same. Although Abraham did not know it, the promise of the Seed would come to the impossible and shocking "single word" of the incarnate, crucified, raised Jesus Christ at the moment of his betrayal by Judas: "I am he" (John 18:5),[23] that is, the keeper of this promise to Abraham.

God Enlarges His Promise

God not only shows his burning heart by swearing, but is not discomposed by knowing exactly to whom he promises: "You, man, are fickle, inconstant, and changeable; therefore I am adding my own oath."[24] It is precisely the sinner's inconstancy that moves God not only to promise, but pledge. It is marvelous enough that God swears to cease being himself apart from his promise, but it is much more astonishing that his unalterable oath is given to a fickle, inconstant, changeable liar. Worse yet, not only are sinners unable to *keep* a promise—despite their oaths to the contrary—they cannot *believe* any other promise made to them. Abraham could not get himself out of this self-referring net until God applied his own unalterable oath to his own promise and made faith where none was possible. The oath demands nothing of us, but gives what sinners cannot.

Before God's promise gives faith, it first removes bad faith from those who do not believe—that is to those who have not actually received this promise. Promises are particular, they are not universal. They serve as the judgment, or dividing line, between condemnation and salvation. God's sacred oath itself is the "breastplate of judgment" (Exod 28:30), or Urim and Thummim, that Aaron was to wear in the Holy Place to remind the people

23. WA 28:234.31.
24. *LW* 4:143; WA 43:238.

(and God!) that the promise of deliverance was sworn by God. A promise presents a grave danger at first because, although *faith saves*, not believing it is already condemnation. God's oath to Abraham was both the yes and the no—the moment of all judgment. The promise condemns unbelief as much as it imparts belief so that God's burning love has both death and resurrection in it—there is the continental divide between uncertainty and certainty.

Subsequently, the oath is not window dressing. God's oath actually does something to the prior promise. It "enlarges" it. God wants to produce faith from his promise in sinners who not only misapprehend the promise, but are offended and repulsed by it. God knows the promise is too easily avoided so he amplifies the thing to make it inescapable. He is not assuring *thinking* of what *faith* faintly holds—the old scholastic canard. That would mean that faith or knowing itself enlarges the promise. But God enlarges his own promise, faith does not. Still, sin is resilient, and assumes that the only thing that matters in life (beyond the trivial things we know for sure, like "this is my hand") are those that one can possibly change in the future. For this, faith is given the exalted position, even over knowledge, of exercising free will that uses law to make its choices between good and evil. In order to give faith this power, however, faith must operate without certainty. This imaginary "empowerment" of faith—at the cost of knowing anything certain of the future—is what Luther is dismantling. As Luther puts it, God's unalterable oath: "By Myself I have sworn, says the Lord," enlarges the promise by surpassing both general faith and thinking. The promise is lifted out of the range of what we can surely know—or even possibly believe—into God's majesty. Neither the object of our knowledge itself (say a hand), nor the limits of subjective knowing ("how I can be certain this is indeed my hand") are the basis for his promise, but rather God's majesty alone is—himself, his essence or existence that not only says things, but makes them by speaking.

But immediately Luther notes another counterintuitive matter of God's self-deprecating oath. While it enlarges the promise beyond human limits into God's own majesty, this act is opposite what we expect from *transcendence*. God is not lifting humans into his majesty and out of their normal created lives, but is himself *condescending*. When God enlarges his promise he descends by "accommodating himself completely to our weakness"—not so that we may exercise our faith's limited power, but so that his promise is so stuffed, plump and humongous even blind and deaf sinners cannot help but trip on it—against their own desires.[25]

After all, what is this weakness of humans that we typically call "sin?" Is our weakness being creatures rather than the Creator, so that our faith must

---

25. *LW* 4:143; WA 43:238.

be uncertain and our knowledge incomplete? No, our weakness is perverse. When God says something we think he may be lying. We must test the word against what we know of the law, otherwise our wills would not be free. Enthusiasm thus seeks God within, in the immediate contact with the law, because it does not trust the God outside us making promises *that we cannot bring to fulfillment*. When Descartes must consider that God is potentially a liar, he is not presuming something contrary to human desire or will, but precisely what sinners really want. The human weakness to which Luther refers is not a creature's natural limit, but a sinner's demand for his preferred, possible—and so uncertain—future where the will has freedom. And all of this can be accomplished with one little word: "what if you are lying?" God knows that Abraham cannot believe under any circumstances, but especially when the promise given by God is itself attacked by its own giver. What else is Abraham to think on this mountain, but that God is lying?

To this "original," or root, weakness God condescends in his oath: "*By Myself*, I have sworn." Whole theologies have been constructed out of theories of divine condescension. But for Luther, condescension is not God giving us a lower dosage of himself to avoid killing people who cannot absorb the whole majesty. That false notion of divine condescension is a basic characteristic of law, misapplied to God, that says if one is too young or confused to know the law, the law's penalty may rightly be reduced. However, God's condescension in his oath is precisely the opposite of lowering the divine dosage. God condescends by doubling his strength and power in his very specific, worldly, word of promise. He not only gives the promise to Abraham but now puts his *full power* in it. He condescends *by cursing him*self. In order to bless us, God curses himself on behalf of the man he had just attacked. There is no greater, divine condescension.

God's oath is not a throw-away line, but an active imprecation, or invocation of evil upon himself. The astounding reality of this self-cursing God is that he is not doing it for his own sake or in order to fulfill his own law—say of humility—but in fact it breaks the law. God self-curses "in order to bless us."[26] It should have been sufficient to overcome Cartesian doubt if God were to "move one finger to bear witness to his fatherly goodwill toward us." God would be gracious just giving us a "sign" or "token"—like a little movement of his finger. We would ask, "do you love us God?"—or, "are you lying now?" and then wait to see if he raises his finger ever so slightly. Seeing such a twitch or movement would then be "faith," and we would ask daily, "have we enough of a sign from God that we can trust him to favor us?" But God does not settle for a sign; instead he condescends—so that

---

26. *LW* 4:143; *WA* 43:238.

we are no longer peering into heaven to read signs, but he speaks in corpulent words. Further, the word he utters is not a "condescending" law, but an inescapable promise: "I will bless you . . . and by your Seed shall all the nations be blessed" (Gen 22:17–18). But the condescension does not stop there. God lays down his promise, then imprecates himself with an oath: "Let there be nothing more of me than this, and *in this* alone I will be your God and you my creature. My majesty is hereby put down into this word, and I will not be found anywhere else, so that you do not fear that I will say something else, or speak as humans do—as if my word were a mere thought or emotion—and not the full being of who I am, without any other reserve. I am God in this word and not God outside it, so that there is no hidden God beyond, above or outside of what I have just said to you."

In this way, the majesty of God is used for our sakes, not as a subject of our inquiry. What we know and believe of the majesty of God is given in its entirety in his self-imprecation: "I will cease being who I am if this Word is merely a token, only a sign, or something fleeting that is here today and gone tomorrow. I am not merely raising a finger for you to determine whether or not I am trustworthy." Luther proceeds to note that once we stumble upon God's condescension in this way, we suddenly forgo (are freed from) the common theological discussions about predestination, evil, suffering. Otherwise these conundrums dog us endlessly since they seek certainty outside of God's word in what is considered to be a higher counsel of knowledge apart from the Word.

By Myself

Enlarging the promise is not what the law means by enlarging, which is to universalize, or extend legal power by increasing its territory and breadth. Enlarging a promise actually makes it spatially or geographically smaller. A fattened promise is more specific, concrete, and particular since it is aimed at only Abraham here, and not Lot or anyone else. But the specific delivery to Abraham is corpulent, heavy and substantial indeed. It makes the promise look like a basketball hoop a thousand feet wide.

Yet the bulk of theologians go sniffing after what they imagine God must be doing when he is not bothering to swear to himself. They conclude that he must be engaged in persuading wills to believe him. Isn't theology about making the case for God to unbelievers, just as Anselm set out to do in *Cur Deus Homo*, so that faith is enhanced by knowledge? Is persuasion not what churches do day in and day out? They take a reluctant, resistant will that turns from belief, and twists it toward belief—at least to some extent—giving the possibility of a saving encounter with God. But not only has this project failed as long as theologians have proffered it, but it completely ignores the real action and power of God in which he deprecates himself in his word. Original sin, either with Adam on earth, or Satan in heaven, is inquisitiveness into God's essence outside his promise: "In Paradise [Adam] sought God apart from the word, just as Satan did in heaven. Both found him, but not without great harm."[27] God is never so hidden that earthly wisdom cannot find him, but what it finds is not divinity or eternal life, but God's unbridled wrath without any promise or oath.

It would be possible, if God had not already taken an oath, to assume his promise always attracts us—offering a moment, perhaps, of decision or commitment on our part. But then God suddenly revokes the insinuation by removing faith from us and taking everything to himself: "*By myself,* I have sworn—says the Lord." The oath forces us to be taken in—*ad amplectendum ea*—so that God's word is esteemed, and nothing else. Reason cannot grasp or esteem this oath, and so God's "by myself" seems like a secondary, simple, foolish matter. Yet, this is how God is "apprehended"—only as he has condescended, or cursed himself. Otherwise, you will discover God's majesty, but it destroys both what you think is certain, and what human faith holds out as possibility—especially the dream that your humility will meet with God's approval. But by God's self-sworn oath, humility in the old, monastic sense is removed entirely. Faith refers to God's "by myself," and so places God's majesty entirely in *God's* own condescension instead of *faith's* act of condescension. God puts his own, and whole, majesty into his oath by amplifying what can only be heard by sinners as an affront. The amplifying neither makes the word heard universally, nor is it heard as a possibility that one person's faith accepts and another's rejects. Instead, the oath is God's own necessity: "By myself," means God's oath is not hopelessly waiting for someone to agree with his prior promise, but it gives certainty from outside of the subject altogether.

Faith's Certain Knowledge

Where there is even a scintilla of trust in God's promise, as with Abraham, faith is always greater than knowledge. It is enough for trust to remain with the "abecedarians"—the teachers of our ABC's—rather than with a doctor or rabbi. Knowing a promise knows little by the measure of the law,

27. *LW* 43:144; WA 43:239.

but what it knows it knows certainly within the enormous oath of God. Human knowledge can teach much about discipline and virtue that preserves life on earth, but when it is ignorant of God's oath it knows neither of mercy nor of sin. Knowledge seeks faith, faith is not seeking knowledge. Moreover, faith is not an act of will, but rather is "spurred on and urged" by God—by Myself—in cursing himself ("if it is permitted to speak this way"). The way faith's knowledge arrives, however, is "not through speculation; it is learned in trial and prayer."[28] Faith's way of knowing is not the logic of propositional statements that everyone already agrees to, like "God is truth," or "God is love." Luther had "no argument about the words/propositions, but there is an argument about the subject matter, namely that God does not lie when he swears and when he promises."[29] The subject of faith is not the proposition of God's essence of love. Faith's subject is the kind of particular, unexpected promise and oath that God applies to us so firmly: "You human being, shall surely live, or I Myself shall not live.... Indeed, in order that you may have no doubt, you have My Son given to you as a gift." This gift, of course, sinners proceed to kill in order to test the oath and self-deprecation: "I Myself shall not live." However, the promise proved stronger than death, even the death on the cross.

For this reason, God gives two gifts to arouse the "confidence of our hearts" over which we have no control. One is the gift of "the oath which he swore to our Father Abraham" (Luke 1:73) that serves as an example to us. But an example itself can do nothing but aggravate our own faith if God does not give the second, greater gift, "giving his own Son for us."[30] Without this promise in the present, there is no church, and Christianity itself falls into the same darkness of all religious movements that trade faith for good works, the gospel for the law, and faith for pyrrhic knowledge.

Faith is not known, and cannot be known, without God actually making a promise to you and sealing it with his oath: "I promise you, and I do not lie." Then faith ceases being "five letters on a page," presented, as it were, to a reader's eyes, which requires our own confirmation rather than God's oath. Luther called that effort a "general" faith that is shared even by the demons. Demons too have rights, and can determine whether the proposition that God is true holds or not. After all, even Satan believes that God gave his oath to Abraham, and that God's only Son died once upon the tree. In that case, faith does become the weak sister of self-reflecting knowledge that is sure: "This is my own hand."

28. *LW* 4:149; WA 43:243.
29. *LW* 4:149; WA 43:243.
30. *LW* 4:149; WA 43:243.

But special F-A-I-T-H ceases being five letters on a page and "draws the following conclusion: God is God for me because he speaks to me. He forgives my sins. He is not angry with me, just as he promises, 'I am the Lord your God.'" Here the First Commandment (and so the first table along with all other commands) is filled, not by human speculation, but by the particular, external word of promise that is delivered by a preacher to a hearer who uses God's elementary promise, "I am the Lord your God." When faith is created thus, even the true threat of the First Commandment can be heard, "You shall have no other gods before me," even though this threat will never manufacture faith. That is why Luther recognized that the enemies of the gospel have even "seized upon the word 'faith' in such a manner that they deny that it alone suffices for salvation and tack on it the merits of works, [so] they lose faith the same time that they lose the works."[31] What makes faith is the promise: "I am your God," not the Commandment or even the fulfillment of the command. Thus, a little further on in the story of Genesis, Luther takes up the case of Isaac's wretched life after the promise: "Thus today the Turk and the pope are raging against us with inhuman hatred and ferocity. Inside, however their consciences are disturbed in various ways; they are wrestling with fear, a lack of confidence, and the terrors of sin. Against all this, of course, we have most powerful consolations: the promise of the Word, Baptism, and the Eucharist, which should be apprehended and held fast with strong faith. But I do not see the forgiveness of sins, eternal salvation, and life. Yet I believe, and I am sustained by hope. And if faith is shaken and weakened either by temptation or by a fall and human frailty, nevertheless I hold fast to the Keys and cling to the promise of God, even if heaven falls. This is worshiping God and fulfilling the First Commandment, the usefulness of which is not perceived until there are trials, when the promise is invisible. I am put off for a long time, and eventually the situation is turned into the opposite."[32]

Luther was well aware that doubts persist in every human being, including those who have been blessed with God's great gift of the promise of his forgiveness of sins. But those doubts are neither a contributing part of the wholeness of faith, nor do they motivate a free will to seek the higher knowledge of God. Doubt is misery, and its only remedy is to treat it "through constant use of the Word of God" just as David and Zechariah did.[33] Even the fact that the First Commandment is filled by faith in the Keys does not merit anything for its doer from the law. One receives not even one little

---

31. *LW* 4:166; WA 43:255.
32. *LW* 4:323–24; WA 43:369.
33. *LW* 4:150; WA 43:244.

"thank you," from God for this accomplishment. It is just as Christ impressed upon his disciples: "Does he [the master] thank the slave because he did what was commanded?" (Luke 17:9). Instead, "faith alone justifies," that is, apart from any command, "set this against God's wrath and judgment, and so be certain."[34] It is never the law (even the First Commandment) that justifies. It was always and is now the promise that God seals with his oath that does this great thing—from nothing. No one places the worth of the servant or the merit of the work, or the fulfillment of the law before God's judgment and wrath, but rather this oath that enlarges the promise: "God cannot deny himself and cast aside his Son, that Seed of Abraham."[35]

Luther figured that the oath continued to enlarge the promise—apart from any debt paid or merit earned by him or the faithful baptized, for Paul as well as Moses and the stories of the patriarchs: "Paul, a servant of God and an apostle of Jesus Christ, for the sake of the faith of God's elect and their knowledge of the truth, which accords with godliness." Yet, what accords with godliness is not the normal expectation of the law. It is the knowledge/faith that when God makes a promise he cannot lie: "in hope of eternal life, which God, *who never lies*, promised before the ages began, and at the proper time manifested in his word through the preaching with which I have been entrusted by the command of God our Savior" (Titus 1:1–3).

Faith clings to this oath against its own knowledge of itself (its lying), and escapes from the inner self's uncertainty, along with the law's fulfillment in myself or even in Christ, into certainty of external things Then, lest faith think God is waiting for some response to an offer or a fulfillment of the law, God—"by myself"—enlarges the promise through a self-deprecating oath, thus giving us himself, outside the law altogether. To this, a blessed sinner says, "without doubt this oath pertains to me too."[36] F-A-I-T-H is certain certainty. No misery is greater than doubt; no joy is greater than God making his certain promise to you and sealing it with his own certainty—the self-denigrating oath he swore to our Father Abraham.

---

34. It is no coincidence that Luther turns the discussion of God's oath to Luke 17:10 and the fulfillment of the law, whether in us or in Christ—that nevertheless receives no reward at all! This passage became the basis of the great fight among the second generation of Lutherans regarding good works that set the pattern for theology ever since. See *LW* 4:166; WA 43:255–56.

35. *LW* 4:166; WA 43:255–56.

36. *LW* 4:166; WA 43:255–56.

Bibliography

Aquinas, Thomas. *Summa Theologica*. Translated by Fathers of the English Dominican Province. London: Burns, Oates & Washbourne, 1911.

Bayer, Oswald. *Promissio. Geschichte der reformatorischen Wende in Luthers Theologie, FKDG*. 2nd ed. Göttingen: Vandenhoeck & Ruprecht, 1989.

———. *Theology the Lutheran Way*. Translated by Jeffrey G. Silcock and Mark C. Mattes. Grand Rapids: Eerdmans, 2007.

Kripke, Saul. *Wittgenstein, On Rules and Private Language: An Elementary Exposition*. Cambridge: Harvard University Press, 1982.

Leibniz, Gottfried Wilhelm. "Reflections on Locke's *Second Reply*." Online. http://www.leibniz-translations.com/locke.htm.

Locke, John. 1698. *Mr. Locke's Reply to the Bishop Worcester's Answer to His Second Letter*. London: C. Baldwin, 2009.

Luther, Martin. *Luther's Works*. Edited by Jaroslav Pelikan and Helmut T. Lehmann. 56 Vols. St. Louis: Concordia; Philadelphia: Fortress, 1955–1986.

Moore, G. E. "Proof of An External World." In *Selected Writings*, edited by Thomas Baldwin, 147–70. New York: Routledge, 1993.

Stillingfleet, Edward. *The Bishop of Worcester's Answer to Mr. Locke's Second Letter*. London: Morlock, 1698.

Wittgenstein, Ludwig. *Ludwig Wittengenstein On Cerrtainty*. Edited by G. E. M. Anscombe, et al. Translated by Denis Paul. Oxford: Blackwell, 1969–1975.

11

Sacraments in the Catechism

Promise, Gift, and Faith

John T. Pless

Oswald Bayer recounts that it was the question of "why have the Lord's Supper if the word does everything?" that prompted his early studies with Ernst Bizer. It was that investigation which, in turn, led him to see Luther's theology through the lens of *promissio,* a performative word by which God is bestowing the forgiveness of sins.[1] This paper, offered in celebration of Dr. Bayer's many contributions to Lutheran theology and pastoral practice, will examine the place of the sacraments in Luther's Catechisms from this perspective.

Werner Elert cautions, "The New Testament does not even contain a common expression for the actions of baptism and communion. Already for this reason every doctrine about them is suspect in advance—suspect of beginning with the nonbiblical term 'sacrament' and then investigating whether and how this general term fits both actions."[2] Elert's warning is reflected in Luther's catechetical approach.

Luther does not begin with a preamble which gives an overarching definition of what constitutes a sacrament. While in the practice of catechesis, Lutheran catechists have not always followed Luther's example, the observation of Hermann Sasse holds true, "The Lutheran church has no dogma *de sacramentis.*"[3] Later dogmaticians would not consistently follow the pattern of the Augsburg Confession in coming to the use of the sacraments[4] only

---

1. See Bayer, "How I became a Luther Scholar," 249–50.
2. Elert, *Lord's Supper Today*, 7.
3. Sasse, *This is My Body*, 21.
4. *CA* 13.

after treating baptism,[5] the Lord's Supper,[6] confession,[7] and repentance,[8] but this is coherent with Luther's approach in the Small Catechism. Luther does not begin with a definition of a sacrament but begins catechetically with the dominical words instituting baptism and the Lord's Supper. How they are to be used in the church is incorporated in both the case of baptism and the Sacrament of the Altar.

If there is no attempt to provide an inclusive definition of a sacrament in the Small and Large Catechisms, how does Luther connect the two? In *The Babylonian Captivity of the Church*, written in 1520, the Reformer clearly rejected the Roman Catholic tradition that Christ had bequeathed to the church seven sacraments.[9] In the Small Catechism, Luther includes baptism and the Sacrament of the Altar with material on confession and absolution incrementally added. How are they—especially baptism and the Sacrament of the Altar—brought together without being made interchangeable?

In his exposition of baptism in the Large Catechism, after asserting that baptism is not a work we do, Luther states that "it is a treasure that God gives us and faith grasps."[10] In its immediate context, Luther is seeking to defend the evangelical teaching on baptism against the charge that this doctrine is against faith. That is to say, salvation is acquired by the act of baptism rather than faith. Luther is actually parsing out the place of faith in baptism in relation to the treasure which God gives. He will use a similar pattern in speaking about the Lord's Supper. Recall here how Luther speaks in the Small Catechism when he says that whoever believes the words "given and shed for you" has what they declare, the forgiveness of sins. Or again the person who has faith in these words is worthy and well-prepared to receive the sacrament. On the other hand, those who do not believe or doubt are unworthy and unprepared "because the words 'for you' require truly believing hearts."[11] This is echoed in the Large Catechism, "And because he offers and promises forgiveness of sins, it can be received in no other way than by faith."[12] In the words of Albrecht Peters: "He [Luther] arranges all of the sacraments by means of the relationship between promise and faith."[13]

5. *CA* 9.
6. *CA* 10.
7. *CA* 11.
8. *CA* 12.
9. See the discussion in Hermann, "Introduction to the Babylonian Captivity," 9–10.
10. LC 4.37; BOC 461.
11. SC 6.9–10; BOC 363.
12. LC 5.34; BOC 470.
13. Peters, *Commentary on Luther's Catechisms*, 15.

Luther retrieves instruction concerning the sacraments and restores them to a place in the catechetical tradition as they had in large part fallen out of the range of catechesis in the medieval church. While the Fourth Lateran Council (1215) gave impetus to preaching on penance and the mass with its requirement of a minimal, yearly reception of Christ's body at Easter, there was little in the way of instruction regarding their benefit or appropriate use. Luther recognized this slippage in the opening lines of his treatment of baptism in the Large Catechism: "We have now finished with the three chief parts of common Christian teaching. We must still say something about our two sacraments, instituted by Christ. For every Christian ought to have at least some brief, elementary instruction about them, because without them no one can be a Christian, although unfortunately nothing was taught about them in the past."[14] The Catechisms are one of his attempts to correct this defect.

Prior to the writing of the Catechisms in 1529, Luther had on numerous occasions sought to teach the salutary use of the sacraments. In his 1519, "A Sermon on Preparing to Die,"[15] Luther urges his readers to make use of the sacraments in the face of death: "We must earnestly, diligently, and highly esteem the holy sacraments, hold them in honor, freely and cheerfully rely on them, and so balance them against sin, death, and hell that they will outweigh these by far. We must occupy ourselves much more with the sacraments and their virtues than with our sins. However, we must know how to give them due honor and we must know what their virtues are."[16] Then Luther continued to connect the "virtues" of the sacraments with faith in God's word joined to the sacramental sign: "I show them due honor when I believe that I truly receive what the sacraments signify and all that God declares and indicates in them, so that I can say with Mary in firm faith, 'Let it be to me according to your words and signs' [Luke 1:38]. Since God himself here speaks and acts through the priest, we would do him in his word no greater dishonor than to doubt whether it is true. And we can do him no greater honor than to believe that his word and work are

---

14. LC 4.1; BOC 456.

15. See Hamm, "Luther's Instructions," 110–53. Hamm notes that this "sermon" was one of several tracts "intended to communicate the essential elements of his [Luther's] theology in a basic, elementary, and catechetical way to a theologically untrained public" (Hamm, "Luther's Instructions," 111). In regard to Luther's evangelical use of the sacraments in this tract, Hamm says "As the saving words and verbal signs of the sacraments make clear, Luther found in them the merciful faithfulness, truthfulness, and omnipotence of God on which this faith could totally depend so that dying could become a 'cheerful venture'" (Hamm, "Luther's Instructions," 147).

16. *LW* 42:100–101.

true and firmly rely on them."[17] Luther repeatedly drives this home as he puts these words in the mouth of the distressed soul: "This sign and promise of my salvation will not lie or deceive me. It is God who has promised it, and he cannot lie in either words or deeds" concluding "He who insists and relies on the sacraments will find his election and predestination will turn out well without his worry and effort."[18] In this pastoral tract, Luther's approach prefigures what he will do more fulsomely in the Catechisms, moving from promise to faith.

While Luther does not deal with the sacraments directly in his "Personal Prayer Book" of 1522, he does speak of "God's particular ordering of things that a lowly Christian person who might be unable to read the Bible should nevertheless be obligated and know" namely "the Ten Commandments, the Creed, and the Lord's Prayer."[19] He says "Three things a person must know to be saved. First, he must know what to do and what he is to leave undone. Second, when he realizes that he cannot measure up to what he should do or leave undone, he needs to know where to go to find the strength he requires. Third, he must know how to seek and obtain this strength."[20] The Ten Commandments make the diagnosis, showing the sickness. The Creed shows the cure, for it "points him to God and his mercy, given and made plain in Christ."[21] The Lord's Prayer teaches the fulfillment of God's Commandments. It is to this catechetical triad—Commandments, Creed, and Lord's Prayer—that Luther will add the sacraments.

If the Creed makes plain that God's cure for sin is in his Son, Jesus Christ, and the Lord's Prayer teaches us how to call on God the Father for every good, then the sacraments serve as the concrete delivery points where God is distributing the treasure of redemption for faith to lay hold of and receive.

Even though Luther does not start with a definition of "sacrament" that would bind baptism and the Lord's Supper together, there is a parallelism in his treatment of both in the Small Catechism.

In a 1528 sermon on the Lord's Supper, Luther reminded the congregation, "Take hold only of the words; they will tell you what the sacrament is."[22] With both baptism and the Sacrament of the Altar, Luther begins with the Lord's words. Baptism is not simply water but "water enclosed in God's

---

17. *LW* 42:101.
18. *LW* 42:109.
19. *LW* 43:13.
20. *LW* 43:13.
21. *LW* 43:14.
22. *LW* 51:189.

command and connected with God's word."[23] The particular word of God is Jesus's mandate in Matthew 28:19 which establishes baptizing in the name of the Father and of the Son and of the Holy Spirit. In like manner, Luther answers the question, "What is the Sacrament of the Altar?" with an appeal to Christ's words of institution.

The words of Christ which institute both Baptism and the Lord's Supper bring together command and promise in such a way as the promise "carries out God's mandate" to use the words of Oswald Bayer.[24] Christ's words give what they declare. It is only from the words of the Lord that he used in instituting baptism and the Lord's Supper that we know what each is and how they are to be used.

Luther catechizes not by drawing analogies with the properties or powers of water; that it is both destructive and life-giving and so forth but with word of God which establishes this sacrament and is in and with the water. Likewise, the Lord's Supper as Bayer puts it "is not some diffuse celebration of life but is defined in a precise way in its essence by means of the connection between the word of Christ that has effective power and faith."[25] In the Large Catechism, Luther asserts "Just as we said of baptism that it is not mere water, so we say here, too, that the sacrament is bread and wine, but not mere bread and wine such as is served at the table. Rather, it is bread and wine set within God's word and bound to it."[26] God's specific word of command and promise distinguishes baptism from all other washings[27] and the Lord's Supper from all other meals.

It is God's Word which makes the sacrament what it is, Christ's body and blood. In the Large Catechism Luther invokes Augustine's dictum "When the word is joined to the external element, it becomes a sacrament"[28] to defend the bodily presence of Christ under the bread and wine. But it is this same word which strengthens the conscience.[29] Luther

---

23. SC 4.1–2; BOC 359.

24. Bayer quoted in Peters, *Baptism and Lord's Supper,* 4.

25. Bayer, *Martin Luther's Theology,* 272.

26. LC 5.9; BOC 467.

27. In the Large Catechism, Luther writes that Holy Baptism is no "bath-keeper's baptism" or mundane washing: "I therefore admonish you again that these two, the word and the water, must by no means be separated from each other. For where the word is separated from the water, the water is no different from the water that the maid uses for cooking and could indeed be called a bath-keeper's baptism. But when the word is with it according to God's ordinance, baptism is a sacrament, and is called Christ's baptism" (LC 4.22; BOC 459).

28. LC 5.10; BOC 468.

29. Luther says: "With this word you can strengthen your conscience and declare: 'Let a hundred thousand devils, with all fanatics, come forward and say, 'How can bread

coordinates the physical eating and drinking with the spiritual eating and drinking in the Sacrament of the Altar: "Eating and drinking certainly do not do it, but rather the words that are recorded: 'given for you' and 'shed for you for the forgiveness of sins.' These words, when accompanied by the physical eating and drinking, are the essential thing in the sacrament, and whoever believes these very words has what they declare and state, namely, 'forgiveness of sins.'"[30]

In the Small Catechism, Christ's words are what make the sacrament sure and certain. For this reason, Luther drives home the point with "a threefold repetition of the two phrases, 'given for you' and 'shed for the forgiveness of sins.'"[31] These words declare what God is doing in the Supper. What Luther does in his unfolding of the Lord's Supper has its parallel in his exposition of baptism. Just as it is not eating and drinking alone which accomplish the forgiveness of sins, so it is not just being washed with water. "Clearly the water does not do it, but the word of God, which is with and alongside the water, and faith which trusts this word of God in the water. For without the word of God the water is plain water and not a baptism."[32]

In Baptism and the Lord's Supper, faith lays hold of what God gives. The treasures of baptism and the Lord's Super are prior to faith. Luther outlines the gifts given in baptism and the Lord's Supper. baptism "brings about forgiveness of sins, redeems from death and the devil and gives eternal salvation to all who believe it, as the words and promises of God declare."[33] The language of the Explanation of the Creed's Second Article is brought into baptism: "He has purchased and freed me from all sins, from death, and the power of the devil, not with gold or silver but with his holy, precious blood and with his innocent suffering and death."[34]

---

and wine be Christ's body and blood?" etc. Still I know that the spirits and the scholars put together have less wisdom than this divine Majesty has in his littlest finger. Here is Christ's word: 'Take, eat this is my body.' 'Drink of this, all of you, this is the New Testament in my blood,' etc. Here we shall take our stand and see who dares instruct Christ and alter what Christ has spoken. It is true, indeed, that if you take the word away from the elements or view them apart from the word, you have nothing but ordinary bread and wine. But if the words remain as is right and necessary, then by virtue of them the elements are truly the body and blood of Christ. For as Christ's lips speak and say, so it is; he cannot lie or deceive" (LC 5.12–14; BOC 468).

30. SC 6.3; BOC 362.
31. Bayer, *Martin Luther's Theology*, 271.
32. SC 4.9; BOC 363.
33. SC 4.5–6; BOC 457.
34. SC 2.4; BOC 355; cf. "That which Christ accomplished for me on the cross becomes fully mine through Baptism" (Peters, *Baptism and Lord's Supper*, 95).

Verbally Luther makes vivid the connection between Christ's passion on the cross and the gift which the Lord has placed in baptism, a connection made even more explicit in Luther's later preaching on baptism and his baptismal hymn. In the sermon preached in Dessau at the baptism of Bernard von Anhalt on April 2, 1540, Luther refers to 1 John 5:6 where the Apostle refers to Christ coming by both water and blood to make the point that to be baptized is to be washed in the blood of Christ: "This blood and its merit he put into baptism, in order that in baptism, we might receive it. For whenever a person receives baptism in faith this is the same as if he were visibly washed and cleansed of sin with the blood of Christ. For we do not attain the forgiveness of sins through our work, but rather through the death and shedding of the blood of the Son of God. But he takes this forgiveness and tucks it into baptism."[35] This thought is also reflected in Luther's hymn, "To Jordan Came the Christ our Lord" written the next year (1541) where he poetically speaks of the baptismal waters as "the crimson flood."[36] In baptism, sinners are joined to the death of Christ which rescues from sin, death, and the devil.

In the Lord's Supper, Christ delivers the fruits of his redeeming suffering and death. "What is the benefit of such eating and drinking?" is answered: "The words 'given for you' and 'shed for you for the forgiveness of sins' show us that forgiveness of sin, life and salvation are given to us in the sacrament through these words, because where there is forgiveness of sin, there is also life, and salvation."[37] The redemption achieved on the cross is distributed in the body and blood of Christ.

In his 1525 treatise "Against the Heavenly Prophets," Luther asserted: "If now I seek the forgiveness of sins, I do not run to the cross, for I will not find it given there. Nor must I hold to the suffering of Christ, as Dr. Karlstadt trifles, in knowledge or remembrance, for I will not find it there either. But I will find in the sacrament or gospel the word which distributes, presents, offers, and gives to me that forgiveness which was won on the cross."[38] This theme lies behind the Small Catechism's question on the benefit of eating and drinking in the Sacrament. It is also echoed in the Large Catechism where Luther confesses the historical reality of Christ's death on the cross for sin and the distribution of this treasure by way of Christ's promise: "Although the work took place on the cross and the forgiveness of sins has been acquired, yet it cannot come to us in any other way than through the

---

35. *LW* 51:325.
36. *LSB* 406.
37. SC 6.5–6; BOC 362.
38. *LW* 40:213–14.

word. How should we know that this took place or was given to us if it were not proclaimed by preaching, by the oral word? From what source do they know of forgiveness, and how can they receive it, except by steadfastly believing the Scriptures and the gospel?"[39] Luther sees in the Lord's Supper the most concentrated form of the gospel[40] because in it the death of Christ is proclaimed and the benefits of that saving death are bestowed in his body and blood given us to eat and drink.

It is often observed that the Small Catechism is remarkable for its lack of polemics.[41] It might be more accurate to say that Luther is only covertly polemical in the Small Catechism. His polemic in the Small Catechism is subversive, under the table. While it is true that he is not aggressively or openly attacking opponents, the Reformation controversies—both with Rome and the Sacramentarians—are lurking in the background and are addressed in the Small Catechism. Luther had already answered the Anabaptist charge that infants were not fitting candidates for Baptism as well as the charge that regeneration by the Spirit does not take place in the sacrament in his 1528 "Concerning Rebaptism."[42] Both Roman and Sacramentarian teachings are subtly countered in Luther's catechesis of the Sacrament of the Altar. As Charles Arand observes, "In four brief questions, Luther provides a single, yet full summary of these debates. Questions one and three appear to have in view the Sacramentarians. Questions two and four appear to be aimed more at the Roman Catholic Church inasmuch as these questions deal with the benefits of the Lord's Supper and the worthiness of those who receive it."[43]

A key issue which Luther is forced to address in the Small Catechism over and against both Rome and Reformers to his left was the place of faith in relationship to the sacraments. Baptism and the Lord's Supper are not founded on faith but Luther incorporates faith into his explanation of

---

39. LC 5.31; BOC 469–70.

40. Also note Peters: "For him [Luther], the Lord's Supper is not an offering and a good work performed by a human being in Christ before God; it is a testament and sacrament of God through Christ for us. As such it is the *summa et compendium Euangelii*" (Peters, *Baptism and the Lord's Supper*, 21).

41. See, for example, the comment of Eero Huovinen: "The *Small Catechism* does not include any direct polemic" (Huovinen, "Common Teacher," 8).

42. Mark Tranvik notes: "But Luther did grasp well the core theological issues at stake. These concerned the nature of faith and the corresponding rationale for infant baptism. As one who upheld the centrality of justification by faith alone, he had to sort out why children should continue to be baptized. The treatise also provided an opportunity for him to explain in detail the relationship between the word and faith" (Robinson, *Annotated Luther*, 3:277).

43. Arand, *That I May be His Own*, 171.

both baptism and the Lord's Supper. As we have observed the words and promises of God precede faith as Luther demonstrates in the second part of the Catechism's treatment of Baptism as he states that Baptism works the forgiveness of sins, redeems from death and the devil, and grants eternal salvation to all who believe "as the words and promises of God declare."[44] The words and promises of God are the words of Christ from Mark 16:16 which state that all who believe and are baptized shall be saved. Then in the third part, Luther goes on to note that it is the word of God "which is with and in the water, and faith which trusts this word of God in the water"[45] that distinguishes baptism from plain water. Faith does not make baptism but it is only by faith that the benefits of baptism are received. A year before writing the Small Catechism, Luther made this clear in his treatise "Concerning Rebaptism" where he goes into significant detail in unpacking the argument that baptism is not constituted by faith nor is it administered on the basis of faith. "Those who would allow themselves to be baptized on the strength of their faith are not only uncertain, but are also idolaters who deny Christ. For they trust in and build on something of their own, namely, on a gift they have received from God, and not on God's word alone."[46] On the basis of God's command and promise, faith does not contribute to baptism and only receives what God gives in word within the water. Or in the words of Gerhard Forde, in Baptism faith is given "something to believe."[47]

Likewise, Christ's body and blood are given in the Lord's Supper even to those who come to the altar without faith but it is only through faith that the benefits of Christ are received. Whoever believes the words "'given for you . . . shed for you for the forgiveness of sins' has what they declare, the forgiveness of sins."[48] The mouth eats and drinks while the heart lays hold

---

44. SC 4.5–6; BOC 359.

45. LC 4.9.

46. Robinson, *Annotated Luther*, 3:305. Also see Luther's sermon on New Year's Day, 1532: "The gospel or faith is what does not demand our works, does not tell to do, but tells us to receive and accept a gift so that something happens to us, that is, so that God promises and sends someone to tell you: 'This is what I am giving to you. You cannot or have not done anything for it; instead, it is my work.' For example, baptism is not something I have made. It is not my work, but God's. He is the one who says to me: 'Hold still; I am baptizing you and washing you from all your sins. Accept it. It shall be yours'" (*LW* 57:68–69). Also see the catechism sermon on baptism from 1528: "My faith does not make baptism but rather receives the baptism: for baptism is not dependent upon my faith but upon God's word" (*LW* 51:186).

47. See Forde, *Preached God*, 131–45. Also note Forde's argument that the sacraments keep the preached word from evaporating in some form of interior spirituality. See Forde, *Preached God*, 89–115.

48. SC 5.8; BOC 362.

of the promise attached to Christ's body and blood, given and shed for you. Peters writes "Both the external human being's body and the inner person of the heart are connected directly with Christ's body that was offered and the blood of the covenant. The Lord draws near to the external, physical man under the gifts of creation and the inner man under the promise of grace."[49] In the Catechism, Luther coordinates the physical eating and drinking with faith in Christ's testamentary words.

The Catechisms address the "use" that the Christian is to make of baptism and the Lord's Supper. Bayer writes: "The fourth baptismal question in the Small Catechism proves that Luther did not think of baptism as an isolated act, but that it decidedly includes the *Christian life* that proceeds from it as well."[50] For Luther, baptism is no longer a rite of initiation in the rear view mirror but the present tense reality of the Christian's existence in repentance and faith. The significance of baptism is found in the rhythm of Christian life: dying and rising (Rom 6). Luther makes this explicit in the Large Catechism: "Thus a Christian life is nothing else than a daily baptism, begun once and continuing ever after. For we must keep at it without ceasing, always purging whatever pertains to the old Adam, so that whatever belongs to the new creature may come forth. What is the old creature? It is what is born in us from Adam, irascible, spiteful, envious, unchaste, greedy, lazy, proud—yes—and unbelieving; it is beset with all vices and by nature has nothing good in it. Now, when we enter Christ's kingdom, this corruption must daily decrease so that the longer we live the more gentle, patient and meek we become, and the more we break away from greed, hatred, envy, and pride."[51]

Luther addresses the use of the Lord's Supper under the question "Who, then, receives this sacrament worthily?"[52] In the catechism sermon from 1528 on the Lord's Supper, Luther uses language that will also show up in the Large Catechism, the Lord's Supper is "not poison; but a remedy and salvation."[53] Pastorally Luther aims to encourage a salutary partaking of the Lord's body and blood which avoids undue fear on the one hand and laxity on the other hand. Fasting and the like are external disciplines which have their usefulness insofar as they go, but as Luther says the person who

---

49. Peters, *Baptism and Lord's Supper*, 196.

50. Bayer, *Martin Luther's Theology*, 267.

51. LC 4.65–67; BOC 465.

52. SC 6.9.

53. *LW* 51.192. Compare with the Large Catechism: "Why, then, do we act as if the sacrament were a poison that would kill us if we ate of it?" (LC 5.68; BOC 474).

has faith in Christ's words "is really worthy and well prepared"[54] because the promise of the forgiveness of sins "can be received in no other way than by faith."[55]

Finally, we would turn our attention to the place of confession and absolution in the Small Catechism. Luther forges a connection with baptism in the Large Catechism when he writes baptism "comprehends also the third sacrament, formerly called penance."[56] The sacramental status of confession and absolution remains ambiguous. Oswald Bayer suggests that we might call it "sign number two and one-half."[57] Whether one calls it a sacrament or not, it is clear that Luther highly values the practice of private or individual confession for the sake of the absolution which is the word of God in human speech.

The original form of the Small Catechism did not contain material on confession or the office of the keys. The brief order for confession was added in June 1529. In 1531, the questions on confession were included to the brief order. Derived from the work of Andreas Osiander (1498–1552), the office of the keys were included in editions of the Small Catechism in Luther's lifetime.[58]

The insertion of a short order of confession between baptism and the Sacrament of the Altar was intended by Luther to catechize Christians in the evangelical use of confession and absolution. "Individual confession and absolution is properly placed between baptism and the Lord's Supper. It marks the point where the *signifiactio* of baptism is made specific, the daily drowning of the old man when the guilt is disclosed in the presence of a Christian brother, as well as the breaking forth of the new man, empowered by the divine absolution; it is what prepares us for the Lord's Supper."[59] Anchored in the final section on baptism ("What then is the significance of such a baptism with water?"), Luther's treatment demonstrates that to confess one's sins is to return to baptism in the confidence of God's promise to forgive. "The eschatological baptismal path for a Christian, to which confession and absolution return us again and again, is and remains encompassed within and protected by God's faithfulness to his gracious promises."[60]

54. SC 6.9.
55. LC 5.34; BOC 470.
56. LC 4.74; BOC 465.
57. Bayer, *Martin Luther's Theology*, 270. See also the discussion in Fagerberg, *New Look*, 5–12.
58. Here see Hinckley, "Andreas Osiander," 37–42. For more on this history, see Ritggers, *Reformation of the Keys*.
59. Peters, *Confession and Christian Life*, 29.
60. Peters, *Confession and Christian Life*, 74.

Confession of sins *coram Deo* is inclusive. Before the God from whom no secrets are hid, we admit guilt of all sins as we pray in the Fifth Petition of the Lord's Prayer. This acknowledgement of sin recognizes its totality and admits no righteousness before God. But before the pastor Luther asserts, "we should confess only the sins we know and feel in our hearts." These sins are brought to light in the self-examination which takes stock of one's life as it is assessed from the perspective of the Ten Commandments as they intersect with one's "place in life," that is, one's calling.[61]

Luther moves quickly from the human act of confession to the divine act of absolution. Confession is defined as consisting of two parts. The first is that we confess our sins. The second is that we receive the absolution from the pastor as from God himself not doubting but firmly believing that the sins confessed are forgiven before God in heaven. When the accent is on the act of confession, questions immediately arise. Was it comprehensive enough to name all the sins committed in thought, word, or deed? Was it motivated out of a pure love? When these questions take over the conscience is left without defense against the monster of uncertainty. Luther recognizes that the broken sinner's only confidence is *extra nos,* outside of the self in the words of God on the lips of the pastor. Luther provides diagnostic questions for the penitent to use along with a template for confession but his focus is ultimately on the absolution which brings comfort in that it actually is the voice of Christ.[62] As with baptism and the Lord's Supper, absolution gives God's treasure of the forgiveness of sins for faith to grasp with the certainty that it is God's doing.

Oswald Bayer has contrasted Luther's approach to theology with that of Anselm as it was configured in the medieval tradition. For Anselm, theology was faith seeking understanding. For Luther, theology was faith enduring attack.[63] So in the Small Catechism, baptism, absolution, and the Lord's Supper are treasures which God gives precisely so that faith might have certainty in the divine promise and so endure the assaults which come from the seductions of the devil, the deceptions of the world, and the pull of our own stubborn flesh. As a handbook for discipleship, the Catechism

---

61. Here note Peters: "Our confession before God is to be comprehensive and complete, but it is to concentrate on specific offenses when it is uttered before human beings. Luther brings this into awareness by linking the Old Testament Decalogue with the New Testament Household Responsibilities, which demarcate our 'estate,' our God-ordained standing within the coordinated system that exists among human beings" (Peters, *Confession and Christian Life*, 9).

62. For more on this point, see Bayer, *Martin Luther's Theology*, 269–70; Pless, "Confession and Absolution," 28–42.

63. See the discussion of this point in Bayer, *Theology the Lutheran Way*, 210–13.

tutors us not simply in an intellectual knowledge of the sacraments but how they are to be used for the strengthening of faith in Christ.

In the Small Catechism, baptism, absolution, and the Sacrament of the Altar are not merely an addendum to the catechetical core of Decalogue, Creed, and Lord's Prayer. They are necessarily connected to the confession of the Third Article, particularly the line which reads "Daily in this Christian church the Holy Spirit abundantly forgives all sins—mine and those of all who believe."[64] This is made even more explicit in the Large Catechism: "Further we believe that in this Christian community we have the forgiveness of sins, which takes place in the holy sacraments and absolution as well as through all the comforting words of the entire gospel. This encompasses everything to be preached about the sacraments and, in short, the entire gospel and all the official responsibilities of the Christian community."[65] Then a few lines later Luther writes "Therefore everything in the Christian community is so ordered that everyone may daily obtain full forgiveness of sins through the Word and signs appointed to comfort and encourage our consciences as long as we live on earth."[66]

Bibliography

Arand, Charles P. *That I May be His Own: An Overview of Luther's Catechisms*. St. Louis: Concordia, 2000.

Bayer, Oswald. "How I became a Luther Scholar." *Lutheran Quarterly* 27 (2013) 249–63.

———. *Martin Luther's Theology: A Contemporary Interpretation*. Translated by Thomas H. Trapp. Grand Rapids: Eerdmans, 2008.

———. *Theology the Lutheran Way*. Translated by Jeffrey C. Silcock and Mark C. Mattes. Grand Rapids: Eerdmans, 2007.

Elert, Werner. *The Lord's Supper Today*. Translated by Martin Bertram. St. Louis: Concordia, 1973.

Fagerberg, Holsten. *A New Look at the Lutheran Confessions 1529–1537*. Translated by Gene Lund. St. Louis: Concordia, 1972.

Forde, Gerhard. *The Preached God: Proclamation in Word and Sacrament*. Edited by Mark Mattes and Steven Paulson. Grand Rapids: Eerdmans, 2007.

Hamm, Berndt. *The Early Luther: Stages in Reformation Reorientation*. Translated by Martin J. Lohrmann. Grand Rapids: Eerdmans, 2014.

Hinckley, Robert. "Andreas Osiander and the Fifth Chief Part." *Logia* 10 (2001) 37–42.

Klän, Werner. "The 'Third' Sacrament: Confession and Repentance in the Confessions of the Lutheran Church." *Logia* 20 (2011) 5–12.

---

64. SC 2.6; BOC 356.
65. LC 2.54; BOC 438.
66. LC 2.55; BOC 438.

Peters, Albrecht. *Baptism and Lord's Supper*. Translated by Thomas H. Trapp. Commentary on Luther's Catechisms. St. Louis: Concordia, 2012.

———. *Confession and Christian Life*. Translated by Thomas H. Trapp. Commentary on Luther's Catechisms. St. Louis: Concordia, 2013.

Pless, John T. "Confession and Absolution." *Lutheran Quarterly* 30 (2016) 28–42.

Ritggers, Ronald K. *The Reformation of the Keys: Confession, Conscience, and Authority in Sixteenth-Century Germany*. Cambridge: Harvard University Press, 2004.

Robinson, Paul W., ed. *The Annotated Luther*. Vol. 3. Minneapolis: Fortress, 2016.

Sasse, Hermann. *This is My Body: Luther's Contention for the Real Presence in the Sacrament of the Altar Revised Edition*. Adelaide: Lutheran, 1977.

Stjerna, Kirsi I., and Brooks Schramm, eds. *Encounters with Luther: New Directions for Critical Studies*. Louisville: Westminster John Knox, 2016.

12

Bayer's Twenty-First-Century Disputation Concerning Lament

Gregory P. Schulz

Do you know Jorge Luis Borges's "book review," "Pierre Menard, Author of the *Quixote*?" If you do, you know why I wrote "book review" in quotes. If not, it's important to know that Borges (1899–1986), a twentieth-century Argentinian author, writes in the forward to his 1944 short story collection *Fictions*: "It is a laborious madness and an impoverishing one, the madness of composing vast books—setting out in five hundred pages an idea that can be perfectly related orally in five minutes. The better way to go about it is to pretend that those books already exist, and offer a summary, a commentary on them." In his fictional review of the fictional Menard's fictional project, Borges writes, "Pierre Menard did not want to compose *another* Quixote, which is surely easy enough—he wanted to compose *the* Quixote. . . . His admirable ambition was to produce a number of pages which coincided—word for word and line for line—with those of Miguel de Cervantes."[1] You can see where this must end up! Menard, seeking to write *the* Quixote for the twentieth century, ended up reproducing word for word the Cervantes classic for contemporary readers.

On this occasion, I would like simply to provide a festive word-for-word version of Matthias Gockel's crisp English translation of Oswald Bayer's "Toward a Theology of Lament,"[2] similar to Pierre Menard's *Quixote*, but I've already done that in an earlier publication by repeating the text of Bayer's call to lamentation digitally.[3] So instead, let me offer a version of

---

1. Borges, *Collected Fictions*, 91.
2. Bayer, "Toward a Theology of Lament," 211–20.
3. Schulz, *Problem of Suffering*.

Bayer's text that may help contemporary readers take to heart and to discuss church-wide his urgent call for a theology of lament. Nearly two decades after his initial call, there are few indications that either theology—systematic or pastoral—or ethics are interested in addressing what I have called "the lamentable lacuna" of the church that degrades our theology of the cross and our witness to the world alike. The biblical texts of lament: the psalms of lament comprising about one-third of the book of Psalms, the books and chapters of lamentations from the Hebrew Prophets, the Old Testament context of Romans, and so on—these are blind spots on the vision of the Western churches today, despite the good-faith efforts of lamentation luminaries such as Oswald Bayer.

Perhaps other readers of professor Bayer would say that his efforts to reintroduce lament into the theology of Lutheran (and Western Christian) churches appears to be a quixotic, or impractical project, to put it charitably. After all, at least in America's Lutheran churches Bayer's call seems to have gone largely unremarked and unheeded, so (these other readers imagine) how important can lament be, after all? As an effort to make Bayer's argument for lament—and this is a mission-critical argument for Christ's church and her pastors—accessible for group study and discussion, let me offer his argument in the form of a disputation, a disputation for the twenty-first century.[4] In a small way, perhaps this disputation will catch and hold the interest of Lutheran systematic theologians and Lutheran philosophers writing in the field of theology and ethics (for whom Bayer's *Freedom in Response* is another goldmine).[5] Or, maybe this dosage of Bayer in disputation form will help to bring the practice of lament into the ministry of faithful pastors who otherwise might remain, lamentably, unaffected by biblical lament.

A *disputation* was one way of having a thoughtful discussion and dialog concerning a critical topic in early sixteenth century universities such as the University of Wittenberg. Today, its appropriation depends largely on our acquaintance with the classical Three Acts of Mind.[6] The online *Stanford Encyclopedia of Philosophy* (SEP) explains that this type of teaching by disputation is essentially an academic form of philosophical dialog (the sort of teaching that Plato did in dialogues such as his *Republic*). It's also significant that this disputation form "comes into the classroom as an outgrowth of the *lectio*, the

---

4. The wording of the numbered propositions in the chapter are Bayer's words in Gock's English translation, but the numbering is my own recommendation. The highlighting is also mine. I've endeavored to respect the section-by-section development of Bayer's article by introducing each with my own commentary.

5. Bayer, *Freedom in Response*.

6. For an introduction to these Three Acts, which are the logical framework for Luther's disputations, please see Schulz, "Session Four—Logic."

careful reading and commentary on authoritative texts" such as Holy Scripture in the first place, but also academic texts such as the writings of Aristotle.[7]

As the SEP explains in detail, disputation "is centered around a systematic rather than a textual question, and the supporting and opposing arguments are supplied by students." By the way, what Luther and the earlier medieval theologians and philosophers called *theses* are what we in philosophy today refer to as *propositions*, statements of fact set out on the common table to be judged as either true or false. Each proposition is an open invitation to say either, "This is true," or, "This is false."

Then the dialog begins.

Theological Theses

Theological Prologue

There is a gaping hole in our Lutheran theology and practice, a lacuna that had consequences for pastoral care during much of the first 500 years of the Lutheran Reformation. This lacuna is *a rejection of lament*. It constitutes a gaping hole in theology and practice that hamstrings our pastoral care and church work today, more than ever.

This doctrinal and practical black hole of ours affects more than Christ's church on earth. It also affects Western culture. This lacuna is a gaping hole that had, and still has, incalculable effect on Christ's ministry and mission in modernity. This lacuna, as Ronald Rittgers explains in his magisterial book, *The Reformation of Suffering,* can be brought to light via a brief catechesis. Q: "What effect has this centuries-long rejection of lament had on the plight of Christianity in the modern Western world?" A: "Perhaps in the (very) long run, the insistence of the Western churches that human beings must face suffering without the possibility of lament has worked to undermine the plausibility of Christian faith."[8] But *do we have the ears to hear what isn't there* (and, by and large, hasn't been present for centuries) in our preaching, teaching and pastoral caregiving?[9]

1. Since the earliest days of Christianity, expressions of lament in worship have largely withered. Because of the influence of Stoic thought, lament was pushed out of the everyday lives of Christians, and where

---

7. See Spade and Yrjönsuuri, "Medieval Theories of *Obligationes*."
8. Rittgers, *Reformation of Suffering*, 261–62.
9. Schulz, "Our Lamentable Lacuna."

it does appear, it does so without form. Even theological reflection has largely ignored it. To this point, lament does not shape any decisive aspect of dogmatics or Christian ethics. This is astonishing!

2. The neglect of lament touches upon no less than the innermost secret of the Christian faith: the cross and resurrection of Jesus Christ.

3. Through the use of Psalm 22 as the foundational element in the Markan and Matthean crucifixion story, the resurrection of Jesus Christ is confessed as the answer to lament. In the Meal, through which this saved one reveals himself, he shares his newly given life in a way that incorporates the previous distress. That is to say, it incorporates lament into thanksgiving. The shared new life does not exclude death and suffering along with lament, but it includes them. The answering of lament does not simply leave them behind as if they were negligible. That can scarcely be overestimated when considering the constitution of Christian and human existence.

4. One may, therefore, with reference to the event of Easter, speak of an "anthropology of answered lament." The thanksgiving of the new human being gives praise to God, who saves from death and resurrects out of death. This praise neither refutes the lament of the old human being nor suffocates or suppresses it; rather, such praise makes room for it all. But obviously, the Christian—the new human being—must relate to the old human being. Thus, he or she has to give room to lament and the questions arising from the deep by making use of the room granted by the promise that the lament is heard.

5. Thus, lament does not become silent in light of the promise of an answer; rather, it becomes louder and sharper. The distress articulated in the lament gains painful depth. The distress is fully known and identified only in the confrontation with the promise of its being overcome.

6. Lament, because it is a request, even a complaint made in the certainty of being answered, lives in "shameless insistence" (Luke 11:8) before God. By exhorting and charging God to grant justice to people and all creatures against the enemy (Luke 18:1–8) and thereby to remain loyal to his own justice, lament calls on God to establish his promise of life: "O Jesus Christ, you are tarrying with your Day of Judgment. . . . Please come!"

7. Therefore, the "eschatology of answered lament" does not only know of the laments and psalms of revenge that are answered when the enemy is overcome by love and evil is overcome by good (Luke 23:34; Matt 5:4–48; Rom 12:19–21). It also knows of an enemy that is vanquished

because it contradicts the promised life in and around us. This, of course, includes death as the "last enemy" (1 Cor 15:26).

8. In the judgment by which the lament is heard and answered, God does not simply judge people's works and deeds analytically. God does not evaluate them in a judgment understood as declaration—this would merely cement evil, eternalize it. No, God is not a bookkeeper. Rather, God judges *creatively*: "See, I am making all things new!" (Rev 21:5). "Creatively" means in boundless goodness, in which the Creator allows and gives the creatures every good thing, and in boundless mercy, in which the Creator saves from all distress.

9. Certainly, God saves by judging and by dependably, as well as exactly, retrieving every single wounding, theft, and destruction of the life that was created by him, not forgetting anybody or anything.

10. All these things have piled up as a *massa miseriae* of world and natural history. Nobody knows it all; none could even name them accurately, much less master them or overcome them. Only God "remembers" this whole unspeakable injustice fully. God remembers it as he remembered Noah (Gen 8:1; 9:15) by saving him, together with all his fellow creatures, from the flood, that is, from the deepest ruin.

11. God saves and judges by retrieving not only the unappreciated good, but also all the world's unspeakable injustice; God saves and judges by again seeking what was irrevocably lost to humanity (Eccl 3:15; Ps 119:176; Luke 15), by healing, "returning," and "restoring" it. Demanding an account, God names injustice in a definitive way and discovers it. God also discovers our complicity in this injustice. "You have set our iniquities before you, our secret sins in the light of your countenance" (Ps 90:8; cf. 19:13).

12. This revelation and conviction of sin by God, as well as God's forgiveness, happens now and also on the last day, if indeed we as human beings are given freedom and called to accountability not above our hearts and heads, but within and through them. The process of judgment and reconciliation does not happen without our mournful remorse and repentance; it does not happen without confronting perpetrators with their victims, not without the process of healthy transformation of both victim and perpetrator. This expectation neither implies the teaching of a purgatory or a universal salvation nor does it necessarily lead there. The decision between faith and disbelief that is made before the death of a person will, in all eternity, be taken seriously. The judgment with which God hears the lament is, as has

been said, not a matter of bookkeeping; it is, rather, creative. Judgment is the world-completing act of the Creator, who in boundless mercy saves from all distress. Once the senses have been sharpened by the Old Testament, one can also recognize the "eschatology of answered lament" in the New Testament.

Ethical Theses

Ethical Prologue

It is the equivalent of Moses's demand that the Israelites choose this day whom they will serve. The demand is for us to choose this day how we will address human suffering: Shall we lament as Job, David and Jeremiah did—or are we going to be Stoics?

Consider a second point from Rittgers, that is, his diagnosis of our malady in the West, an addiction to Stoicism in preference to reliance on God. "Why this exclusion of lament?"[10] The malady, or *mala habitus*—call it "the chronic bad habit" that hamstrung the premodern church—was its acceptance in theory and practice of Stoicism. To put it charitably (much too charitably), it is rather odd that the philosophy of Cicero, Epictetus and Marcus Aurelius should have become our default philosophy of life in times of suffering. It is dumfounding to realize that we have pondered this Stoicism in our hearts after the time of ignorance had passed, following the accomplishment of Christ's suffering and resurrection for all.

Recall Acts 17 and Paul's demolition of Stoicism in the course of his argument to the Stoic and Epicurean philosophers in first-century Athens. Then, have a look at what Stoicism teaches. Here is an excerpt from the Stoic Epictetus, the mentor of the Stoic Marcus Aurelius.

> Men are disturbed, not by things, but by the principles and notions which they form concerning things. Death, for instance, is not terrible, else it would have appeared so to Socrates. But the terror consists in our notion of death that it is terrible. When therefore we are hindered, or disturbed, or grieved, let us never attribute it to others, but to ourselves; that is, to our own principles. An uninstructed person will lay the fault of his own bad condition upon others. Someone just starting instruction will

---

10. See Rittgers, *Reformation of Suffering*, 259.

lay the fault on himself. Someone who is perfectly instructed will place blame neither on others nor on himself.[11]

While there is a fine narrative commentary on Paul's deconstruction of the Stoic and Epicurean dogma that there can be no life after biological death (a dogmatically-held opinion on which the very viability of Stoicism depends) available in Barclay,[12] Augustine's sarcastic, pastoral judgment of Stoicism will do for our purposes. He touches on what we could call *The Stoic Fallacy*, the fallacy that what seems to work for a time, even for a relatively long time, is an adequate philosophy for a lifetime—a fallacy that withers and blows away like chaff in the sirocco of the resurrection of Jesus Messiah, as Augustine proclaims:

> And I am at a loss to understand how the Stoic philosophers can presume to say that these are no ills, though at the same time they allow the wise man to commit suicide and pass out of this life if they become so grievous that he cannot or ought not to endure them. . . . O happy life, which seeks the aid of death to end it? If it is happy, let the wise man remain in it; but if these ills drive him out of it, in what sense is it happy?[13]

Not that Saint Paul or Augustine has eradicated Stoicism from among us. This is due, I have discovered, to the fact that we as a church not only do not read the Stoics to see for ourselves what the Apostle recognized and deployed against this philosophy, but we are by and large not reading Augustine or Paul either. Our failure to read, but *especially our failure to read and to pray the psalms of lament* ("Take and read!" to co-opt Augustine), are the reason that we practice a sort of closet Stoicism and talk ourselves into "toughing things out" in the face of suffering, rather than lamenting to the Lord, employing His God-breathed words to us and praying to Him as dear children to their dear father.[14]

By neglecting to pray the psalms of lament, we reject God's work of terraforming, or better *cruciforming* our very being as individual human beings. Stoicism works by means of a vague sort of hope against hope that we can get ourselves through suffering; by contrast, in the psalms of lament (and the other lamentations of Scripture), which are His own words and His ways and means of affecting us, the suffering Servant of Calvary takes us up

---

11. See Epictetus, *Works*, 5.
12. Barclay, *Daily Study Bible*, 129–34.
13. Augustine, *City of God* 19.4.
14. See Schulz, "Our Lamentable Lacuna," 11–14.

into His own suffering. Choose ye this day which way of life (or which Way, Truth and Life [John 14:6]) ye will serve.

13. A theology of lament that stands in radical contradiction to the Stoic theology of submission. This implication touches on God's own being.

14. Job is not only a rebel, he is also a sufferer.

15. Moreover, one should not forget the Pauline question: "But who indeed are you, a human being, to argue with God?" (Rom 9:20), though it should not at all be made absolute, as does the already mentioned Stoic theology of submission.

16. Certainly, the last day will not begin without question or lament, but it will end without question or lament. "On that day [at its end] you will ask nothing of me" (John 16:23).

17. This is certainly true. What exactly does this certainty mean? What does it imply? What follows from it, above all, for the lingual mode of theological propositions and, correspondingly, for their kind of rationality? This question determines the layout and structure of a work of systematic theology.

18. However, it takes time to turn away from wrath and turn toward mercy, time in which the turning away and the turning toward are completed—time to pray a psalm such as Psalm 51. It is thus notable that in Psalm 22, for instance, lament is presented in no less than three approaches (Ps 22:2-6, 7-12, 13-22). The psalm leaves room for lament, even for repetition and expansion. Evidently, lament cannot be completed immediately. Patience is required—as in suffering, so also in the lament of this suffering.

19. Still, lament takes place—apparently paradoxically—in impatient anticipation of the promised saving mercy. Therefore, one must live in waiting and in hurrying (2 Pet 3:12). So the mode of speech and life may be determined both by Spirit-effected patience and by equally Spirit-effected impatient lament and petition. Luther expressed this especially clearly and impressively in his sermon on 2 Cor 15:23, offered on October 20, 1532, with reference to Rom 8:26 ("but that very Spirit intercedes with sighs too deep for words"): "O how I would love to be saved! Help from death! That is a call, such as no language and no fleshly human being [knows it], and [it wants] nothing other than salvation from death. Therefore, every Christian must learn that this sighing and lamenting will be heard and makes a noise in heaven, that the Lord will come and help."

Concluding Pastoral Postscript

Lament is not a principle; rather, lament is an existential (or non-theoretical, true-to-life) reality that involves us in God's very being via His verbatim Word to us. The biblical-verbatim reality of lamentation means that we must reconsider our understanding of what it means to be human beings and, at the same time, upgrade our philosophy of language to put our thinking in sync with the nature of the means of grace.[15]

We are hamstrung in our work of the ministry by deficient anthropologies or views of what it means to be human beings. There is a remedy in Luther's 1536 *Disputation Concerning Man*. The key insight that Bayer derives from this disputation comes from Luther's thirty-second thesis or proposition: "32. Paul in Romans 3[:28], 'We hold that a man is justified by faith apart from works,' briefly sums up the definition of man, saying, 'Man is justified by faith.'" The impact of Bayer's appropriation of Luther's biblical anthropology depends on our understanding Luther's appropriation of Aristotle, so we need a brief philosophical excursus.

Since our thesis (32. Paul in Romans 3[:28], "We hold that a man is justified by faith apart from works," briefly sums up the definition of man, saying, "Man is justified by faith.") is an anthropological, or essential definition of the human being, as Oswald Bayer says, we would do well to translate it as "The human being is human in that he is justified by faith." This relies on the broader and deeper understanding of *logos* that we receive only in the biblical text, but this does not mean that we can do without Aristotle as the first staging point, so to speak, for Luther's expedition that we know as his *Disputation Concerning Man*. As Bayer explains:

> The human being is human *insofar as* he is justified by faith. . . . Justifying faith for Luther is not something *about* a human being, no qualitative element, which comes only secondarily, as that which is accidental to the substance. *Hominem justificari fide* (a human being is justified by faith) is, instead, a *fundamental* anthropological thesis.[16]

In other words, we have grown up learning to think of the human being as *homo sapiens*; but on the basis of the thicker, more authoritative biblical anthropology, it would be much more accurate to think of the human being as *homo justificans*, since we are the kind of being that seeks to be justified. The definition of our kind of being, namely, that a human being is justified by faith, depends on Aristotle's essential definition of our kind of being as *zōon*

---

15. See Schulz, "Pain, Suffering, Lament," 7–12.
16. Bayer, *Martin Luther's Theology*. 155–56.

logon echōn (ζῷον λόγον ἔχων) in his *Politics*.[17] Our essential characteristic of *logos* does not mean merely that we can talk, reason, discourse, inquire, and so on just for the fun of it. Aristotle recognizes that, since our species is essentially *logos*-like we are going to use *logos*. Then the question is: use *logos* for what purpose, to what end? The contemporary philosopher Robert Sokolowski translates Aristotle's definition of the human being as "agents of truth,"[18] but this too invites the same question of the purpose of our nature. Bayer, following Luther in beginning with Aristotle's minimum daily required definition, and then following Luther's 1536 expedition into the heights of Scripture (undreamed of by Aristotle and the Greeks, 1 Cor 2:9), to discern that the *logos* of the human being finds its telos in justification.

Therefore, as the kind of being that we human beings are, we will ultimately use *logos* to justify our existence: either we acknowledge that we are justified by God's grace alone in Christ, or we spend our time of grace seeking to justify ourselves apart from Christ—an inherently undoable and unsatisfying project!

We find ourselves blind, dead and enemies of God by nature, a lamentable situation. But God is not content to leave us on our own, so He becomes incarnate. Then, He creates in us a right spirit (that is, a spirit in tune with His will) by the process of lament in His own words. We human beings are *homo sapiens* (a decent definition), *homo justificans* (a thicker, biblical definition) and *homo lamentes* (the best pastoral definition).

The biblical text is the means through which God actually works on actual people. There is no other Way. Just as the Words of Scripture are more in character with the way in which a husband talks with his wife, rather than a systematic treatise, so too lament is a personal interaction over time between people and their incarnate God. As we have been saying for half

---

17. "Therefore it is clear that the city-state is a natural growth, and that man is by nature a political animal, and a man that is by nature and not merely by fortune citiless is either low in the scale of humanity or above it (like the "clanless, lawless, heartless" man reviled by Homer, for one by nature unsocial is also 'a lover of war') inasmuch as he is solitary, like an isolated piece at draughts. And why *man is a political animal* in a greater measure than any bee or any gregarious animal is clear. For nature, as we declare, does nothing without purpose; and *man alone of the animals possesses speech.* The mere voice, it is true, can indicate pain and pleasure, and therefore is possessed by the other animals as well (for their nature has been developed so far as to have sensations of what is painful and pleasant and to indicate those sensations to one another, but speech is designed to indicate the advantageous and the harmful, and therefore also the right and the wrong; for it is the special property of man in distinction from the other animals that he alone has perception of good and bad and right and wrong and the other moral qualities, and it is partnership in these things that makes a household and a city-state" (Aristotle, *Politics* 1.1253a).

18. Sokolowski, *Phenomenology of the Human Person*, 1.

a millennium in the Lutheran church, "God cannot be treated with, God cannot be apprehended *nisi per verbum*, except through the Word."[19] Lament—biblical, Psalm 22-lament, cannot take place *nisi per verbum*. Just as important: We cannot lament if we are going to neglect and thus reject the lamentations of the Bible.

Extreme care is necessary because the certainty of being heard is not simply available as a principle, which one could always presuppose and reckon with at any given time (timelessly!). On the other hand, a skepticism on principle is not acceptable either because no lament exists entirely without remembered trust or, finally, expected answer. In a specific way, God's hearing and fulfilling is always assumed, otherwise even lament would be impossible and meaningless.

Too often, systematic theology reaches a happy ending much too quickly and does not take seriously the uncertainty and hopelessness along the way. It surely takes time to walk the way in prayer, meditation, and affliction (*oratione, meditatione, tentatione*). Yet when the precarious temporality of the way often interrupted is considered seriously, it decisively shapes the layout and structure of a systematic theology. It determines the grammar of its statements and, correspondingly, the nature of its rationality and integrity. But temporality is not to be taken into account only with respect to us, but also with respect to God's own being.[20]

The crucial point here is that *lament requires time (lots and lots of time!) with the means of grace as such*. Perhaps lament, for this very reason, cannot be at home in systematic theology. While the *stuff* of theology, that is, the biblical *logos*, is alive and active (Heb 4:12), the *form* of theology, that is, the philosophical arrangement of the Word,[21] tends toward intellectualism and principlism. This is a problem as well for philosophy and ethics, which always want to substitute universal ethical principles for the living person's living encounter with the living and personal God of the Bible, as Kierkegaard brings to light in *Fear and Trembling*, his Lutheran dialog on the Genesis 22 account of Abraham being commanded to sacrifice Isaac.

To be crystal clear, lament works this way not on account of our praying the psalms of lament liturgically and thus committing ourselves to a mindset or course of action in an especially impactful manner, as in Gordon Wenham's intriguing book titled *Psalms as Torah*:

19. *Ap* 4. See Schulz, "NISI PER VERBUM."

20. Schulz, "Toward a Theology of Lament," 216.

21. "The two main sources of Christian theology are the Bible and Hellenic culture, especially Greek philosophy" (Allen and Springfield, *Philosophy for Understanding Theology*, xv).

> Prayer has an impact on ethical thought. For example, when we pray, "forgive us our trespasses, as we forgive those who trespass against us," we are committing ourselves to forgiving other people.... This makes the ethics of liturgy uniquely powerful. It makes a stronger claim on the believer than either law, wisdom, or story, which are simply subject to passive reception: one can listen to a proverb or a story and then take it or leave it, but if you pray ethically, you commit yourself to a path of action.[22]

On the contrary, in the case of biblical lament, the message is the means. Lament is not plain lamenting only; it is lament instituted by God's command (as in the psalms of lament, Lamentations, and so on) and intimately connected with the Word of God. Lament is sacramental because lament is Word of God activity—God's work on our human being in, with, and under the words of Scripture.

In the introduction to this version of Bayer's twenty-first century Disputation Concerning Lament, I referred to Borges's "book review" of a fictional project to reach twentieth-century people with the text of Cervantes's *Don Quixote*. Let me conclude by repurposing Borges this way: "Oswald Bayer does not want to compose *another* theology, which is surely easy enough—he wants to compose *the* theology.... His admirable ambition is to produce a theology which coincides—word for word and line for line—with those laments of David in the Psalms, Jeremiah in his Lamentations, the Prophets in their writings, Paul in his Epistle to the Romans, and in the very person of *God incarnate in the words of His only-begotten Son on the cross* (Ps 22)."

You can see where this must end up! Before God expired the words and David inspired Psalm 22, this is what Yahweh commanded His people regarding their kings.

> And when he sits on the throne of his kingdom, he shall write for himself in a book a copy of this law, approved by the Levitical priests. And it shall be with him, and he shall read in it all the days of his life, that he may learn to fear the Lord his God by keeping all the words of this law and these statutes, and doing them. (Deut 17:18–19)

Perhaps the way for us to learn and to teach lament has to do with pen and paper. It requires time. It requires the Scriptures. This is most certainly true.

---

22. Wenham, *Psalms as Torah*, 57.

Bayer's argument for biblical lament ends up with us in sackcloth and ashes, the Word of God open in our hands. Those psalms of lament and the laments of the prophets and apostles—we really ought to write them out by hand, so that we are paying attention and so that we are reading, learning and inwardly digesting lamentation. To thank and praise, to serve and obey the God who suffered under Pontius Pilate for all, we must lament. To minister faithfully and fully to the sick and the dying, we must lament. To be theologians of the cross, we must lament.

Brothers, we . . . must . . . lament.

Bibliography

Allen, Diogenes, and Eric O. Springfield. *Philosophy for Understanding Theology*. 2nd ed. Louisville: Westminster John Knox, 2007.

Barclay, William. *The Daily Study Bible*. Rev. ed. Philadelphia: Westminster, 1976.

Bayer, Oswald. *Freedom in Response: Lutheran Ethics: Sources and Controversies*. Translated by Jeffrey F. Cayzer. Oxford: Oxford University Press, 2007.

———. *Martin Luther's Theology: A Contemporary Interpretation*. Grand Rapids: Eerdmans, 2008.

———. "Toward a Theology of Lament." In *Caritas et Reformatio: Essays on Church and Society in Honor of Carter Lindberg*, edited by David M. Whitford, 211–20. Translated by Matthias Gockel. Concordia Academic, 2002.

Borges, Jorge Luis. *Collected Fictions*. Translated by Andrew Hurley. London: Penguin, 1999.

Epictetus. *The Works of Epictetus: His Discourses, in Four Books, the Enchiridion, and Fragments*. Translated by Thomas Wentworth Higginson. New York: Nelson, 1890. Online. http://www.perseus.tufts.edu/hopper/text?doc=Perseus%3Atext%3A1999.01.0237%3Atext%3Denc%3Achapter%3D5.

Rittgers, Ronald K. *The Reformation of Suffering: Pastoral Theology and Lay Piety in Late Medieval and Early Modern Germany*. New York: Oxford University Press, 2012.

Schulz, Gregory P. "NISI PER VERBUM: A Disputation Concerning Postmodernism and the Pastoral Ministry." *Logia* 27.4 (2018) 23–36.

———. "Our Lamentable Lacuna: How Western Churches Have Undermined the Plausibility of Christian Faith." *Logia* 21.1 (2019) 7–14.

———. "Pain, Suffering, Lament." *Logia* 24.2 (2015) 7–12.

———, ed. *The Problem of Suffering: A Companion Study Guide + Resources for Pastors and Christian Caregivers*. St. Louis: Concordia, 2011.

———. "Session Four—Logic." *Open Education*. Concordia University, Wisconsin, 2017. https://openeducation.blackboard.com/mooc-catalog/courseDetails/view?course_id=_1630_1.

Sokolowski, Robert. *Phenomenology of the Human Person*. Cambridge: Cambridge University Press, 2008.

Spade, Paul Vincent, and Yrjönsuuri, Mikko. "Medieval Theories of *Obligationes*." Stanford Encyclopedia of Philosophy (2017). Edited by Edward N. Zalta. https://plato.stanford.edu/archives/win2017/entries/obligationes.

Wenham, Gordon J. *Psalms as Torah: Reading Biblical Song Ethically.* Grand Rapids: Baker Academic, 2012.

13

Hearing and Seeing (Eye & Ear)

Word and Image in the Bible, Luther, and the Lutheran Tradition

Jeffrey G. Silcock

Introduction

The underlying thesis of this paper is that in Lutheran theology hearing is given primacy over seeing, the word over the image, and faith over sight. Counterintuitive as it may sound, it will become clear that seeing in fact arises from hearing. Although the word is given priority, the image is still important because it is the means by which the word takes hold of the heart so that we not only hear the word with our ears but also perceive it with our other senses as well.

I will begin by looking at the topic from a biblical perspective and then consider it from the standpoint of Luther and the Reformation. In the final section, I will show how the priority of hearing over seeing in the Bible and in Luther carries over into the Lutheran tradition with priority being given to the oral word over the visual image. We will see that art, though subordinate to the word, supports and reinforces the word and allows it to impress itself on the heart and stir the emotions more powerfully than it could by itself.

Hearing and Seeing in the Bible

Outside the Bible, especially in the Greek mysteries, the normal way of apprehending God is by seeing him. Hearing is subordinated to seeing. The moment of revelation is the moment of seeing the divine epiphany rather than hearing the divine voice.[1] Unlike the Greco-Roman world, seeing God plays no major role in the Bible—although the psalmists often express the desire to see the face of God in the sanctuary.[2] Both the Old and New Testaments testify to the priority of hearing over seeing, and of faith over sight. In the biblical world, the priority of speech and orality even extends to prayer and meditation. Devout Israelites and Jews not only read Scripture aloud, or whisper it to themselves, but they also mediate on it and even pray it in an audible voice.[3]

Old Testament

We begin at the beginning. In the beginning, God created through his word: he spoke, and it came to be (Gen 1:3). This is the biblical basis for referring to God's spoken word as a creative or performative word. God can be relied on to do what he says, and he can do it because his word is all-powerful. The theme of God's word is picked up again in the Prologue to the Fourth Gospel where we learn that the word with which God *spoke* the world into being became enfleshed in the person of his Son, Jesus Christ (John 1:1); the *logos asarkos* became the *logos sarkos*. The theme of the creative word in Genesis 1 is echoed in Psalm 33:6 where the psalmist confesses that the heavens were made "by the word of the Lord" and all things by the "Spirit [breath] of his mouth." This is one of the foundational texts for the doctrine of creation *ex nihilo*.[4] It is also the main text that teaches the inseparability of word and Spirit,[5] reminding us that the *spiritus creator*[6] works through the word, and not apart from the word.

---

1. *TDNT* 1:217.

2. See Ps 42:2: "My soul thirsts for God, for the living God [a polemic against idols]. When shall I come and appear before God?" The psalmist is longing to go to God's temple, the Lord's earthly dwelling place, where his word is heard, and his face is seen, in faith (Ps 27:8). Both hearing and seeing come together in Song of Songs: "Let me see your face, let me hear your voice" (Song 2:14).

3. Bunge, *Earthen Vessels*, 123. The Hebrew word for "meditate" (*hgh*) means to ruminate on God's word, to chew it over, like a cow chewing its cud, to murmur it aloud.

4. For a theological rather than a scientific interpretation of this concept in Romans 4:17, see Bayer, *Martin Luther's Theology*, 96–97.

5. Silcock, "Luther on the Holy Spirit," 297–300.

6. The hymn *Veni, Creator Spiritus* ("Come, Creator Spirit"), believed to have been written by Rabanus Maurus in the ninth century, links together creation theology and soteriology. For an English translation, based on Luther's German version (*Komm, Gott Schöpfer, Heiliger Geist*), see *LW* 53:261–62.

Hamann captures a profound truth of the Lutheran doctrine of creation in his classical formula: "Speak, that I may see you." He says, "this wish was fulfilled by creation, which is a speech [*Rede*] to the creature through the creature[7]; for day to day pours forth speech, and night to night declares knowledge" (Ps 19:2).[8] In other words, God has already responded to our desire to see him and know something about him with the gift of creation. However, because of sin, we cannot hear God.[9] Our ears must first be opened—and indeed God does that first in baptism when he speaks into our ears his performative word *ephphatha*, be opened! (Mark 7:34), so that we can hear him speak to us in his word. No one has ever seen God, except his only Son who has told us of the Father (John 1:14) and who now speaks the Father's word to us. The great mystery of the incarnation is that Christ not only *speaks* the word of the Father, he *is* God's word to us in the flesh.

One emphasis, common in the Old Testament, is that God's voice is heard but his face remains hidden. The classical text that underscores this is Deuteronomy 4:12 where Moses says to the people at Sinai, "You heard the sound of words, but saw no form; there was only a voice." This text, as well the prohibition of images in Deuteronomy 4:15–19, has been at the center of the debate over whether images are permissible in the liturgical spaces of our churches. I will return to that question in the final part of this essay.

No sinner is permitted to see the face of God (John 1:14; 1 John 4:12), since no one can see God and live (Exod 33:20), "for God dwells in unapproachable light" (1 Tim 6:16). For this reason, all that Moses sees of God, who hides him in a rock as his glory passes over, is his back, not his face. Admittedly, we read that God *spoke* to Moses "face to face" (Exod 33:11), but this means that he spoke with him intimately, as a friend, but he did not see his face.

On the other hand, the account of Jacob's all-night wrestling bout with a mysterious figure at the ford of the Jabbok River reveals an altogether different side of God, the God who is utterly silent and reveals nothing of himself—although in the end he allows Jacob to overpower him and to wrest a blessing from him (Gen 32:22–32). Jacob was petrified with fear.

---

7. See Bayer, *Contemporary in Dissent*, 76–77, for an explanation of the significance of the two prepositions "to" and "through" in Hamann's dictum that creation is the address *to* the creature *through* the creature.

8. Betz, "Glory(ing) in the Humility," 146. For a fuller description of the significance of God's creative word that he speaks to us through the creation, see Bayer, *Martin Luther's Theology*, 106–12, where he takes Luther's sermon on Jesus's healing of a deaf man (Mark 7:31–37) and, following Hamann, uses it to give a new twist to the notion of "natural theology."

9. Already the second half of Ps 19 shows that human beings are unable to hear God speak to them through creation, and so God has to give Israel the Torah (Ps 19:7–13).

Who was this uncanny figure he was wrestling with? Was it God or was it the devil, or was it God disguised as the devil? Luther notes that Jacob only recognized in hindsight that it was God[10]—Luther calls this God the hidden God, the *Deus absconditus*.[11] He interprets this story as paradigmatic of the encounter of believers with the hidden God, who contradicts the promise of the revealed God (*Deus revelatus*) and so causes great spiritual turmoil and anguish (*Anfechtung*). In such times of doubt, all we can do is hold on to the promise of the preached God (*Deus praedicatus*), for there he is unambiguously the God for us.

New Testament

It is the unanimous witness of both testaments that God is hidden from our eyes, and that faith and hope belong to the realm of the things not seen (Heb 11:1). It is only in Christ Jesus that God steps out of his hiddenness and reveals himself in a definitive way in the mystery of the incarnation, where the eternal Logos takes on flesh[12] in the person of the God-Man and becomes the visible Word so that whoever sees him sees God, in faith. But even though God's Son walked the streets of Palestine, most who saw him did not believe in him, as we will see. Just seeing him persuaded no one who did not believe in him already.

John the Evangelist says of the Word incarnate, "*We* have seen his glory" (John 1:14), where the "we" is the apostolic circle, those who already believe that "Jesus is the Christ, the Son of God" (John 20:31). Only the eyes of faith can perceive his glory hidden under the form of an ordinary

---

10. See also Bayer, *Theology the Lutheran Way*, 18–19. Compare Luther's sermons on Gen 31; 32 (WA 14:433–42); Gen 32 (WA 14:443–50); Gen 32 (WA 24:566–81); Gen 32–34 (WA 14:450–57). See also WA 44:93–116.

11. See Miller, *Hanging by a Promise*, 257–302, for a discussion of Bayer's claim that Luther makes a critical distinction between the hiddenness of God in revelation and the terrible hiddenness of God outside revelation. It is this latter experience of the *Deus absconditus* that can drive people to unbelief and despair because it feels as if God has become our enemy. As Luther says in the section on the three lights at the end of his treatise on *The Bound Will* (WA 18:784–85; *LW* 33:289–92), this unfathomable contradiction within God himself will never be resolved in the light of nature (*lux naturae*), and not even in the light of grace (*lux gratiae*), but only in the light of glory (*lux gloriae*).

12. The use of *sarx* in John 1:14 rather than the usual *soma* is decidedly anti-docetic and anti-gnostic. John's Gospel has not only a high Christology but also a strong emphasis on the full humanity of Christ. In the same way, the writer of the First Epistle of John testifies of the Word of life that we (the apostolic circle) have heard him [with our ears], seen him with our eyes, and looked upon and touched him with our hands (1 John 1:1–2). In both cases, the emphasis on the reality and physicality of the incarnation, the enfleshment of the Son of God, is unmistakable.

human being. To those whose eyes are closed in unbelief, Jesus's miraculous signs (*semeia*) are only deeds (*erga*) of power, not signs pointing to his messianic identity. When Jesus multiplies the loaves and feeds the five thousand, the crowd wants to make him king (John 6:15), a bread king, but his true kingship they reject (John 19:14: Behold, your king). They miss the sign pointing to Jesus, the bread of life, and see only the bread that perishes (John 6:27). Again, when Jesus turns the water into wine at the wedding in Cana, the text says that his disciples—not the crowd—begin to believe (ingressive aorist) in him (John 2:11). Finally, the man born blind in John 9 can "see" Jesus even before he opens his eyes, because he believes in him, while the Pharisees who claim to see are blind (John 9:41), because they do not believe that Jesus is the Son of God, the light of the world (John 8:12). In John's Gospel, word and sign are interrelated. The word interprets the sign and the sign confirms the word.

Thomas's Easter confession to Christ as the risen Lord forms the climax of the Fourth Gospel and, together with the Prologue, is one of the two great testimonies to the full divinity of Christ in this Gospel (20:28: My Lord and my God). Thomas's confession elicits from Jesus a great beatitude: "Blessed are those who have not seen and yet believe" (20:29). Thomas believes because he saw the risen Christ in the flesh (we don't need to posit that he actually touches his wounded side; his invitation to do so is enough). But Jesus now affirms that all who belong to the post-Easter church and did not see the historical Jesus with their eyes are at no disadvantage. Indeed, with his exaltation and return to the Father, the way of perceiving Jesus changes. Visual perception must now give way to the perception of faith. Mary Magdalene also has to learn this lesson when she wants to hold on to Jesus in a physical way (John 20:17: "Do not cling to me"). However, it is this same Mary who demonstrates the truth of Jesus's words: "My sheep hear my voice, and I know them, and they follow me" (John 10:27). For when Jesus, the Good Shepherd, calls Mary by name, she recognizes who he is (John 20:16). It is his voice, not his appearance, which reveals Jesus to Mary. Here clearly, seeing is not believing, but hearing is seeing and believing.

Luther often reflects on the paradoxical nature of divine revelation where God hides himself under the form of his opposite (*absconditus sub contrario*).[13] And nowhere does God hide himself more deeply than on the

---

13. Luther explicates this in his *Heidelberg Disputation* of 1518 (WA 1:353–65; *LW* 31:39–58) in connection with his *theologia crucis*, where he stresses that God reveals himself by hiding himself. This is a genuinely reformational topos in an otherwise largely pre-reformational document. Luther develops the topic further in his *Bound Will*. On the theology of the cross, see also Lexutt and Neumeister, *Alles hängt am Kreuz*. This book offers a truly evangelical meditation on the theme of the cross through

cross (*cruce tectum*) and in the cry of dereliction, where God cries out to God against God: "My God, my God, why have you abandoned me" (Matt 27:46).[14] Only faith can penetrate the covering mask that conceals God under the form of his humanity. The Fourth Gospel in particular emphasizes that only *believing is seeing* (see John 6:40; 12:45; 20:29) and that mere seeing is blind. Spiritual seeing is always the seeing of faith. Only in faith can we join St. John in saying of the Word made flesh, "We have seen his glory, glory as of the only Son from the Father," and so too only faith can see in the crucifixion of the man, Jesus of Nazareth, the glorification of God's Son (John 7:39; 12:16, 23; 13:31).[15]

The Promise of the Word in Luther

In this section I will explore Luther's understanding of the word and show that he continues the biblical tradition of ascribing priority to the word and so of privileging the ear over the eye, and faith over sight.

The Priority of the Word

When Luther says, "Do not look at anything with your eyes, but put your eyes in your ears,"[16] he is reversing an ancient Greek tradition, perpetuated by the scholastic theology of his day, which gave preeminence to the eye rather than the ear, and so put the image before the word. For him the emphasis is rather on God's word.[17] However, although reformational theology stresses the priority of the word—indeed, of the external, oral word (*verbum externum*)—the image or sign, as we will see, is not unimportant and the two cannot be separated, for what we see is determined by what

---

words (Lexutt) and images (Neumeister). On the concept of God hidden under the opposite, see also the Explanation of thesis 58 of the *Theses on Indulgences* (WA 1:613-14, 27; *LW* 31:225-27). For a fresh perspective, see Silcock, "New Look."

14. "The cross demands faith *contrary to what our eyes see*" (Sasse, *We Confess*, 50).

15. On "signs" in John, see Brown, *Gospel According to John*, 527-31.

16. WA 37:202, 215-16.

17. See Heal's aptly titled article (Heal, "Catholic Eye and the Protestant Ear," 321), where she notes this reversal. She refers to Peter Blickle's research on the "Christianization" of peasant belief in Saxony where he poses the telling question: "Why did people in 1515 want to '*see*' the Host, and why in 1525 did they want to '*hear*' the plain word of God?" We know that in pre-Reformation times, the holy bread was worshipped more than it was consumed, and that ocular communion (*manducatio per visum*) overshadowed communion by the mouth. See Koerner, *Reformation of the Image*, 341-42.

we hear. So, it is consonant with the preeminence Luther gives to hearing when he claims that "the ears alone are the organs of a Christian."[18] Luther obviously exaggerates here to drive home a crucial point: that priority must be given to hearing rather than seeing because it accords with the general thrust of the biblical witness.[19]

In parallel to the early Christian belief that Christ's conception in Mary's womb took place when the seed of God's word, spoken by the angel, entered Mary's ear (*conceptio per aurem*),[20] Luther teaches that the same word of God also enters the heart of every believer through the ear, in keeping with Paul's words that faith comes from hearing (Rom 10:17). Mary's pregnancy through the agency of the Spirit-filled word means that she took the word into herself and treasured it in her heart (Luke 2:19). And after the period of gestation, the Word is born that saves the world.

Oswald Bayer perceptively notes that Hebrews 11:3 along with Genesis 1 and John 1 show the creational and ontological basis for why the biblical texts as a whole break with the Western tradition that gives primacy to seeing. The Hebrews text states clearly that "the universe was created by the word of God, so that what is seen was not made out of things that are visible." Bayer observes that in human perception therefore "primacy is given to hearing because the world was *called* into being out of nothing.[21] He then makes a crucial link with faith and justification because God's creation by his powerful word was a creation of out nothing, without any conditions, "without any merit or worthiness on our part,"[22] a pure gift, which is to be received in faith. This is the language of justification, which Paul also, in speaking of Abraham's faith, links with creation (Rom 4:17).

The priority of the oral word also implies the priority of hearing over reading.[23] This has implications for the nature of the liturgy, saturated as

---

18. WA 57/3:222, 4–7, esp. 7 (on Heb 10:5). Similarly, Jesus commends Mary above Martha because Mary had chosen to listen to Jesus's word rather than serve him (Luke 10:42). It is not a question of one or the other. Both are important, but listening to Jesus's word, which is faith, comes before doing, just as for Luther the *vita passiva* must come before the *vita activa*. On the latter, see WA 5:165, 33–166, 16.

19. On hearing and seeing in Luther, see Preuss, *Martin Luther*, 130–35.

20. Following Mary's *fiat* (Luke 1:38), she conceives according to the promise of the angel. No word that God speaks is impossible, no word lacks the power to do what he says (see also Isa 55:11).

21. Bayer, "Schöpfungslehre als Rechtfertigungsontologie," 32.

22. Bayer, "Schöpfungslehre als Rechtfertigungsontologie," 33.

23. We note in passing that Luther also privileges the oral word over the written word, since for him the word is first and foremost the *viva vox Dei*. He emphasizes in an Advent sermon that the church is a "mouth-house, not a pen-house" (WA 10/1.2:48, 5–6). On the other hand, Luther knows that these two forms of the word cannot be

it is with God's word, which is read, sung, preached, and sacramentally enacted. It is this external, bodily word (*das leibliche Wort*) of the gospel, confessed in Article V of the *Augsburg Confession*, which was rejected by the *Schwärmer*, the anti-sacramental spiritualists of the day. Luther continually stresses the external, bodily word, as it is proclaimed and enacted in the divine service, for one reason and one reason only: to preserve the integrity of the gospel for the sake of troubled consciences.[24]

The apostle Paul stresses that in this life "we walk by faith and not by sight" (2 Cor 5:7). Luther puts it this way, "The kingdom of God is a hearing kingdom (*Hör-Reich*), not a seeing kingdom (*Sehe-Reich*). For the eyes do not guide and lead us to discover Christ and to learn to know him, but this is a task for the ears."[25] Nevertheless, as already mentioned, hearing and seeing are inseparably connected: we only see through hearing. So even our seeing is never apart from the word. As Hamann says, "God makes himself visible only by allowing himself to be heard."[26]

The Word Liturgically and Sacramentally Enacted

In this section we will consider in summary fashion the threefold way in which the word is enacted: through the absolution, the sermon, and the sacrament (including baptism).

Part of Luther's reformational discovery is that God's word is constitutive of the sacrament and does and delivers what it promises, because God does not lie. Bayer has carefully laid out the story of how Luther's exegetical labors gradually led him to understand God's promise as the crystallization of the gospel, which is the promise of forgiveness, orally and sacramentally enacted, and received here and now in faith.[27] Crucial to Luther's reformational breakthrough is his overcoming of the Augustinian

---

separated, for the proclaimed word is grounded in the written word and needs the written word as a normative criterion to preserve it from error (*BSLK* 767, 1; *BC* 1216, 9–19). The oral word and the written word belong together because in and through both the Holy Spirit communicates and mediates Jesus Christ the Savior, whose person and work form the chief content of the Scriptures.

24. This emphasis runs throughout Luther's writings. For some examples, see Bayer, *Promissio*, 168–69, 174–75, 184–85, 187, 190, 197–202, 209, 211, 226–29, 240–53, 257–58, 261–65, 267, 269, 272, 277, 283n62, 286–93, 296–97, 306–7, 311–37, 341, 347–48, 350.

25. WA 51:9, 25–30.

26. Bayer, *Contemporary in Dissent*, 75.

27. For a summary of Luther's reformational discovery, turn, or breakthrough, see Bayer, *Promissio*, 339–51.

split between *signum* and *res* and returning to the sacramental realism (the *est*) of the New Testament. According to Augustine, the sacramental sign (*signum*) points away from itself to an inner or heavenly reality (*res*). However, Luther's decisive hermeneutical insight is that the *signum* points to itself and is itself the *res*.[28] Faith believes the word of promise and grasps hold of the *signum* and *res* at the same time so that the human word of the preacher *is* God's word, the bread *is* Christ's body, the wine *is* Christ's blood, the water of baptism *is* a washing of regeneration and renewal in the Holy Spirit. God makes himself audible to human ears, visible to human eyes, and tangible to human touch. It is through these means of grace that God enters the senses and engages the human heart.[29]

As we have been saying, the word has priority, but the sign also plays a role. Luther points out that "Christ has attached a most powerful and noble seal and sign to the words of his testament [*verba testamenti*]. This seal and sign is his own true flesh and blood under the bread and wine." But he notes that, "since we live in our five senses," we need an outward sign besides the word to cling to. Christ has so arranged things that he draws us to the spiritual through the external, "comprehending the external with the eyes of the body and the spiritual or inward with the eyes of the heart."[30]

Along with his reformational insight, Luther recovers the ancient teaching of the *communicatio idiomatum* (communication of attributes) which enables him to say that God entrusts his word to humans and puts it in their mouths and on their lips so that we have no doubt that it is God himself who speaks.[31] The minister is the servant of Christ and the mouthpiece of God in both the sermon and the sacraments.[32] Sasse reminds us that after a pastor has finished his sermon, he can join Luther in saying with joyful confidence that he has preached God's word.[33] The most his Reformed colleague can say is that he hopes God has seen fit to add his Spirit

---

28. See Bayer, *Promissio*, 240; Ringleben, *Gott im Wort*, 154–65. For Augustine's understanding of the sacrament, see Sasse, *This Is My Body*, 25–26n10.

29. See Bayer, *Living by Faith*, 47–49; Cooper, *Life in the Flesh*, 108–30.

30. WA 6:359, 4–12; *LW* 35:86. Also noted in Sasse, *This is My Body*, 114.

31. WA 12:493, 3–7.

32. Luther, therefore, says in *The Babylonian Captivity of the Church* (1520), that we should "receive Baptism at human hands just as if Christ himself, indeed, God himself, were baptizing us with his own hands" (WA 6:530, 19–31; *LW* 36:62–63; cf. 29, 82).

33. Many older churches have the words of John 12:21 engraved on the pulpit lectern: "We wish to see Jesus." It serves as a good reminder that people come to church, not to hear the eloquent words of the preacher, but to hear Jesus, indeed, to "see" Jesus in the words of their pastor. Paul's resolve to preach nothing but "Jesus Christ and him crucified" should be our model (1 Cor 2:2).

to his human words so that they become his divine words.[34] The Lutheran pastor's claim is not arrogance; it is made out of the conviction that, as an ordained servant of the word, he stands in the place of Christ (2 Cor 5:20) and speaks Christ's word. The basis for this confidence is the dominical institution of the office together with the seminal reformational teaching of the *communicatio idiomatum*, which has been called the linchpin or the axle and motor of Luther's theology.[35]

The promise, "God is for you"[36] and "your sins are forgiven," are physical words spoken into my ear by the mouth of the pastor. They are biblical words, but for them to become words of gospel for me, they need to be addressed to me by a preacher. A Lutheran sermon should never just speak about the gospel but deliver it, for God's word is performative, it does things: it opens ears and eyes, it releases from captivity, it heals body and soul, and forgives sins.[37] For Luther, preaching is thoroughly sacramental.

Luther believes that the Lord's Supper is a form of proclamation and so urges that the altar be moved forward so that the presiding minister can consecrate the elements in the full view of the people and they hear the words of institution (*verba*) as proclamation of the gospel promise.[38] The emphasis on hearing the words marks a shift from Luther's earlier focus on seeing that we noted earlier. Before the Reformation, the element or sign is the dominant part of the mass, but as Luther's exegetical work leads him to understand the centrality of the spoken word, specifically the *verba*, which are pure promise, the element or sign loses its prominence and becomes subordinated to the word.[39]

Luther not only stresses the priority of the word but he also has to insist, *contra* the radical spiritualists (*Schwärmer*), on the priority of the *external* preached word of promise over the inner word of the Spirit, so that those troubled by doubts and spiritual attack (*Anfechtung*) have something objectively certain that they can take hold of and rely on. Luther is at heart a pastoral theologian who always wants to give comfort and confidence to the

---

34. Sasse, *Here We Stand*, 169. He notes Luther's words in *Against Hanswurst* (1541) where he says that a preacher can say with St. Paul and all the apostles and prophets: "*Haec dixit Dominus*, 'God himself has said this'" (WA 51:517, 8–9; *LW* 41:216).

35. See Steiger, "Communicatio Idiomatum," 125–58. Luther applies this doctrine chiefly to Christology. For a thorough discussion of its significance in Luther, see Bayer, "Das Wort ward Fleisch," 5–34.

36. On the reformational understanding of Luther's *pro me/pro te* formula, see Bayer, *Promissio*, 274–97.

37. On the sermon as a speech act, see Bayer, "Preaching the Word," 254–55.

38. WA 19:80, 28–30; *LW* 53:69.

39. See Bayer, *Promissio*, 245–46.

troubled conscience. He argues that the outward things (the oral word and the material sacraments) come first because these are certain; they in turn give rise to inward experiences. Luther is emphatic: "God has determined to give the inward to no one except through the outward."[40]

Luther insists not only that the outward word must precede the inner word, but also that the downward movement of God's word to us must precede the upward movement of our words to God in response. In this he is simply echoing the Bible's own testimony that the sacramental (*beneficium*) comes before the sacrificial (*sacrificium*) and is the basis for it. This, in a nutshell, is the foundational principle of Lutheran worship[41] and grows out of Luther's equally fundamental hermeneutical principle that law and gospel must be properly distinguished.[42] In a similar way, Luther insists that the *sacramentum* must always come before the *exemplum*.[43]

Word and Image in the Lutheran Tradition

In this final section I will consider the Lutheran attitude to images, in the sense of the visual arts. Luther and his colleagues are forced to grapple with the image question when faced with the rising unrest in Wittenberg due to the teaching of Karlstadt, Münster, and their fellow iconoclasts (*Bilderstürmer*). They want to remove all images and pictures from the churches because they claim they are idolatrous and contrary to Scripture. While Luther is initially cool towards images,[44] he later changes his mind and sees their value in furthering the cause of the Reformation.

---

40. WA 18:136, 9–15; *LW* 40:146. In the *Smalcald Articles*, Luther says bluntly: "God gives no one his Spirit or grace apart from the external Word which goes before" (*BC* 322, 3; *BSLK* 770, 12–14).

41. On *beneficium* and *sacrificium*, see Vajta, *Lutheran Worship*, 27–66.

42. See WA 38:8–42. See the translation by Willard L. Burce in Luther, "Distinction." Luther's law-gospel distinction is also the basis of his cardinal reformational teaching of justification by faith.

43. See Nagel, "*Sacramentum et Exemplum*," 172–99. Luther says that the "chief article and foundation of the gospel is that before you take Christ as an example, you accept and recognize him as a gift, as a present that God has given you and that is your own" (WA 10/1.1:12–5; *LW* 35:119).

44. This criticism of images is most apparent in his early period and arises mainly from his disapproval of the Catholic use of images and his skepticism over externals; as he saw it then, since they are merely shadows of the real thing, they are unnecessary. However, once Luther comes to appreciate that material things are God's good gifts, which can be used in the service of the gospel, he embraces the visual arts and begins a long and productive collaboration with the Wittenberg artist and entrepreneur, Lucas

His single most sustained rebuttal of the iconoclasts comes in his famous 1525 tract *Against the Heavenly Prophets*. It is there that he sets out one of his most incisive arguments in favor of images.

> It is impossible for me to hear [the gospel story of the Passion] and bear it in mind without forming mental images of it in my heart. For whether I will or not, when I hear of Christ, an image of a man hanging on a cross takes form in my heart, just as the reflection of my face naturally appears in the water when I look into it. If it is not a sin but good to have the image of Christ in my heart, why should it be a sin to have it in my eyes? This is especially true since the heart is more important than the eyes.[45]

Luther holds that it is impossible to have an imageless faith. However, he promotes images primarily for didactic rather than aesthetic purposes. If he had his way, he would see Bible pictures painted on the walls of houses, inside and outside, so that they can better be remembered and understood.[46] Here he agrees with the ancient Gregorian view of art as a means of educating people in the faith.[47] But there is a difference. While Gregory thinks that images are like biblical texts ("the Bible of the laity") which can be read by heathens and Christians alike, and so have a kerygmatic function, for Luther they can only be used properly when accompanied by the word. "Here Luther joins word and image in much the same way he joined word and sacramental matter: the latter is the creation of the former, the former interprets the latter. The image is a 'creature' of the word."[48]

Meditation on the cross by itself without the word of promise is not a source of comfort. The cross itself is ambiguous. It can just as easily accuse us of our sin as comfort us with the reminder that sin has been overcome by the crucified. However, the crucifix on the altar, which is an old Lutheran custom, ties it to the Lord's Supper and is meant to reinforce the promise that in this holy meal we receive the body and blood of the crucified Lord, the one who died for us (*pro nobis*) and who in this meal gives us the full remission of all our sins. The crucifix on the altar is meant to remind us of

---

Cranach the Elder.

45. WA 18:83, 7–15; *LW* 40:99–100. Although Luther says he forms a mental image in his heart of what he hears, this is not an idol. See Goeser, "Luther," 6. On the portrayal of the word generally, see Mattes, *Beauty*, 147–51.

46. WA 18:82, 23–83, 5; *LW* 40:99.

47. For a critical examination of the famous thesis of Pope Gregory the Great that "what writing (*scriptura*) does for the literate, a picture does for the illiterate looking at it," see Duggan, "Book of the Illiterate," 227–51.

48. Torvend, "Whole Bible Painted," 55.

the real bodily presence of Christ in the sacrament and the comfort and consolation that this gives.[49]

Stirm maintains that the crucifix has a completely different effect on the viewer today than it had in Luther's day.[50] She suggests that we see it less, like Luther, as a victory over death but more like Good Friday without Easter, and quotes Barth as saying that "the crucified Christ is for us no image of comfort but an image of accusation (*Anklage*)."[51] However, Barth says this because he does not distinguish between law and gospel. The cross by itself is not yet gospel, it needs to be proclaimed as gospel, for it can be understood from the angle of both law and gospel. Seen as law, it tells us the extent of our sin (Jesus died *because* of us) but seen as gospel it tells us the profound depth of God's love for us (Jesus died *for* us).

In Lutheran territories, in contrast to the Reformed lands, the visual arts flourished.[52] The work of Lucas Cranach and his workshop is one instance of this—but probably the most important. One of his greatest achievements is the illustration of the 1534 *Lutherbibel* with its 117 colored woodcuts. The Old Testament has most of the images and the first dozen books are profusely illustrated. The most lavishly illustrated book in this Bible is the last one, the book of Revelation, with twenty-six woodcuts.[53] In Reformed lands, images were permitted in the homes and in books, and both the Zurich Bible (1531) and the Geneva Bible (1560) contained woodcuts.[54] But images were not permitted in the worship space for fear that they would prove a distraction or become a source of idolatry.

The illustrations of the Luther Bible offer a way of appropriating the words of the biblical story by means of our imagination. They invite us to meditate on certain aspects of the story that the artist highlights. This can be a helpful way of entering the world of the biblical text. Luther says that first we need to read the text. Then let the image stimulate our imagination so that the picture speaks to our heart and leads us more deeply into

---

49. See Koerner, *Reformation of the Image*, 308–10.

50. Stirm, *Bilderfrage*, 129.

51. Stirm, *Bilderfrage*, 129n27.

52. Tonkin observes: "The arts may have grown cold in Basel—and in Zurich and Geneva, and many other cities under the spell of Zwingli and Calvin. But in Wittenberg, Nuremberg and other cities where Luther's more 'catholic' spirit prevailed, this was not so" (Tonkin, "Word and Image," 53).

53. Christensen notes that the 1534 Wittenberg Bible contains an illustration of the enthroned Deity based on Isaiah 6:1, one of the key texts that sanctions such a portrayal. Other biblical warrants are to be found at Ps 11:4; Heb 12:2; Rev 4:2; 7:15. See Christensen, *Luther and the Woodcuts*, 397.

54. See Christ-von Wedel, "Bilderverbot," 299–320.

a meditation on God's word. This in turn will lead us to Christ, for, as Luther remarks, "Scripture is the swaddling clothes and manger in which Christ lies."[55]

The Cranach workshop produced four Reformation altarpieces that visually portray Luther's theology: the Schneeberg (1539), the Wittenberg (1547), the Weimar (1555), and the Dessau (1565). The Wittenberg is without doubt the most comprehensive of these retables. Its central panel features the Last Supper, whereas the Dessau puts the focus on the Lord's Supper.[56] This is in line with Luther's judgment that the Lord's Supper is the most appropriate subject matter for evangelical altar paintings.[57] Also worthy of mention are Cranach's visual depictions of the law-gospel theme both in woodcuts and in painted panels at Prague and Gotha dated to 1529. This theme, which also appears in the Schneeberg altarpiece,[58] lies at the heart of the Reformation faith and underpins its central doctrine of justification.[59]

Art historians are generally critical of Lucas Cranach's work because they believe that his emphasis on "didacticism," with its focus on doctrinal content rather than aesthetic style, contributed to the decline of the German art tradition which was eclipsed by the works of the Italian Renaissance.[60] Zweck rightly notes that Cranach "took the spotlight off the art itself, as well as the artist, and put it on to Christ." This is especially evident in Cranach's altarpiece in the city church at Wittenberg which most accurately expounds the center of Luther's theology: the sacramental enactment of the word.[61] Cook opines, "Cranach and his sons have given us what appear to be painted sermons, at once confessional, scriptural, and deeply theological. They are not art for art's sake but art in the service of the word."[62] Word and image are closely

---

55. WA DB 8:12; LW 35:236.

56. This is the first retable known to have been created for an evangelical church. It was installed in the Church of St. Wolfgang in Schneeberg. On the interpretation of the images, see Pöpper and Wegmann, *Das Bild*, 87–162.

57. WA 31.1:415, 23–31; LW 13:375.

58. See Noble, *Lucas Cranach*, 67–96.

59. See Rosebrock, "Luther's Visual Theology," 332–39.

60. Lucas Cranach, of course, was originally inspired by the Italian Renaissance. This is evident especially in his early nudes and his portraiture. However, with his "conversion" to the Lutheran faith and his partnership with Luther, he used his art in the service of the church and its theology.

61. Zweck, "Luther and Art," 105. See Koerner, *Reformation of the Image*, who discusses the Wittenberg altarpiece from an art historical perspective. For a comprehensive theological treatment, see Thulin, *Cranach Altäre der Reformation*, 5–32.

62. Cook, "Picturing Theology," 39.

connected. The word comes first, but without the image, which is a form of language, it lacks the power to touch the affections and the heart."[63]

Luther knows that the eyes can deceive us. We can become distracted and seduced by the spectacles and images of the world, which deflect our attention away from listening to God's word. Siedell, an art critic, observes that "a robust and practical theological approach to artistic practice must begin, counter-intuitively, with the ear, not the eye; with the particularity of the preached word of God, not the image. It is through the theology of ear that a theology of modern art begins."[64] Therefore, he insightfully remarks that when he views a piece of art he first asks, what is it saying to me.

We have seen that the promise of the word means that the word is given precedence over the image, and that therefore the ear comes before the eye. We say: Speak, that we may *see* you.[65] For those who have ears to hear will surely see. We see *par excellence* by listening to God's word. In approaching art, Luther's theology, grounded as it is in the proclaimed word, teaches us to give priority, not to the image and to what the eye sees, but to the word and to how the work of art is heard.

Bibliography

Bayer, Oswald. *A Contemporary in Dissent: Johann Georg Hamann as Radical Enlightener*. Translated by Roy A. Harrisville and Mark C. Mattes. Grand Rapids: Eerdmans, 2012.

———. "Das Wort ward Fleisch: Luthers Christologie als Lehre von der Idiomenkommunikation." In *Creator est Creatura. Luthers Christologie als Lehre von der Idiomenkommunikation*, edited by Oswald Bayer and Benjamin Gleede, 5–34. Berlin: de Gruyter, 2007.

———. "Justification as the Basis and Boundary of Theology." Translated by Christine Helmer. *Lutheran Quarterly* 15.3 (2001) 273–92.

———. *Living by Faith: Justification and Sanctification*. Translated by Geoffrey W. Bromiley. Grand Rapids: Eerdmans, 2003.

———. *Martin Luther's Theology: A Contemporary Interpretation*. Translated by Thomas H. Trapp. Grand Rapids: Eerdmans, 2008.

———. "Preaching the Word." Translated by Jeffrey G. Silcock. *Lutheran Quarterly* 23.3 (2009) 249–69.

63. Goeser, "Luther," 6. Werner Brändle, in his work on the wall art in the historic St. George Church on the Island of Reichenau, also speaks about the power of the image to portray the message of Jesus's healing miracles in an *affective* way. See Brändle, *Die Macht der Bilder*, 11–13.

64. Siedell, "They Who Have Ears to Hear."

65. On this famous phrase coined by Hamann, see Schulte, *Rede, daß ich Dich sehe!*, 7–10.

———. *Promissio: Geschichte der reformatorischen Wende in Luthers Theologie.* 2nd ed. Darmstadt: Wissenschaftliche Buchgesellschaft, 1989. [Translation: Minneapolis: Fortress, forthcoming].

———. "Schöpfungslehre als Rechtfertigungsontologie." In *Word—Gift—Being*, edited by Bo Kristian Holm and Peter Widmann, 17–41. Religion in Philosophy and Theology 37. Tübingen: Mohr/Siebeck, 2009.

———. *Theology the Lutheran Way.* Translated and edited by Jeffrey G. Silcock and Mark C. Mattes. Lutheran Quarterly Books. Grand Rapids: Eerdmans, 2007.

Betz, John R. "Glory(ing) in the Humility of the Word: The Kenotic Form of Revelation in J. G. Hamann." *Letter and Spirit* 6 (2010) 141–79.

Brändle, Werner, and Theo Keller. *Die Macht der Bilder: Die ottonischen Wandbilder in der Kirche St. Georg auf der Klosterinsel Reichenau.* Beuron: Beuroner Kunstvlg, 2011.

Brown, Raymond E. *The Gospel according to John I–XII.* Anchor Bible Series 29. New Haven: Yale University Press, 1995.

Bunge, Gabriel. *Earthen Vessels: The Practice of Personal Prayer According to the Patristic Tradition.* Translated by Michael J. Miller. San Francisco: Ignatius, 2002.

Christ-von Wedel, Christine. "Bilderverbot und Bibelillustrationen im reformierten Zürich." In *The Myth of the Reformation*, edited by Peter Opitz, 299–320. Göttingen: Vandenhoeck & Ruprecht, 2013.

Christensen, Carl C. "Luther and the Woodcuts of the 1534 Bible." *Lutheran Quarterly* 19.4 (2005) 392–413.

Cook, John W. "Picturing Theology: Martin Luther and Lucas Cranach." In *Art and Religion: Faith, Form, and Reform*, edited by Osmund Overby, 22–39. 1984 Paine Lectures in Religion. Columbia: University of Missouri–Columbia, 1986.

Cooper, Adam G. *Life in the Flesh: An Anti-Gnostic Spiritual Philosophy.* Oxford: Oxford University Press, 2008.

Duggan, Lawrence G. "Was Art really the 'Book of the Illiterate'?" *Word and Image* 5.3 (1989) 227–51.

Goeser, Robert. "Luther: Word of God, Language, and Art." *Currents in Theology and Mission* 18.1 (1991) 6–11.

Heal, Bridget. "The Catholic Eye and the Protestant Ear: The Reformation as a Non-Visual Event?" In *The Myth of the Reformation*, edited by Peter Opitz, 321–55. Göttingen: Vandenhoeck & Ruprecht, 2013.

Kittel, Gerhard, and Gerhard Friedrich, eds. *Theological Dictionary of the New Testament.* Translated by Geoffrey W. Bromiley. 10 vols. Grand Rapids: Eerdmans, 1964–1976.

Kleinig, John W. "Where Is Your God? Luther on God's Self-Localisation." In *Perspectives on Luther; Papers from the Luther Symposium held at Luther Seminary, Adelaide, South Australia 22–23 March 1996, Commemorating the 450th Anniversary of the Reformer's Death*, edited by Mark W. Worthing, 91–103. North Adelaide, South Australia: Luther Seminary, 1996.

Kloha, Jeffrey J., and Ronald R. Feuerhahn, eds. *Scripture and the Church: Selected Essays of Hermann Sasse.* Concordia Seminary Monograph Series 2. St. Louis: Concordia Seminary, 1995.

Koerner, Joseph Leo. *The Reformation of the Image.* Chicago: University of Chicago Press, 2008.

Lexutt, Athina, and Elisabeth Neumeister, OSB. *Alles hängt am Kreuz: Eine Annäherung in Wort und Bild*. Münster: Bonifatius, 2018.

Luther, Martin. "The Distinction Between the Law and the Gospel. A Sermon preached on January 1, 1532." Translated by Willard L. Burce. *Concordia Journal* 18.2 (1992) 153–63.

Mattes, Mark C. *Martin Luther's Theology of Beauty: A Reappraisal*. Grand Rapids: Baker Academic, 2017.

Miller, Joshua C. *Hanging by a Promise: The Hidden God in the Theology of Oswald Bayer*. Eugene, OR: Pickwick, 2015.

Nagel, Norman. "*Sacramentum et Exemplum* in Luther's Understanding of Christ." In *Luther for an Ecumenical Age*, edited by Carl S. Meyer, 172–99. St. Louis: Concordia, 1967.

Noble, Bonnie. *Lucas Cranach the Elder: Art and Devotion of the German Reformation*. New York: University Press of America, 2009.

Peters, Albrecht. *Ten Commandments*. Commentary on Luther's Catechisms. Translated by Holger K. Sonntag. St. Louis: Concordia, 2009.

Pöpper, Thomas, and Suzanne Wegmann, eds. *Das Bild des neuen Glaubens. Das Cranach-Retabel in der Schneeberger St. Wolfgangskirche*. Regensburg: Schnell & Steiner, 2011.

Preuss, Hans. *Martin Luther: Künstler*. Gütersloh: Bertelsmann, 1931.

Ringleben, Joachim. *Gott im Wort: Luthers Theologie von der Sprache her*. Hermeneutische Untersuchungen zur Theologie 57. Tübingen: Mohr/Siebeck, 2010.

Rosebrock, Matthew. "Luther's Visual Theology: The Lectures on Galatians and Cranach's Law and Gospel Paintings." *Concordia Journal* 42.2 (2016) 332–39.

Sasse, Hermann O. *Here We Stand. Nature and Character of the Lutheran Faith*. Translated by Theodore G. Tappert. 1966. Reprint, Adelaide: Lutheran, 1979.

———. *This is My Body: Luther's Contention for the Real Presence in the Sacrament of the Altar*. Minneapolis: Augsburg, 1959.

———. *We Confess: Jesus Christ*. Volume 1. Translated by Norman Nagel. St. Louis: Concordia, 1984.

Schulte, Susanne, ed. *Rede, daß ich Dich sehe!* Aachen: Rimbaud, 2007.

Siedell, Daniel A. "They Who Have Ears to Hear, Let them See?" *Comment: The Word of God and the City of Man* 30.2 (2012). https://www.cardus.ca/comment/article/they-who-have-ears-to-hear-let-them-see.

———. *Who's Afraid of Modern Art? Essays on Modern Art and Theology in Conversation*. Eugene OR: Cascade Books, 2015.

Silcock, Jeffrey G. "Luther on the Holy Spirit and His Use of God's Word." In *The Oxford Handbook of Martin Luther's Theology*, edited by Robert Kolb, et al., 294–309. Oxford: Oxford University Press, 2014.

———. "A New Look at the Theology of the Cross: What it Meant for Luther and Its Significance for us Today." In *Luther@500 and Beyond: Martin Luther's Theology Past, Present and Future*, edited by Stephen Hultgren, et al., 75–104. Adelaide: ATF, 2019.

Steiger, Johan Anselm. "The Communicatio Idiomatum as the Axle and Motor of Luther's Theology." *Lutheran Quarterly* 14.2 (2000) 125–58.

Stirm, Margarete. *Die Bilderfrage in der Reformation*. Gütersloh: Gütersloher, 1977.

Tonkin, John. "Word and Image: Luther and the Arts." *Colloquium* 17 (1985) 45–54.

Torvend, Samuel. "'The Whole Bible Painted in Our Houses': Visual Narrative and Religious Polemic in Early Lutheran Art." In *Institute of Liturgical Studies: Occasional Papers 11*, edited by Rhoda Schuler, 45–62. Valparaiso: Institute of Liturgical Studies, 2006.

Vajta, Vilmos. *Lutheran Worship: An Interpretation*. Eugene, OR: Wipf & Stock, 2004.

Zweck, Pamela E. "Luther and Art: The Role of Images and Their Artists in the Wittenberg Reformation." *Gesher* 5.3 (2017) 103–9.

14

Keep a Low Profile!

*Observations from a Translator
of Oswald Bayer*

Thomas H. Trapp

Let me begin by adding my greetings and congratulations to Professor Bayer on the occasion of his 80th birthday. May the Lord continue to provide joy and blessings and peace in Christ in the years ahead!

Now to the topic of translating a work by Professor Bayer, to make his work available to the English-speaking audience. A variety of comments and observations about translating have come to me over the years: "Do you mean that you just sit there with a dictionary and look up words?"; "How can you stand to translate?"; "I would want to publish my own ideas"; "How can you keep from adding your views along the way?"; "The first translation is always the first 'mistranslation'"; "Do you make it completely 'accurate,' word for word, or only thought for thought?"; "Translate only books and articles of those who are no longer alive"; "The dead will not give you trouble and second guess when you are done"; "No one but another translator will ever know what goes into making a good translation."

In late 2007 I was just entering into a sabbatical semester at Concordia University in Saint Paul, seeking to research themes that unite the entire Isaiah corpus, when I was contacted by Tom Raabe from Eerdmans Publishing Company. His brother Paul (at Concordia Seminary in Saint Louis) was familiar with my translation work of Hans Wildberger's three-volume commentary on Isaiah 1–39, which I had translated for Fortress Press for their *Continental Commentary Series*, along with Keel and Uehlinger's *Gods, Goddesses, and Images of God*. Those four volumes came to about 2,500 pages in print. Paul suggested his brother contact me about taking over the translation of Oswald Bayer's *Martin Luthers Theologie. Eine Vergegenwärtigung*.[1]

I began translating after my Heidelberg Doktorvater, Hans Walter Wolff, suggested that I translate his Haggai commentary for Fortress. Since that had been assigned already, I took on the much larger Isaiah project (1,753 pages in German). At least when you translate you know where the last page is.

Fulltime teaching at the college level, along with evening programs and summer school, left little time for in-depth research. Translating meant that I could delve into the prophets and archaeology and act as bridge for others into these subjects. That became the key thought in translating for me: to be a bridge from a world-class scholar or scholars for an interested group that otherwise would not have access. That is really teaching at its finest as well.

Professor Bayer's book would give me access to another world class scholar and his work. I had only had limited exposure to current Luther scholarship. Yet, I had a friend in Luther studies: Bob Kolb. Bob taught at Concordia University, Saint Paul during my first years at the school in the 1980s and was talking German with me by the coffee pot at 6:30 a.m. most mornings. So, I contacted him in Saint Louis, asking if he would be willing to "check my work." Bob is at the top of my list as one who always has time and is willing to share his expertise; he is a real rarity in the world of scholarship. As I engaged in initial discussions with Eerdmans, Professor Bayer came up with the same idea. He, as well, asked Bob if he would be willing to review my work. Tom Raabe was also a wonderful and supportive participant in the process. So began the project now titled *Martin Luther's Theology: A Contemporary Interpretation*.[2]

I became aware of translations that existed in English for some other works by Professor Bayer. But *Martin Luthers Theologie* was a different type of work. When Professor Bayer was at the end of his teaching career in Tübingen, he fashioned a series of two-hour lectures for the general student population. He shared with them, in summary, the aspects of Luther's theology and of his own more formal studies, which had appeared over the years in print and in public lectures. So, I was aware that this book was "technically" aimed toward a general audience, not to specialists who knew the inside vocabulary. Professor Bayer told me subsequently that the students were tracking with him during these lectures. Impressive students! I

---

1. Bayer, *Martin Luthers Theologie*.
2. Bayer, *Martin Luther's Theology*.

thought it important to do more than just replicate technical jargon and let the novice wonder about what it meant.

Only rarely did I consult translations of other works by Professor Bayer, sometimes noting that a term I thought carried a unique meaning had not been thus rendered elsewhere. "Secular" did not mean what was divorced from God and the church, but was our world at large and in parallel with the church. I went with "temporal" instead, and then "spiritual." God reigns in both spheres.

The translation process itself can be daunting, but was best managed by breaking the full book into manageable sections. The first decision I made was to have the Concordia University print shop make a copy for me, blowing up each chapter onto larger paper and print size, color coded by chapter so that I could measure my progress. A big project has to be reduced to smaller projects and goals. Never in what is now over 4,000 total pages of published translations have I ever seen a word jump from a German page to my English translation in the computer without help. Just the typing itself is a big issue. I never hand-wrote a single sentence for any translation I ever did. Everything went right from the German sentence through my head into a rough draft English sentence, repositioned and rearranged. Yes, the dictionary was ever present. Many times, I did not know the meaning of a word. Sometimes I was looking for a range of possible nuances. I would make notes on small pieces of paper or lists of things to check on later. Most often, I would note questions in brackets in the rough translation. Such was certainly not at a level to share with anyone. I should also note, for good or for ill, that I never read any book in its entirety in advance. I always went page-by-page and line-by-line. I wanted to follow the thinking as the book unfolded.

Professor Bayer emphasized repeatedly in our private communication over the year that consistency was of the essence, especially in a systematic work. I knew I would have to educate myself on current issues. Before it went to the press, the entire work would end up consuming nine months of work, as many hours as I could squeeze in; usually it would entail much more than a regular work day. Further time was spent on the project later, during its final production. Everything else possible was set aside. If there was something that did not make sense at the moment, I knew I could come back to it later. From my best recollection, I worked most of the winter and all spring of my sabbatical just to get the rough draft done. Thus, it consumed a large part of 2008, until it was finished, and I received my copy on November 10, 2008, Martin Luther's 525th birthday.

While translating, I looked forward to the citations from Luther, since they seemed to be easier to render into English! I was not, however, always in agreement with the American Edition. I felt it most important to render the train of thought in Professor Bayer's work and to make that flow. When it came to rendering the hymn "*Nun freut euch, lieben Christen g'mein* [Dear Christians, One and All, Rejoice],"[3] I provided the translation from the *Lutheran Service Book* as a whole, but then translated each line literally within the discussion that followed, since hymns are never rendered exactly in translations and the points Professor Bayer was emphasizing would have made little sense if the English were just incorporated into the discussion.

Now came the hard part. In my past work, the second time through would generally see things fall into place, but that was not happening. The sentences that were puzzling the first time were puzzling the second time too. Some of that I knew occurred because, not being a specialist, I was unaware of the nuances of terminology and the debates in which Luther scholars and philosophers had engaged in the succeeding centuries. Often, I would have to read and reread the entire paragraph or section for the discussion to make sense. It was then that whole paragraphs often fell into place.

Some translators are specialists in their own right. I considered myself to be a very interested observer, standing in the back of the room but never expecting to offer or be asked for my opinions. It was satisfying just to be the bridge. Still others who seek to translate might know the language but not the discipline. My wife and I figured that out when I tried to help her read abbreviations for crocheting a baptismal gown for our newborn son in Heidelberg back in 1973. The German Hausfraus were far ahead of me when consulted about the technique the next morning. My theological training certainly helped prepare me for the project. One must, however, read, search, and try to make sense of fine point discussions on the fly, or else do background reading and research. Even a seemingly simple word such as *sermo* was not to be translated as "sermon."

Another issue that dawned on me over time was that many of the chapters represented distillations of much longer treatments elsewhere. The chapter on *promissio* proved to be the most challenging, and at one point seemed insurmountable. This was the topic for Professor Bayer's *Doktorarbeit* and *Habilitationsschrift*.[4] There was one particular sentence, about ten or so lines long, which I can no longer even find. This problem caused me to sit, trying to figure it out for four hours. That never happened again, and I must have gotten it right. That was unique in my experience, and I do not remember it pleasantly. There were so many variables in that long sentence that it had to be diagrammed repeatedly. Many sentences were later divided into several in the translation.

3. *LSB* 556.
4. Bayer, *Promissio*.

After I finished each chapter, I would go back in a second pass and rework it. Everyone who works with the German language knows that word order is very different from English and complex. I would continue to massage the structure of each sentence to the way I thought Professor Bayer would present the material as a lecture in English. I kept in mind that these were verbal presentations, and they ought to be as easy as possible to follow in the target language. Some might think that translating is simply sitting down, typing it out, and turning it in. Yet, for me, the first rough draft was probably about a third to a half of the work that needed to be done. The second time through called for a careful check, for resolving as many issues as possible, followed then by a reexamination of the text to get the flow of the entire paragraph or chapter. But even that was followed by much rearranging. That was also the time to look at technical terminology to look for consistency throughout the book. At that point what had been mentioned in the introduction or early chapters took on a clearer sense. I probably went over most of the chapters five or six times each.

Two terms called for special attention: *Anfechtung* and *Leibliches Wort*. Fred Danker shared the challenges that he faced in updating the Third Edition of the BDAG.[5] He said that he finally had to come to grips with finding a way to render "blasphemy, etc." and other terms that had been merely transliterated in the past. It would not do just to let people try to figure out what it meant. Since I was translating Professor Bayer for, among others, a somewhat neophyte audience, as well as for those who had a deeper background, I took Fred Danker's counsel seriously as my own methodology. As I was at work on the translation, I asked various Luther scholars (sorry, folks!) how they rendered *Anfechtung* in English. A puzzled look usually followed. Just keep the word! Why translate it? But that solution leads to writing for the inside crowd! I finally came up with "agonizing struggle." That could have been the title for this little article too, as well as for every life in general! I know that any translation somewhat limits the possibilities of what a seemingly open-ended term might mean. I knew one word would not do it for *Anfechtung* (e.g., steadfast love). In Reformation-related reading that I have done in retirement, I have found references close to "agonizing struggle" in some Luther studies in English from earlier in the last century.

So what about *Leibliches Wort*? Even Bob Kolb thought that "bodily word," as it is often translated, was sufficient. But what does that mean? I must admit here that I am still looking for help in all the ramifications of that term. Some help is provided in the Latin *verbum externum* in Article 5 of

---

5. BDAG 178.

the Augsburg Confession (*verbo externo*).[6] It is rendered on the same page in the German as *Das leiblich Wort*. So, I thought "external word" would not be too far off, even though I assume that the Word of God Incarnate is wrapped within the concept as well. "The physical word" seemed to be too weak.

After each chapter was done, I sent it off to Bob Kolb for an evaluation, first in Saint Louis, then in Germany. I even wondered out loud in a phone conversation with him at one point whether I would ever be successful in completing the project. This was the day of the four-hour sentence. My undying gratitude goes to Bob for his help. He was generally supportive and affirming. From time to time he would explain what was at issue and help me to clarify a rendering. Only rarely did he wonder why I went against the way he would translate a term. His responses morphed from English to German as he made his yearly pilgrimage with his wife, Pauline, during the summer to Germany. The process of sending chapter by chapter continued right to the end of the summer. Terms that might appear in several chapters would have to be standardized later still.

I would sometimes seek out Bob's special counsel about certain renderings. One stands out: *Was Christum treibet*. The Latin *Christus* is in the nominative, but *Christum* is in the accusative. If I translated that "What drives Christ," which admittedly keeps one word for one word, it could mean what drives Christ as subject to do what he did, as if "Christ" was in the nominative. Latin is more precise at this point. Luther, however, obviously saw Christ present(ed) in the accusative throughout the entire Old Testament. Bob said that his practice was to render it "What drives Christ home." The point is driven home in the Old Testament that it is all about Christ. That rendering later proved a point of contention but it remains in the English rendering.

My *modus operandi*, hence the title for this brief narrative, was to keep a low profile. I kept in mind that I was a bridge between a highly respected German Luther scholar and an English-speaking audience that would possibly have this as their first and maybe only introduction to Luther. Yes, scholars would profit. But this was for a wider audience, admittedly with special interest in the topic. I expected it would play a role in the 500th anniversary of the Reformation. (The work has appeared in a list of the best ten books in English to introduce the Reformation.)[7] What that meant for me most of all was to make sure that the sentences flowed as one would hear them in a public lecture delivered in English. That meant shortening sentences and rearranging, rather than trying to keep word order. I have found

---

6. *BSLK* 58.
7. Grandquist, "Planning for 2017," 172.

it to be infuriating as a reader when working through translations that are "too wooden." Not every translation is up to the challenge. Most scholars know of books that have been the first mistranslation, often without a follow-up. Even if technically correct, my view of the translator's task was to go beyond, to get rid of as many roadblocks for the listener as possible. Usually that meant placing phrases at the beginning of sentences that would otherwise be set off by a double comma. Such translating does not mean playing fast and loose with subject matter, or guessing that the reader will figure it all out in the end, and certainly not introducing my own opinions. An email sent to me late one night from a pastor in northern Minnesota, the father of a former student, during the winter after publication, thanked me for the translation. He said it felt as if he were reading a good mystery novel, and spoke of his disappointment that the book did not keep going for more chapters yet. That is the type of compliment that warms the heart and makes it all worthwhile and the greatest reader-response possible.

I was more aware of the difficulty of the task and the need for accuracy after I had finished. What had I gotten myself into? How would Professor Bayer and others react? This was not a private project. Was I setting back the effect that he would have? Hearsay evidence suggested that my translation underwent detailed examination both in the States and in Germany and that many individual sentences and terms were carefully weighed and found to be accurate. Apparently the work passed muster, at least with those who delved deeply into it. I struggled mightily about a caption under the picture of Luther on page three. I even called up a full professor of German at the University of Minnesota for help. Martin Luther is "*inwendig voller Figur.*" Inwardly a full figure? Full of figures? Dürer speaks of an artist as "*inwendig voller Figur.*" Sometimes the translator must take a shot and hope it is not too far astray. I am not sure even today about that one! No one has mentioned anything about it, yet.

I can only imagine how Professor Bayer was filled with trepidation when the major results of his life's work were put into a different language, where precious and precise ideas might be open to misinterpretation. I know that he was deeply involved in examining the translation as well, and that is as it should be. If I were to misunderstand and mischaracterize what he was trying to bring across, I would have done him a disservice. As I stated in my introduction to the translation, the best compliment that I could get would be that no one would think of it as a translation when reading it. Keep a low profile! Content would win out, not choppy style or rank errors. A friend once told me about a translation done by someone else that so infuriated him that he threw the book down on the ground in disgust. I hoped to avoid that. Knowing that I had made blunders and that I had missed typos in earlier translations has kept me from being flippant or defensive or boastful. And yet, I also sought to remember an audience of neophytes as the target.

So, what did I personally garner from the content? Probably first and foremost is the entire emphasis on the word effecting something when it was uttered. It became clear rather quickly that Luther's *Small Catechism* repeated frequently that it is not water only, but water connected with God's word. Baptism is in the name, essentially into the power of the Father, Son, and Holy Spirit, and is, as such, a restoration of an original relationship. The words of institution for the Lord's Supper emphasize the bread and wine are given to us as the body and blood of Christ, right then and there, for you and me. According to Professor Bayer, what moved the entire Reformation forward was Luther articulating how the sinner is forgiven right then and there, when the words of absolution are spoken following the command of the Lord behind closed doors, through the mouth of the priest, not only after some satisfaction is performed. To me, that is the chief argument for considering absolution to be on the same level with the other two sacraments. To my mind, there are not just two and one-half sacraments, but three ways in which the power of God's word applies grace, affording the benefits of the Lord's death and resurrection. The relationship is initiated in holy baptism. The connection is strengthened both in holy absolution and in the Lord's Supper. Who but those helped by Luther see the change in the relationship with God to be so completely tied in with the new birth? The Triune God makes the decision. It never gets any better, not until the eschaton and its fulfillment.

This leads to another important insight for me. Lutherans have generally spoken about justification and sanctification in terms of human beings before God and in his world. Bayer's emphasis on the nascent restoration of the entire creation has proved most helpful. Those who want little to do with the church and its teachings about sin and grace appear to have hijacked the natural world as their own project, devoid of a God who created all things; the natural world itself is their god and humans must be stopped from sinning against it. One almost gets the idea that the best thing a human could do would be to remove their carbon footprint by simply ceasing to exist; nature would then clean up the mess humans have made. The problem is real. But how different it is to treasure the creation as God's gift, to be cared for even in the midst of the brokenness! One need not give up on attempting to keep our world clean and safe, but it is the Triune God's world, and humans are the crown of the creation. Professor Bayer helped me to hear that emphasis coming through in Luther.

In addition, in my own ministry, I found myself gravitating toward Luther's emphasis on the three estates, the family, the church, and government.

The third seems a bit slippery, since I wonder if it would have existed apart from the fall into sin. Professor Bayer's way of highlighting Luther's emphasis on the church as existing already in the Garden of Eden provided a nice way to see the unity of the Scriptures. God was at work from the beginning to have a relationship of peace and fellowship with all humanity. That thrust goes over against the false dichotomy which suggests today that church and state are different entities, in different spheres. The church supposedly has no business in the state, which is countermanded by Luther who notes that God's interest remains in both, whether it be Christ's hanging on the cross or the hangman for the wicked. These are certainly areas that those who consider themselves to be modern thinkers quarrel with and reject.

Other chapters gave foundational support and emphasis to topics with which I had been familiar. But this opportunity to delve deeply into Professor Bayer's insights garnered from a lifetime of work with Luther and with those who used his ideas in all sorts of ways was most satisfying. I know that my teaching and preaching were impacted regularly by the volume I was privileged to translate. I also know that many who could profit from Professor Bayer's insights would be robbed of that if they had to struggle through the German. It seems strange to pick up the volume now and to think that I had anything to do with it.

A particular joy for me was that Professor Bayer worshiped at Emmaus Lutheran Church in Saint Paul where I served as pastor. He also joined the congregation in Bible Class. I introduced him and explained the contribution he made to understanding the *promissio* concept, which by the way was the most compact and hardest chapter of all.[8] He seemed pleased that I not only understood what he had researched but that I conveyed it clearly to the members. He shared his observation with my member Joshua Miller, one of our Festschrift editors. Josh and Katie came to Emmaus when I was translating this volume. When Josh was getting interested in Professor Bayer's theology, he met probably the only parish pastor around who was in on the discussion to that level. The point of mentioning so many people, and others who could be named, is that translation is much more than a dry, dull exercise in typing. For the joy set before me!

Steve Paulson spoke at a reception at Concordia University, Saint Paul to celebrate the publication of the English translation. He noted that only other translators could appreciate the depth of work that goes into a translation, the long and deep searching to find the best way to communicate words from one language into another. So it is. Communication of the gospel is what makes it worthwhile, through translators, scholars, back to the

---

8. Bayer, *Martin Luther's Theology*, 44–67.

Lord and Savior who reset us onto the original path of life through his dying and rising, as he has PROMISED! I have been welcomed into the circle of those who spend their life studying and sharing and teaching the faith and Luther's contributions. I am most honored and grateful, even if I am standing in the back of the room!

Bibliography

Bauer, Walter. *A Greek-English Lexicon of the New Testament and Other Early Christian Literature*. Edited by Frederick William Danker. 3rd ed. Chicago: University of Chicago Press, 2000.

Bayer, Oswald. *Martin Luthers Theologie: Eine Vergegenwärtigung*. 3rd ed. Tübingen: Mohr/Siebeck, 2007.

———. *Martin Luther's Theology: A Contemporary Interpretation*. Translated by Thomas H. Trapp. Grand Rapids: Eerdmans, 2008.

———. *Promissio: Geschichte der reformatorischen Wende in Luthers Theologie*. Göttingen: Vandenhoeck & Ruprecht, 1971.

Dingel, Irene, ed. *Die Bekenntnisschriften der evangelisch-lutherischen Kirche*. Vollständige Neuedition. Göttingen: Vandenhoeck & Ruprecht, 2014.

Grandquist, Mark A. "Planning for 2017: Reformation Resources for Your Library." *Word & World* 36 (2016) 168–76.

15

Oswald Bayer and Postmodernism

Gene E. Veith

"My own approach to being involved with systematic theology," commented Oswald Bayer, "grew out of the highly controversial task of trying to relate Luther's theology to contemporary problems."[1] This does not entail creating a contemporary version of Luther or revising his theology so that it conforms to contemporary thought. Rather, says Bayer, "We discover that he speaks to our contemporary situation."[2]

Despite the historical gap between Luther and today and despite the changing modes of thought and kinds of experience over the course of the last five centuries, certain primal concerns, while perhaps taking different forms, keep manifesting themselves:

> We cannot get away from the fact that our own contemporary existence must be examined in light of the same questions that occupied Luther for his entire life: What is the correct way to talk about God and his relationship to human beings? How do salvation, life, and blessedness enter into a world of sin, the devil, and death? How does one become confident about this salvation, precisely at the time when things happen every day to contradict it? Is the church necessary, and if so, who needs it? How does the Christian live in a world that is viewed apocalyptically? These questions were clearly not resolved by the transition from the Middle Ages to the present age and into the postmodern world.[3]

---

1. Bayer, *Martin Luther's Theology*, xx.
2. Bayer, *Martin Luther's Theology*, xix.
3. Bayer, *Martin Luther's Theology*, xx.

Bayer dealt both with modernity, with its faith in scientific rationality, and with postmodernity, which reacted against that rationality. Both ways of being "contemporary" are caught up in futile attempts at "self-justification," compounded by an inadequate understanding of physical existence and a sense of meaninglessness related to confusions over language. Bayer, with the help of Luther, responds to postmodernism with reinvigorated proclamations of the doctrines of creation, God's word, and justification by faith in Christ.

Postmodern Theologian

Bayer offers a succinct explanation of the terms: "'Postmodernism' as some call it, whereby what is proposed by or what seeks to be explained by 'postmodern' can be interpreted only as a serious *metacriticism* of the modern era."[4] By that definition, Bayer can himself be considered a postmodern theologian.

"Modernist" theologians sought to "demythologize" Christianity by revising out or reinterpreting its supernatural elements, assuming that "modern man" can no longer believe in non-scientific claims. Thus the different "liberal theologies" of the twentieth century offered an array of this-worldly gospels that had nothing to do with salvation for eternal life: the "social gospel" of political reform, a psychologized gospel of self-actualization, an existentialist gospel of creating meaning for oneself, etc.

But these proved too anemic for the spiritual traumas and upheavals of the twentieth century—for World War and Holocaust, totalitarianism, revolutionary social changes, aggressive secularism, and the like. In the years before, during, and after World War II, "neo-Orthodox" theologians, such as Karl Barth, were challenging conventional liberal theology. In the latter part of the century, as modernist projects such as political utopias had devolved into tyrannies and were starting to collapse and as a Christian revival broke out in the non-European world, Thomas Oden identified a "postmodern" theology, which brought the "premodern" insights of the historic Christian faith into a contemporary context and addressed to the contemporary condition.[5] This clearly describes the work of Oswald Bayer; what Oden was doing with the church fathers and Joseph Ratzinger was doing with Medieval Catholicism, Bayer was doing with the Reformation.

---

4. Bayer, *Martin Luther's Theology*, 20.

5. Oden, *After Modernity*. See also his autobiographical account, Oden, *Change of Heart*.

In the meantime, though, "postmodernism" took on another meaning. In academia, the reaction against "modernism," with its rationalism and scientific reductionism, intensified. The Enlightenment assumption of a detached observer applying reason to the world so as to understand and control it came under withering critique. There is no such thing as objective meaning, argued academics in field after field. Meaning—whether in a literary text, a philosophical commitment, or in language itself—is inherently subjective and perspectival. Truth claims are not so much discoveries as constructions. The mind constructs its own realities. Ideas, institutions, laws, customs, arts, and religions are all *cultural* constructions.

As such, according to postmodernists who built on Nietzsche and Marx, cultural constructions are impositions of *power*. The so-called "post-Marxists," who substituted other groups for Marx's social classes, taught that the artifacts of culture at any given time are designed to maintain the power of the privileged groups and to oppress the "marginalized," such as women, racial minorities, the poor, homosexuals, the transgendered, etc. With this dimension of post-Marxist identity politics, postmodernist scholars promoted the "construction" of new histories, new canons, and new paradigms that put the "marginalized" into the "center."

In theology, this meant feminist, black, and "queer" theology. In historical theology, this meant, for example, asserting the legitimacy of Gnosticism, which was allegedly suppressed by the male-dominated Orthodox faction of the early church because of its openness to female leadership. Consequently, the Gnostic gospels, pseudepigrapha, and visionary writings were improperly "excluded from the canon" and now deserve acceptance.

Such radical scholarship, of course, leaves almost nothing standing, with some postmodernists embracing the ultimate meaninglessness of nihilism. Not all postmodernists go quite so far as the post-Marxists or the nihilists. Despite its appropriation by political radicals, postmodernism also accords well with today's consumerism, with its hedonism and its exaltation of "choice." Postmodernism is practically embodied in today's information technology, with its proliferation of "fake news" and "virtual reality." In its more popular manifestations, postmodernism is evident in the moral and intellectual relativism pervasive throughout contemporary culture.

In light of this more extreme form of postmodernism and in partial answer to it, another theological movement has arisen: Radical Orthodoxy. Started by the Anglicans John Milbank, Catherine Pickstock, and Graham Ward,[6] and adopted by some Catholic and Orthodox theologians, radical orthodoxy adopts the postmodernist critique of the Enlightenment, scientific

---

6. Milbank et al., *Radical Orthodoxy*.

rationalism, and modernist culture to attack liberal theology and to cultivate an all-encompassing Christian vision of the world.

Although it would be wrong to classify Oswald Bayer with this movement (we will explain why later), he played a part in its inception. Bayer describes postmodernism, quoted above, as a "serious *metacriticism* of the modern era." He is alluding here to Johann George Hamann, the eighteenth-century German thinker who coined the word in his *Metacritique of the Purism of Reason*. Though quite prominent in his time—being a major influence on Goethe, Herder, and Kierkegaard, among others—Hamann (1730–1803) fell into obscurity, pigeonholed as an "irrationalist" who played a role in German romanticism, but otherwise all but forgotten. One of Bayer's major contributions to contemporary thought is his role in the rediscovery of Hamann, who is now recognized as offering a definitive refutation of Enlightenment rationalism while also providing an alternative to the postmodernist relativism, political reductionism, and nihilism that would emerge in its place.

Bayer's 1988 book on Hamann, translated into English in 2012 as *A Contemporary in Dissent: Johann Georg Hamann as Radical Enlightener*,[7] as well as his extensive additional scholarship in German, helped to bring this friend, neighbor, and adversary of Immanuel Kant back into the history of ideas. Hamann, with his distinctive approach to questions that have become preoccupations of contemporary thought, has been received with great enthusiasm. The prominent philosopher Charles Taylor draws on Hamann in developing his important new study of language,[8] and the Radical Orthodox theologians use Hamann in their critique of modernity and their attempt to forge a new approach to theology.[9] John Betz says that Hamann's contributions are so significant that he deserves to be included with the "postmodern triumvirate" of Nietzsche, Heidegger, and Derrida. But Betz goes on to say that the approach of those three postmodernists leads ultimately to nihilism, and that the *only* way forward is through the "post-secular" vision of J. G. Hamann. "Simply put," says Betz, "the alternative is one between Hamann and postmodernity." Or, indeed, between Hamann and nihilism.[10]

---

7. Bayer, *Contemporary in Dissent*.

8. Taylor, *Language Animal*.

9. The opening chapter in the manifesto of the movement is John Milbank's "Knowledge: The Theological Critique of Philosophy in Hamann and Jacobi" (Milbank, *Radical Orthodoxy*, 21–37).

10. Betz, *After Enlightenment*, 319.

Betz describes this alternative as "post-secular" because Hamann's thought is profoundly, foundationally, *Christian*. In fact, it is a very sophisticated application of a distinctly *Lutheran* theology.

This is what Bayer understands, though others who attempt to make use of Hamann often do not. The Radical Orthodox, who are among those who hold Luther responsible for modernity, reject the Reformation. They are essentially Platonists—which puts them at odds also with the Aristotelianism of classic Catholicism—who are attempting to recover a "spirituality" grounded in church authority. As such, they misappropriate Hamann,[11] who is applying the distinctly Lutheran doctrines of creation, the word of God, the sacraments, and justification by faith in Christ.

In fact, for Bayer, *Luther* emerges as the true postmodern theologian. Postmodernists have been maintaining that reason has its limits; Luther taught that in the sixteenth century. But Luther's analysis of the human condition is deeper and more penetrating than what today's secularists can offer. Observes Bayer, "Luther's insights, gained from an intimate struggle with evil, were not surpassed by such masters of the hermeneutics of suspicion as Marx, Freud, and Nietzsche."[12]

Postmodernists practice the "hermeneutics of suspicion," rejecting the surface meaning of texts, institutions, and values to find their ulterior, disguised meanings: For Marx, behind the façade of every cultural expression is the class struggle, as laws and religions and works of art all serve to justify the economic ruling class and to keep the working class under control. For Freud, the hermeneutics of suspicion means interpreting all human expressions in terms of sex. For Nietzsche, cultural expressions are veils for the will to power. But Luther recognizes an even more fundamental reality, which human beings seek to hide from others and from themselves, a reality that manifests itself in evasions and rationalizations and false belief systems, including those of Marx, Freud, and Nietzsche: namely, *sin*. Luther employs a "hermeneutics of suspicion" when he exposes the idolatry that looms behind so many human enterprises. And yet Luther's critical method does not stop there: Once sin is disclosed and recognized and all attempts at self-justification are deconstructed (so to speak), he proclaims justification through the work and the promises of Jesus Christ.

---

11. For the misreading of Hamann by the Radical Orthodox, see Terezakis, "J. G. Hamann" (Isherwood and Zlomislic, *Poverty of Radical Orthodoxy*, 32–57). Although it seems that this author, too, is missing the centrality of Hamann's Lutheran convictions.

12. Bayer, *Martin Luther's Theology*, 2.

The Postmodern Condition

Bayer has perceptively described the postmodern condition, seeing in its contradictions and rebellions the need for law and gospel:

> When one tries to formulate a theological assessment in regard to the connections between morality and legalism, freedom and determinism, compulsion and insight, spontaneity and nomism, one can still not avoid coming to terms with the reformational distinction between law and gospel. This distinction should also provide help with respect to the postmodern reshaping of the modern age, as regards memory, diagnosis, and therapy if it is valid, to cite one example, to offer an assessment about the radical constraint to justify oneself, as well as the way the postmodern world seeks to compensate for this judgmental activity. This kind of compensation becomes visible in the flight from such excessive constraint to justify oneself into a hedonistic individualism and into the much-loved transformation of everything into aesthetics, as well as the attempt to cover our entire context in anonymity.[13]

Transforming everything into aesthetics: that is, reducing questions of belief, religion, and morality into what "I like." An obsession with self, combined with a craving for anonymity. Above all, however, is "the radical constraint to justify oneself": to insist that "I am right"; "I am good."

Bayer shows that, far from being an arcane theological concept, "justification" is a major preoccupation of contemporary life. We have a need to be "right." We insist that "I am a good person." We need to feel this ourselves, and we need others to acknowledge it about us. Thus, when we are criticized, we defend ourselves. We feel accused and judged, and—in part to justify ourselves—we accuse and judge others. This is why we get into arguments and why we quarrel with ones we love. We rationalize our actions and make excuses for our shortcomings, all in an attempt to justify ourselves.

Bayer's treatment of "self-justification," in which he demonstrates the psychological imperative of affirming our goodness and our rightness—that is, our righteousness—is one of his distinctive contributions. He is not simply psychologizing this critically important theological and moral concept; rather, he is showing how the human need for justification persists even in our highly secularist and morally permissive context. Thus, his observations in his powerful little book, which he himself wrote in English, *Living by Faith*:

---

13. Bayer, *Martin Luther's Theology*, 66.

> We cannot reject the question that others put to us: Why have you done this? What were you thinking about? Might you not have done something else? In the other's view of us, and also in our own view, we always find ourselves to be the ones who are already being questioned and who have to answer. Complaints are made against us. We are forced to justify ourselves, and as we do so, we usually want to be right. . . . There is no escaping the questions and evaluations of others. If one accepts and welcomes the other or not, if one greets the other or not, if one acknowledges the other—either through praise or reproach, affirmation or negation—or if one does not acknowledge the other and regards the other as worthless, a decision is made concerning our being or non-being.[14]

Bayer could be describing life on social media, with its "likes" and its "judgmental" comments; its strenuously positive self-presentations and its shaming; and why, despite everything, it is so addictive:

> We want constant recognition of ourselves because it is vitally necessary. We need its confirmation and renewal. If it is lacking, we try to regain it or even to coerce it. We want to produce something which others will say gives pleasure and ought to be recognized, so that it is rewarded by a glance or a word, and thus finds an answer. . . . As social beings we live by the word given and heard. This word either grants or denies us recognition and justification. This basic human feature has been particularly intensified in modern times and has given rise to ruthless questioning and complaining. With what right do you exist at all, rather than not exist? With what right do you exist the way you do and not some other way? Pressured by such questions, we must submit the authorization of our existence to the proof. We must inexorably offer persuasive reasons for our right to exist and to exist the way we are.[15]

In our postmodern culture, which has stripped away traditional social roles and authorities, we are typically insecure, preoccupied by what other people think about us, and uncertain about what we think of ourselves. "I am constantly trying to ascertain others' judgment about me and my own judgment of myself; I arrive at some point of calm, and then become unsure of myself again."[16]

---

14. Bayer, *Living by Faith*. Bayer based this book, which he wrote in English, on an earlier German monograph published in 1990.

15. Bayer, *Living by Faith*, 2–3.

16. Bayer, *Living by Faith*, 3.

Such a penchant for self-justification, ironically, accounts for today's climate of moral relativism and permissiveness. "I am a good person," we tell ourselves and others. Therefore, when we do something that is *not* good, we justify ourselves by repudiating the standards according to which we are condemned. This is why, as Bayer observes, our "age is antinomian, but at the same time it is increasingly nomistic."[17] Postmodernists tend to be simultaneously immoral and moralistic; self-righteous without being righteous.

But there can come a point when all attempts at self-justification fail, when we face up to the fact that we are *not* good, that we are not "right," that our self-righteousness has been a lie. Instead of evading the word of condemnation, we agree with it. Then we can hear another word: a message that though we cannot justify ourselves, Christ has justified us. He has borne our guilt and our shame, and his goodness is ascribed to us. God has declared us righteous. We are justified by faith.

Bayer echoes Luther in describing what happens when the law, finally putting to death our pretensions at self-justification, gives way to the gospel:

> Grace can only be freely granted. It is experienced only as a gift. This justification and righteousness which cannot be attained and won by us is the righteousness of faith. It is neither a justifying thinking nor justifying acting, neither contemplative nor active righteousness. It is a passive righteousness.[18]

Bayer also specifically rejects the postmodernist catchphrases: "Faith is wholly and entirely God's work. It is not our own decision, interpretive activity, or construction of meaning."[19]

This, in turn opens up a new life: "The passive righteousness of faith with its new relation to God and the self creates a new relation to all creatures, to the world, including a new perception of time and space."[20]

Critique of Postmodernism

Three themes in Bayer's theology directly counter and give an alternative to the postmodernists: creation, language, and the estates.

---

17. Bayer, *Martin Luther's Theology*, 65.
18. Bayer, *Living by Faith*, 19.
19. Bayer, *Living by Faith*, 20.
20. Bayer, *Living by Faith*, 27.

Creation

It may seem odd that those who hold to a worldview of naturalistic materialism—who believe that physical matter is the only reality—should nevertheless have a tendency to reject the physical world. And yet, this is the case, both for the scientific rationalists of modernism and the social constructivists of postmodernism. The modernists posit a universe of inert, dead matter. The human being is an observer, who, by application of reason and the scientific method, can fully comprehend that matter and exploit it for human purposes. But strictly speaking, the objective universe has no meaning, no purpose, no value, much less moral or religious significance. These are all facets of the *human* mind. Thus, morality and religion are held to be intrinsically subjective. For the postmodernists, the human mind, with all of its subjectivities, is actively *constructing* the world, taking in sense perceptions but organizing them according to its own mental categories, as shaped by culture and the will to power.

In both perspectives, the human being stands outside of nature, either as a detached observer and manipulator, or as a god-like demiurge. The Enlightenment's new rational religion of Deism taught that God created the universe but now observes it at a distance. Once belief even in this kind of God faded, human beings took his place. But the God they emulated was not the active, saving God of Christianity, but the detached watchmaker of Deism.

Kant represented the apex of Enlightenment philosophy, with its exaltation of reason, thus making him one of the great formative thinkers of modernity. But, in showing how the mind organizes the sense perceptions that it takes in, Kant also laid the foundations for constructivism, and thus for postmodernity. This is why Hamann, in refuting Kant, has such applicability for ideas that would not be formulated for another two hundred years. Bayer makes those applications to contemporary thought.

Hamann believed that we need to recover physical reality and our own place within this physical order. He did so by emphasizing, exploring, and applying the Christian—specifically, the Lutheran—doctrine of creation.

Bayer notes "the modern way of designing the world and controlling the world—with very specific reference to the claim of instrumental reason for dominion."[21] He contrasts this stance with that of Luther: "*The central point of Luther's understanding of creation is that the whole world and all creatures call upon him [God] and that God uses this medium to promise and to give himself completely to us.*"[22]

---

21. Bayer, *Martin Luther's Theology*, 112.
22. Bayer, *Martin Luther's Theology*, 111.

God created and continues to sustain the physical universe—including us as his creatures—continuing to providentially care for all that he has made. Furthermore, he employs *physical means* "to give himself completely" to us *physical creatures*. In Jesus Christ, God became incarnate, making himself a physical being, to redeem us. Christ makes us his own with the physical water of Baptism. Christ gives us not just his spirit but his body and his blood in the bread and wine of Holy Communion. The Holy Spirit creates faith by means of the language—ink imprinted on paper; sound waves travelling in air; digital words on a screen—of God's Word.

Bayer quotes Hamann, who says that "Creation" is "address to the creature through the creature."[23] Our justification by faith, says Bayer, not only reconciles us to God, but also reconciles us to his creation. This is because God uses his creation—water, bread, wine, paper, other people, a pastor standing in a wooden pulpit—to bring us to himself. We ourselves are "a new creation" (2 Cor 5:17). Comments Bayer, discussing Luther:

> The "new creation" is a return to the world, not a retreat from it. The new creation is a conversion to the world, as a conversion to the Creator, hearing God's voice speaking to us and addressing us through his creatures. Augustine was wrong to say that his voice draws us away from God's creatures into the inner self and then to transcendence. Counteracting Augustine's inwardness in its withdrawal from the world, Luther emphasizes the penetrating this-worldliness of God. God wills to be the Creator by speaking to us only through his creatures.[24]

Elsewhere, Bayer discusses Luther's "turn from radical denial of the world to an impressive affirmation of everything that is of the world and nature."[25]

> After Luther was thoroughly convinced, because of his new understanding of word and sacrament, that the spiritual is constituted in the form of what was earthly—not only negatively but also positively—the spiritual importance of all things earthly was opened to him in a positive sense as well.[26]

Such affirmations grow out of a distinctly Lutheran understanding of creation. They would be difficult for Reformed theology, which considers

---

23. Bayer, *Martin Luther's Theology*, 108. The quotation is from Hamann, *Aesthetica in Nuce*.
24. Bayer, *Living by Faith*, 28.
25. Bayer, *Martin Luther's Theology*, 141.
26. Bayer, *Martin Luther's Theology*, 141.

any physical manifestation of God to be an idol.[27] It would be difficult for Eastern Orthodoxy, with its Platonic hierarchies. Roman Catholicism with its sacramentalism and natural law would come closer, but its split between the spiritual and the secular orders, its ascetism and mysticism, and its docetic view of Holy Communion, that the earthly elements only seem to be present, would prevent it from fully embracing such a "penetrating this-worldliness of God." Luther and Lutherans like Hamann and Bayer hold to a "sacramental union" of Christ's body and blood with the bread and wine. Luther warned against contemplating God as an abstraction and attempting to comprehend him in his infinite transcendence, apart from his self-revelation in Christ. Rather, he said, "We must look at no other God than this incarnate and human God."[28] Lutheran Christology combines this strong emphasis on the Incarnation with the teaching that the resurrected Christ ascended bodily into heaven, so that he now "fills all in all" (Eph 1:23). "That the spiritual is constituted in the form of what [is] earthly," in turn, as we will see, has a bearing on the spiritual significance of the earthly estates and human vocation. For Bayer, as for Hamann and Luther, recovering this understanding of creation—including our own creatureliness—can serve as an antidote both to the modernist's attempt to dominate nature and to the postmodernist's attempt to deny it altogether.

Language

One of Hamann's most important contributions to philosophy is his insistence on the centrality of language. Part of his "metacritique" of Kant is that his Konigsberg neighbor was attempting to erect an edifice of "pure," disembodied reason while ignoring language. Actually, Hamann pointed out, we cannot think without language. There can be no reason apart from language. "Reason is language."[29] And along with language, which shapes our thoughts and our reasoning, comes culture and tradition and other human beings. The figure of the disinterested rationalistic observer, working with no preconceptions or biases and without any personal investment, applying reason and

---

27. As opposed to Luther's definition of idolatry as putting your faith in anything other than the true God. For the difference between the Reformed and the Lutheran understandings of idolatry, see Lockwood, *Unholy Trinity*.

28. *LW* 26:29.

29. Hamann quoted in Bayer, *Contemporary in Dissent*, who also devotes a chapter to these issues (see Bayer, *Contemporary in Dissent*, 156–70).

reason alone—the human being as deistic god—is a myth. Any philosophy or account of human nature must take language into account.[30]

Thus, Hamann can be given credit for the "linguistic" turn in modern philosophy, which culminated with Ludwig Wittgenstein.[31] But this emphasis on language would take different forms. A strain of analytic philosophers who held to the modernistic assumptions of logical positivism engaged in "linguistic analysis," purporting to show that classic philosophical problems are nothing more than "language games." Some of the formative postmodernist thinkers were literary critics who stressed the instability of language. The arbitrary relationship between the "sign" (e.g., the word) and the "signified" (what the word refers to in the world) was emphasized so as to cast doubt on the ability of language to convey any kind of objectively reliable meaning. The meaning of a text, whether a novel or a law, is a linguistic construction—indeed, all cultural expressions and institutions can be thought of as a "text"—which can, by attention to their linguistic contradictions and power relationships, be deconstructed. The point is, neither the modernists nor the postmodernists had a positive basis for language that did justice to its all-encompassing place in human thought and human life.

Hamann, on the other hand did: Human language is related to the language of God; that is, to God's word. In fact, God's word is fundamental to creation itself. God spoke the universe into existence, so that his word, the *Logos*, underlies all things. This is why we language-bound human beings can know the world. This is why reason, though it has its limits, does give us truth about the world, because *Logic* presupposes the *Logos*. And this is how we can know God, whose word became flesh in Jesus Christ and whose word is written down in the Book of the Holy Scriptures.

Bayer, in pursuing these lines of thought, shows how Luther himself anticipates the current debates about the nature of language. He shows how Luther undermines the distinction between sign and signified, which goes back to Augustine, replacing the "hermeneutics of signification": "According to this approach, language is a system of signs that refer to matters or circumstances, or else it uses signs that express an emotion. In both cases the sign—whether as an assertion or as an expression—does not equate with the matter itself."[32] Bayer quotes Luther: "The philosophical sign is the mark of something absent; the theological sign is the mark of something present."[33] Bayer concludes, "That the *signum* itself is already the *res*,

30. See Betz, *After Enlightenment*, 248–57.
31. See Snellman, "Hamann's Influence on Wittgenstein," 59–82.
32. Bayer, *Martin Luther's Theology*, 52.
33. Bayer, *Martin Luther's Theology*, 52. The quotation is from Luther's *Table Talk*.

that *the linguistic sign is already the matter itself*—that was Luther's great hermeneutical discovery."[34]

That is to say, language is not simply a set of arbitrary signs that point to facts or experiences outside themselves, as both modernists and postmodernists had assumed. Yes, language is referential, but it also can be performative. Bayer draws on contemporary linguistics—specifically "speech-act theory"—to illuminate what Luther says about language (indeed, for Bayer, Luther anticipates speech-act theory). Words can make things happen: "I command you"; "I sentence you to prison"; "I accept your offer." Words can call new realities into being: "I now pronounce you husband and wife"; "I install you into office"; "I apologize." And words can establish relationships: "I promise you"; "I forgive you"; "I love you."

The word of God is supremely performative. It accomplishes what it says. God spoke the universe into existence. "And *God said*, 'Let there be light,' and there was light" (Gen 1:3). And God's word continues its creative work:

> For as the rain and the snow come down from heaven
> and do not return there but water the earth,
> making it bring forth and sprout,
> giving seed to the sower and bread to the eater,
> so shall my word be that goes out from my mouth;
> it shall not return to me empty,
> but it shall accomplish that which I purpose,
> and shall succeed in the thing for which I sent it. (Isa 55:10–11)

"For the word of God is living and active, sharper than any two-edged sword, piercing to the division of soul and of spirit, of joints and of marrow, and discerning the thoughts and intentions of the heart" (Heb 4:12).

An example of this performative word of God, as Luther describes it, is the law, which pierces the heart and exposes its sin, and the gospel, which brings Christ to the repentant heart. Thus, the word of God can create faith in the heart of its hearer. The message of forgiveness through Jesus Christ is a *promise*, which the Christian can hold onto through all trials and doubts. Other words of God that accomplish his purpose can be found in Baptism: "I baptize you in the name of the Father, the Son, and the Holy Spirit." In Holy Communion, the words of Christ constitute a new reality: "This is my body. . . . This is my blood." The bread and wine are not mere signs, as Zwingli insisted; rather, Jesus Christ is truly present in these elements, on the basis of his Word.

34. Bayer, *Martin Luther's Theology*, 52.

Human words are also performative when they communicate God's promises, as in a pastor's sermon or in the words of absolution: "In the stead and by the command of my Lord Jesus Christ I forgive you all your sins in the name of the Father and of the Son and of the Holy Spirit."

All of this, of course, is the ordinary Lutheran theology of the word and sacraments. The Bible is not simply a book that gives doctrinal information about God and a record of historical facts about Jesus and the Israelites. While it does give doctrinal information and record historical facts, the Bible is also a means of grace. That is, the word of God addresses us personally, as his efficacious communication to us, convicting us of sin, giving us guidance, and bringing us the promises of Christ. Just as Christ is present in the sacraments, bringing us to faith by means of God's creation, the Holy Spirit is present in God's word, bringing us to faith, by means of language.[35]

The Estates

Postmodernists tend to be radically hostile to cultural institutions of every kind. They regard them with the "hermeneutics of suspicion," seeing in marriage, parenthood, governments, economics, churches, and other human relationships, a mask for the exercise of power and oppression. But in light of the doctrine of creation and of God's word, Bayer, along with Hamann and Luther, sees them as masks of God's love.

Luther teaches that God actively and lovingly reigns in his creation, as well as in his eternal kingdom. Christians are citizens of both realms, but they are to live out their faith in the created order. God works through human beings and is present in their vocations, giving daily bread by means of farmers and bakers, creating new life by means of mothers and fathers, healing by means of physicians, and protecting by means of lawful magistrates. The purpose of every vocation is to love and serve one's neighbors. Vocation is the realm of good works, cross-bearing, and the struggle against sin, through which the Christian grows in holiness.

These vocations, or callings, are multiple, and they are to be found in three estates that God has ordained for human life: The church, the household, and the state. These, according to Bayer, are the "three fundamental forms of life, in which God's promise organized human existence and organizes it still."[36] The church consists of those who have been called by the gospel and thus have been brought into a community of faith, where they

---

35 See Bayer, *Martin Luther's Theology*, 50–54.
36. Bayer, *Martin Luther's Theology*, 122.

are nourished by the word and the sacraments. The household consists of both the family and the workplace. Bayer explains it as "the relationship between parents and children, between a husband and a wife, between human being and field, thus, as work: the interrelationship of the human being with nature, the acquisition of his means of sustenance, his daily bread."[37] The state is the realm of citizenship, of government and our obligations to the society as a whole.

Human beings are not made to exist as isolated individuals, but are to exist in relationships with others, as made possible by language. Says Bayer, "A human being's dignity and his freedom are located in the communal interchange between hearing and speaking, providing and acquiring, receiving and passing on, authority and critique thereof."[38]

To be sure, sin infects all of the estates. "But in spite of their depravity, they are not destroyed," says Bayer. "Even though they are corrupted, they are still held fast by God's promise and are thereby sanctified. Even through their depravity one can still recognize and believe in the power of the word of God that creates and forgives."[39]

Bayer thus gives an alternative way of looking at human roles and social institutions, valuing them highly as provisions of God, while also recognizing their potential for human evil, which is all many postmodernists allow themselves to see. But Bayer addresses their concerns about power and freedom, while making the case that power is not evil in itself. "From the time of its origin according to God's creative will, 'freedom' as a form of interaction within community does not exist within a power vacuum, but in a relationship that views power as that which always seeks to benefit the life of the other."[40]

Conclusion

If you reject the word of God, says Bayer, "then the world is no longer the medium that delivers on the promises to me." Instead, the world becomes fearful and oppressive. "You must squeeze some sense out of this chaos, this fearful natural realm in all its uncertainty; you have to be in charge

---

37. Bayer, *Martin Luther's Theology*, 123.
38. Bayer, *Martin Luther's Theology*, 150.
39. Bayer, *Martin Luther's Theology*, 123.
40. Bayer, *Martin Luther's Theology*, 150.

of making sense in this and out of this chaotic world; you yourself have to establish its order!"[41]

But this alienation from reality itself, this lostness, can be healed through the word of God, which reveals and reconciles. Bayer echoes Hamann in underscoring the self-giving quality of each Person of the Trinity:

> The *Father* gives himself to us absolutely in the creation; the *Son* gives himself to us in the redemption and opens for us thereby once again the access to the Father; finally, the *Spirit* gives himself to us in the *promissio*, which constitutes faith, and at the same time gives us the Son and the Father.[42]

This is the answer to the postmodern condition.

Bibliography

Bayer, Oswald. *A Contemporary in Dissent: Johann Georg Hamann as Radical Enlightener*. Translated by Roy A. Harrisville and Mark C. Mattes. Grand Rapids: Eerdmans, 2012.

———. *Living by Faith*. Minneapolis: Fortress, 2017.

———. *Martin Luther's Theology: A Contemporary Interpretation*. Translated by Thomas H. Trapp. Grand Rapids: Eerdmans, 2008.

Betz, John R. *After Enlightenment: The Post-Secular Vision of J. G. Hamann*. Oxford: Wiley-Blackwell, 2012.

Isherwood, Lisa, and Marko Zlomislic, eds. *The Poverty of Radical Orthodoxy*. Eugene, OR: Pickwick, 2012.

Lockwood, Michael A. *The Unholy Trinity*. St. Louis: Concordia, 2016.

Milbank, John, et al., eds. *Radical Orthodoxy: A New Theology*. London: Routledge, 1999.

Oden, Thomas C. *After Modernity . . . What?: An Agenda for Theology*. Grand Rapids: Zondervan, 1990.

———. *A Change of Heart: A Personal and Theological Memoir*. Downers Grove, IL: InterVarsity Academic, 2014.

Snellman, Lauri. "Hamann's Influence on Wittgenstein." *Nordic Wittgenstein Review* 7 (2018) 59–82.

Taylor, Charles. *The Language Animal: The Full Shape of the Human Linguistic Capacity*. Cambridge: Harvard University Press, 2016.

---

41. Bayer, *Martin Luther's Theology*, 102.
42. Bayer, *Martin Luther's Theology*, 341.

16

The Significance of *Oratio, Meditatio,* and *Tentatio* for Abraham Calov's Understanding of Theology

Roland Ziegler

Oswald Bayer has consistently emphasized the significance of Luther's triad *oratio, meditatio,* and *tentatio* for the concept of theology.[1] Not all of later Lutheranism followed Luther's example, and those who did use the triad used it in a modified way.[2] One of the Lutherans that did use Luther's advice extensively was Abraham Calov, a chief representative of the silver age of Lutheran orthodoxy in Wittenberg.[3] The question of the significance of the triad raises the issue of the relation between erudition and piety, between the academic character and the spiritual nature of theology. Changes in the un-

---

1. See, e.g., Bayer, "Oratio, Meditatio, Tentatio," 7–59; *Theologie*, 55–105; "Urteilskraft als theologische Kompetenz," 307–8; "Twenty Questions," 442: "Is your theological existence determined by prayer (*oratio*), meditation (*meditatio*) and attack *(tentatio)*; that is, by the fact that, driven as you are by *Anfechtung*, you enter prayerfully into Holy Scripture and are interpreted by it, in order that you can interpret it for others who are under spiritual attack, so that they too enter prayerfully into Holy Scripture and are interpreted by it?"

2. "Auch so unzweideutig der lutherischen Orthodoxie zuzurechnende Theologen wie Förster, Hütter oder Hülsemann kennen die Lutherische Trias in ihren Anweisungen zum Theologiestudium nicht. Sie war vielmehr seit der Repetitionsrede des Chytraeus als strukturgebendes Prinzip aus den Wittenberger Anweisungn verschwunden" (Nieden, *Erfindung,* 231).

3. On Calov in general, see Wallmann, "Abraham Calov," 563–68; Jung, *Das Ganze.* On Calov's concept of theology and the study of theology, see Preus, *Theology of Post-Reformation Lutheranism,* 194–207; Appold, *Abraham Calov's Doctrine,* 46–66; Kang, *Frömmigkeit und Gelehrsamkeit,* 125–40; Nieden, *Die Erfindung des Theologen,* 225–36. The periodization of Lutheran orthodoxy in a "golden age," "high orthodoxy," and a "silver age" is in Preus, *Theology,* 44–47.

derstanding of theology in the seventeenth century among Lutherans led to the relation of faith to theology an issue. Marcel Nieden describes the way of the Wittenberg theologians as a "via media" between those who identify the pious and the theologian and those who separate them, a way "not without tensions."[4] How, then, does Calov see the relation between faith and theology, and what importance does *oratio, meditatio,* and *tentatio* have for his question and for his understanding of theology?

Calov defines theology in his "Systema locorum theologicorum" in this way: "Theology is a practical aptitude of knowledge derived from divine revelation, concerning the true religion, through which man after the fall is to be led to eternal salvation through faith."[5] Theology is first an aptitude (*habitus*). Calov follows here the understanding of science as an aptitude that Lutheran orthodoxy had adopted from Zabarella.[6] For Zabarella, there are theoretical and practical disciplines, each with its own method.[7] Theoretical disciplines (physics, mathematics, metaphysics) follow the synthetic method: they start with first principles and then progress from these. Practical disciplines (logic and ethics) follow the analytical method: they start with the purpose, and then progress to first principles.

4. Nieden, *Erfindung,* 243.

5. "Theologia est Habitus Practicus cognitionis è revelation divinâ haustae, de verâ Religione, qua homo post lapsum per fidem ad salutem aeternam perducendus" (Calov, *Systema locorum theologicorum,* 1:1).

6. "Scientiae itaque & artes omnes in animo considerandae sunt, tanquam in subiecto primo: & eas ita co[n]siderauit Aristoteles in sexto libro Ethic. ad Nicomachum vt habitus animi, nam habitu[m] mentis vt earum genus accepit: quod non rectè factum esst, si aequè extra mentem, ac in mente earum natura consisteret, sic enim habitus mentis non esset earum genus, sed accidens quiddam sine quo existere possent" (Zabarella, "De Doctrinae ordine apologia," 1.2.5c). On Zabarella's influence on German Lutheran philosophy in the late sixteenth and seventeenth century, see Petersen, *Geschichte der Aristotelischen Philosophie,* 195–218; Sparn, "Die Schulphilosophie," 482–87. The application of the concept of *habitus* for theology was not uncontroversial as the debate between Andreas Cramer and Sigismund Evenius shows (Friedrich, *Die Grenzen der Vernunft,* 193–202).

7. For the distinction between contemplative and practical disciplines see Zabarella, *On Methods,* 150–55. For comtemplative disciplines, the appropriate method is compositive, starting from beginning-principles (prima principia); for practical disciplines, the appropriate method is the resolutive method. Zabarella defines the resolutive method, which was later called the analytical method, thus: "The other is resolutive, which, once the ultimate end to be done or effected by us is set out, progresses to the first beginning-principles being tracked down and by means of which we can afterward produce and procure that end.... But arts and all other disciplines can use only resolutive, not compositive at all" (Zabarella, *On Methods,* 153). "Zabarella's philosophy was used above all in the text-books on natural philosophy at the turn of the seventeenth century, and his logic and methodology were adopted in protestant Germany to legitimate the new protestant theology" (Mikkeli, *Aristotelian Response,* 181).

With the adoption of Zabarella's philosophy of science came the adoption of the analytic method in theology among Lutherans who had a strong anti-speculative view of theology.

Calov is no exception and thus views theology as a practical discipline. Theology does not find its goal in knowing, but in accomplishing something outside of the subject of the aptitude.[8] The purpose of theology and of the theologian is to lead men to salvation. Thus, theology begins with man as sinner and then develops how man is to be saved.[9] Gerhard and Calov both use the analogy of a physician and medicine: the purpose of medicine is not only to know but also to heal; the physician is the one who has the acquired skill to heal others.[10] Calov's acceptance of the theory of science of his time, though, means that theology is framed into the alternative of knowing or doing, belonging either to the *vita activa* or *contemplativa*. And with theology belonging to the *vita activa*, there is now a distinction between faith and the *habitus* of the theologian: Faith is one of the goals of theology, but to be a theologian and to be a Christian is conceptually not the same. Does this open the door to *a theologia irregenitorum*? Preus rejects this possibility, and Calov does not entertain the question which has its origin in pietistic controversies after Calov.[11] Appold sees here a similarity to Calixt in Calov's distinction between faith and theology and a shift from an older understanding according to which theology is essentially connected with faith.[12]

Appold is right in pointing out that Johann Gerhard and Calov differ in their concept of theology. For Calov, theology is primarily connected with the ecclesiastical office and its functions, though also Gerhard can say that theology can be used for the functions of the ministry. For Gerhard, theology can be used in three ways: for the knowledge that every Christian has, for the functions of the ministry, and for the deeper knowledge of

---

8. "Cujus disciplinae finis est practicus, ea est practica, quando quidem à fine practico dependeat ratio formalis disciplinae practicae; At Theologiae finis est, practicus tùm *externus,* DEI fruitio, tùm *externus & intermedius,* hominum conversio, & *ultimus,* ad salutem aeternam perductio" (Calov, *Systema* 1.28).

9. Here the impulse of Luther's soteriological understanding of theology continues. See the definition of the subject matter of theology in Luther's lecture on Psalm 51 as the justifying God and man condemned and guilty (WA 328:17–18; *LW* 311).

10. Calov, "Tractatus," 1144–45. For Gerhard, see Wallmann, *Der Theologiebegriff,* 51–52.

11. "Calov is not teaching a theology of the unregenerate here, nor do any of the theologians of his day.... This disastrous teaching came later as the orthodox Lutherans battled with Pietism" (Preus, *Theology I,* 250).

12. "Calov is not the first Lutheran to distinguish theology from faith; Georg Calixt, known, ironically, as Calov's arch-rival and intellectual opponent, had preceded him with such a distinction in the 1619 *Epitome*" (Appold, *Vocatio,* 54).

the divine mysteries.[13] For Calov, not all Christians are theologians. Calov seems to separate theology from faith even further when he mentions that theologians are not necessarily elect. Theology, though a gift of God, is a ministerial gift, not identical with the gift of faith.[14] But Calov's point is not that theology and faith are divorced. Calov does not say that not all theologians are believers, but that those who are temporal believers but do not persist to the end and thus are not elect can be theologians *while they believe.* Thus, Appold's thesis that Calov's concept of theology comes close to Calixt is not supported by this quotation. For Calov, the theologian can only become a theologian if he is a believer, even if he later loses faith. For Calixt, saving faith is not a prerequisite for a theologian, but only a humanly attainable faith. Indeed, the faith of the theologian is the same faith as the faith of the demon (Jas 2:19).[15]

Calov does not include in his definition that theology is a God-given *habitus.*[16] Appold sees in this a further indication of the division of faith and theology in Calov's concept of theology. Instead of a divine operation in the acquisition of the *habitus,* its supernatural character lies solely in the content it learns: "For Calov, any supernatural quality of theology lies less in the mental operations by which it is practiced than in the nature of its unique object. Hence, the term occupies a position of considerably less prominence in Calov's *Systema* than it had for previous Lutherans."[17] For

---

13. Gerhard, "Exegesis," 2. "Bei Calov ist es auch begrifflich durchgedrungen, daß die Theologie wesentlich als Funktion des kirchlichen Amtes zu bestimmen und darum wiederum die kirchliche Amtsfunktion als Theologie zu begreifen ist. Calov kann in Fortführung der bei Gerhard noch nicht ausgezogenen Linie der Ineinssetzung von Theologie und functio ministerii sämtliche Pflichten des kirchlichen Amtes aus dem Begriff des ‚Theologen' geradezu ableiten: das docere, adhortari, dehortari, consolare, poenitentes absolvere, sacramenta dispensare, examina instituere, disciplinam ecclesiae coercere gehört zur ‚functio theologorum'" (Wallmann, *Theologiebegriff,* 41. The reference is to Calov, *Systema,* 1:29).

14. "Non autem *omnes Theologi sunt electi,* nec *omnes electi sunt Theologi* propriè dicti, prout hîc vox Theologiae accipitur. Theologia est quidem donum Dei, sed pertinent ad *dona ministrantia,* non autem ad *sanctificantia*; quanquam nec dona sanctificantia solùm electorum propria sint, sed etiam cadant in reprobos ad tempus credentes. V. cumprimis *Ebr. VI, v.4.5*" (Calov, *Systema,* 1:56).

15. Wallmann, *Theologiebegriff,* 113. The quote from Calixt's *Epitome* can be found in the modern edition (Calixt, *Dogmatische Schriften,* 218).

16. "Calov gives only perfunctory attention to the so-called proximate genus of theology, theology classified as a gift of God. Unfortunately he is again too wrapped up in the polemics of his day" (Preus, *Theology,* 1:206).

17. Appold, *Vocatio,* 65.

Calov, so Appold, theology is God-given only in the sense that the content of theology comes from God.[18]

For such a view speaks that the term θεόσδοτος is rather rare in Calov's discussion of the nature of theology.[19] But is it true that there is a difference between Calov and Johann Gerhard in regard to the God-given nature of the *habitus*? Calov does not include θεόσδοτος in his definition of theology.[20] There, in the place one would expect θεόσδοτος one finds theology is a *habitus practicus* "*cognitionis e revelatione divina haustae.*"[21] This suggests that theology is θεόσδοτος because of its divinely given content. Calov does mention as a reason for theology's character as θεόσδοτος the content of theology.[22] But is that the only way in which God acts when a person acquires the *habitus*?

Volker Jung points out that the theological *habitus* can be paralleled to the *claritas externa* of Scripture. Though Jung sees the danger that the *habitus* can become independent and turn into a mere intellectual knowledge of Scripture, he argues, that this is not the intention of Calov because of his use of the triad. This shows that the means by which the theological *habitus* is acquired are anything but intellectualistic.[23]

The triad *of oratio, meditatio*, and *tentatio* is therefore of great importance for the understanding of Calov's concept of theology. For if theology would be only a human ability whose content is given in the Bible and nothing more, then this would be a step toward a secularization of theology. But if the way one becomes a theologian is a spiritual process, then faith and piety are not external to theology.[24]

Calov mentions the triad in the discussion of theology in the first volume of his *Systema locorum theologicorum*.[25] He places the triad in

18. "Theology is θεόσδοτος simply because its subject-matter, contained in Holy Scripture, is given by God. All cognitive functions which have their origin in an encounter with that subject-matter could therefore be described as 'God-given' operations, and when 'habitualized,' as a God-given *habitus*" (Appold, *Vocatio*, 65).

19. Calov does assert that *forma* of theology is a *habitus practicus* θεόσδοτος (Calov, *Systema*, 1:5).

20. Calov, *Systema*, 1:1.

21. Calov, *Systema*, 1:1.

22. Calov, *Systema*, 1:5.

23. Jung, *Das Ganze*, 249.

24. Niedner states that the theologians in Wittenberg in the seventeenth century had the problem of combining erudition and piety because of the changed understanding of theology. "Die Frömmigkeit wurde zu einem unverzichtbaren Teil des normativen Selbstverständnisses erklärt, ohne doch noch aus dem Theologiebegriff schlüssig abgeleitet werden zu können" (Niedner, *Erfindung*, 243).

25. Calov, *Systema*, 10–11. The section on sanctity because of the means verbatim

the discussion of the chief attributes of theology (unity, truth, necessity, dignity, and sanctity) under sanctity. Theology is holy because it comes from the three-holy God, mediated by the most holy word of God, deals with holy things, and demands a holy person. It is also holy because of the means which are necessary for the study of theology: prayer, meditation, affliction, as Luther said. The scriptural proof for prayer which begins the sacred study is found in Prov 3:3; Jas 1:5; meditation which continues it (Ps 1:1); and affliction consummates it (Isa 28:19; 1 Pet 1:7). Thus, a student ought to have time for prayer, since he always needs divine grace and blessing (Luke 11:13; John 16:23); for meditation, because the word of God is to be kept by a faithful heart (Luke 11:28), and for the spiritual and holy fight, since the flesh fights against the spirit (Gal 5:17; Isa 28:19). For a more extensive discussion, Calov refers to his introduction to the study of theology, the *Isagoge*.

Thus, the triad does not structure the discussion of the concept of theology as such in *Systema*, but is part of the discussion of its holiness, a specific property that distinguishes theology from other branches of knowledge.[26]

When we follow Calov's reference for a further discussion on *oratio, meditatio, tentatio* in his *Isagoges ad SS Theologia Libri Duo*, we find an extensive discussion of the triad.[27] The *Isagoges* consists of two parts. The first volume, titled *De Natura Theologiae*, analyzes the concepts of theology and revelation in numerous distinctions, ending in a definition of theology as "Theology is a practical *habitus* of knowledge, drawn from the divine revelation, concerning the true religion, through which man after the fall is to be led through faith to eternal salvation."[28]

The second volume is titled *Paedia theologica, De Methodo Studii Theologici piè, dextrèm felicitèr* [sic] *tractandi*. In his definition of *paedia theologica*, Calov introduces God as agent: "Theological education is the practical aptitude concerning the study of theology, to be conducted skillfully and fruitfully according to the leadership of the Holy Spirit; to the praise of the

---

also Calov, *Isagoges*, 300.

26. This differs from the approach in the third edition of Haffenreffer's *Loci Theologici* (1–22), in which the Prolegomena are structured by *oratio, meditatio*, and *tentatio*.

27. I use the second edition. The two parts have different pagination. Subsequently, part one is referenced as *Isagoges, De Natura Theologiae*; part two is *Isagoges, Paedia*.

28. "Theologia est habitus Practicus cognitionis, ê revelatione Divinâ haustus, de verâ religione, qvâ homo post lapsum, per fidem ad saltutem æternam perducendus" (Calov, *Isagoges, De Natura Theologiae*, 29). Preus gives an extensive overview of Calov's understanding of theology, including the *Isagoges* (Preus, *Theology*, 1:194–207). Contrary to what his bibliography indicates, he is using the second edition, not the first of the *Isagoges*.

divine name, our salvation and the edification of the church."[29] The effective cause for theology is the Holy Spirit.

The Holy Spirit is the "principal efficient cause, without which there is certainly no fruitful or beneficial undertaking of anybody ever."[30] Calov quotes right at the beginning of the *Paedia* Luther's advice from the preface of the collection of the German writings as "golden advice."[31] He engages *oratio*, *meditatio*, and *tentatio* more comprehensively in the second chapter, "Praecepta de mediis studii theologici, sectio prima generalis caput I. DE reqvisitis in Genere."[32]

Oratio, meditatio, and *tentatio* are the general requirements for the student, because they are not associated with a specific discipline of theology. Prayer is connected with the holiness of life.[33] *Meditatio* is connected with the hearing, reading, writing, and practice (*exercitatio*) of Scripture. *Tentatio* refers to the continual internal wrestling between spirit and flesh and what comes to individual men, and external struggle.[34] A student of theology devotes himself always to prayer, meditation, and struggle because he is always in need of prayer, the word of God is to be retained in the heart always (Luke 11:28), and the struggle against the flesh is perpetual.[35] The three are, though distinct, intimately connected. Prayer needs meditating on the Scriptures and is necessary in affliction. Meditation needs prayer and meditation, enlivened by prayer, makes affliction bearable. The relationship between *oratio, meditatio,* and *tentatio* can also be described as a sequence: studying theology starts with prayer, it continues with meditation, and affliction completes the sacred studies.[36]

Prayer is necessary for the study of theology because of man's natural blindness, the sublimity and difficulty of the subject matter, the necessity of the illumination by the Spirit, the gravity of the danger, the usefulness of prayer, and the weight of the example of the saints.[37]

---

29. "Paedia theologica est habitus Practicus de Studio Theologiae, ad ductum Spiritûs S. dextrè ac feliciter tractando, ad Nominis divini laudem, nostram Salutem, & Ecclesiæ ædificationem" (Calov, *Isagoges Paedia*, 1).

30. "*Causa Efficientis Principis* . . . quippe sine quâ *nullius est felix conatus & ultilis unqvam*" (Calov, *Isagoges, Paedia*, 2).

31. Calov, *Isagoges, Paedia*, 49.

32. Calov, *Isagoges, Paedia*, 6.

33. Calov, *Isagoges, Paedia*, 33. Calov references Isa 1:15; 1 Tim 1:8.

34. Calov, *Isagoges, Paedia*, 33–34.

35. Calov, *Isagoges, Paedia*, 34.

36. Calov, *Isagoges, Paedia*, 35.

37. Calov, *Isagoges, Paedia*, 37.

Meditation is the attentive consideration of Scripture and what is to be learned from it and concerning it, so that it is retained in the faithful mind and applied to a beneficial use. The ways of meditation are reading, hearing, lecture (*recitatio*), writing, declamation, sermon, disputation, repetition and other exercises.[38] We see here that Calov, following the tradition since Chytraeus, widens the understanding of meditation and draws into it also specific academic ways of engaging with the Scriptures.[39] Meditation is necessary, it has to be based on Scripture, it should be undertaken rather during the day than during the night and follow a definite order and includes the listening to lectures by the professors and the use of secondary sources.[40] Since not all of them are good or clear, the student is to ask his professor for recommendation. The exercises following include first repetition with others, then declamations, then disputations, then homiletical exercises. Again, we see how Calov includes the then usual academic pedagogical way under Luther's "meditation," thus following the tradition of a creative relecture of Luther.

Tentatio or affliction for Calov is first the struggle between flesh and Spirit, the divine cross put on the Christian, and the sifting of Satan, through which faith is made firmer and one becomes a practical theologian.[41] This distinction between internal and external *tentatio* has been traditional in manuals on the study of theology since Chytraeus.[42] Affliction is thus either from man, from God, or from the devil. Affliction educates the mind and perfects the will. Affliction affects the will of man, because God wants a humble heart (2 Cor 12:7). Quoting Luther, Calov sees affliction effecting a spiritual sense and a practical experience of the divine oracles, so that affliction is not only to create understanding, but to sense (*sentire*) and experience the certainty, truth, sweetness, efficacy, and comfort of the word.[43] It is necessary against interior afflictions that the student fortifies himself with the spiritual armament (Eph 5).

For Calov, the theological *habitus* is not something that can be acquired by natural means alone, as his discussion shows. Even though the aptitude of theology is not identical with faith, if prayer, meditation, and affliction are necessary for the acquisition of it, then faith is a prerequisite of becoming a theologian.

38. Calov, *Isagoges, Paedia*, 52.
39. Nieden, *Erfindung*, 93.
40. Calov, *Isagoges, Paedia*, 54–60.
41. Calov, *Isagoges, Paedia*, 64.
42. Nieden, "Anfechtung," 90.
43. Calov, *Isagoges, Paidia*, 67.

There are other points in Calov's view that connect the personal faith of the theologian and the studying and exercise of theology. In the discussion of the goals of theology, he mentions that the purpose of studying theology is not only to acquire the ability to lead others to salvation, but to care for one's own salvation. Thus, the *finis* of theology includes the faith of the theologian.[44] Hence, Calov mentions that the student is not to neglect his own salvation (1 Tim 4:16). The study of theology serves also the purpose that the student himself progresses in his knowledge of the content of salvation and his faith is made more certain, so that he can teach with *plerophoria*.[45]

When Calov emphasizes the transitive nature of the theological habit in his *Tractatus novo de methodo* and distinguishes it from faith, he does not thereby exclude that the object of the theologian is also himself. Indeed, the theologian is a theologian if he has the *habitus* to lead others to the faith, even if he does not lead others to the faith, since there is a difference between having the habit and actualizing the habit. There is the possibility of a theologian who does not care about his own salvation, just as there is the possibility of a doctor that does not take care of his own illnesses. Such a situation is possible, but of course not desirable. Appold is wrong when he writes: "Theology is, to Calov, no more a matter of 'coming' to salvation than medicine a science of healing one's own body. It focuses, rather, on others."[46] The analogy between medicine and theology is: As medicine is the discipline of healing (and not the state of being healthy), so theology is the discipline of leading to salvation (not the state of being on the way to heaven). But just as the doctor should not only be concerned about the health of others, but also his own, so the theologian should be not only concerned about leading others to salvation, but also being on the way to salvation. As a doctor does not cease to be a doctor when he neglects his health, so a theologian does not cease to be a theologian if he has no concern for his salvation. The point is twofold: first, that theology is a *habitus* directed to action, second, that the *habitus* exists, even when it is not applied to the theologian himself—even though it should! The theologian is, if one wants, under his own care, and he

---

44. "Datur horum finium quaedam subordinatio, ita ut *supremus* sit Gloria DEI: *medius* salus Hominis: *infimus*, profectus in Studio Sacro. Proficere enim in Sacris studemus, ut tùm nostrae, tum aliorum saluti consulamus, gloriamq[ue] DEI propagemus, & quicquid ad nostram, quicquid ad aliorum salute facit, id omne ad Gloriam nominis divini ampliandam facere certum est: cùm in eâ sit etiam salus nostra, nempe in fruitione & celebratione DEI" (Calov, *Isagoges Paedia*, 27).

45. Calov, *Isagoes, Paedia*, 30.

46. Appold, *Vocatio*, 52.

is not a good theologian if he neglects the application of the means of grace to himself. Then he should be told: Physician, heal yourself![47]

And even though there is a strong link between theology and the pastoral office, Calov also states: "As the study of theology is necessary for everybody, thus it ought not to be utterly disregarded by anybody."[48] The reason that all Christians need to study theology is because they for themselves and for their neighbor and their household need to be able to test the spirits (1 John 4:1), avoid false prophets (Matt 7:15), and avoid those who cause divisions and offenses (Rom 16:17). Lawyers and politicians need to study theology so that they conduct everything in the fear of God, their consciences are formed, and, as the custodians of both tablets, act in such a way that they do not violate the foundation of good administration, the divine law. Physicians need theology, so that they can talk in a pious manner with the sick, can comfort and admonish them with the divine word and know when to ask for help from pastors.[49]

Calov thus gives a reason why every Christian and the students of the other professional schools, law and medicine, should also be conversant in theology. Thereby theology is not exclusively tied to the pastoral office. But as his examples show, theology is still mostly directed outwardly, to serve others, even if the aspect that the Christian as a Christian for himself has to judge doctrine is not lacking.

There are obvious differences between Luther's and Calov's understanding of theology. As Bayer has pointed out, for Luther theology was neither *vita contemplative* nor *vita active*, neither theory nor "Handlungswissenschaft." (theory of action)[50] But there is an aspect in which theology and the theologians do not relate only to God and themselves, but to other men.[51] Thus, the concept of theology refers to the work of the word

---

47. "*Verum enim verè licet omnes* fideles *habere debeant aliquam notitiam articulorum fidein, non tamen ideo* omnes fideles propriè *dicuntur* theologia, *sed alius* est habitus fidei, *alius* Theologiae; & *quanquam Theologus suae salutis non minorem habere curam debeat, quam alienae, tamen audire cogitur sua ipsius merito;* Medice cura te ipsum." (Calov, "Tractatus," 1144–45). Calov uses the analogy medicine also in *Isagoges, De Natura Theologiae*, 186–87.

48. "Studium Theologiae ut omnibus necessarium, ita à nemine prorsus negligendum est" (Calov, *Isagoges, Paedia,* 13).

49. Calov, *Isagoges, Paedia*, 13–14.

50. Bayer, *Theologie*, 59. For the concept of theology as a theory of communicative action (Theorie des kommunikativen Handelns), see Peukert, *Wissenschaftstheorie*.

51. "In Kürze lassen sich Luthers Ausführungen so zusammenfassen: Ein Theologie ist, wer von der Heiligen Schrift ausgelegt wird, sich von ihr auslegen läßt und sie als von ihr Ausgelegter anderen Angefochtenene auslegt" (Bayer, *Theologie*, 61).

of God in regard to the theologian, but also takes into account that the theologian serves others.

That the theologian is the one who serves others becomes more explicit when the academic study of theology is considered which aims at becoming able to perform the duties of the pastoral office. Hence, there is a strong tendency to see theology as a "Handlungswissenschaft," as something that aims at making people, i.e., pastors, able to *do* something.

In the definition of theology as a practical *habitus*, there is a shift in the understanding of theology from Luther that creates the tendency to a more exclusive association of theology and the pastoral office. Nevertheless, as the use of the triad shows, theology does not become simply a theory of action in this Lutheran tradition. For theology and personal faith are inseparable. There are, though, differences in Lutheran Orthodoxy. In Gerhard's definition, the concept of theology combines the personal faith and the ability to teach, since theology is defined as wisdom. For Gerhard, theology is a *habitus intellectualis* in the Aristotelian scheme, most like the Aristotelian scheme of wisdom, though better defined as *habitus* θεόσδοτος.[52] But when he discusses if it is speculative or practical, he sides with practical, since the purpose of theology is not mere knowledge, but doing.[53] In his final definition of theology though, he defines theology not only as a *habitus* directed at doing to others, but also directed to the one who has it.[54]

Calov does not define theology in this way, because for him the concept of the practical *habitus* excludes that it is directed primarily towards the theologian. When Calov talks about theology as being practical, the reasons for him are the goal, which is the enjoyment of God and for the conversion of men and the leading to eternal salvation; from the means, since the means do something to the goal, namely from the side of God sacraments and the word of God, from the side of man, faith; from what the theologian does, namely teaching, exhorting, warning, comforting, absolving, administering the sacraments etc.; from the principle of theology, namely divine revelation, which is practical (John 20:20; Rom 15:4; 1 Tim 3:16–18); from the means of the study of theology, which are practical,

52. Gerhard, "Exegema, Prooemium," x.
53. Gerhard, "Exegema, Prooemium," xii.
54. "[Theologia] est *doctrina ex verbo Dei extructa, qua homines in fide vera & vita pia erudiuntur ad vitam aeternam.* Theologia (habitualiter & concretive considerate) est habitus θεόσδοτος, per verbum a Spiritu sancto homini collatus, quo non solum in divinorum mysteriorum cognitione per mentis illuminationem instruitur, ut quae intelliget in affectum cordis & executionem operis salutariter traducat, sed etiam aptus & expeditus redditur de divinis illis mysteriis, ac via salutis alios informandi, ac coelestem veritatem a corruptelis contradicentium vindicandi, ut homines fide vera & bonis operibus rutilantes ad regum coelorum perducantur" (Gerhard, "Exegema, Prooemium," xxx).

namely *oratio, meditatio,* and *tentatio*.[55] The triad confirms the practical nature of theology. If the requirements for a discipline are practical, not theoretical, then the discipline is practical. But the requirements for theology are practical, not theoretical. Therefore, theology is practical. The requirements for theology are prayer, meditation, and affliction, which are practical, insofar as they work towards theology (*quatenus ad Theologiam faciunt*). Thus, the practical character of theology is taken in a wide sense. Theology is not only practical because it refers to the practice of the church in preaching and administering the word of God, but because the goal is practical: the salvation of man.

Here Calov follows Luther. For Luther, the subject of theology is not simply God, but it is God in relation to man and man in relation to God. Since God and faith belong together, the study of theology and the existence of the Christian cannot be separated. Hence, the basic situation of the Christian in his dependence on God, in his listening to the word of God, and his affliction by the assaults of the enemies of God, is also constitutive for the existence of the theologian.[56]

Though Calov's definition of theology does not contain the practice of faith, his prominent use of *oratio, meditatio,* and *tentatio* does show that for Calov theology without faith is not possible.

Bayer states in his chapter on Luther's understanding of what it means to be a Christian that the believer cannot sustain himself and thus faith cannot become a *habitus*. Rather there is continual dependence on the Holy Spirit in life-long, listening, and reading.[57] When Calov uses *habitus* as genus for theology, does he succumb to the danger of making theology something the theologian has once and for all? Gerhard saw the danger and used *habitus* not in the same sense as Aristotle or Zabarella for theological reasons.[58] Thus, Gerhard emphasizes the θεοσδότος of theology: because

---

55. Calov, *Systema*, 1:28–30. Calov sees himself in agreement with "Magnus noster Gerhardus" (Calov, *Systema*, 1:31).

56. "Luther erblickte den Gegenstand der Theologie nicht mehr, dem Wortsinn des Begriffs entsprechend, einfach in Gott, sondern in der Beziehung zwischen Mensch und Gott. Er war der Überzeugung, dass die Theologie Gott nicht anders als im Glauben habe. Das hatte zur Folge, dass damit der Mensch in den Gegenstandsbereich der Theologie gehörte. Es bedeutete aber auch, dass die Theologie selbst als Glabuen zu konzipieren war, wenn sie es wirklich mit Gott zu tun haben wollte. Das Theologiestudium, wie es Luther in seiner Vorrede beschrieb, war daher im Grunde eine fromme Praxis, die sich vom Glaubensvollzug aller anderen Christinnen und Christen nicht prinzipiell unterschied" (Nieden, *Erfindung*, 86).

57. Bayer, *Theologie*, 92.

58. "Die Theologie ist nicht einem Genus menschlicher Wissenschaft zu unterstellen, nicht als Spezialfall menschlicher Erkenntnis zu begreifen. So wie der Glaubensbegriff

theology depends on God's action, it cannot be subsumed under what is regularly understood as a *habitus*, an accident inhering in the soul of man making a person able to do something at all times.

If the statement that theology is God-given marks a difference to the philosophical understanding of *habitus*, what about the second point that Bayer makes, that faith and theology as theologizing depend on the continual action of God and thus are not an accident in the Aristotelian sense? Calov does affirm that becoming a theologian is a work of the Holy Spirit, but does he address the ongoing work of the Holy Spirit in the life of the theologian, something the concept of *habitus* does not include?

Calov, even with all his interest in giving advice to the academic study of theology, does state that the study of theology is a life-long process.[59] Together with Calov's reception of *oratio, meditatio,* and *tentatio*, this indicates that Calov does not think of theology as a *habitus* that, once acquired, then naturally inheres in the soul. Rather, if the triad describes the study and thus the life of the theologian, the theologian can be theologian only in the school of the Holy Spirit, so to speak.

Calov thus takes up essential elements of Luther's approach to theology under the conditions of the seventeenth century. Because Calov identifies theology as a practical *habitus*, there is the danger that theology is understood like any other discipline in the theoretical scheme of disciplines or sciences of his day. Calov avoids this danger by insisting that theology is God-given because it deals with the divinely inspired Scriptures, and by his adoption of *oratio, meditatio,* and *tentatio* as essential for becoming and being a theologian.

Bibliography

Appold, Kenneth G. *Abraham Calov's Doctrine of* Vocatio *in Its Systematic Context*. Tübingen: Mohr/Siebeck, 1998.

Bayer, Oswald. "Oratio, Meditatio, Tentatio." *Lutherjahrbuch* 55 (1988) 7–59.

———. "Theologie." In *Handbuch Systematischer Theologie 1*, 55–105. Gütersloh: Gütersloher Verlagshaus, 1994.

———. "Twenty Questions on the Relevance of Luther for Today." *Lutheran Quarterly* 29 (2015) 439–43.

---

die Kategorien der philosophischen Seelenlehre sprengt, weil er Verstand und Willen zugleich umfaßt, so sprengt auch der Theologiebegriff das Schema der aristotelischen habitus intellectuales" (Wallmann, *Theologie*, 73).

59. "Theologiae Studium amplissimum est, cui non pauci anni impendendi sunt, imò cui nec tota Hominis vita sufficit" (Calov, *Isagoges, Paedia*, 17).

---. "Urteilskraft als theologische Kompetenz. Was macht einen Theologen zum Theologen?" In *Zugesagte Gegenwart*, by Oswald Bayer, 303–312. Tübingen: Mohr/Siebeck, 2007.

Calixt, Georg. *Dogmatische Schriften*. Vol. 2 of *Werke in Auswahl*. Edited by Inge Mager. Göttingen: Vandenhoeck & Ruprecht, 1982.

Calov, Abraham. *Isagoges ad SS Theologia Libri Duo, De Natura Theologiae, Et Methodo Studii Theologici . . . Editio secunda, recognita, et alicubi aucta*. n.p.: Andreae Hartmanni, 1666.

---. *Isagoges ad SS Theologiam Libri Duo, De Natura Theologiae, Et Methodo Studii Theologici, pie, dextre, ac feliciter tractandi Cum examine Methodi Calixtinae*. Wittenberg: Andreae Hartmanni, 1652.

---. *Systema locorum theologicorum*. Vol. 1. Witebergae: Andreae Hartmanni, 1655.

---. "Tractatus novus de methodo docendi et disputandi." In *Scripta philosophica*. Wittenberg: Literis Meyeranis, 1673.

Friedrich, Markus. *Die Grenzen der Vernunft. Theologie, Philosophie und gelehrte Konflikte am Beispiel des Helmstedter Hofmannstreits und seiner Wirkungen auf das Luthertum um 1600*. Schriftenreihe der Historischen Kommission bei der Bayerischen Akademie der Wissenschaften. Vol. 69. Göttingen: Vandenhoeck & Ruprecht, 2004, 193–202.

Gerhard, Johann. "Exegesis sive uberior explicatio articuli de scriptura sacra." Prooemium, §4. In *Loci theologici*, edited by J. F. Cotta. Vol. 2. Tübingen: Cotta, 1763.

Haffenreffer, Matthias. *Loci Theologici*. Tübingen: Georgij Gruppenbachij, 1603.

Jung, Volker. *Das Ganze der Heiligen Schrift. Hermeneutik und Schriftauslegung bei Abraham Calov*. Stuttgart: Calwer Verlag, 1999.

Kang, Chi-Won. *Frömmigkeit und Gelehrsamkeit. Die Reform des Theologiestudiums im lutherischen Pietismus des 17. und des frühen 18. Jahrhunderts*. Gießen, Basel: Brunnen Verlag, 2001.

Mikkeli, Heikki. *An Aristotelian Response to Renaissance Humanism: Jacopo Zabarella on the Nature of Arts and Sciences*. Helsinki: SHS, 1992.

Nieden, Marcel. "Anfechtung als Thema lutherischer Anweisungsschriften zum Theologiestudium." In *Praxis Pietatis. Beiträge zu Theologie und Frömmigkeit in der Frühen Neuzeit. Festschrift Wolfgang Sommer*, edited by Hans-Jörg Nieden and Marcel Nieden, 83–102. Stuttgart, Berlin, Köln: W. Kohlhammer, 1999.

---. *Die Erfindung des Theologen. Wittenberger Anweisungen zum Theologiestudium im Zeitalter von Reformation und Konfessionalisierung*. Tübingen: Mohr/Siebeck 2006.

Petersen, Peter. *Geschichte der Aristotelischen Philosophie im protestantischen Deutschland*. 1921. Reprint, Stuttgart-Bad Cannstatt: Friedrich Frommann Verlag (Günther Holzboog), 1964.

Peukert, Helmut. *Wissenschaftstheorie—Handlungstheorie—Fundamentale Theologie. Analysen zu Ansatz und Status theologischer Theoriebildung*. 3rd ed. Frankfurt: Suhrkamp, 2009.

Preus, Robert D. *The Theology of Post-Reformation Lutheranism: A Study of Theological Prolegomena*. Vol. 1. St. Louis: Concordia, 1970.

Sparn, Walter. "Die Schulphilosophie in den lutherischen Territorien." In *Das Heilige Römische Reich Deutscher Nation. Nord- und Ostmitteleuropa*, edited by Johannes

Rohbeck and Helmut Holzhey, 475–606. Vol. 4 of *Die Philosophie des 17. Jahrhunderts*. Basel: Schwabe, 2001.

Wallmann, Johannes. "Abraham Calov (1612–1686)." In *Theologische Realenzyklopädie*. Vol. 7. Berlin/New York: de Gruyter, 1981.

———. *Der Theologiebegriff bei Johann Gerhard und Georg Calixt*. Tübingen: Mohr/Siebeck, 1961.

Zabarella, Jacopo. "De Doctrinae ordine apologia." In *Opera Logica*, edited by Wilhelm Risse. 2 vols. Hildesheim: Georg Olms Verlangsbuchhandlung, 1966.

———. *On Methods*. Edited and translated by John P. McCaskey. Volume 1. Books 1–2. Cambridge: Harvard University Press, 2014.

Oswald Bayer Bibliography

Compiled by Joshua C. Miller

Works by Oswald Bayer

Bayer, Oswald. "A priori willkürlich, a posteriori notwendig: die sprachphilosophische Verschränkung von Ästhetik und Logik in Hamanns Metakritik Kants." *Neue Zeitschrift für systematische Theologie und Religionsphilosophie* 42 (2000) 117–39.

———. "Angels are Interpreters." English translation of "Engel sind Hermeneuten." In *Gott als Autor: Zu einer poietologischen Theologie*, 230–39. Tübingen: Mohr/Siebeck, 1999. Translated by Christine Helmer. *Lutheran Quarterly* 13 (1999) 271–84.

———. *Aufbruch und Orientierung: Zur Gegenwart der Theologie Luthers*. Veröffentlichungen der Luther-Akademie Ratzeburg 31. Erlangen: Martin Luther, 2000.

———. *Aus Glauben leben: Über Rechtfertigung und Heiligung*. Stuttgart: Calwer, 1990.

———. *Autorität und Kritik: Zu Hermeneutik und Wissenschaftstheorie*. Tübingen: Mohr/Siebeck, 1991.

———. "Barmen zwischen Barth und Luther." In *Luther und Barth*, edited by Joachim Heubach, 21–36. Veröffentlichungen der Luther-Akademie Ratzeburg 13. Erlangen: Martin Luther, 1989.

———. "Barmherzigkeit." In *Dass Gott eine grosse Barherzigkeit habe*, edited by Doris Hiller and Christine Kress, 77–84. Leipzig: Evangelische Verlagsanstalt, 2001.

———. "The Being of Christ in Faith." Translated by Christine Helmer. *Lutheran Quarterly* 10 (1996) 135–50.

———. "Creation as History." In *The Gift of Grace: The Future of Lutheran Theology*, edited by Niels Henrik Gregersen, et al., 253–63. Translated by Martin Abraham. Minneapolis: Fortress, 2005.

———. "Das Problem der natürlichen Theologie." In *Einfach von Gott reden: Ein theologischer Diskurs: Festschrift für Friedrich Mildenberger zum 65. Geburtstag*, edited by Jürgen Roloff and Hans G. Ulrich, 151–58. Stuttgart: Kohlhammer, 1994.

———. "Das Wort ward Fleisch: Luthers Christologie als Lehre von der Idiomenkommunikation." In *Jesus Christus—Gott für uns*, edited by Friedrich-Otto Scharbau, 58–101. Veröffentlichungen der Luther-Akademie Ratzeburg 34. Erlangen: Martin Luther, 2003.

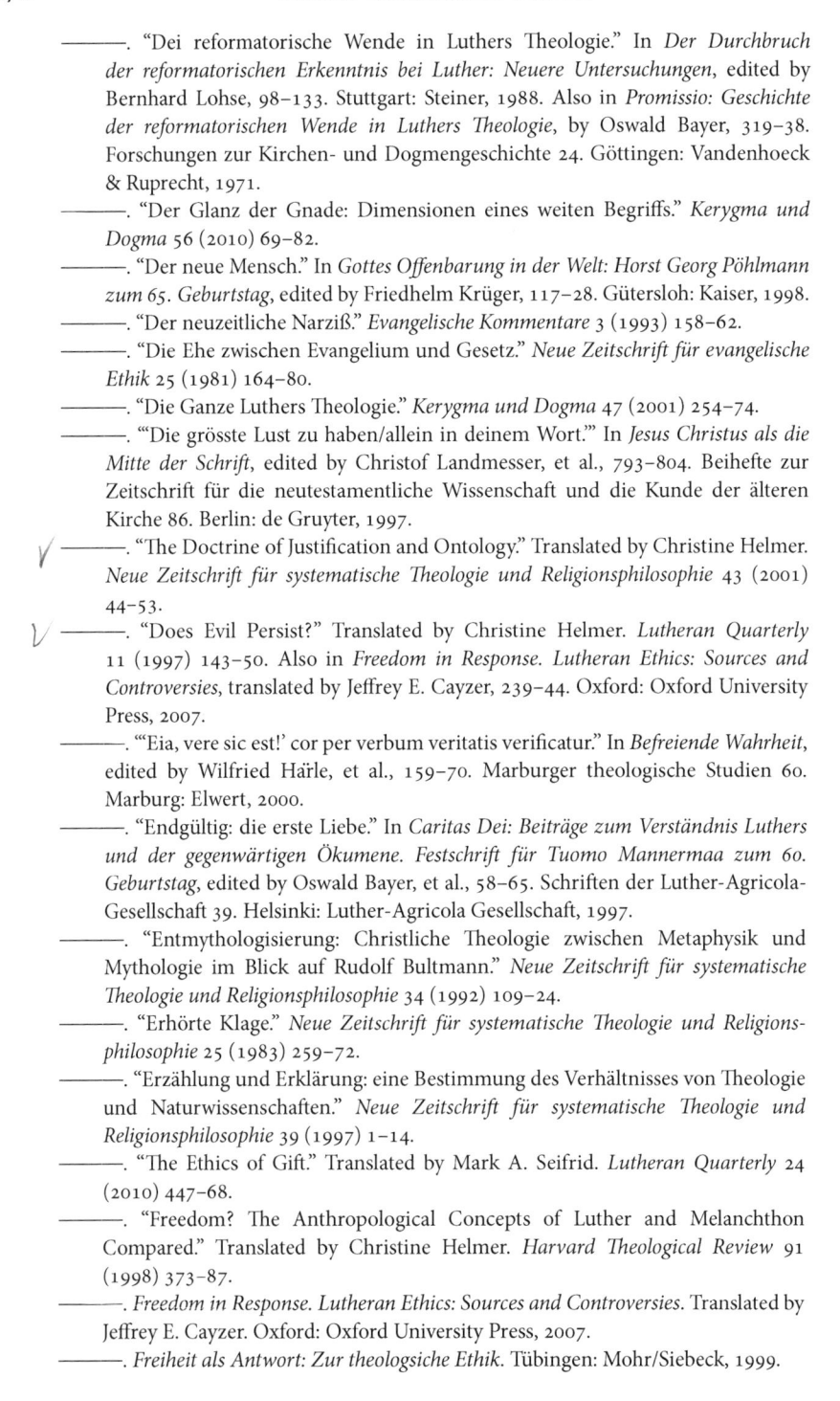

———. "Dei reformatorische Wende in Luthers Theologie." In *Der Durchbruch der reformatorischen Erkenntnis bei Luther: Neuere Untersuchungen*, edited by Bernhard Lohse, 98–133. Stuttgart: Steiner, 1988. Also in *Promissio: Geschichte der reformatorischen Wende in Luthers Theologie*, by Oswald Bayer, 319–38. Forschungen zur Kirchen- und Dogmengeschichte 24. Göttingen: Vandenhoeck & Ruprecht, 1971.

———. "Der Glanz der Gnade: Dimensionen eines weiten Begriffs." *Kerygma und Dogma* 56 (2010) 69–82.

———. "Der neue Mensch." In *Gottes Offenbarung in der Welt: Horst Georg Pöhlmann zum 65. Geburtstag*, edited by Friedhelm Krüger, 117–28. Gütersloh: Kaiser, 1998.

———. "Der neuzeitliche Narziß." *Evangelische Kommentare* 3 (1993) 158–62.

———. "Die Ehe zwischen Evangelium und Gesetz." *Neue Zeitschrift für evangelische Ethik* 25 (1981) 164–80.

———. "Die Ganze Luthers Theologie." *Kerygma und Dogma* 47 (2001) 254–74.

———. "'Die grösste Lust zu haben/allein in deinem Wort.'" In *Jesus Christus als die Mitte der Schrift*, edited by Christof Landmesser, et al., 793–804. Beihefte zur Zeitschrift für die neutestamentliche Wissenschaft und die Kunde der älteren Kirche 86. Berlin: de Gruyter, 1997.

———. "The Doctrine of Justification and Ontology." Translated by Christine Helmer. *Neue Zeitschrift für systematische Theologie und Religionsphilosophie* 43 (2001) 44–53.

———. "Does Evil Persist?" Translated by Christine Helmer. *Lutheran Quarterly* 11 (1997) 143–50. Also in *Freedom in Response. Lutheran Ethics: Sources and Controversies*, translated by Jeffrey E. Cayzer, 239–44. Oxford: Oxford University Press, 2007.

———. "'Eia, vere sic est!' cor per verbum veritatis verificatur." In *Befreiende Wahrheit*, edited by Wilfried Härle, et al., 159–70. Marburger theologische Studien 60. Marburg: Elwert, 2000.

———. "Endgültig: die erste Liebe." In *Caritas Dei: Beiträge zum Verständnis Luthers und der gegenwärtigen Ökumene. Festschrift für Tuomo Mannermaa zum 60. Geburtstag*, edited by Oswald Bayer, et al., 58–65. Schriften der Luther-Agricola-Gesellschaft 39. Helsinki: Luther-Agricola Gesellschaft, 1997.

———. "Entmythologisierung: Christliche Theologie zwischen Metaphysik und Mythologie im Blick auf Rudolf Bultmann." *Neue Zeitschrift für systematische Theologie und Religionsphilosophie* 34 (1992) 109–24.

———. "Erhörte Klage." *Neue Zeitschrift für systematische Theologie und Religionsphilosophie* 25 (1983) 259–72.

———. "Erzählung und Erklärung: eine Bestimmung des Verhältnisses von Theologie und Naturwissenschaften." *Neue Zeitschrift für systematische Theologie und Religionsphilosophie* 39 (1997) 1–14.

———. "The Ethics of Gift." Translated by Mark A. Seifrid. *Lutheran Quarterly* 24 (2010) 447–68.

———. "Freedom? The Anthropological Concepts of Luther and Melanchthon Compared." Translated by Christine Helmer. *Harvard Theological Review* 91 (1998) 373–87.

———. *Freedom in Response. Lutheran Ethics: Sources and Controversies*. Translated by Jeffrey E. Cayzer. Oxford: Oxford University Press, 2007.

———. *Freiheit als Antwort: Zur theologsiche Ethik*. Tübingen: Mohr/Siebeck, 1999.

———. "Für eine bessere Weltlichkeit: Ernst Steinbach zum Gedenken." *Zeitschrift für Theologie und Kirche* 83 (1986) 238–60.

———. "Gegen Gott für den Menschen: zu Feuerbachs Lutherrezeption." *Zeitschrift für Theologie und Kirche* 69.1 (1972) 34–71.

———. "Gegen System und Struktur: die theologische Aktualität Johann Georg Hamanns." In *Johann Georg Hamann: Acta des Internationalen Hamann-Colloquiums in Lüneburg 1976*, edited by Bernhard Gajek, 40–50. Frankfurt: Klostermann, 1979.

———. "Gegenwart: Schöpfung als Anrede und Anspruch." *Luther: Zeitschrift der Luther-Gesellschaft* 59.3 (1988) 131–44.

———. "Gesetz und Evangelium." In *Bekenntnis und Einheit der Kirche: Studien zum Konkordienbuch*, edited by Martin Brecht and Reinhard Schwartz, 155–74. Stuttgart: Calwer, 1980.

———. "God as Author of My Life-history." *Lutheran Quarterly* 2 (1988) 437–56.

———. "God's Hiddenness." Translated by Nicholas Hopman. *Lutheran Quarterly* 28 (2014) 266–79.

———. "God's Omnipotence." Translated by Jonathan Mumme. *Lutheran Quarterly* 23 (2009) 85–102.

———. *Gott als Autor: Zu einer poietologischen Theologie*. Tübingen: Mohr/Siebeck, 1999.

———. "Grundzüge der Theologie Paul Tillichs, kritisch dargestellt." *Neue Zeitschrift für systematische Theologie und Religionsphilosophie* 49 (2007) 325–48.

———. "Hermeneutical Theology." *Scottish Journal of Theology* 56 (2003) 131–47.

———. "How I Became a Luther Scholar." Translated by Jeffrey G. Silcock. *Lutheran Quarterly* 27 (2013) 249–63.

———. "'I Believe That God Has Created Me with All That Exists': An Example of Catechetical-Systematics." Translated by Christine Helmer. Edited by Richard Bliese. *Lutheran Quarterly* 8 (1994) 129–61.

———. *Johann Georg Hamann: Der hellste Kopf seiner Zeit*. Tübingen: Attempto, 1998.

———. "Justification." *Lutheran Quarterly* 24 (2010) 337–40.

———. "Justification as the Basis and Boundary of Theology: Monotony or Concentration." Translated by Christine Helmer. *Lutheran Quarterly* 15 (2001) 273–92.

———. "Law and Morality." Translated by Christine Helmer. *Lutheran Quarterly* 17 (2003) 63–76.

———. "Leibliches Wort: Öffentlichkeit des Glaubens und Freiheit des Lebens." *Kerygma und Dogma* 27 (1981) 82–95.

———. *Leibliches Wort: Reformation und Neuzeit im Konflikt*. Tübingen: Mohr/Siebeck, 1991.

———. *Living by Faith: Justification and Sanctification*. Translated by Geoffrey W. Bromiley. Grand Rapids: Eerdmans, 2003.

———. "Lutheran Pietism, or *Oratio, Meditatio, Tentatio* in August Hermann Francke." *Lutheran Quarterly* 25 (2011) 383–97.

———. "Lutherischer Pietismus: *Oratio, Meditatio, Tentatio* bei August Hermann Francke." In *Festschrift für Ulrich Köpf zum 70. Geburtstag*, edited by Albrecht Beutel and Reinhold Rieger, 1–12. Religiöse Erfahrung und wissenschaftliche Theologie. Tübingen: Mohr/Siebeck, 2011.

———. "Luther's Ethics as Pastoral Care." *Lutheran Quarterly* 4 (1990) 125–42.

———. "Macht, Recht, Gerechtigkeit." *Kerygma und Dogma* 30 (1984) 200–212.

———. "Marcuse's Critique of Luther's Concept of Freedom." *Lutheran Quarterly* 32 (2018) 173–204.

———. "Marcuses Kritik an Luthers Freiheitsbegriff." *Zeitschrift für Theologie und Kirche* 67 (1970) 453–78.

———. "Martin Luther." In *The Reformation Theologians: An Introduction to Theology in the Early Modern Period*, edited by Carter Lindberg, 51–66. Oxford: Blackwell, 2002.

———. "Martin Luther as Interpreter of Holy Scripture." In *The Cambridge Companion to Martin Luther*, edited by Donald K. McKim, 73–85. Translated by Mark Mattes. Grand Rapids: Eerdmans, 2003.

———. *Martin Luthers Theologie: Eine Vergegenwärtigung*. Revised ed. Tübingen: Mohr/Siebeck, 2007.

———. *Martin Luther's Theology: A Contemporary Interpretation*. Translated by Thomas H. Trapp. Grand Rapids: Eerdmans, 2008.

———. "Mercy from the Heart." Translated by Jonathan Mumme. *LOGIA* 19 (2010) 29–32.

———. "Metakritik in nuce: Hamanns Antwort auf Kants Kritik der reinen Vernunft." *Neue Zeitschrift für systematische Theologie und Religionsphilosophie* 30 (1988) 305–14.

———. "Middle—Beginning and End: Johann Georg Hamann's Comprehensive Understanding of Nature and History." Translated by John R. Betz. *Lutheran Theological Journal* 50 (2016) 190–200.

———. "The Modern Narcissus." Translated by Christine Helmer. *Lutheran Quarterly* 9 (1995) 301–13.

———. *Mythos und Religion: interdisziplinäre Aspekte*. Stuttgart: Calwer Verlag, 1990.

———. "Nachfolge in der Welt." In *Zwei Kirchen, eine Moral?*, by Oswald Bayer, et al., 53–75. Regensburg: Pustet, 1986.

———. "Narration and Explanation: The Relationship between Theology and Natural Sciences." Translated by Roy A. Harrisville. *Lutheran Quarterly* 31 (2017) 172–88.

———. "Nature and Institution: Luther's Doctrine of the Three Orders." Translated by Luis Dreher. *Lutheran Quarterly* 12 (1998) 125–59. Also in *Freedom in Response. Lutheran Ethics: Sources and Controversies*, translated by Jeffrey E. Cayzer, 90–118. Oxford: Oxford University Press, 2007.

———. "Necessary Transformation? The Reformation and Modernity in Controversy over Freedom." Translated by Piotr J. Malysz. *Pro Ecclesia* 22 (2013) 290–306.

———. *Neuer Geist in alten Buchstaben*. Neuendettelsau: Freimund, 1994.

———. "Notae ecclesiae." In *Lutherische Beiträge zur Missio Dei*, edited with a new introduction by Heinrich Foerster, 75–90. Veröffentlichungen der Luther-Akademie Ratzeburg 3. Erlangen: Martin Luther, 1982. First printed as "Leibliches Wort: Öffentlichkeit des Glaubens und Freiheit des Lebens." *Kerygma und Dogma* 27 (1981) 82–95.

———. *Ökumenische Sozialethik als gemeinsame Suche nach christlichen Antworten*. Stuttgart: Kohlhammer, 1996.

———. "Paradox: Eine Skizze." In *The Theological Paradox: Interdisciplinary Reflections on the Centre of Paul Tillich's Thought*, edited by Gert Hummel, 3–8. Theologische Bibliothek Töpelmann 74. Berlin: de Gruyter, 1995.

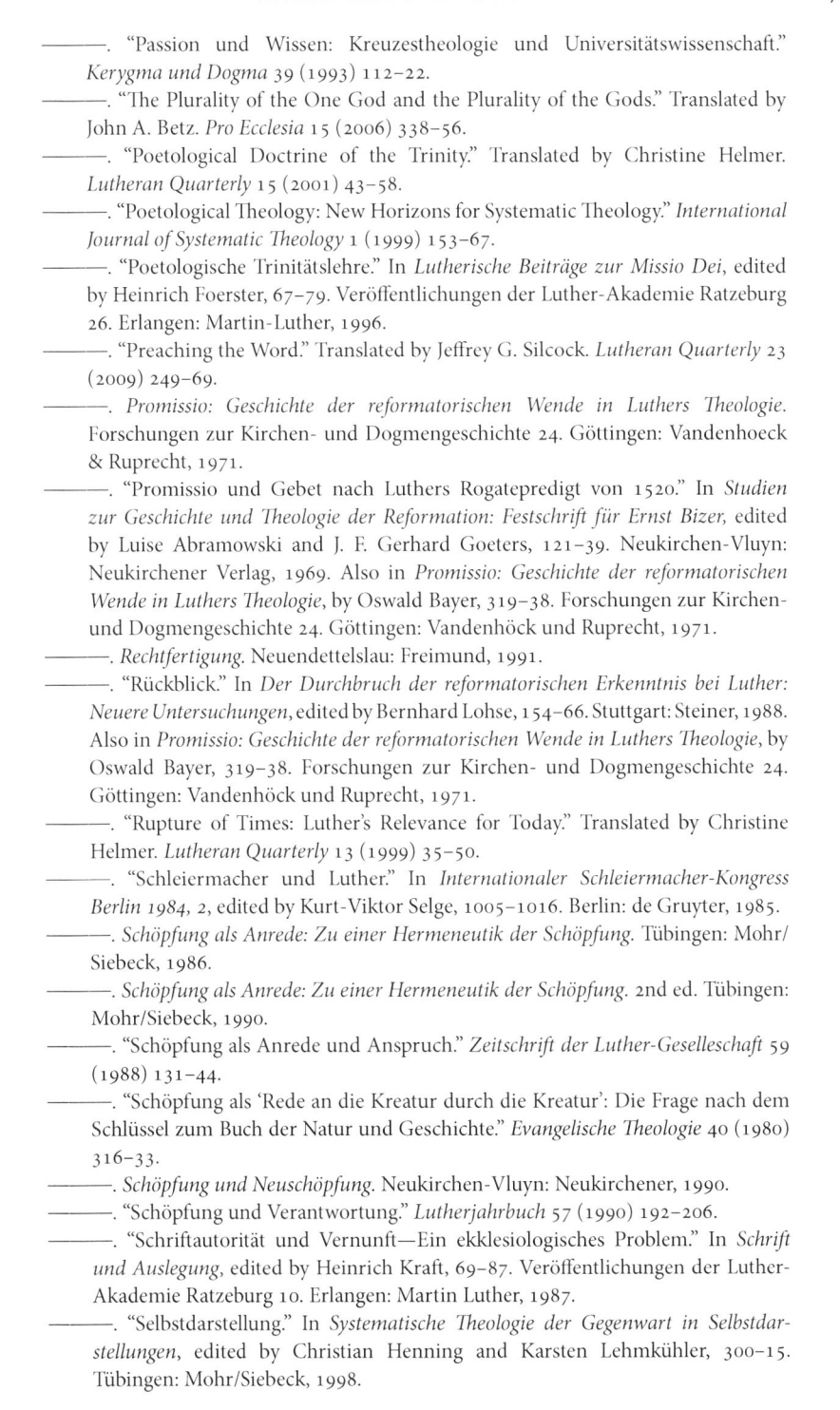

———. "Passion und Wissen: Kreuzestheologie und Universitätswissenschaft." *Kerygma und Dogma* 39 (1993) 112–22.

———. "The Plurality of the One God and the Plurality of the Gods." Translated by John A. Betz. *Pro Ecclesia* 15 (2006) 338–56.

———. "Poetological Doctrine of the Trinity." Translated by Christine Helmer. *Lutheran Quarterly* 15 (2001) 43–58.

———. "Poetological Theology: New Horizons for Systematic Theology." *International Journal of Systematic Theology* 1 (1999) 153–67.

———. "Poetologische Trinitätslehre." In *Lutherische Beiträge zur Missio Dei*, edited by Heinrich Foerster, 67–79. Veröffentlichungen der Luther-Akademie Ratzeburg 26. Erlangen: Martin-Luther, 1996.

———. "Preaching the Word." Translated by Jeffrey G. Silcock. *Lutheran Quarterly* 23 (2009) 249–69.

———. *Promissio: Geschichte der reformatorischen Wende in Luthers Theologie*. Forschungen zur Kirchen- und Dogmengeschichte 24. Göttingen: Vandenhoeck & Ruprecht, 1971.

———. "Promissio und Gebet nach Luthers Rogatepredigt von 1520." In *Studien zur Geschichte und Theologie der Reformation: Festschrift für Ernst Bizer*, edited by Luise Abramowski and J. F. Gerhard Goeters, 121–39. Neukirchen-Vluyn: Neukirchener Verlag, 1969. Also in *Promissio: Geschichte der reformatorischen Wende in Luthers Theologie*, by Oswald Bayer, 319–38. Forschungen zur Kirchen- und Dogmengeschichte 24. Göttingen: Vandenhöck und Ruprecht, 1971.

———. *Rechtfertigung*. Neuendettelslau: Freimund, 1991.

———. "Rückblick." In *Der Durchbruch der reformatorischen Erkenntnis bei Luther: Neuere Untersuchungen*, edited by Bernhard Lohse, 154–66. Stuttgart: Steiner, 1988. Also in *Promissio: Geschichte der reformatorischen Wende in Luthers Theologie*, by Oswald Bayer, 319–38. Forschungen zur Kirchen- und Dogmengeschichte 24. Göttingen: Vandenhöck und Ruprecht, 1971.

———. "Rupture of Times: Luther's Relevance for Today." Translated by Christine Helmer. *Lutheran Quarterly* 13 (1999) 35–50.

———. "Schleiermacher und Luther." In *Internationaler Schleiermacher-Kongress Berlin 1984*, 2, edited by Kurt-Viktor Selge, 1005–1016. Berlin: de Gruyter, 1985.

———. *Schöpfung als Anrede: Zu einer Hermeneutik der Schöpfung*. Tübingen: Mohr/Siebeck, 1986.

———. *Schöpfung als Anrede: Zu einer Hermeneutik der Schöpfung*. 2nd ed. Tübingen: Mohr/Siebeck, 1990.

———. "Schöpfung als Anrede und Anspruch." *Zeitschrift der Luther-Gesellschaft* 59 (1988) 131–44.

———. "Schöpfung als 'Rede an die Kreatur durch die Kreatur': Die Frage nach dem Schlüssel zum Buch der Natur und Geschichte." *Evangelische Theologie* 40 (1980) 316–33.

———. *Schöpfung und Neuschöpfung*. Neukirchen-Vluyn: Neukirchener, 1990.

———. "Schöpfung und Verantwortung." *Lutherjahrbuch* 57 (1990) 192–206.

———. "Schriftautorität und Vernunft—Ein ekklesiologisches Problem." In *Schrift und Auslegung*, edited by Heinrich Kraft, 69–87. Veröffentlichungen der Luther-Akademie Ratzeburg 10. Erlangen: Martin Luther, 1987.

———. "Selbstdarstellung." In *Systematische Theologie der Gegenwart in Selbstdarstellungen*, edited by Christian Henning and Karsten Lehmkühler, 300–15. Tübingen: Mohr/Siebeck, 1998.

———. "Selbstschöpfung? Von der Würde des Menschen." *Veröffentlichungen der Luther-Akademie Ratzeburg* 32 (2001) 179–99.

———. "Selbstverschuldete Vormundschaft: Hamanns Kontroverse mit Kant um wahre Aufklärung." In *Wirklichkeitsanspruch von Theologie und Religion. Herausforderung: Ernst Steinbach zum 70. Geburtstag*, edited by Dieter Henke et al., 3–34. Tübingen: Mohr/Siebeck, 1976.

———. "Self-Creation? On the Dignity of Human Beings." Translated by Martin Abraham et al. *Modern Theology* 20 (2004) 275–90.

———. "A Sermon on Psalm 46." *LOGIA* 25 (2016) 67–69.

———. "Staunen, Seufzen, Schauen: Affekte der Wahrnehmung des Schöpfers." In *Schöpfung und Neuschöpfung*, edited by Ingo Baldermann, et al., 191–204. Jahrbuch für Biblische Theologie 5. Neukirchen-Vluyn: Neukirchener, 1990.

———. "Systematische Theologie als Wissenschaft der Geschichte." In *Verifikationen: Festschrift für Gerhard Ebeling zum 70. Geburtstag*, edited by Eberhard Jüngel et al., 341–61. Tübingen: Mohr/Siebeck, 1982.

———. "Tempus creatura verbi." In *Eschatologie in der Dogmatik der Gegenwart*, edited by Heinrich Foerster, 91–102. Veröffentlichungen der Luther-Akademie Ratzeburg 11. Erlangen: Martin Luther, 1988.

———. *Theologie*. Gütersloh: Gütersloher Verlagshaus, 1994.

———. "Theologie, Glaube und Bildung." *Zeitschrift für Theologie und Kirche* 72 (1975) 225–39.

———. "Theologie und Philosophie in produktivem Konflikt." *Neue Zeitschrift für systematische Theologie und Religionsphilosophie* 32 (1990) 226–36.

———. *Theology the Lutheran Way*. Translated and edited by Jeffrey G. Silcock and Mark C. Mattes. Grand Rapids: Eerdmans, 2007.

———. "Theses on the Renewal of Lutheranism by Concentrating on the Doctrine of Justification." *Lutheran Quarterly* 22 (2008) 72–75.

———. "Tillich as a Systematic Theologian." In *The Cambridge Companion to Paul Tillich*, edited by Russell R. Manning, 18–36. Cambridge Companions to Religion. Cambridge: Cambridge University Press, 2009.

———. "Tod Gottes und Herrenmahl." *Zeitschrift für Theologie und Kirche* 70 (1973) 346–63. Also in *Leibliches Wort: Reformation und Neuzeit im Konflict*, by Oswald Bayer, 289–305. Tübingen: Mohr/Siebeck, 1991.

———. "Toward a Theology of Lament." In *Caritas et Reformatio*, edited by Carter Lindberg and David Whitford, 211–20. Translated by Matthias Gockel. St. Louis: Concordia, 2002.

———. "Trust." Translated by Nicholas Hopman. *Lutheran Quarterly* 29 (2015) 249–61.

———. "Twenty Questions on the Relevance of Luther for Today." Translated by Jeffrey G. Silcock. *Lutheran Quarterly* 29 (2015) 439–43.

———. "Twenty-Four Theses on the Renewal of Lutheranism by Concentrating on the Doctrine of Justification." *Lutheran Quarterly* 5 (1991) 73–75.

———. *Umstrittene Freiheit: Theologisch-philosophische Kontroversen*. Uni-Taschenbücher 1092. Tübingen: Mohr/Siebeck, 1981.

———. "Uns voraus: Bemerkungen zur Lutherforschung und Lutherrezeption." *Lutherjahrbuch* 84 (2017) 170–89.

———. "Unsere Hoffnungen und das Reich Gottes." In *Reich Gottes und Kirche*, edited by Heinrich Foerster, 53–76. Veröffentlichungen der Luther-Akademie Ratzeburg 12. Erlangen: Martin Luther, 1988.

———. *Vernunft ist Sprache: Hamanns Metakritik Kants. Spekulation und Erfahrung*. Abteilung II, Untersuchungen 50. Stuttgart-Bad Connstatt: Frommann-Holzboog, 2002.

———. *Was ist das: Theologie? Eine Skizze*. Stuttgart: Calwer, 1973.

———. "What Is Evangelical? The Continuing Validity of the Reformation." Translated by Jeffrey G. Silcock. *Lutheran Quarterly* 25 (2011) 1–15.

———. "What Keeps Faith Alive, or, On What Does It Depend?" Translated by Roy A. Harrisville. *LOGIA* 27 (2018) 72–74.

———. "With Luther in the Present." Translated by Mark A Seifred. *Lutheran Quarterly* 21 (2007) 1–16.

———. "The Word of the Cross." Translated by John R. Betz. *Lutheran Quarterly* 9 (1995) 47–55. English translation of "Das Wort vom Kreuz." In *Autorität und Kritik: Zu Hermeneutik und Wissenschaftstheorie*, by Oswald Bayer, 117–24. Tübingen: Mohr/Siebeck, 1991.

———. "A Year with Luther: From the Great Reformer of Our Times." Translated by Roy A. Harrisville. *Lutheran Quarterly* 31 (2017) 198–200.

———. "Zeit zur Antwort." In *Ehe: Zeit zur Antwort*, edited by Oswald Bayer. Neukirchen-Vluyn: Neukirchener, 1988.

———. *Zeitgenosse im Widerspruch: Johann Georg Hamann als radikaler Aufklärer*. Serie Piper 918. Munich: Piper, 1988.

———. *Zugesagte Freiheit: Zur Grundlegung theologischer Ethik*. Gütersloher Taschenbücher 379. Gütersloh: Gütersloher, 1980.

———. *Zugesagte Gegenwart*. Tübingen: Mohr/Siebeck, 2007.

———. *Zum gedenken an Carl Heinz Ratschow 22.7.1911–10.11.1999: Reden bei der Gedenkfeier der Theologischen Fakultät der Universität Marburg am 15. November 2000*. Berlin: de Gruyter, 2000.

———. "Zur Theologie der Klage." *Jahrbuch für Biblische Theologie* 16 (2002) 289–301.

Bayer with Others:

Bayer, Oswald, and Alan M. Suggate. *Worship and Ethics: Lutherans and Anglicans in Dialogue*. Theologische Bibliothek Töpelmann 70. Berlin: de Gruyter, 1996.

Bayer, Oswald, and Benjamin Gleede, eds. *Creator est Creatura*. Theologische Bibliothek Töpelmann 13. Berlin: de Gruyter, 2007.

Bayer, Oswald, and Christian Knudsen. *Kreuz und Kritik: Johann Georg Hamanns Letztes Blatt: Text und Interpretation*. Beiträge zur historischen Theologie 66. Tübingen: Mohr/Siebeck, 1983.

Bayer, Oswald, and Christof Gestrich. *Die biologische Machbarkeit des Menschen: Der Traum der Selbstschöpfung*. Beiheft 2001 zur Berliner theologischen Zeitschrift. Berlin: Wichern, 2001.

Bayer, Oswald, and Robert Kremer. "L'héritage paulinien chez Luther." *Recherches de science religieuse* 94 (2006) 381–94.

Bayer, Oswald, and Susanne Schulte. *Rede, dass ich Dich sehe!: Wortwechsel mit Johann Georg Hamann*. Aachen: Rimbaud, 2007.

Thompson, Virgil, ed. *Justification Is for Preaching: Essays by Oswald Bayer, Gerhard Forde, and Others*. Eugene, OR: Pickwick Publications, 2012.

Secondary Literature Addressing Bayer's Theology

Grube, Dirk Martin. "Luthers reformatorischer Durchbruch: zur Auseinandersetzung mit Oswald Bayers Promissio-Verständnis." *Neue Zeitschrift für systematische Theologie und Religionsphilosophie* 48 (2006) 33–50.

Helmer, Christine. "The Subject of Theology in the Thought of Oswald Bayer." *Lutheran Quarterly* 14 (2000) 21–52.

Herrmann, Erik. "Writing a Theology of Luther: A Review Essay on Contributions New and Old." *Concordia Journal* 35 (2009) 380–89.

Hütter, Reinhard. *Suffering Divine Things: Theology as Church Practice.* Translated by Doug Stott. Grand Rapids: Eerdmans, 2000.

Jonkers, Peter. "Theologie und (Post)modernität: philosophische Fragen zu Oswald Bayers Luther-Buch." *Neue Zeitschrift für systematische Theologie und Religionsphilosophie* 48 (2006) 4–17.

Link, Christian. *Schöpfung: Schöpfungstheologie angesichts der Herausforderungen des 20. Jahrhunderts.* 2 vols. Handbuch Systematischer Theologie 7. Gütersloh: Gütersloher, 1991.

Lüpke, Johannes von, and Edgar Thaidigsmann, eds. *Denkraum Katechismus: Festgabe für Oswald Bayer zum 70. Geburtstag.* Tübingen: Mohr/Siebeck, 2009.

Mattes, Mark C. *The Role of Justification in Contemporary Theology.* Grand Rapids: Eerdmans, 2004.

Miller, Joshua C. *Hanging by a Promise: The Hidden God in the Theology of Oswald Bayer.* Eugene, OR: Pickwick Publications, 2015.

Sauter, Gerhard. "Katechismus-Grammatik: Katechismusunterricht als Pendant des Theologiestudiums." In *Denkraum Katechismus: Festgabe für Oswald Bayer zum 70. Geburtstag*, edited by Johannes von Lüpke und Edgar Thaidigsmann, 19–34. Tübingen: Mohr/Siebeck, 2009.

Schaeffer, Hans. *Createdness and Ethics: The Doctrine of Creation and Theological Ethics in the Theology of Colin E. Gunton and Oswald Bayer.* Theologische Bibliothek Töpelmann 137. Berlin: de Gruyter, 2006.

Rikhof, Herwi. "Luther und die Trinitätstheologie zu Oswald Bayer: Martin Luthers Theologie. Eine Vergegenwärtigung." *Neue Zeitschrift für systematische Theologie und Religionsphilosophie* 48 (2006) 74–82.

Wyller, Trygve. *Glaube und autonome Welt: Diskussion eines Grundproblems der neueren systematischen Theologie mit Blick auf Dietrich Bonhoeffer, Oswald Bayer und K. E. Løgstrup.* Theologische Bibliothek Töpelmann 91. Berlin: de Gruyter, 1998.

Zwanepol, Klaas. "Zur Diskussion um Gottes Verborgenheit." *Neue Zeitschrift für systematische Theologie und Religionsphilosophie* 48 (2006) 51–59.

Works in Honor of Oswald Bayer

Dietrich, Theodor, ed. *Aufmerksam aufs Wort: Freundesgabe für Prof. Dr. Oswald Bayer zum 50. Geburtstag am 30. September 1989.* Tübingen: T. Dieter c/o Inst. für Christl. Gesellschaftslehre, 1989.

Lüpke, Johannes von, und Edgar Thaidigsmann, eds. *Denkraum Katechismus: Festgabe für Oswald Bayer zum 70. Geburtstag.* Tübingen: Mohr/Siebeck, 2009.

Name Index

Abraham, 27–8, 59, 90, 166–70, 172–77, 179, 205, 215
Adam [and Eve], 24, 28, 50, 59, 77n29, 106, 120–21, 125, 126n51, 142–43, 156, 158–60, 164, 176, 190
Althaus, Paul, 43, 43n14, 47
Aristotle, 197, 203–204n17, 264
Aquinas, Thomas, 180
Austin, J. L., xi, 325n69

Barclay, John M., 128, 128n58, 130, 103n62, 134, 201, 201n12, 207
Barth, Karl, 221, 238
Betz, John, xin10, 211n8, 224, 240–41, 240n10, 248n30, 252
Bielenberg, Steven, 152, 152n56, 154
Bizer, Ernst, ix, 49n2, 63, 181
Bultmann, Rudolf, 47

Cajetan, Cardinal, x, 161n2
Calov, Abraham, 253–67
Calvin, John, 44n16, 126, 126n49, 134, 221n52
Concordists. *See Formula of Concord.*

Daniel, 17
David, 19, 27, 101–9, 140–41, 146, 160, 167, 178, 200, 206

Ebeling, Gerhard, 45n19, 47
Elert, Werener, 181, 181n2, 193
Elijah, 90
Ezekiel, 17

Feuerbach, Ludwig, 5
Forde, Gerhard, 40n6, 42n12, 45n20, 46–47, 46n3, 57, 118, 120n24, 122, 134, 189, 189n47, 193
Francis I, Pope, 38, 38n2, 47–48

Gerhard, Johann, 255–57, 255n10, 256n13, 263–64, 263n52–54, 266–67
Giertz, Bo, 142–43, 142n29, 143n31, 154
Gnesio-Lutherans, 68, 79
Goethe, Johann Wolfgang von, 240

Habakkuk, 140
Haggai, 228
Hamann, Johann Georg, viii, ix-xii, 17–36, 211, 211n7–8, 216, 223–24, 223n65, 240–41, 240n9, 241n11, 245–48, 246n23, 247n29, 248n31, 250, 252
Harrison, Matthew C., 147, 147n42, 150–51, 150n50, 150n52–53, 151n55
Harrisville, Roy A. Jr., 133, 133n73–75, 134
Herder, Johann Gottfried, 4, 240
Hinlicky, Paul, 122n33
Hobbes, Thomas, 33, 119
Holl, Karl, 121
Hutter, Reinhard, 253n2

Isaiah, 17, 143

278

NAME INDEX

Jacob, 27, 36, 59, 141, 211–12
Jeremiah, 17, 200, 206
Job, 18, 19, 23, 90, 140, 200, 202
John the Baptist, 56
Jonah, 27, 87n77

Kant, Immanuel, x, 17, 33, 128, 162, 164, 240, 245, 247
Kierkegaard, Soren, 120, 205, 240
Kolb, Robert, 73n16, 93, 120n24, 135, 228, 231–32

Leibniz, Gottfried Wilhelm, 162–64, 163n4, 180
Locke, John, 162–65, 163n6–7, 180
Lohse, Bernhard, 115, 135

Mannermaa, Tuomo, 118
Marx, Karl, 239, 241
Masaki, Naomichi, 97n19, 104n53, 105n60, 113
Mattes, Mark, 135, 138n12, 220n45, 225
Melanchthon, Philip, 49, 51, 70, 95
Melchizedek, 28
Milbank, John, 239, 239n6, 240n9, 252
Miller, Joshua C., ixn1–3, xn4–7, xin9, xin12–14, xiin15, xiin17, 136n1, 137n4, 137n6–8, 138n10, 140n19–22, 146n36–37, 154, 212n11, 225, 235
Moses, 22–29, 35, 40, 59, 84, 84n64, 115n2, 127, 140, 171, 179, 200, 211
Musaeus, Simon, 66–93

Nestingen, James Arne, 107, 107n73, 113

Oden, Thomas, 238, 238n5, 252

Paul, 28, 39n3, 40n8, 54, 59, 62, 130n62
Pauli, Simon, 66–93
Paulson, Steven D., 116n5, 117, 121, 135, 148, 145n45, 154, 235

Philipists, 53
Peter, 28, 62, 156, 161–62
Peters, Albrecht, 182, 182n13, 185n24, 186n34, 188n40, 190–92, 190n49, 191n59–60, 192n61, 194, 225
Praetorius, Peter, 52n12, 55, 55n32, 64
Pickstock, Catherine, 239
Pless, John T., 149n47, 150, 150n51, 154, 194

Rahab, 90
Ratzinger, Ernst (Pope Benedict XVI), 38–40, 38n2, 39n4, 47–48, 238
Rogers, Fred, 150n54

Saarinen, Risto, 118, 118n17, 128, 128n60, 130, 130n63–64, 135
Sartre, Jean Paul, 10,13
Sasse, Hermann, 104, 181, 181n3, 194, 214n14, 217, 217n28, 217n30, 218n34, 224
Scaer, David P., 149n48, 154
Schulz, Gregory P., 195n3, 196n6, 197n9, 201n14, 203n15, 223n19–20, 207
Silcock, Jeffrey, 210n5, 124n13, 243
Spangenberg, Cyriacus, 52n12, 52n15, 53–58, 53n20–21, 54n23, 55n30, 57n44–46, 58n56, 61, 61n71, 64
Spangenberg, Johann, 59n61, 61–2, 61n72, 62n77, 62n79, 64

Tranvik, Mark D., 147, 147n41, 154, 188n42
Trapp, Thomas, 138n12

Ward, Graham, 239
Wolff, Hans Walter, 228

Zacchaeus, 19
Zechariah, 178
Zwingli, 221n52, 249

Subject Index

absolution, 49–65, 107–112, 121, 155–58, 166, 182, 191–94, 216, 234, 250
Anfechtung (tentatio), x–xi, 35, 80, 103, 116, 138–41, 138n12, 145, 149, 177, 212, 218, 231, 253–54, 259–60, 260n42
Anglicanism, 17, 97, 239
Apology to the Augsburg Confession, 71n10
Aristotelianism, 197, 203–4, 264
assurance, 50, 148, 162–65, 170–12
Augsburg Confession, 49, 71, 71n10, 157, 161n2, 181, 216, 232
Augustinianism, 26, 33, 78, 95, 216

the Bible. *See* Scripture.
Baptism, 15, 24, 27, 50, 50n5, 52–53, 52n14, 53n20, 58–61, 68, 78, 96–97, 106–112, 116, 120, 125–27, 132–33, 178, 181–93, 185n24, 185n27, 186n34, 188n40, 188n42, 189n46, 190n40, 191n59, 211, 216–17, 217n32, 230, 234, 246, 249

Calvinism, 58
catechesis, 53n18, 183, 188, 197
Christendom, 106
Christology, 71n11, 143, 212n12, 217–18, 218n35, 247
the church, ix, xii, 9, 27–32, 38–41, 39n3, 39n5, 51, 54–6, 60–61, 83, 86–90, 95–97, 104, 108–113, 114–21, 125–27, 132–34, 137, 145–52, 149n46, 177, 182–83, 193, 196–97, 200–201, 211–13, 215n23, 217n33, 222n60, 229, 234–35, 237–41, 250, 259, 264
communicatio idiomatum, 36, 217–18, 218n35
communion of saints, see the church
creation, xi–xii, 18–20, 22–26, 30, 34–35, 39n5, 44–46, 74, 83–86, 98, 114–19, 118n18, 123, 127–29, 129n61, 136–53, 139n18, 155–60, 171–72, 190, 211, 210n6, 211n7–9, 215, 220, 234, 238, 214, 244–52
cross, 27, 30, 37–48, 54, 59, 75, 86, 110, 124, 127, 133, 144–45, 158–60, 177, 186n84, 187, 196, 198, 206–7, 213–14, 213n13, 214n14, 220–21, 235, 250, 260

the devil, 22–6, 39, 50–1, 59–61, 70, 80–2, 87, 105, 111, 117, 129, 137–38, 158–59, 176–77, 185n29, 186–89, 192, 212, 237, 260

Eastern Orthodoxy, 247
the Enlightenment, viii, x, 10, 17, 20, 33, 36, 239–40, 245
election, 184
eschatology, 46, 155–60, 198, 200
ethics, 3, 8–14, 67n2, 126, 130, 132, 196, 198, 205–6, 254

Eucharist. *See* Holy Communion.
evil. *See* problem of evil.

Formula of Concord, 7, 66–72, 72n14, 77, 107, 211
freedom, 3, 9–15, 40, 45n19, 47, 67, 108, 119, 148, 157, 162, 174, 196, 199, 242, 251

God, as author, 18–20
God, love of, xii, 23, 26, 30–34, 38n3, 39, 42, 115, 170–74, 177, 192, 221, 250
God, preached, 212
God, Triune. *See* Trinity.
God, unpreached, 138
God, wrath of, xiii, 22, 45–46 45n22, 55, 74, 102–7, 137–38, 144–47, 176, 179, 202
God, wrestling of, 23, 141, 211–12
the gospel, x-xi, 13–15, 32–3, 38, 40–2, 45n19, 46–7, 49–51, 58–9, 61, 66–9, 72–85, 72n15, 73n17, 89, 91, 95, 107–21, 125–27, 130, 137, 142, 148, 150n52, 157–60, 169, 177, 188, 189n46, 216–20, 219n43, 235, 244, 249–50

hermeneutics, 217–19, 241, 248–50
hiddenness of God, 138–42,140n21–22, 211–12, 212n11
Holy Communion, 15, 50, 50n5, 51, 52n14, 53n20, 55–9, 61–2, 71, 71n11, 95–7, 101, 109–112, 116, 125, 145–47, 152, 159, 178, 181–93, 188n40, 214n17, 218–34, 246–49
Holy Spirit, 18, 27, 49, 56, 59–60, 66–76, 72n15, 79, 82–83, 89–90, 95, 108–110, 114–34, 146, 155, 159, 170, 185, 193, 210n5, 216n23, 217, 234, 246, 249–50, 258–59, 264–65

justification, x-xii, 14, 37–9, 39n5, 42–4, 42n10, 47, 66–9, 72n15, 74, 78, 91, 96, 106–8, 116–21, 125, 131–34, 132n72, 138–39, 160, 164, 167–69, 188n42, 204, 215, 219n42, 222, 234, 238, 241–46

Kantianism, x

Large Catechism, 114–34,181–93
lament, xii, 9, 107n73, 136–53, 195–207
the law, xi, 2–7, 14, 20, 24–9, 35–40, 40n8, 42–6, 45n19, 66–9, 74–8, 77n32, 80, 88–92, 95–7, 102–3, 107–8, 115, 115n2, 126, 129–30, 144, 147, 157–59, 162–71, 174–79, 222, 244, 249
law and gospel, 16–18, 28–29, 37–40, 38n3, 43, 46–47, 56, 62, 69, 76–80, 80n44, 89, 91, 97, 105n60, 107, 219–21, 242
law, third use of, 77, 97
liberation, 38, 49–51, 61, 137
linguistics, 17, 248–49
liturgy, 95–97, 104, 112, 145–46, 152, 205–6, 211, 215–16
Lord's Supper. *See* Holy Communion.
love for neighbor, 14, 25, 31, 66, 121, 126–27, 132, 132n72, 147–48, 150–51, 150n52, 151n54, 198, 250
Lutheran orthodoxy, 117, 253–54, 253n3, 263
Lutheranism, vii-xii, 15, 44n16, 62, 66–80, 78n38, 87n77, 92, 97, 104, 106, 120–21, 126–29, 136, 181, 196–97, 205, 209–211, 218–21, 222n60, 234–35, 241, 245–47, 247n27, 250–56, 253n3, 254n6, 255n11–12, 263

Marxism, 8, 239–41
meditation, *meditatio*, x-xi, 18, 99, 132–33, 205, 210, 213n13, 220–22, 253n1, 258–60, 264
monasticism, 129n61, 176

new creation, xii, 83–6, 118n18, 129n6, 137–41, 151, 155, 246

pietism, 88, 255n11

SUBJECT INDEX

prayer, *oratio*, xii, x-xi, 21, 30, 53-4, 81, 86-7, 87n77, 90, 95, 100, 103-6, 116, 132-33, 140n19, 146, 149, 168-69, 177, 184, 192-93, 205-6, 210, 253, 253n1, 258-60, 264

preaching, ix, xi, xvii, 16, 46, 51, 58, 66-70, 73, 79-86, 79n41, 80n14, 89-92, 96, 106-7, 109, 112, 115, 124, 133, 137, 144, 148-51, 179, 183, 187-88, 197, 218, 235, 264

predestination, 175, 184

problem of evil, xi-xii, 2, 43, 45, 50, 60, 70-5, 81, 90, 105, 122-23, 136-53, 175, 198-99, 241, 251

proclamation. *See* preaching.

promise, ix-xii, 1, 15, 45n19, 45n22, 46, 46n22, 49-63, 85, 91, 104, 107, 115-16, 121, 124, 127, 132, 136-53, 160, 161-62, 166-79, 181-92, 198-99, 202, 212, 214-20, 223, 236, 241, 245, 249-51

radical orthodoxy, 239-47

the Reformation, x-xi, 15, 37-38, 40, 51, 56, 62, 67, 188, 197, 209, 216-19, 222, 231-35, 241-42

Reformed tradition, 44n16, 106, 126-27, 217, 221, 246, 247n27

Roman Catholicism, vii, 33, 38, 39n3, 97, 115, 120, 182, 188, 214n17, 219n44, 238-41

romanticism, 20n10, 240

rupture of the ages, 136-42, 151

Sacraments, *See also* baptism, absolution, Holy Communion.

Sacrament of the Altar. *See* Holy Communion.

sanctification, 66-92, 114, 117-23, 134, 234

Satan, *See* the devil

Scripture, x-xi, 18-23, 28, 41n9, 56, 95-98, 100-101, 104, 114-18, 133, 144, 165-67, 188, 197, 201, 204-6, 210, 216n23, 219, 222, 235, 248, 253n1, 257, 257n18, 259-60, 265

self-creation, 44-46, 123

self-justification, 14, 39n3, 44, 91, 238, 241-44

Small Catechism, 39n3, 50, 57, 83, 90, 108, 113-34, 158-59, 181-93, 234

speech act, 45, 218n37, 249

suffering, xi-xii, 8n29, 12, 34, 41, 41n9, 58, 67n2, 75-76, 79, 98-9, 117, 125, 136-53, 158-59, 175, 186-87, 195-207

tentatio. *See Anfechtung*.

theology of the cross, 37-47, 196, 213n13

the three lights, 212n11

Trinity, 23, 34-35, 114, 252

vita passiva, the passive life, 35, 110, 129-31, 215n18

vocation, 95, 145-49, 247, 250

will bound, 13-16, 212n11

will, free, 108-9, 130, 130n63, 162, 166, 173, 178

Scripture Index

Genesis

1	84n64, 210, 215
1–2	84
2:3	20
3	28
22	166–79
31	30, 34
32:11–14	141
33:19	19n8

Exodus

3:14	171
20:2	166
28:30	172
29	109
32:6	18
33:11	211
33:20	211

Leviticus

16	28

Deuteronomy

4:12	211
4:15–19	
8:1–3	32
17:18–19	206

1 Samuel

9:10	18

2 Samuel

1	26

Job

	2:13
3:19	21
23–31	141n23

Psalms

22	141, 144, 146, 198, 202, 205–6
33:6	210
51	87n37, 94–113, 160, 202, 255n9
119:36	81

Song of Songs

2:14	2

Ecclesiastes

1:8	44n17
3:15	199

Isaiah

1–39	227
1:15	259n33
6:1	221
11	143
14:24	167
28:19	258
45:15	41n9
55:10–11	249
55:11	215n20

Matthew

4	28
4:1	82
4:4	82
5:17	35
5:18	24
5:35–36	169
6:6	103
7:7	36
7:15	262
9:2–6	54
10:27	111
11:28	58
13:17	109
13:24–30	86
16:19	55
18:21–22	62
18:15–20	55
20:28	47
25:31–46	86
26:26	103
27:46	144, 214
28:19	185
28:19–20	148
28:20	110

Mark

7:31–37	211n8
7:34	143, 211
7:34–35	137n8
9:7	42
9:49–50	25
10:45	47
14:50	156
16:16	189

Luke

1:38	183, 215n20
1:73	167, 177
2:19	215
4:1–13	82
7:41–50	54
10:24	109
10:25–37	25
10:42	215
11:8	198
11:13	258
11:28	258–59
14:17	143
15	199
17:9	179
17:10	179n34
18	106–7
18:1–8	198
18:9–14	54
20:1–8	22
22:19	110
23:34	198
23:43	54
24:47	96

John

1	215
1:1	210
1:1–2	212n12
1:14	211–12, 212n12
1:48	25, 33
2:11	213
3	59

4:13	44n17	\multicolumn{2}{c}{Romans}
6:15	213		
6:26	213	1:16	21, 28, 84
6:67–69	161	1:17	7, 50, 166
6:40	214	3:20	165
7:16–18	61	3:28	116n7, 203
7:39	214	4:16–17	170
8:12	213	4:17	210n4, 215
8:14–16	61	4:25	106, 117
9	213	5:12–21	143
9:41	213	6	50, 59, 190
10:7–10	58	8:14	118n18
10:9	41n9	8:19–22	142
10:17	25–26	9:20	202
10:27	213	10:4	108
11	31	10:17	215
12:16, 23	214	16:17	262
12:21	217n33		
12:44–45	61	\multicolumn{2}{c}{1 Corinthians}
13:32	214		
14:1–3	145		
14:6	41n9, 202	1:18	42
14:8	41n9	1:21	41n9
14:9	41n9	1:25	41n9
14:23	108	1:30	58
16:5–15	73	2:2	59, 217n33
16:23	202, 258	2:6–16	40n8
18:5	172	2:9	204
19:14	213	4:7	123
20	60–61	5:1–5	54
20:7	213	6:11	118
20:16	213	11:27	103
20:19–23	155–60	15:20	157
20:20	263	15:20–28	143
20:21–23	55	15:26	199
20:31	212		
		\multicolumn{2}{c}{2 Corinthians}
\multicolumn{2}{c}{Acts}		
		3:6	168
1:11	145	5:7	216
7:42	96	5:17	246
9	40n8	5:20	218
17	200	5:21	41n8
22	40n8	5:23	202
26	40n8	12:7	260
26:18	117–18	13:5	87

Galatians

2:19	41n8
3:13	42
5:17	258
6:1	62

1 Timothy

4:12	85
4:16	261
6:16	211

Titus

1:1–3	179

Hebrews

4:12	205, 249
6:4–6	62
6:13–20	167
10:14	118
10:22	163
10:26–31	62
11	30
11:1	212
11:3	215

James

1:16–27	69–92
2:19	256

I Peter

1:23	74
3:4	23

1 John

2:20	30
4:1	211, 262
5:6	187

3 John

9–10	31

Revelation

21–22	143
21:3–4	143
21:5	199

Made in the USA
Columbia, SC
17 February 2020